THE BIRTH OF THE TRINITY

How and when did Jesus and the Spirit come to be regarded as fully God? *The Birth of the Trinity* offers a new historical approach by exploring the way in which first- and second-century Christians read the Old Testament in order to differentiate the one God as multiple persons. The earliest Christians felt they could metaphorically "overhear" divine conversations between the Father, Son, and Spirit when reading the Old Testament. When these snatches of dialogue are connected and joined, they form a narrative about the unfolding interior divine life as understood by the nascent church. What emerges is not a static portrait of the triune God, but a developing story of divine persons enacting mutual esteem, voiced praise, collaborative strategy, and self-sacrificial love. The presence of divine dialogue in the New Testament and early Christian literature shows that, contrary to the claims of James Dunn and Bart Ehrman (among others), the earliest Christology was the highest Christology, as Jesus was identified as a divine person through Old Testament interpretation. The result is a Trinitarian biblical and early Christian theology.

Matthew W. Bates is Assistant Professor of Theology at Quincy University in Quincy, Illinois.

The Birth of the Trinity

Jesus, God, and Spirit in New Testament and Early Christian Interpretations of the Old Testament

MATTHEW W. BATES

OXFORD
UNIVERSITY PRESS

OXFORD
UNIVERSITY PRESS

Great Clarendon Street, Oxford, OX2 6DP,
United Kingdom

Oxford University Press is a department of the University of Oxford.
It furthers the University's objective of excellence in research, scholarship,
and education by publishing worldwide. Oxford is a registered trade mark of
Oxford University Press in the UK and in certain other countries

First published 2015
First published in paperback 2016

Published in the United States of America by Oxford University Press
198 Madison Avenue, New York, NY 10016, United States of America

British Library Cataloguing in Publication Data
Data available

Library of Congress Cataloging in Publication Data
Data available

ISBN 978-0-19-872956-3 (Hbk.)
ISBN 978-0-19-877924-7 (Pbk.)

Nowhere else can the self-giving love of the triune God
—persons in intimate fellowship—
be more joyfully experienced than in Christian family life.
Thus, in praise of the three-in-one God, I dedicated this book
to my beloved wife,
Sarah Nicole Bates,
and to our five delightful children:
Thaddaeus, Ezekiel, Adeline, Lydia, and Evelyn

Acknowledgments

In bringing this book to completion I have the privilege of thanking many people who have helped me along the way. In addition to the two anonymous Oxford University Press reviewers, highest accolades rightfully belong to those who read the entire manuscript at various draft stages and gave much-needed constructive criticism: Daniel L. Smith, Assistant Professor of Biblical Studies at Saint Louis University; Matt Lynch, Dean of Studies and Old Testament Lecturer at Westminster Theological Centre; Jonathan K. Miles, Assistant Professor of Philosophy at Quincy University; and Zeke Nelson, Pastor of Church of the Cross/Iglesia de la Cruz in Delhi, California. In addition, a number of others gave helpful comments on portions of the manuscript: Bradley C. Gregory, Assistant Professor of Biblical Studies at the Catholic University of America; Kent J. Lasnoski, Assistant Professor of Theology at Quincy University; Eric Rowe, Postdoctoral Teaching Fellow at the University of Notre Dame; and Greg Barnhill, a graduate student. Several of my advanced undergraduate students at Quincy University also opted to read a preliminary draft of the manuscript to fulfill requirements for my New Testament course in the spring term of 2013. Undoubtedly their student-oriented feedback helped make this a more reader- and classroom-friendly book: Jamie Grady, Michael Crotteau, Elizabeth Cramsey, and Paul Blum. The editorial team at Oxford University Press also deserves recognition for excellence—they made the publishing experience a true delight: Tom Perridge, Karen Raith, Alexander Johnson, Rachel May, Caroline Hawley, Aimee Wright, Sylvie Jaffrey, and others. I am especially grateful for my parents, Mike and Linda Bates, who have supplied constant support, good humor, and unflagging encouragement throughout my life. Many thanks to all of you!

Contents

List of Abbreviations   xi

Introduction   1

1. Reading as Birth—The Trinity Emerges   12

2. Divine Dialogues from the Dawn of Time   41

3. Theodramatic Stratagems—The Son's Mission   85

4. Cross-Shaped Conversations   115

5. Praise for Rescue   136

6. Triumphant Talks   157

7. Reading God Right   175

Epilogue: The Read God   203

References   207
Index of Biblical References   219
Index of Other Ancient Sources   226
Index of Modern Authors Cited   230
Index of Concepts and Other Names   232

List of Abbreviations

AB	Anchor Bible
ABRL	Anchor Bible Reference Library
AGJU	Arbeiten zur Geschichte des antiken Judentums und des Urchristentums
AnBib	Analecta biblica
ANF	Ante-Nicene Fathers
BDAG	*A Greek-English Lexicon of the New Testament*, edited by Danker, 3rd edn.
BHT	Beiträge zur historischen Theologie
BIS	Biblical Interpretation Series
BZNW	Beihefte zur Zeitschrift für die Neutestamentliche Wissenschaft
CBET	Contributions to Biblical Exegesis and Theology
CBQ	*Catholic Biblical Quarterly*
Comm.	*Communio*
EKKNT	Evangelisch-katholischer Kommentar zum Neuen Testament
FOTC	Fathers of the Church
ICC	International Critical Commentary
Int.	*Interpretation*
JBL	*Journal of Biblical Literature*
JR	*Journal of Religion*
JSNT	*Journal for the Study of the New Testament*
JSNTSup	Journal for the Study of the New Testament: Supplement Series
JTI	*Journal of Theological Interpretation*
LCL	Loeb Classical Library
LXX	Septuagint
MT	Masoretic Text
NICNT	New International Commentary on the New Testament
NIGTC	New International Greek Testament Commentary
NT	New Testament
OT	Old Testament
OTL	Old Testament Library
PG	Patrologia graeca
PGL	*A Patristic Greek Lexicon*, edited by Lampe

PTS	Patristische Texte und Studien
RB	*Revue biblique*
RevQ	*Revue de Qumran*
SBL	Society of Biblical Literature
SBLDS	Society of Biblical Literature Dissertation Series
SBLMS	SBL Monograph Series
SBLSymS	SBL Symposium Series
SBLWGRW	SBL Writing from the Greco-Roman World
SC	Sources chrétiennes
SPCK	Society for Promoting Christian Knowledge
SupNovT	Supplements to Novum Testamentum
TGl	*Theologie und Glaube*
THNTC	Two Horizons New Testament Commentary
TS	*Theological Studies*
TynBul	*Tyndale Bulletin*
WBC	Word Biblical Commentary
WUNT	Wissenschaftliche Untersuchungen zum Neuen Testament
ZNW	*Zeitschrift für die neutestamentliche Wissenschaft und die Kunde der älteren Kirche*

Introduction

When the author of Hebrews takes up the lyrics of the psalmist, "Sacrifice and offering you did not desire, but a body you prepared for me," the author forthrightly identifies the Christ as the speaker of the poetic lines that he has recited. But how? Why? The Christ does not appear as an overt or obvious character in the psalm itself in the Old Testament—indeed, he is not mentioned at all. So what could possibly have led the author of Hebrews to posit that the Christ is the speaker? If one merely skims the outer shell of the problem, it might be tempting to conclude that the author of Hebrews was either an inept or a brazenly tendentious reader. Yet even when one probes deeper and begins to sense that the author's reading strategy is more refined than a surface perusal might indicate, rather than the murkiness immediately dissipating, other puzzles churn up. For instance, if the Christ speaks in this psalm, then *when* was he thought to be speaking?—and *to whom* did the author of Hebrews think the Christ was uttering these lines?

Even if several enigmas persist, we can at least give a reasonably certain answer to this last *to-whom* question. The broader context in Hebrews indicates that the words of the Christ have been taken as addressing God (the Father), so that we might paraphrase the author's startling interpretation of these lines from the psalm as follows:

JESUS CHRIST (speaking to GOD): Sacrifice and offering *you, O my Father*, did not desire, but a body you prepared for *me*, that is for *me, your Son*.[1]

That is, the author of Hebrews, with his "a body you prepared for me" language, has construed this as a dialogue between the Son and the Father about the incarnation.[2] When the author of Hebrews and various early Christians read this psalm and other Old Testament passages as containing conversations between Jesus Christ, God (the Father), and others, what allowed this imaginative move? Can anything be said about the quality or legitimacy of such interpretations? And most vitally, what theological and Christological

---

[1] Heb. 10: 5 citing Ps. 40: 6 (= Ps. 39: 7 LXX).
[2] For a detailed discussion of Heb. 10: 5, see "A Body You Have Prepared for Me" in Ch. 3.

implications can be teased forth regarding how the earliest Christians viewed God? These are the overarching question that will occupy us in this book.

My thesis is that a specific ancient reading technique, best termed *prosopological exegesis*, that is evidenced in the New Testament and other early Christian writings was irreducibly essential to the birth of the Trinity. Since at this time prosopological exegesis remains largely unknown, even in circles traversed by seasoned biblical scholars and theologians, it will be explained fully in due course. To the best of my knowledge no one has ever systematically explored Trinitarian inner dynamics or Christology in the New Testament and second-century Christianity from this angle. Accordingly, this book seeks to provide a panoramic view of the relationship between Father, Son, and Spirit as it was conceptualized through a specific mode of interpreting Old Testament dialogues in the earliest church. In essence, I am attempting to tell the story of the interior of the divine life as perceived by the first Christians.

As such, this book is written for general readers of theology, history, and religion, as well as for professional scholars and students. Although the general reader will need to wait for the story to unfold in order to learn the major players and positions, specialists should immediately recognize that in discussing how Jesus came to be regarded as God, the *Christology of Divine Persons* model I favor differs but relates to the Christology of Divine Identity proposed by Richard Bauckham and furthered by N. T. Wright. Like the latter model, in advocating for an early high Christology, my proposal stands at considerable distance from the backward movement of Christology schema that is supported by James D. G. Dunn, Bart Ehrman, and others. Regarding students, instructors who prefer to teach through integrative monographs rather than traditional textbooks may, it is hoped, find this book suitable for courses and seminars emphasizing the Trinity, Christology, New Testament theology, biblical theology, the use of the Old Testament in the New Testament, and the like. Yet as we begin to explore the great Trinitarian mystery together, I submit that all readers who are willing to heed the advice of Saint Augustine will find something profitable. I myself have certainly sought to pay careful attention to it while penning this book.

SAINT AUGUSTINE ISSUES THREE WARNINGS

If theology were a mountain range, then many theologians would consider Saint Augustine's *On the Trinity* (*De Trinitate*) not just a grassy hill, or a carved peak, but the loftiest pinnacle of the most majestic mountain in the range. Augustine is usually regarded as the greatest post-biblical Christian theologian, and *On the Trinity*, in which he fully and directly treats the most central Christian mystery, is his *magnum opus*. Yet, since this mystery is so precious and vital to the church, Augustine is compelled to open his discussion with a warning to his reader about three types of people who have unwittingly erred or intentionally connived to distort a true conception of the triune God—a warning as relevant now as then.

The first type permit themselves to be "deceived through an unreasonable and misguided love of *reason*," that is, in their overbearing concern to let rational thought thread them through the labyrinth of the divine mystery, they confuse physical things with God's true eternal nature—believing, for instance, that God the Father has an actual tangible face, since Scripture reports that Adam and Eve hid from God's face. In a like manner, the second type simplistically apply descriptions of human moods to God, such as jealousy, on the basis of the scriptural witness, but in failing to appreciate metaphor and other literary devices, this group falls prey to "distorted and misleading *rules of interpretation*," that is, they fail hermeneutically when they attempt to synthesize the biblical testimony.[3]

Indeed, in whatever guise they might appear, misguided rationalism and inappropriate means of scriptural interpretation can truly result in faulty assessments of God. In a way, this book is my attempt to correct the former in the history of scholarship by reassessing neglected features in the latter. That is, the doctrine of the Trinity did not emerge as a late philosophical imposition predicated on Hellenistic assumptions, as Adolf von Harnack and the heirs of his legacy have posited. Nor did it predominantly arise as an extension of the concept of divine agency or divine intermediaries within the matrix of Jewish monotheism, as James Dunn and others have argued. Rather, in conjunction with early Christian experiences of Jesus and certain philosophical and mediatorial factors, the idea of separate persons in timeless, intimate communion within the Godhead—Father, Son, and Spirit—was especially fostered and nurtured *by a specific reading technique* that the earliest Christians utilized as they engaged their ancient Jewish Scripture. Although a more sophisticated explanation will be provided at the proper time, in short this technique—*prosopological exegesis*—involved assigning dramatic characters to otherwise ambivalent speeches in inspired texts as an explanatory method. In addition to its presence in the earliest church, it is also discernible in ancient Homeric scholarship and philosophical Judaism, although the technique has not yet been adequately recognized by biblical scholarship.[4]

Yet for Augustine, in terms of those who err regarding the Trinity, there is a third category of people—perhaps the most pernicious—those who "*strive to*

---

[3] Augustine, *Trin.* 1. 1 (§1); trans. Hill, emphasis mine. For the specific examples, on God's face, see *Trin.* 2. 4 (§§17–18; cf. Origen, *Princ.* 4. 3. 1); on God's jealousy, see *Trin.* 1. 1 (§2). All abbreviations follow Patrick H. Alexander et al., (eds.), *The SBL Handbook of Style* (Peabody, Mass.: Hendrickson, 1999).

[4] See Ch. 1 for discussion of scholarship.

climb above the created universe," which is "so ineluctably subject to change" in hope that they can entirely escape their creaturely limitations, gain a transcendent vantage point on the unchangeable God, and from that lofty height, then speak about God apart from any creaturely analogy.[5] The warning issued by Augustine is as fresh and timely for contemporary biblical and theological studies today as it was some 1,600 years ago. There is real danger, indeed a radical hubris, when scholars seek to decree authoritatively on the true nature of God, as if the contemporary theologian can—apart from the aid of special revelation—ascend above the created order to gain a true perspective on God.

The author of a book with so audacious a title as *The Birth of the Trinity* is particularly sensitive to these concerns. The builders of the tower of Babel sought to reach the heavens, and regardless of whether they hoped to overrun the divine court itself, as many ancient interpreters suspected, or merely sought to make a name for themselves in some more innocuous way, undoubtedly this tale cautions the theologian against a presumptuous arrogance with respect to the Holy One.[6] No matter how much I might wish that I could, as Annie Dillard puts it, "climb up the blank blue dome" of the sky and "with a steel knife claw a rent in the top" in order to poke my head through and gaze in wonder at all the divine mysteries, such is not possible.[7] I certainly do not believe that I personally am somehow able to escape the cosmic confines which God has deemed my suitable mortal limitations so as to gain a transcendent view of divine affairs. Nor as a finite human can I or anyone else talk about God apart from suitable creaturely metaphorical language. As such, in speaking of "the birth of the Trinity," I do not refer to the ultimate "real" or ontological starting point for the Trinity—traditionally, Christians have affirmed that the triune God is eternal, with no origin in time, and this study ultimately finds much early Christian testimony to support that claim. Rather, in speaking of "the birth of the Trinity" I refer to the arrival and initial sociolinguistic framing of this doctrine in human history by the nascent church.

DIVINE DIALOGUES AND TRINITARIAN ORIGINS

Yet this arrival and framing, this Trinitarian birth, did not occur in a vacuum, but as I shall argue throughout this book, largely through a specific method of reading the Old Testament. For not only Augustine, but also the very earliest

---

[5] Augustine, *Trin.* 1. 1 (§1); trans. Hill, emphasis mine.

[6] For the leitmotif of the tower of Babel as a means of war against God, see James L. Kugel, *Traditions of the Bible: A Guide to the Bible as It Was at the Start of the Common Era* (Cambridge, Mass.: Harvard University Press, 1998), 229.

[7] Annie Dillard, *Pilgrim at Tinker Creek* (New York: Bantam Books, 1975), 33.

Christians were convinced that a few special humans in the past had in fact obtained an otherworldly glimpse into divine affairs—the ancient Hebrew prophets. For the first Christians these prophets—Isaiah, Jeremiah, David, and others—were in fact able to climb through a divinely ordained tear between heaven and earth, in order to overhear and report certain celestial conversations. As such, these prophetic visitors could listen as God the Father spoke with the preexistent Son, as the Father, for instance, lovingly described the way he was preparing a human body for him. Or more often, so the earliest Christians believed, the prophets themselves actually *participated* in the conversations as actors, alternately taking on the person of the Son and then the Father, as, for instance, the now-glorified Son reminisced with his heavenly Father about the concern he felt for the Father when he was enduring the agony of the cross. The earliest Christians believed that the ancient prophets had in fact gained a supernatural view of the divine as these prophets participated in what we might term "a grand theodrama," taking on various *prosōpa* (persons, masks, characters)—and these Christians were prone to read the ancient Jewish Scripture in a person-centered fashion in order to recover the transcendentally revealed information about the nature of God latent therein.[8]

Although innumerable theologians have thoroughly and repeatedly combed the earliest Christian writings—the New Testament, Apostolic Fathers, and early Apologists—for proto-Trinitarian statements, such as are found in the Gospel of John, "*I* and the *Father, we are one*" (10: 30), or the Great Commission in Matthew, "Therefore go and make disciples of all nations, baptizing them in the name of the *Father* and of the *Son* and of the *Holy Spirit*" (28: 19), or Paul's mention of all three in Galatians, "Because you are sons, *God* sent the *Spirit* of his *Son* into our hearts, the *Spirit* who calls out, '*Abba, Father*'" (4: 6), and a myriad of other texts, there has never been a detailed study that looks specifically at the Trinitarian assumptions and implications of person-centered reading strategies as these first- and second-century Christian authors engaged what would come to be termed the Old Testament—the very interpretative matrix that first lent impetus to Trinitarian dogma.

Thus, I would argue, surprisingly, some of the deepest and richest aspects of the interior life of the persons who would later come to be identified as members of the Trinity, as these are expressed in the very pages of the New Testament itself, have not yet been plumbed. For now, one further example

---

[8] Although I share the term *theodrama* with Hans Urs von Balthasar (*Theo-Drama: Theological Dramatic Theory* [trans. Graham Harrison; 5 vols.; San Francisco: Ignatius, 1988–98]) and with Kevin J. Vanhoozer (*The Drama of Doctrine: A Canonical Linguistic Approach to Christian Theology* [Louisville, Ky.: Westminster John Knox, 2005]), among others, I intend something decidedly more specific. By *theodrama* I refer to the dramatic world invoked by an ancient reader of Scripture as that reader construed a prophet to be speaking from or observing the person (*prosōpon*) of a divine or human character. For a more detailed explanation, see "Prosopological Exegesis and the Birth of the Trinity" in Ch. 1.

must suffice. Paul, in seeking to reconcile the strong and the weak factions in the Roman house-churches, writes: "Let each of us please our neighbor, for the common good, in order to edify. For even the Christ did not please himself, but just as it is written: 'The insults of those who were insulting you fell upon me'" (Rom. 15: 2–3 citing Ps. 68: 10 LXX]).[9] Although of course Paul would have understood David to be the author of Psalm 68 LXX, in this bold prosopological interpretation, Paul has construed Psalm 68: 10 LXX by assigning an unexpected character as the speaker. For Paul it is not David who speaks, but the Christ, who is not directly mentioned in this Old Testament text at all. And if for Paul it is the Christ who speaks, then David was necessarily writing as a Spirit-inspired prophet, speaking about the future suffering of the Christ on the cross. Yet, this in turn implies for Paul that the Christ preexisted in fellowship with the Father during the days of David in such a way that *the Spirit* could speak through David in the person of *the Christ* from his future position in the divine drama (in an anticipatory way) to *his Father* about the sufferings that he had undergone in the past. So Paul reads this passage from the Psalter:

THE CHRIST (speaking to GOD): The insults of those who insulted *you*, O *Father*, they fell upon *me*, on *the Christ, the Son*, when *I* was on the cross.

That is, Paul reads these words as spoken in the past by David, but nonetheless as containing a real future conversation between the Father and the Son as facilitated by the Spirit that looks backward in time on the crucifixion. Yet from Paul's vantage point this future has now already come and gone, this fragmentary snippet of Father–Son dialogue has transpired, so it is now in the past when Paul incorporates it into his letter to the Romans.

Vital information about the Father, the Son, and the Spirit, and their relationship with one another, can be drawn forth from Paul's reading of this psalm—briefly, that the Son loves the Father so much that the Son, speaking via the Spirit in the past tense as if the cross is a fait accompli, tells the Father that he voluntarily bore in the passion the reviling insults by which the godless cursed the Father. An intimate concern for one another among the divine persons in the Godhead is hereby revealed, to such a degree that the Son is willing to suffer intensely here not because of his love for humanity per se, but because he loves *his Father* so much that he wants to shoulder the hostile words aimed at him. This passage is not discussed in detail in any of the major works on the Trinity of which I am aware, showing that it is precisely this sort of rich Trinitarian fruit—fruit connected with prosopological exegesis of the Old Testament—not just in the later Fathers of the church, but also in the New

---

[9] In the versification of the English Bible—which differs from the versification employed for ancient Hebrew and Greek modern editions of the Bible—the reference is to Ps. 69: 9.

Testament and in the second century—that has not yet been plucked by scholarship.

THE STORY OF THE CONVERSATIONAL GOD—THESIS AND PROGRAM

When this reading strategy is unveiled in the early Christian writings, a theological wealth shines forth as we are privileged to listen in on the intimate conversations among the persons within the Godhead. For example, by the personal agency of the Spirit, the preexistent Son is found to be speaking in advance to the Father about his suffering on the cross; the Father speaks of the Son as his begotten and beloved; the Son expresses his obedient trust in the Father; the Son passionately praises the Father in the midst of the gathered assembly by testifying to the Father's ability to rescue those who trust—and much more. By unfolding the logic and implications of person-centered exegesis of the Old Testament in the New Testament and the early post-New Testament church by a theologically attuned exposition of select passages, what emerges is not a philosophically defined Godhead internally differentiated by procession or subordination, such as is portrayed by scholarly models dependent on the late patristic era, but rather a Father, Son, and Spirit who are characterized by relentless affection and concern for one another. This, of course, is not to say that these later philosophical models are wrongheaded or unnecessary, but rather to show that the emphasis in the earliest church lies elsewhere. In other words, prosopological exegesis affirms and further develops the notion that for the earliest Christians the God of Israel had revealed himself as a *personal* God.

Thus, what is offered in this book is a window into the inner life of God as discerned via person-centered reading of the Old Testament in the early church. Moreover—and this is the central thesis I wish to argue—prosopological exegesis contributed decisively to the development of the concept of the Trinity, since it was this way of reading that especially led to the consolidation of "person" language to express the three-in-one mystery. Accordingly with regard to the divinity of Jesus, it is best to speak of a Christology of Divine Persons. This thesis is contextualized in terms of other scholarship and theoretical modeling in Chapter 1, "Reading as Birth—The Trinity Emerges."

The person-centered Trinitarian conversations in the earliest church between the Father, the Son, and sometimes even the Spirit, with the Spirit always supplying the words, covers the full chronological range of the revealed divine life, from before creation to the final consummation, and the heart of the book, Chapters 2 through 6, traces this unfolding divine drama. In other words, to borrow Karl Rahner's economic/immanent distinction, person-centered interpretation pulls back the veil on the *economic* Trinity—that is, God's triune self-revelation by active engagement with the world through the flow of time. This in turn gives us true, albeit not comprehensively exhaustive, information about the *immanent* Trinity—namely, the eternal existence of the triune God within God's own self.[10] More specifically, Chapter 2 explores early Christian interpretations of the Old Testament that feature conversations between the Father and the Son pertaining to happenings at or before the dawn of time. Chapter 3 examines moments of Old Testament dialogue between the Father and the Son that were felt by early Christians to have bearing on the unique mission of the Son. Chapter 4 enters into the most intimate of intra-divine conversations, as the suffering Son speaks words of anguish and trust to his Father from the cross, and the Father declares his love for the Son. In Chapter 5, the Son speaks words of praise to the Father for deliverance, while the entire human family is invited to join the exultant chorus. The divine story culminates in Chapter 6, where discussions pertaining to the enthronement of the Son, the final conquest of evil, and new creation are explored. In this way for the early church intra-divine dialogue covers the full spectrum of the life of the Godhead as economically revealed in the Old Testament.

The book concludes in Chapter 7, "Reading God Right," with a reflection on the hermeneutical questions raised by the study. For example, when the earliest church read its Scripture—primarily the Greek Old Testament—in this person-centered fashion, was it a *good* reading? In keeping with the historical tone of this book as a whole, this question of interpretative normativity is broached by an exploration of the procedures and principles of prosopological exegesis within second-century Gnosticism and emerging orthodoxy.

---

[10] Karl Rahner, *The Trinity* (trans. Joseph Donceel; New York: Seabury, 1974), 21–4. More precisely, Rahner's dictum regarding the Trinity is: "*The 'economic' Trinity is the 'immanent' Trinity and the 'immanent' Trinity is the 'economic' Trinity*" (p. 21). I would qualify this rule as an ontological statement inasmuch as the economic Trinity assuredly does truly reveal the immanent Trinity, but given (among other limitations) the accommodating (analogical) nature of scriptural God-language and Scripture's testimony to God's transcendence beyond what can be known through a time-bound economy, the economic Trinity does not unambiguously and exhaustively reveal the immanent Trinity. That is, there are aspects of God's own intra-divine life that have not been fully revealed to us, such as a complete description of all the details of precisely what "love for the other" might have entailed in God's own self-life prior to God's creation of the cosmos. Thus, in my judgment the second half of Rahner's dictum ("*the 'immanent' Trinity is the 'economic' Trinity*") is invalid as an ontological statement, although it does accurately describe the epistemological boundary of constructive theology, inasmuch as we can make no definite, positive statements about the immanent Trinity beyond what is revealed to us economically. A more precise dictum that blends ontological and epistemological concerns would be: "The economic Trinity truly reveals the immanent Trinity, so the immanent Trinity cannot be less than the economic Trinity, but is undoubtedly more, although we cannot know or describe this 'more.'"

Purposes and Presuppositions

Although my basic aim in this book is quite simply to describe the birth of the Trinity as it is manifest in the theologically rich yet underexplored matrix of theodramatic New Testament and early Christian scriptural interpretation, I have subsidiary intentions.

Types, Typology, and Prosopological Exegesis. First, in recovering an ancient historical model for how the Christ was understood to converse with the Father in the Old Testament, I desire to show that, contrary to a widespread consensus in biblical scholarship, the interpretative strategy employed by the earliest church with respect to these conversations was *not* generally *typological* but rather *prosopological* or *theodramatic.* For instance, the leading and most articulate advocate for the typological model for how Christ speaks in the Old Testament, Richard Hays, believes that David was regarded by the early church as a *type* or pattern for the future Christ, while at the same time, because the king embodied Israel's national sorrows and hopes he was also a type in the sense of a corporate symbol, allowing early Christians to see an imitative correspondence between David, Israel, and the future Christ. So according to this typological model Jesus Christ, it was felt by the earliest Christians, could appropriately be assigned as the true speaker of David's words.[11] Although there is plenty of reasoning around "types" in the New Testament in general (and Hays is an outstanding guide), the typological model as applied to the special case of Christ as one who speaks in the Old Testament, in my judgment, has decisive weaknesses—especially the lack of evidence that the earliest Christians had sufficient interest in the suffering of David so as to provide an imitative link. Accordingly, this book, by way of the cumulative force of the examples presented and evidence from reception history, seeks to advocate for a new way of understanding the interpretative logic of the earliest church:[12] When the Christ was found to speak or to be addressed in the Old Testament, this was generally because the first Christians were reading these particular texts in a prosopological rather than typological fashion.

Toward Connecting Biblical Studies and Theology. Second, I write as a confessing Christian, who as a trained scholar of Second Temple Judaism and Christian origins, has chafed at the frustrating, artificial divide between biblical studies and theology. Although there are extraordinary signs of a healthy rapprochement budding forth in every direction, especially the intense conversations about theological interpretation of Scripture, apart from

---

[11] Richard B. Hays, "Christ Prays the Psalms: Israel's Psalter as Matrix of Early Christology," *The Conversion of the Imagination* (Grand Rapids: Eerdmans, 2005), 101–18.

[12] On method, see "Historical Probability, Reception History, and Intertextuality" in Ch. 2.

several noteworthy gains, the practical pay-off has hitherto been slender.[13] I hope that this book shows something of my own vision for how the two can intertwine in a mutually beneficial synthesis. I am convinced that the theological interpretation of Scripture matters deeply for church and world, so if somehow this book helps stimulate readers to make like-minded attempts to reconnect the close study of Scripture and the early Christian Fathers (and any relevant but neglected Mothers) with the larger theological enterprise, then I shall be grateful.

In accordance with my desire to build cross-disciplinary bridges, I have attempted to make the book as approachable as possible for the non-specialist while still doing full justice to the subtleties of the ancient texts. In other words, although I have made ample use of the relevant ancient languages in writing, frequently supplying my own translations, I always immediately provide a translation of any ancient language that appears in the main body of the book, while restricting technical discussion to the notes whenever possible.[14] Accordingly, my hope is that the book will prove helpful not just to professionals and clergy, but also to general readers and students. A premium has been placed on the ancient texts themselves rather than on the staggeringly voluminous secondary literature of other scholars on the Trinity, early Christology, the historical Jesus, the New Testament, and related matters, so my engagement with other scholars is illustrative and representative rather than comprehensive, even though I have read more widely. I must beg the indulgence of anyone whose work merits more discussion but has not been treated.

Worldviews and Historical Research. Finally, since I am a Christian who researches, teaches, and writes in a confessional context—previously at the University of Notre Dame and now at Quincy University—I would like to say a few words about this "situated-ness" for a professional historian and theologian. For many, free intellectual inquiry into Christian origins is highly contentious and emotionally fraught. Even twenty-five years ago it would have been deemed inappropriate in a scholarly work involving historical reconstruction for an author to be frank in stating that she or he thinks and

---

[13] For a concise overview of theological interpretation, see Daniel J. Trier, *Introducing Theological Interpretation of Scripture: Recovering a Christian Practice* (Grand Rapids: Baker Academic, 2008). Exceptional practical achievements in theological interpretation include the Two Horizons New Testament Commentary series (ed. Joel B. Green and Max Turner; Grand Rapids: Eerdmans, 2005–), the Brazos Theological Commentaries on the Bible (ed. R. R. Reno; Grand Rapids: Brazos, 2005–), and the founding of the excellent new *Journal of Theological Interpretation* (ed. Joel B. Green; Winona Lake, Ind.: Eisenbrauns, 2007–). See the rationale for the THNTC series in Max Turner and Joel B. Green (eds.), *Between Two Horizons: Spanning New Testament Studies and Systematic Theology* (Grand Rapids: Eerdmans, 2000), 1–22.

[14] Throughout this volume all translations are my own unless otherwise noted, with the exception of Irenaeus's *Epideixis*. Since the *Epideixis* is extant mainly in Armenian, all translations are those of John Behr (trans. and intro.), *St. Irenaeus of Lyons, On the Apostolic Preaching* (Crestwood, NY: St Vladimir's Seminary Press, 1997).

writes about matters pertaining to Christian origins from within a Christian framework, because this would have been viewed as a distorting bias that precluded truly critical inquiry. Accordingly, despite the I-am-merely-a-historian claim offered by some working in this field, I am grateful that we live in an era in which it is increasingly recognized that there is no neutral, objective, independent ground that is unsullied by prior commitments and worldviews upon which any historian might stand when examining these matters. With respect to the study of anything, Christian origins included, *everyone* is equally intellectually positioned while undertaking the task—those outside, inside, on the fence, self-avowedly neutral, bitter, "in love with Jesus," intrigued, congenial, hostile. Yet, this inescapable perspectivalism when doing historical theology must not become an excuse for lack of fair-mindedness or intellectual rigor in seeking the truth. The best that we can do is to try to be honest with ourselves and with others about the lenses that we bring, exercise a healthy self-suspicion, and then to pursue the truth wherever it might lead.

* * *

For reasons that will become clear in the body of the book itself my own examination of early Christology and Trinitarian origins has led me as a historian to reject the view of specialists such as James D. G. Dunn and Bart Ehrman, who claim that the first Christians believed Jesus was adopted as "Son of God" (regarded originally only as a messianic title) at his resurrection but did not preexist as such, only more gradually coming to be regarded as preexistent and begotten before time. On the contrary, I conclude that it is more probable that the earliest Christians regarded Jesus as both a distinct divine person in relationship to God the Father and as the Son begotten before time, perhaps, although this is much more speculative, even beginning with the historical Jesus himself. Indeed, I believe the adoptionist hypothesis has flourished partly because scholarship has not yet come to appreciate the subtleties of the prosopological reading strategy deployed by the earliest church in a number of crucial passages in the New Testament.

At the end of this study, I find myself even more warmly affirming the Trinitarian dogma as traditionally described in the Niceno-Constantinopolitan creedal synthesis: there is one God who subsists as three distinct persons—uncaused Father, eternally begotten Son, and sent-forth Spirit.

1

Reading as Birth—The Trinity Emerges

There has been a significant revival of interest in the Trinity in the last century within systematic theology,[1] and there are undoubtedly an incalculable number of ways in which the doctrine of the Trinity has informed and continues to shape systematic and constructive theology.[2] However, in terms of the basic storyline of the *historical* development or emergence of this doctrine as can be discerned in the New Testament and other ancient sources, four basic positions can be discerned. The first three are quite well known and are easily represented and described, but the fourth is more like cargo on a sunken battleship. A few are privy to its approximate location and possible worth— and their initial soundings have signaled as much to the broader scholarly community—but nobody has really attempted to extract the submerged goods so that their value can be assessed.

There is, of course, a healthy measure of truth in all four scholarly narratives about the way Father, Son, and Spirit came to be regarded as differentiating the one God for early Christians, so that to a significant degree the approaches overlap and are blended by most scholars. Indeed there is a certain

---

[1] Although the main conversation partners for this book are those engaged in the study of Christological and Trinitarian origins in the NT and earliest church, we will occasionally take sideways glances at the theological edifices constructed by leading Trinitarian architects in contemporary theology—e.g. Barth, Rahner, and Moltmann. Yet, most of these efforts have little to do with the rise and unfolding of Trinitarianism itself in the earliest sources, but rather with the constructive conclusions for theology that result once the Trinitarian dogma is assumed as the necessary starting point—e.g. Barth's notion of the self-revealing triune God; Rahner's intimate linkage of the immanent Trinity with the economic Trinity; Boff's emphasis on the Trinity as the basis for authentic human community and relationality. For an excellent survey, see Stanley J. Grenz, *Rediscovering the Triune God: The Trinity in Contemporary Theology* (Minneapolis: Fortress, 2004). Stephen R. Holmes, *The Quest for the Trinity: The Doctrine of God in Scripture, History and Modernity* (Downers Grove, Ill.: IVP Academic, 2012), also briefly but ably surveys the contemporary Trinitarian revival in dogmatic theology while demonstrating that many of these recent contributions substantially depart from the classical articulation of Trinitarian dogma.

[2] Something of the dizzying current diversity can be seen in the parts V–VII of the recent contribution in Gilles Emery and Matthew Levering (eds.), *The Oxford Handbook of The Trinity* (New York: Oxford University Press, 2011).

danger in associating specific scholars with any singular approach given the fine-combed subtleties in their positions. Nonetheless, a heuristic can help us identify the dominant strands, even if these strands are in the final analysis intertwined for virtually every scholar. This is not a comprehensive attempt to describe the history of scholarship on the origins and growth of the doctrine of the Trinity or of how Jesus and the Spirit came to be viewed as fully divine alongside or within the one God of Israel—far from it. Especially since, focusing on initial impetus and not wishing to tread overly much upon ground already well covered by others, apart from some very brief orienting words near the end of this chapter, I say virtually nothing about Nicaea, Constantinople, and other crucial post-Tertullian developments[3]—rather it is a means of organizing the scholarship and briefly exemplifying the principle approaches to help the reader discern precisely where this study hopes to make a unique contribution.[4] My specific claim is that the church's ultimate preference for primarily speaking of God's *oneness* in terms of distinct *persons*— rather than, let's say, powers or luminaries—was predominately established by a prosopological reading of certain dialogical shifts in the Old Testament, and that this reading strategy was widely deployed by New Testament and second-century Christian authors.

FOUR APPROACHES TO THE GROWTH OF THE DOCTRINE OF THE TRINITY

Trinitarianism by Encounter with the Historical Jesus

The first approach might be termed "Trinitarianism by encounter with the historical Jesus," and its advocates tend to be staunch defenders of the full-flowered bloom of the doctrine of the Trinity, so much so that they are

---

[3] For a concise yet accurate standard account of the development of Trinitarian dogma, see Franz Dünzl, *A Brief History of the Doctrine of the Trinity in the Early Church* (trans. John Bowden; London: T&T Clark, 2007). A selection of primary sources is collected by William G. Rusch (trans. and ed.), *The Trinitarian Controversy* (Philadelphia: Fortress, 1980). On the era between the first century and the fourth, I particularly appreciate John Behr, *The Way to Nicaea: The Formation of Christian Theology, Volume i* (Crestwood: NY, St Vladimir's Seminary Press, 2001), especially for the emphasis on the role of Scripture in doctrinal development. For particularly outstanding recent syntheses of Nicaea and its aftermath as it pertains to the Trinity, see Lewis Ayres, *Nicaea and Its Legacy: An Approach to Fourth-Century Trinitarian Theology* (Oxford: Oxford University Press, 2004) and Khaled Anatolios, *Retrieving Nicaea: The Development and Meaning of Trinitarian Doctrine* (Grand Rapids: Baker Academic, 2011).

[4] For an alternative way of organizing the field based on varieties of monotheism, see James F. McGrath, *The Only True God: Early Christian Monotheism in Its Jewish Context* (Urbana, Ill.: University of Illinois Press, 2009), 5–22.

particularly keen to show that this doctrine is inchoately present even if not quite fully formed in the New Testament. It is not just a bare seed sprinkled with dirt and hope—a blossom has emerged, and even if the blossom has not yet fully opened, the bud has already appeared and is beginning to unfurl. The main claim here is that Trinitarian theology developed because *the experience of meeting Jesus*, and perhaps the subsequently sent Spirit as well, *forced the issue*. That is to say, quite simply, the historical Jesus claimed and did things that no ordinary human could possibly have done, culminating in the resurrection. This compelled his earliest followers to revere him as a divine *person* and stimulated an ineluctable movement toward the full Trinitarian flower of three persons having the same divine essence.

This approach is especially favored by older studies that touch on emerging Christology and the rise of Trinitarian dogma, although it continues to find a contemporary hearing, especially in the works of Christian apologists and in catalogue-type studies that aim primarily to collect Trinitarian data as "proof" in the scriptural sources. For example, Jules Lebreton, whose classic study remains the single most comprehensive treatment of the growth of the Trinitarian doctrine before the Council of Nicaea (325 CE), places the heaviest weight on "Trinitarianism by encounter with the historical Jesus"—even though he is well aware of other approaches—when he claims that any fair-minded historian, "will attribute to Jesus himself the decisive role" in the revelation of Trinitarian and Christological dogmas, and "will consequently give primary attention to the part played" by him.[5] In a like-minded manner, such a view of the eventual development of the Trinity is also intimated, even if not made explicit, in popular apologetic works. For example, C. S. Lewis's justly famous *trilemma*—that the historical Jesus was necessarily one of three things: (1) a liar, (2) a lunatic, as Lewis so memorably puts it, "on a level with the man who says he is a poached egg," or (3) the very Lord God almighty.[6] In short, Jesus' strange claims and mighty deeds compelled an acknowledgment of his full divinity, stimulating an inevitable growth toward the mature Trinitarian dogma.

And although obviously attributing the growth of Trinitarian doctrine solely to an experiential encounter with the historical Jesus would be a gross oversimplification—as even those who place special weight upon this element are generally ready to admit—it should not be rejected or despised for its artlessness, for such a view can claim ample warrant in the early sources, even

---

[5] Jules Lebreton, *History of the Dogma of the Trinity: From Its Origins to the Council of Nicæa, i. The Origins* (trans. Algar Thorold; London: Burns Oates & Washbourne, 1939), 191. Lebreton emphasizes that it was only the distinctive encounter with Jesus (and subsequently the Spirit) by his early followers that could have amalgamated the various Jewish and Hellenistic religious and philosophical traditions: "it is impossible to find in the Christian faith a single concept that was not transformed and elevated by contact with him" (pp. xv–xxiii, here p. xv).

[6] C. S. Lewis, *Mere Christianity* (rev. edn.; New York: Touchstone, 1996), 52–6, here 56.

if thorny questions must still be asked regarding how precisely these sources contribute toward a composite portrait of the historical Jesus. Accordingly, the temple guards who are commissioned to seize Jesus, but who cannot quite bring themselves to do it, testify: "No person has ever spoken in this way" (John 7: 46). Or, as the Roman centurion is compelled to say after watching the strange events surrounding Jesus' crucifixion, "Truly this man was God's son" (Mark 15: 39). Indeed, Jesus' forceful claim that his own identity is bound up with God in such a way that he shares attributes and functional prerogatives that appropriately belong to God alone can be found not only in passages, the historical value of which skeptically minded critics might question, such as John 8: 58 ("Jesus said to them, 'Truly truly I say to you, Before Abraham came into existence, I am'"), but also in synoptic tradition that is widely regarded as historical (e.g. Mark 14: 61–2 and Matt. 19: 28).[7]

In addition to the older studies and to works of popular apologetics that emphasize "Trinitarianism by encounter with the historical Jesus," related catalogue-type studies have generally tended to find support for this notion by their presuppositional starting points. The most comprehensive of these catalogue-type studies of which I am aware is Arthur W. Wainwright, *The Trinity in the New Testament*. Here one finds an extensive collection of statements of God's oneness (e.g. "God is one"—Rom. 3: 30), dyadic statements (e.g. "*I am in the Father* and the *Father* is in *me*"—John 14: 10), triadic groupings (e.g. "The grace of the Lord *Jesus Christ* and the love of *God* and the fellowship of the *Holy Spirit* be with you all"—2 Cor. 13: 14; cf. 1 Pet. 1: 2), and the like that do prove that something approaching the future Trinitarian dogma can be found in the New Testament. Yet Wainwright is typical of this sort of study inasmuch as he definitively—at least to my mind—shows that the New Testament speaks of Father, Son, and Spirit in terms that demonstrate that these are regarded as three divine entities, but without really attempting an explanation of *how* the doctrine originated and grew—apart from raw presuppositional assertions affirming a high Christology such as "Christians believed Jesus was divine" that align with "Trinitarianism by encounter with the historical Jesus."[8]

---

[7] On the controversial and complex issue of historicity and Jesus, see "The Historically Plausible Jesus" in Ch. 2. On the historicity of Mark 14: 62, see N. T. Wright, *Jesus and the Victory of God* (Minneapolis: Fortress, 1996), 519–28; on the general plausibility of Jesus uttering this sort of logion, see Dale C. Allison, Jr., *Constructing Jesus: Memory, Imagination, and History* (Grand Rapids: Baker Academic, 2010), 246–7. On Matt. 19: 28, see Allison, *Constructing Jesus*, 68–74; John P. Meier, *A Marginal Jew* (4 vols.; ABRL; New York: Doubleday, 1991–2009), iii. 135–9.

[8] Arthur W. Wainwright, *The Trinity in the New Testament* (London: SPCK, 1962), 3. Although Wainwright does briefly sketch some helpful background information in his second chapter, "The Trinity in Hebrew Religion," his main burden is to show that the Trinitarian problem—that is, the question of the nature and relationship between Father, Son, and Spirit— emerged in the NT era itself rather than in subsequent church history. As such, his main task is

For strong adherents of this position, even though the distinctive technical Trinitarian language—*hypostasis, ousia, substantia, prosōpon, persona, homoousios*, and the like—would not be employed in the church to describe the Trinity until centuries later, nonetheless the move from the New Testament to the Nicene and post-Nicene creeds is miniscule, because the Trinitarian dogma is for all practical purposes functionally present already in the ideas of the New Testament itself. As we shall see, it is perhaps safest to affirm a soft version of this approach. The encounter with Jesus and the Spirit as refracted through early Christian memory was undeniably indispensable to Christological and Trinitarian origins, while at the same time it must be acknowledged that other approaches are necessary to bridge the distance between the first-century church and the fourth-century Trinitarian creeds.

Trinitarianism by Hellenistic Philosophical Imposition

The second scholarly avenue for describing the historical emergence of the Trinity might be called "Trinitarianism by Hellenistic philosophical imposition." What defines this approach is the assertion that Jewish monotheism was incapable of a linear growth toward a high Christology and Trinitarian conceptions apart from the borrowing of alien Hellenistic philosophical language and categories that twisted Christianity into a form far removed from its roots. The tireless and enormously influential champion of this position in the twentieth century was Adolf von Harnack in his *History of Dogma*, and the reverberations from Harnack's impact are still being felt today.

Harnack, building on the legacy of F. C. Baur, argued that a history of Christian dogma must presuppose a definitive separation between Judaism and nascent Christianity within the first two generations after the death of Jesus. In light of this definitive break, emergent Christianity was in need of a rich cultural heritage by means of which it could transform itself away from Judaism and house its unique developing ideas, thus: "The Christian Church and its doctrine were developed within the Roman world and Greek culture in opposition to the Jewish Church."[9]

As such, Christianity—beginning especially with the Apologists—borrowed heavily from Hellenistic philosophy in conceptualizing God. For example, even though the *Logos* ("Word") of John 1: 1—"In the beginning was the *Logos*, and the *Logos* was with God, and the *Logos* was God"—is rooted in the

---

to list and discuss all the pertinent NT evidence, and this he achieves quite admirably (excluding much of the prosopological data to be discussed in this book).

[9] Adolf von Harnack, *History of Dogma* (trans. Neil Buchanan; 7 vols.; London: Williams & Norgate, 1894–9), i. 43–50, here i. 46. See further Harnack's remarks about the dominance of the "Hellenic spirit" (i. 48–9).

creation story of Genesis, in which God creates the cosmos through *speech*, the *Logos* theology of John was nonetheless articulated in a milieu that was very much indebted to earlier Hellenistic philosophy. In Stoicism, *Logos* is the rational principle that permeates the entire universe, making it knowable. Meanwhile, in Middle Platonism, the transcendent divinity actualizes itself in the world through "mind" or "idea" or *Logos*, bringing order to the cosmos. Indeed, for Jesus' contemporary, the Jewish middle-Platonic philosopher Philo of Alexandria, the *Logos*, which could be termed the "image of God" and even "first-born" of God, is the intermediate reality standing between the transcendent God and the material universe, while the *Logos* also serves as the instrument through which the universe is organized.[10]

Since disagreements over the precise relationship between the preexistent *Logos*, the human Jesus of Nazareth, and God the Father indisputably played a central role in subsequent Trinitarian and Christological developments, the strong influence of Hellenistic ideas at this juncture cannot seriously be questioned by any responsible account of Trinitarian growth; indeed, by the time of Origen the *Logos* could be viewed as a distinct, subordinate *hypostasis* ("discrete individual being") that mediates between the uncreated God and the created order, much as in Middle Platonism.[11]

The claims of "Trinitarianism by Hellenistic philosophical imposition" are quite different than "Trinitarianism by encounter with the historical Jesus"— yet some but not all of the tenets of the two positions are mutually compatible in principle. For example, agreement can potentially be reached that Jesus' own person stands at the origin of the rise of Trinitarianism. In fact, in line with the softer version of "Trinitarianism by encounter with the historical Jesus," Harnack himself felt that the historical Jesus did play an integral role in inaugurating Christian dogma[12]—even though Harnack personally rejected many orthodox fundamentals such as the incarnation and resurrection. Yet to Harnack's mind, the Hellenistic move ultimately (but sadly) dwarfed and eclipsed any impetus prompted by Jesus' earthly teachings and activities. For advocates of Harnack's position, the sharp division and dichotomy between the ideas of the Jewish Jesus and his earliest Jewish followers about God and those of the later Hellenistic church are difficult to reconcile with the more simple model of "Trinitarianism by encounter with the historical Jesus," inasmuch as they suggest that an ordinary, faithful, monotheistic Jew could

---

[10] E.g. see Philo, *Conf.* 146 (cf. *Somn.* 1. 215) for "his [God's] first-born *Logos*" (*ton prōto-gonon autou logon*); see *Fug.* 101 (cf. *Spec. Leg.* 1. 81) for "the divine *Logos* . . . itself being an image of God" (*logos theios . . . autos eikōn hyparchōn theou*). On the *Logos* as chief intermediary and agent of cosmic ordering, see Philo, *Opif.* 19–25; *Sacr.* 8; *Cher.* 127.

[11] On the *Logos* in the Apologists, see Harnack, *History of Dogma*, ii. 206–14. For Harnack's reconstruction of the transformation of the doctrine of the *Logos* as it moved through the Alexandrian platonic grid and interfaced with emerging Trinitarianism, see ii. 352–61.

[12] Harnack, *History of Dogma*, i. 42.

not have believed in a triune God apart from a dramatic, foreign Hellenistic influence.

Harnack's reconstruction cast a long shadow in the scholarly community devoted to studying Christian origins, and the shadow can still be seen today, even though—as we shall see—many of its assumptions and conclusions have been decisively undermined. For example, Harnack's influence can be observed in the Christological synthesis of Wilhelm Bousset, *Kyrios Christos*, who argued that the Jewish-Christian titles "Christ" and "Son of Man" came to be superseded by the preferred title of the Gentile Christians, "Lord," in service of an incipient mysticism that conflated Christ and the Spirit.[13] The likeminded assumption of dogmatic growth predicated upon a drastic split between Jewish and Gentile Christians is also at the heart of Rudolph Bultmann's *Theology of the New Testament*.[14]

This same logic persists today and continues to be featured even in some of the most prestigious New Testament commentaries. To choose just one example among many, in his contribution to the highly regarded Hermeneia series, Robert Jewett argues that the pre-Pauline Jewish-Christian community believed that Jesus was neither preexistent nor born of a virgin, but that he was *adopted* as God's Son at his resurrection. Subsequently the Hellenistic community sought to undermine this Jewish-Christian emphasis on Jesus' messianic qualifications by accenting the Spirit. For Jewett, in response to this early Christological disagreement, Paul is trying to reconcile these disharmonious positions in his letter to the Romans.[15]

Although nobody should deny that the earliest church made liberal use of the Greek language and Hellenistic philosophical resources in wrestling with the identity of God, both at its inception and in the subsequent centuries, nonetheless the thesis of "Trinitarianism by Hellenistic philosophical imposition" has justifiably fallen on hard times as the dominant explanation.[16] For in the first place, subsequent scholarship has shown, in what would appear to be

---

[13] Wilhelm Bousset, *Kyrios Christos: A History of the Belief in Christ from the Beginnings of Christianity to Irenaeus* (trans. John E. Steely; Nashville: Abingdon, 1970).

[14] Although Rudolph Bultmann, *Theology of the New Testament* (trans. Kendrick Grobel; 2 vols.; London: SCM, 1952–5), i. 35, decisively rejected the notion—so prevalent in earlier studies—that the personality of the historical Jesus was decisive to the development of early Christian doctrine, he did persist in seeing a strong Jewish/Hellenistic dichotomy, as can be seen by comparing in vol. i his Ch. 2 (focused on the eschatological setting of the Jerusalem-based church) with his Ch. 3 (describing the Hellenistic church).

[15] See Robert Jewett, *Romans: A Commentary* (Hermeneia; Minneapolis: Fortress, 2007), 98, which builds on his earlier work: Robert Jewett, "The Redaction and Use of an Early Christian Confession in Romans 1:3–4," in D. E. Groh and R. Jewett (eds.), *The Living Text: Essays in Honor of Ernest W. Saunders* (Lanham, Md.: University Press of America, 1985), 99–122.

[16] An exception to this trend is the recent effort by Marian Hillar, *From Logos to Trinity: The Evolution of Religious Beliefs from Pythagoras to Tertullian* (Cambridge: Cambridge University Press, 2012). Hillar, who situates himself in the stream of radical criticism, sees orthodox Trinitarian dogma as an illegitimate Middle Platonic outgrowth of *Logos* theology, favoring a

a decisively irreversible manner, the high degree to which Hellenism had thoroughly penetrated Palestinian Judaism by the time of Jesus, showing the hypothesis of a phased dogmatic development from Jewish Christianity to Hellenistic Christianity to be implausible.[17] Second, not only is there no evidence supporting hermetically sealed Jewish-Christian and Hellenistic-Christian factions, the decisive break between Judaism proper and what would later come to be termed Christianity does not appear to have been as decisive as Harnack (and others) imagined—rather the communities remained somewhat fluid while polemicizing against one another as a means of self-definition, and all the while offering divergent answers to some basic worldview questions.[18]

In other words, the growth of Trinitarian dogma could not result from an *alien* Hellenistic tainting not because the thesis of Hellenistic philosophical influence was spurious, but rather because the *pure* Jewish monotheism of Jesus and his earliest followers is chimerical—Hellenism had already decisively encroached into Palestinian Judaism well before Jesus. If the second-century church (and beyond) would continue to use Hellenistic philosophical resources in conceptualizing God, this was not a break with the earliest church, but an extension of its original setting and practices. Finally, and most importantly, the third approach—to be discussed next—has shown to the satisfaction of many that Judaism itself (through ongoing Hellenistic engagement) had more than adequate resources that could account for an organic move from faithful Jewish monotheism to the Nicene-Christian conception of a plurality of distinct divine persons having the same divine essence or being.

Trinitarianism as the Outgrowth of Mediated Jewish Monotheism

The third way of describing the origin and development of the doctrine of the Trinity can be termed "Trinitarianism as the outgrowth of mediated Jewish monotheism." Here emphasis is placed upon various beings that mediated the

---

unitarian conception of God. But among other problems, I do not believe his position can be sustained in light of early Christian scriptural interpretation.

[17] See Saul Lieberman, *Hellenism in Jewish Palestine: Studies in the Literary Transmission, Beliefs and Manners of Palestine in the I Century B.C.E–IV Century C.E.* (New York: Jewish Theological Seminary of America, 1962); Martin Hengel, *Judaism and Hellenism: Studies in Their Encounter in Palestine During the Early Hellenistic Period* (trans. John Bowden; 2 vols.; Philadelphia: Fortress, 1974).

[18] On fluidity, see Daniel Boyarin, *Border Lines: The Partition of Judeo-Christianity* (Philadelphia: University of Pennsylvania Press, 2004); on polemics and self-definition, see Judith Lieu, *Image and Reality: The Jews in the World of the Christians in the Second Century* (London: T&T Clark, 1996); on worldview differences, see N. T. Wright, *The New Testament and the People of God* (Minneapolis: Fortress, 1992), 444–64.

divine, were quasi-divine, or were highly venerated as divine agents alongside God within the bounds of monotheistic Second Temple Judaism. Such Jewish categories—which under this analysis perhaps strained but did not break monotheism—include personified Wisdom, the *Logos*, elevated patriarchs, the Son of Man in Daniel and the Enochic literature, kings/messiahs, priests, various archangels who might rule from the divine throne (especially as is evidenced in the Dead Sea Scrolls), and platonic categories. As James McGrath, one of the leading proponents of this approach, puts it: "Numerous Jewish texts allow for the existence of a 'second figure' alongside God—of high rank and at times almost blending into God, yet at other times clearly subordinate and distinct."[19] This is far and away the most popular explanation today for how Jesus was elevated to divine status and for the ultimate development of the doctrine of the Trinity within New Testament and early Christian studies—although, of course, it can be (and usually is) combined with the two other approaches that have just been discussed.

Although he rejects the notion that any of these intermediaries (except angels) had a truly autonomous status vis-à-vis God, the decidedly influential work of James D. G. Dunn nonetheless exemplifies this well, as he places a definite emphasis on mediatorial Jewish categories, seeing Wisdom and Adam Christologies as especially important in the earliest church. But he also argues that for the earliest Christians, Jesus was understood as having been appointed to divine sonship only on the day of his resurrection, not preexisting as such— what is frequently termed an adoptionist Christology.[20] For Dunn, the movement of Jesus from human to divine status within the earliest church, and hence the road to anything approaching the full-blown Trinitarian dogma, is a lengthy, complex, and convoluted process that was ultimately facilitated by ransacking language about transcendent brokers of the divine—such as Wisdom—in late Second Temple Judaism as it collided with Hellenism. As will be discussed in Chapter 2, I think there are methodological problems present in Dunn's study that undermine some of his results.[21]

Working along a trajectory similar to Dunn's (but coming to quite different conclusions), Larry Hurtado has explored the interface between Christology and Jewish monotheism in a wave of stimulating and carefully researched projects that culminate in his magisterial *Lord Jesus Christ*.[22] For Hurtado, late

---

[19] McGrath, *The Only True God*, 16.

[20] James D. G. Dunn, *Christology in the Making: A New Testament Inquiry into the Origins of the Doctrine of the Incarnation* (2nd edn.; Grand Rapids: Eerdmans, 1989), on which see esp. pp. 33–6, 163–212. For an updated statement engaging with more recent proposals, see James D. G. Dunn, *Did the First Christians Worship Jesus?: The New Testament Evidence* (Louisville, Ky.: Westminster John Knox, 2010).

[21] See esp. nn. 31 and 32 in Ch. 2.

[22] Larry W. Hurtado, *Lord Jesus Christ: Devotion to Jesus in Earliest Christianity* (Grand Rapids: Eerdmans, 2003). For his earlier work, see especially Larry W. Hurtado, *One God, One Lord: Early Christian Devotion and Ancient Jewish Monotheism* (Philadelphia: Fortress, 1988).

Second Temple Judaism as a whole was characterized by a belief in a diverse multitude of exalted divine agents. Nonetheless it was perfectly capable of maintaining belief in these agents without Jews feeling that their unique brand of "exclusivist" monotheism had been compromised, because these divine agents were *not worshiped* alongside God. In other words, the divine could be (and was) readily construed as mediated in a wide variety of ways—and God was even believed in many quarters to have a chief vizier that represented God in a relatively full sense, but this was not felt to violate the monotheistic principle embedded in the Shema (see Deut. 6: 4), that there truly is only one God, the God of Israel. This principle was concretely affirmed by worshipping *only* this singularly real God.

Yet Hurtado gives an interesting further twist, because he argues that the very earliest Christian devotion emerges from exclusivist Jewish monotheism, borrowing from its conceptual categories of divine agency, but shows a significant realignment that can be called binitarian (although not yet fully Trinitarian) inasmuch as Jesus was worshiped *from the beginning* in the nascent church alongside God in a fashion entirely without precedent within the bounds of contemporaneous Jewish monotheism. Hurtado is compelled to conclude, correctly in my estimation, that the earliest sources indicate that the earthly ministry of Jesus and convictions about the reality of his resurrection and exaltation served to bring about this explosively rapid and unprecedented shift. So Hurtado largely accepts both the soft version of "encounter with the historical Jesus" and the *mediatorial* approach—as does this present author as well. How does all of this relate to Trinitarianism? As Hurtado puts it in speaking about the later Trinitarian syntheses of Nicaea and Chalcedon,

> It would be simplistic and naïve to collapse the distinctions between these later stages of Christian reflection and the foundational stage.... But it would also be simplistic to ignore the fact that the intricate and often heated doctrinal discussion leading to these later formulations was set in motion quite early in the Christian movement by the appropriation of the divine agency category.[23]

That is, for Hurtado and others it was the experiences of the earliest Christians of Jesus when combined with Jewish conceptions of divine agency (as they mutated into binitarian worship of Jesus in earliest Christianity) that above all compelled the church in the Trinitarian direction. In sum, although both Hurtado and Dunn concur that Jewish categories of divine agency were important vehicles for expressing early Christology, for Hurtado over against Dunn, the stress is on the explosive immediacy of the rise of Jesus to divine status rather than on a gradual, developmental process.

This mediatorial approach nears its extreme in the recent book by Adela Yarbro Collins and John J. Collins, *King and Messiah as Son of God*, in which

---

[23] Hurtado, *One God*, 127.

they argue, correctly, that the title "Son of God" was a fairly ordinary way of speaking about the king or the emperor in the ancient Near Eastern environment in which late Second Temple Judaism flourished.[24] Hence, they contend that the title Son of God as applied to Jesus was at first a messianic title with no real, literal ontological overtones. That is, they conclude that although Paul, the first Christian author, speaks of Jesus as the preexistent messiah, the title "Son of God" came to entail something more than messiahship only as part of a gradual development in the early church. Much the same conclusion is reached in the popularizing work of Bart Ehrman, *How Jesus Became God*.[25] However, I believe that a proper assessment of the Christology displayed in our earliest Christian documents (not least with respect to person-centered scriptural exegesis as discussed in the chapters that follow), does not allow for these developmental conclusions.

If Yarbro Collins and Collins move a long way down the path, the full zenith of Trinitarianism as a developmental outgrowth of mediatorial figures within Second Temple Judaism has now been attained by Daniel Boyarin. For Boyarin, in the final analysis the doctrine of the Trinity is quite simply a Jewish notion: "The ideas of Trinity and incarnation, or certainly the germs of those ideas, were already present among Jewish believers well before Jesus came on the scene to incarnate in himself, as it were, those theological notions and to take up his messianic calling."[26] According to Boyarin, then, the distinctive ideas of additional divine figures alongside God (the Father) were already highly developed during the time of Jesus Christ, so the Trinity is as much (or more?) a Jewish concept as a Christian one!

Meanwhile despite the enormous popularity of the approach of Dunn, Hurtado, Yarbro Collins and Collins, Ehrman, Boyarin, and others in recent scholarship—what I have called "Trinitarianism as the outgrowth of mediated Jewish monotheism"—one prominent scholar is skeptical that this avenue can sufficiently explain the overlapping conceptions of Jesus and God in the earliest sources. Richard Bauckham, in his *God Crucified*, does not deny that

---

[24] Adela Yarbro Collins and John J. Collins, *King and Messiah as Son of God: Divine, Human, and Angelic Messianic Figures in Biblical and Related Literature* (Grand Rapids: Eerdmans, 2008).

[25] Bart D. Ehrman, *How Jesus Became God: The Exaltation of a Jewish Preacher from Galilee* (New York: HarperOne, 2014). Ehrman is to be commended for recognizing that Paul does truly identify Jesus as a preexistent being. Yet Ehrman thinks Jesus was regarded by Paul as a preexistent *angel* (see pp. 252–4, 267–9), which is to overemphasize an idiosyncratic detail capable of several competing explanations in Gal. 4: 14, and to downplay inappropriately a much more obvious category that is ubiquitously and unambiguously present in Paul's letters— Jesus is consistently regarded not as an *angel* by Paul, but as God's *Son* (e.g. Rom. 1: 3; 1: 9; 5: 10; 8: 3; 8: 29; 1 Cor. 1: 9; 15: 28; 2 Cor. 1: 19; Gal. 1: 16; 2: 20; 1 Thess. 1: 10; etc.). No additional category beyond *Son* is needed to make sense of the data regarding preexistence in Paul, so why multiply categories unnecessarily?

[26] Daniel Boyarin, *The Jewish Gospels: The Story of the Jewish Christ* (New York: The New Press, 2012), 102.

there were numerous mediatorial figures that were occasionally thought to be capable of brokering the one God in late Second Temple Judaism; moreover, he thinks, in essential agreement with Hurtado, that the "uniqueness of God" was by and large stressed in this period. Yet Bauckham parts company with the majority in stating that intermediary figures are idiosyncratic and of tangential rather than central import: "Intermediate figures who may or may not participate in divinity are by no means characteristic of the literature of Second Temple Judaism."[27] Thus, generally speaking, Bauckham denies that organic growth from mediatorial roles facilitated the early Christian elevation of Jesus to divine status, favoring instead the idea that God and Jesus were directly correlated in the earliest church because they were regarded as having the same *unique personal identity*.[28]

N. T. Wright, in his monumental study *Paul and the Faithfulness of God*, has given Bauckham's Christology of Divine Identity proposal a resounding endorsement while seeking to build upon it further.[29] Like Bauckham, Wright contends that scholarship has begun its investigation in the wrong direction. Previous scholarship has analyzed in minute detail exaltation-categories that were extant in pre-Christian Judaism in hope of showing how it is that these categories might explain the upward movement of Jesus to divine status. Wright provocatively queries: "Why should we not begin, not with 'exalted figures' who might as it were be assimilated into the One God, but with the One God himself? Did Judaism have any beliefs, stories, ideas *about God himself* upon which they might have drawn to say what they now wanted to say about Jesus?"[30] For Wright, the answer is explicitly "yes," Judaism did have stories about the one God that were drawn upon to show that Jesus participates in the divine identity. For Wright, who correctly insists that Second Temple Jews (including the earliest Christians) were eschatological monotheists, it is above all the story of "the long-awaited return of YHWH to Zion," the idea that God would return in person to be with his people, that is "the hidden clue to the origin of christology."[31]

---

[27] Richard Bauckham, *God Crucified: Monotheism and Christology in the New Testament* (Grand Rapids: Eerdmans, 1998), 5. He has expanded this seminal study by adding supplemental essays in Richard Bauckham, *Jesus and the God of Israel: God Crucified and Other Studies on the New Testament's Christology of Divine Identity* (Milton Keynes: Paternoster, 2008).

[28] Note, however, that Bauckham, *God Crucified*, 20–2, 26, does include Wisdom and Word within God's unique divine identity, so his reticence toward divine agents as a beachhead for establishing a high Christology needs to be tempered in this way.

[29] N. T. Wright, *Paul and the Faithfulness of God* (2 vols. in 4 parts; Minneapolis: Fortress, 2013), ii. 3. 644–56 esp. 651. Note well, Wright's massive monograph appeared subsequent to the drafting of my full manuscript, so apart from some brief notices here and elsewhere, regretfully I was not able to engage its entirety.

[30] Wright, *Paul and the Faithfulness of God*, ii. 3. 653.

[31] Wright, *Paul and the Faithfulness of God*, ii. 3. 654.

Bauckham and Wright have advanced innovative and exciting proposals—and in general I am sympathetic to their detailed readings of specific texts and their criticism of previous scholarly approaches. In short, I agree with them that stories about God within eschatological monotheism took precedent over (but did not obviate) ready-made mediatorial categories with regard to Christological origins. However, at least until further studies are done, at the same time I would recommend caution in embracing a Christology of Divine Identity as presently formulated for three reasons.

A Looming "Identity" Crisis? First, as he forthrightly acknowledges, Bauckham is using a modern category—identity—that lacks a clear ancient counterpart.[32] And although in and of itself this is not problematic, in this particular case it causes difficulties for the overall model. As Dunn has correctly noted, "identity" is not self-interpreting, and the introduction of this modern term probably raises more questions than it answers.[33] By "unique personal identity," as best as I can discern, Bauckham intends something akin to human personal identity inasmuch as this is formed for a human person via a journey through time, resulting in certain character qualities, actions, relations, roles, and so forth.[34]

God as Eternally Differentiated. Second, in formulating his Christology of Divine Identity model, Bauckham stresses identity forged *through time* and, whether wittingly or not, de-emphasizes the ontic ("being") relationship between the Father and the Son *outside time*. This diminishes the utility of the distinct divine "person" concept in considering how the one God is *eternally* differentiated. If we discover in the earliest sources that divine persons are found to speak to one another beyond the ordinary boundaries of time, then how precisely can the identity model accommodate such conversations? In other words, if the earliest sources indicate that the economic Trinity points to an immanent Trinity, then how does this result integrate with the identity-through-time model?[35] I think that these questions can potentially be answered—perhaps Bauckham will clarify in subsequent publications—but I am not presently convinced that the answers are not *best* given by upholding the Niceno-Constantinopolitan language of three persons subsisting in one divine essence. Thus, even for our earliest Christian sources I currently support what is perhaps best termed a *Christology of Divine Persons*, signaling that prosopological exegesis (and its multi-person dialogical nature) was essential both to an early high Christology and to Trinitarian

---

[32] See Bauckham, *Jesus*, 6 esp. n. 5.   [33] Dunn, *Did the First Christians*, 141–4.

[34] Bauckham, *God Crucified*, 3–13. Bauckham is also particularly leery of the perceived need to choose between a functional and ontic Christology, seeing the choice as a false dilemma that puts an unhealthy emphasis on categories alien to the earliest church (pp. 40–2).

[35] On the economic and immanent Trinity, see n. 10 in the Introduction.

dogmatic development. Meanwhile I remain open to further conversation about how, beginning with stories about Israel's God, we can best speak about the essence or nature of God.

The Primacy of the Person Metaphor. Third, I want to raise another cautionary flag with respect to a Christology of Divine Identity as it pertains to the person metaphor. As much as I appreciate the overall contributions of Bauckham and Wright, this study, I believe, shows that all Trinitarian proposals that dance away from the time-honored concept of *persons* having the same divine essence are at least somewhat infelicitous. Why? Because they risk severing the person-centered exegetical thread that connected the earliest Christians to their ancient Scripture, cloaking how the early church came to the realization that the one God subsists as three distinct *persons*. The Christology of Divine Identity schema is not the only model that obscures the primacy of the person metaphor with respect to Trinitarian origins. For example, Karl Barth undermines the person metaphor even more radically when he glibly substitutes out the standard person model in favor of "modes of being" (*Seinsweise*), and also when he uses terms such as "revelation," "Scripture," and "proclamation" in place of the traditional names of Father, Son, and Spirit.[36] It may be that newer models such as a Christology of Divine Identity can supplant or be successfully harmonized with the traditional three-persons-sharing-one-divine-essence model—I am certainly open to the possibility. In fact, reflection on early Christian prosopological exegesis might prove helpful in clarifying what the "in person" actually means, for instance, in N. T. Wright's frequent refrain that incarnational Christology developed from the promise of Israel's God to return "in person" to rescue his people and the world.[37] But I submit that more work needs to be done to show how such Christological schemata can account for the emergence of the doctrine of the Trinity in conjunction with prosopological exegesis as it was practiced in the earliest church.

So, in sum, although I do not endorse Bauckham's identity proposal as presently formulated, I do share with Bauckham, Wright, and others a reticence in certain regards toward the dominant explanation of "Trinitarianism as the outgrowth of mediated Jewish monotheism."[38] More precisely, although I judge that advocates of this approach have indeed convincingly demonstrated that the earliest Christians did draw upon Jewish conceptual categories of

---

[36] Karl Barth, *Church Dogmatics* (4 vols.; Edinburgh: T&T Clark, 1956–75), i. 1. 121.

[37] For this "in person" language in conjunction with YHWH's return, see e.g. Wright, *Paul and the Faithfulness of God*, ii. 3. 653, 655, 688, and *passim*.

[38] In addition to Bauckham and Wright, see David B. Capes, *Old Testament Yahweh Texts in Paul's Christology* (WUNT 42; Tübingen: Mohr [Siebeck], 1992), who shows that in his scriptural citations Paul deliberately applies OT Yahweh texts to Jesus, asserting that Jesus is in some fashion a direct manifestation of Yahweh. Meanwhile Chris Tilling, *Paul's Divine Christology* (WUNT 323; Tübingen: Mohr [Siebeck], 2012), sees a unique overlap in relational-language patterns with respect to the Christ and Yahweh as the key to Paul's divine Christology.

divine agency, such as Wisdom, in describing the exalted status of Jesus (e.g. Col. 1: 15–20), I think that stories about God within eschatological monotheism as reworked in light of the experience of Jesus and the Spirit better explain the origins of Christology. So although Hurtado in particular has done a marvelous job debunking many of the overly speculative conjectures about mediators while still showing that these categories played a vital role in describing early Christian experiences,[39] I do agree with Bauckham and Wright that stories about God's own character and actions provide the overarching framework within which mediatorial categories tended to function.

Nonetheless, despite all the valuable work that has already been done by other scholars with regard to the story of how Jesus of Nazareth came to be described as God, I am convinced that something crucial is being neglected by all the Christological and Trinitarian approaches we have thus far discussed. That is, the impetus lent by prosopological exegesis was equally essential in paving the way to the Niceno-Constantinopolitan Creed. The birth of the Trinity is best located in the confluence of prosopological exegesis with experiential, mediatorial, and philosophical factors, all of which collectively shaped the fuller metaphysical models of the third and fourth century and beyond. So when properly nuanced to affirm the primacy of stories about God's own self and early experiences of Jesus and the Spirit, I deem the leading paradigm of "Trinitarianism as the outgrowth of mediated Jewish monotheism" as helpful in explaining how early Christians came to describe Jesus and the Spirit as divine, but also as overreaching so that it requires urgent supplementation.

Trinitarianism by Continuity in Prosopological Exegesis

Finally, the fourth approach to describing the developmental growth of the doctrine of the Trinity—and this is the approach which I compared to cargo on a sunken vessel that is known by a few, but is still awaiting full exploration and retrieval—is "Trinitarianism by continuity in prosopological exegesis." Although there are ad hoc exceptions (mainly the scholars of the patristic era to be discussed momentarily), this avenue of approach to the doctrine of the Trinity has been almost entirely neglected by New Testament and early Christian scholarship. It is my hope that this present study will make at least a small contribution in the direction of retrieval and illumination, and it is the burden of this book to show just how much information about intra-divine relationships can be gleaned by paying attention to this reading strategy as it was used in the earliest church. As such, this study as a whole does not seek to

---

[39] See especially the carefully nuanced discussion of personified divine agents, exalted patriarchs, and elevated angels in Hurtado, *One God*, 41–92.

cover the same ground or somehow supplant the many excellent, sophisticated, and helpful studies of Jewish monotheism, early Christology, and the rise of Trinitarianism that have been produced by other scholars, but rather to supplement, draw out implications, and show that certain correctives are in order. Thus, in what follows in this chapter I seek to describe in some detail "Trinitarianism by continuity in prosopological exegesis"—an approach that largely complements the approach of Hurtado and others, but also suggests that certain revisions to the scholarly story of Trinitarian and Christological growth are in order.

PROSOPOLOGICAL EXEGESIS AND THE BIRTH OF THE TRINITY

Tertullian and the "Person" Concept

Tertullian has long been recognized as the father of the doctrine of the Trinity, since he is the one who first used the term "Trinity" (Latin: *trinitas*) and who coined much of the distinctive Trinitarian nomenclature that would subsequently come to dominate Western theology. Yet, Tertullian himself was heir to a robust exegetical tradition that decisively shaped his Trinitarian discourse. This can be illustrated by looking at the curious method he employs in interpreting the Old Testament, such as in *Against Praxeas* (written *c.*213), which can be shown to rely on still earlier traditions, such as can be found in Justin Martyr's *Dialogue with Trypho* (*c.*160) and Irenaeus's *Against Heresies* (*c.*185). What is of import here is not just Tertullian's dependence on an earlier exegetical tradition, but the person-centered reading strategy that he and his predecessors undertook—assigning dramatic speakers or addressees that are unmarked, and indeed in some cases, seemingly totally foreign to the Old Testament text. For example, Tertullian reads his Old Testament thus:

No, but almost all the psalms which sustain the role [*personam*] of Christ represent the Son as speaking to the Father, that is, Christ as speaking to God. Observe also the Spirit speaking in the third person concerning the Father and the Son: *The Lord said unto my lord, Sit at my right hand until I make your enemies the footstool of your feet* [Ps. 110: 1]. Again, through Isaiah: *Thus says the Lord to my lord Christ* [Isa. 45: 1] . . . .

So in these texts, few though they be, yet the distinctiveness of the Trinity [*Trinitate*] is clearly expounded: for there is the Spirit himself who makes the statement, the Father to whom he makes it, and the Son of whom he makes it. So also the rest, which are statements made sometimes by the Father concerning the Son or to the Son, sometimes by the Son concerning the Father or to the

Father, sometimes by the Spirit, establish each several Person [*personam*] as being himself and none other.[40]

As Tertullian mentions, when he interprets his Old Testament text—and this is but one of many possible examples that could be used for Tertullian—the Spirit makes the basic prophetic utterance, obviously through the human medium, who then takes on different characters or acting-roles, and as such he steps into the role of the Father as the speaker, sometimes the role of the Christ, and at other times the Spirit speaks as the Spirit's own self—indeed, the person addressed by the speaker also shifts. In short, for Tertullian, there are traces of divine conversation in the Old Testament. On what basis were such role assignments made and justified by early Christian interpreters such as Tertullian?—and what are the theological implications of such assignments? And vitally, *when* did the church begin using this reading strategy in conceptualizing God? Here I want to introduce the reader more thoroughly to a vehicle that I shall argue was irreducibly essential to the birth of the Trinity—a theodramatic reading strategy best termed "prosopological exegesis."

Previous Scholarship Related to Prosopological Exegesis

In 1961 Carl Andresen's landmark study, "Zur Entstehung und Geschichte des trinitarischen Personbegriffes" ("Toward the Origin and History of Trinitarian Conceptions of the Person"), foregrounded the degree to which early Christian exegesis contributed to the rise of Trinitarian dogma, bringing this critical dimension to the attention of patristic and systematic theologians.[41] Andresen showed that Tertullian's scriptural exegesis was definitive for his formulation of persons (Latin: *personae*) of the Trinity, and argued that this reading strategy—which Andresen termed *prosopographische Schriftexegese* ("prosopographic exegesis")—had roots in both the ancient church and pagan antiquity. And although Andresen's insights were to stimulate a variety of studies in systematic and patristic theology, exploring how the concept of "the person" impacted the growth of Trinitarian thought from Tertullian forward in time,[42] surprisingly, no serious full-scale study of which I am

---

[40] Tertullian, *Prax.* 11; trans. Evans (slightly modified).

[41] Carl Andresen, "Zur Entstehung und Geschichte des trinitarischen Personbegriffes," *ZNW* 52 (1961): 1–39.

[42] See e.g. Aloys Grillmeier, *Christ in Christian Tradition: From the Apostolic Age to Chalcedon (451)* (trans. John Bowden; 2nd rev. edn.; Atlanta: John Knox, 1975), 125–7; Helga Offermanns, *Der christologische und trinitarische Personbegriff der frühen Kirche: ein Beitrag zum Verständnis von Dogmenentwicklung und Dogmengeschichte* (Berne: Herbert Lang; Frankfurt am Main: Peter Lang, 1976); Marie-Josèphe Rondeau, *Les Commentaires patristiques du Psautier (3e–5e siècles), i. Les Travaux des Pères grecs et latins sur le Psautier: Recherches et bilan; ii. Exégèse prosopologique et théologie* (2 vols.; Orientalia Christiana Analecta 220; Rome:

aware has sought to trace this concept backward into the early church that preceded Tertullian, although there have been some brief notices that signal such an attempt is feasible and desirable. Marie-Josèphe Rondeau, who has introduced the nomenclature *exégèse prosopologique* ("prosopological exegesis") that I prefer to follow for reasons to be mentioned in due course, devotes a few suggestive pages to the origins of prosopological exegesis in the New Testament and Justin Martyr.[43] Michael Slusser succinctly treats Justin Martyr, and Stephen Presley helpfully explores Irenaeus.[44]

Meanwhile on the biblical studies front A. T. Hanson,[45] Richard Hays,[46] and Harold Attridge[47] have all made valuable attempts to decipher what is

---

Institutum Studiorum Orientalium, 1982–5); Basil Studer, "Zur Entwicklung der patrististichen Trinitätslehre," *TGl* 74 (1984): 81–93 esp. 85–6; Hubertus R. Drobner, *Person-Exegese und Christologie bei Augustinus: Zur Herkunft der Formel Una Persona* (Leiden: Brill, 1986); Bernd J. Helberath, *Der Personbegriff der Trinitätstheologie in Rückfrage von Karl Rahner zu Tertullians "Adversus Praxean"* (Innsbruck; Vienna: Tyrolia-Verlag, 1986); Cardinal Joseph Ratzinger, "Concerning the Notion of Person in Theology," *Comm.* 17 (1990): 439–54 esp. 440–3; David J. Downs, "Prosopological Exegesis in Cyprian's *De opere et eleemosynis*," *JTI* 6 (2012): 279–93.

[43] On the preference for the terminology "prosopological exegesis" over against "prosopographic exegesis," see Rondeau, *Les Commentaires patristiques*, i. 8 n. 7; on the NT origins, see ii. 21–4; on Justin, see ii. 24–9.

[44] Michael Slusser, "The Exegetical Roots of Trinitarian Theology," *TS* 49 (1988): 461–76 esp. 466–8 on Justin Martyr; Stephen O. Presley, "Irenaeus and the Exegetical Roots of Trinitarian Theology," in Paul Foster and Sara Parvis (eds.), *Irenaeus: Life, Scripture, Legacy* (Minneapolis: Fortress, 2012), 165–71.

[45] Although undoubtedly a plethora of biblical scholars have suggested related ideas, the only (relatively) comprehensive attempt to look at how "prophetic dialogue" contributes to Christological and Trinitarian origins of which I am aware is that of Anthony T. Hanson, *Jesus Christ in the Old Testament* (London: SPCK, 1965), *passim* but esp. pp. 37–47, 75–82, 139–60. Hanson has by and large not been followed, probably due to his preference for conjecture over demonstrated historical probability. For example, Hanson does not explain how or why early Christians might have identified the "real presence" of Jesus in OT prophetic dialogues (p. 8). This book seeks to establish prosopological exegesis a historically grounded alternative.

[46] Richard B. Hays, "Christ Prays the Psalms: Israel's Psalter as Matrix of Early Christology," *The Conversion of the Imagination* (Grand Rapids: Eerdmans, 2005), 101–18. For an overview of Hays's typological model, see my remarks in the Introduction.

[47] Harold W. Attridge, "Giving Voice to Jesus: Use of the Psalms in the New Testament," in Harold W. Attridge and Margot E. Fassler (eds.), *Psalms in Community: Jewish and Christian Textual, Liturgical, and Artistic Traditions* (SBLSymS 25; Atlanta: SBL, 2003), 101–12, here 102, explores NT examples "in which the voice of the psalmist becomes the voice of Jesus." Attridge's article bristles with ground-breaking insights, but apart from quibbles about some of the exegetical details, I would offer four macro-criticisms. (1) Apart from correctly seeing that David was construed as a prophet, Attridge does not really offer a cogent theoretical model for why Jesus was felt by early Christian readers to be voicing the psalms. He does not connect it to prosopopoeia, nor to ancient reading strategies in general, nor to emerging patristic exegesis (except for his casual remarks about later developments in Justin Martyr's *Logos* theology—p. 107). (2) Attridge posits a liturgical *Sitz im Leben* for this phenomenon but what precisely he means by "liturgical" remains vague. A broader *Sitz im Leben* of interpretative reading coheres better with the evidence. (3) Attridge's puzzling assertion that this phenomenon appears "only in texts that focus on the passion of Jesus" (p. 102) in the NT cannot be sustained. Indeed Attridge himself provides several examples that do not cohere with this claim. (4) Attridge is imprecise in delineating the way the psalms were used literarily by one person to speak on behalf of another,

happening when Jesus Christ is found to be speaking via an Old Testament citation. And although none of these latter studies draw upon the ancient prosopological model that I am advocating, they all offer useful seminal insights. I myself have sought to demonstrate in my previous book, *The Hermeneutics of the Apostolic Proclamation*, through a detailed engagement with the primary sources, that the prosopological reading method was definitely current in the Greco-Roman world of the first century CE, as evidenced by the Jewish philosopher Philo and various interpreters of Homer,[48] and moreover that the Apostle Paul uses this method numerous times.[49] Paul's use is vital because it locates the prosopological method in the very earliest stratum of Christian literature that we possess. Hence, this book builds irreducibly upon the foundational theoretical and practical work on prosopological exegesis I have already undertaken in *The Hermeneutics of the Apostolic Proclamation*. It seeks to explore more extensively prosopological exegesis in the New Testament and second-century church, testing its potential for describing Christology and Trinitarian origins and growth, and so to fill the general void in scholarly treatments of this phenomenon in the earliest church.[50]

---

saying, "Jesus becomes David and David Jesus" (p. 107). My study suggests that it is not that the Son of David "is given the persona of his purported ancestor" (p. 102), but rather, I would argue, consistently the other way around—early Christian readers felt David had prophetically adopted the *persona* of the Christ, and if Jesus had played out that part subsequently, it was with this recognition.

[48] On its roots in the Greco-Roman world, especially for the interpretation of Homer, see Hans Dachs, *Die λύσις ἐκ τοῦ προσώπου: Ein exegetischer und kritischer Grundsatz Aristarchs und seine Neuanwendung auf Ilias und Odysee* (Erlangen: Junge & Sohn, 1913). This reading technique is also evidenced in Heraclitus, *Allegoriae*; Ps-Plutarch, *De vita et poesi Homeri*; the works of Philo; and elsewhere—for evidence see Matthew W. Bates, *The Hermeneutics of the Apostolic Proclamation: The Center of Paul's Method of Scriptural Interpretation* (Waco, Tex.: Baylor University Press, 2012), 209–12.

[49] Bates, *The Hermeneutics of the Apostolic Proclamation*, chs. 4–5; see also Matthew W. Bates, "Prosopographic Exegesis and Narrative Logic: Paul, Origen, and Theodoret of Cyrus on Psalm 69:22–23," in Daniel Patte and Vasile Mihoc (eds.), *The Greek Fathers' and Eastern Orthodox Interpretations of Romans* (Romans through History and Culture 9; London: Bloomsbury [T&T Clark], 2013), 105–34.

[50] The noteworthy effort of Simon J. Gathercole, *The Preexistent Son: Recovering the Christologies of Matthew, Mark, and Luke* (Grand Rapids: Eerdmans, 2006), shows that there is need for a more robust model in explaining OT "prophetic dialogues" (to use the phrase of Hanson, *Jesus Christ in the Old Testament*, 140). Gathercole himself appears, on my reading, to be conflicted about the utility of prophetic dialogues. On the one hand he cites specific words from Heb. 1: 10 (Ps. 101: 26 LXX) and 10: 7 (Ps. 39: 8 LXX) as evidence in favor of preexistence (pp. 34–5), but then goes on in an excursus (pp. 43–5) to state that although the notion of preexistence in the prophetic dialogues of Hebrews is "in some ways attractive" (p. 44), such a conclusion is hazardous because the author of Hebrews uses the OT to construct a dialogue between God and the believer in Heb. 13: 5–6. Gathercole concludes that the author of Hebrews "uses the OT as a dramatic script to construct imaginary lines or speaking parts for God, the Son, and Christian believers" (p. 45). Yet later Gathercole uses prophetic dialogues in Mark 1: 2–3 (pp. 249–52) and Mark 12: 35–7 (pp. 236–8) as part of an argument for preexistence, while declaring that prophetic dialogue is "potentially a fascinating exegetical device" that merits more attention from scholarship (p. 252). All of this indicates, I think, that Gathercole (and

The Greco-Roman Background to Prosopological Exegesis

In ancient Greek theater characterization was achieved by using a mask, a *prosōpon*, in order to establish audience expectations. Furthermore, in ancient drama dialogical shifts between speaking characters were frequent. Moving from the stage to the public courtroom or forum, rhetoricians sometimes would employ in-character speeches as a persuasive technique—for example, Cicero in the midst of a speech might temporarily take on the character of the entire nation of Italy as a way of heightening audience interest and adding emotional appeal.[51] This rhetorical strategy—called *prosopopoeia* (literally "character-making")—was discussed extensively in ancient rhetorical handbooks.[52] In fact, as practice exercises, students were compelled to write suitable in-character speeches, crafting fictional orations and putting them into the mouths of ancient characters to gain practice with the technique.[53] This dramatic device came to be used by ancient authors, sometimes without the technique being explicitly marked, so that ancient readers had to read with care in order to identify dialogical shifts—that is, they had to engage in prosopological exegesis. The use of this technique to interpret ancient texts is attested beginning in the second century BCE.[54] For a much fuller treatment of the Hellenistic roots of prosopological exegesis (and its origins as a self-conscious reading strategy appear primarily to be Hellenistic rather than Jewish), see Chapter 4 of my *The Hermeneutics of the Apostolic Proclamation*.

New Testament scholarship is well aware of the rhetorical device of *prosopopoeia*, indeed, it is generally accepted that Paul makes ample use of it.[55]

---

presumably others) finds something intriguing in these moments of prophetic dialogue, but that a plausible explanatory model remains a *desideratum*. For criteria that might be used to show that Heb. 1: 10 and 10: 7 are plausible instances of prosopological exegesis, but Heb. 13: 5–6 is not (thus addressing Gathercole's methodological concern), see Bates, *The Hermeneutics of the Apostolic Proclamation*, 219–20.

[51] Quintilian *Inst.* 9. 2. 32; cf. Cicero *Cat.* 1. 11. 27.

[52] For primary source references and a concise yet extremely helpful discussion, see R. Dean Anderson, Jr., *Glossary of Greek Rhetorical Terms Connected to Methods of Argumentation, Figures and Tropes from Anaximenes to Quintilian* (CBET 24; Leuven: Peeters, 2000), 106–7.

[53] E.g. Aelius Theon (probably first century CE) gives some specific examples of possible compositional exercises involving prosopopoeia: "What words would a man say to his wife when leaving on a journey? Or a general to his soldiers in a time of danger? Also when the persons are specified; for example, What words would Cyrus say when marching against the Massagetae?" Text in Leonardus Spengel (ed.), *Rhetores Graeci* (3 vols.; Leipzig: Teubner, 1854–6), ii. 115; George A. Kennedy (trans.), *Progymnasmata: Greek Textbooks of Prose Composition and Rhetoric* (SBLWGRW 10; Atlanta: Society of Biblical Literature, 2003), 47.

[54] Dachs, *Die λύσις ἐκ τοῦ προσώπου*, 8–11, finds that this "solution by person" technique was used to interpret Homer by Aristarchus of Samothrace (c.214–144 BCE), who succeeded Apollonius as head of the library in Alexandria c.153 BCE.

[55] For *prosopopoeia* in Paul, see Rom. 2: 1–5, 17–29; 3: 1–9; 3: 27–4: 2; 7: 7–8: 2; 10: 6; and 11: 19. The ground-breaking study of *prosopopoeia* in Paul was Stanley K. Stowers, *The Diatribe and Paul's Letter to the Romans* (SBLDS 57; Chico, Calif.: Scholars Press, 1981); an important

What is new in this study (building on my earlier book on Pauline hermeneutics) for biblical scholarship, at least to the best of my knowledge, is the claim that *prosopopoeia* was not just a rhetorical strategy adopted by New Testament authors to persuade the audience, but also was employed by these authors as a theodramatic reading technique vis-à-vis the Old Testament.[56]

An Ancient Description of Prosopological Exegesis

We have already seen, albeit briefly, a practical example of the dialogical nature of theodramatic interpretation in Tertullian, *Against Praxeas* 11—and we shall have many more opportunities to explore it in the chapters that follow. But how can we get a handle on what ancient practitioners of prosopological exegesis thought they were doing in terms of both *the how* and *the why*? Fortunately, we are not left entirely on our own in surmising, because we have some theoretical statements from antiquity that explain the technique. Although there are other explanations of the method, the fullest, clearest, early statement in our sources comes from Justin Martyr in his *1 Apology*:[57]

> But whenever you hear the sayings of the prophets spoken *as from a person* [*hōs apo prosōpou*], you must not suppose the sayings to be spoken from the inspired persons themselves, but from *the divine Logos* [*theiou Logou*] who moves them. For sometimes he speaks as one announcing in advance things which are about to happen; sometimes he speaks as from the person of God, the Master and Father of all; sometimes as from the person of Christ; sometimes as from the person of the people giving answer to the Lord and his Father—such as is seen in your own writers, when one person is the writer of the whole, *but many people*

synthesis and rejoinder to criticisms can be found in Stanley K. Stowers, "Romans 7:7–25 as Speech-in-Character (προσωποποιΐα)," in T. Engberg-Pederson (ed.), *Paul in His Hellenistic Context* (Edinburgh: T&T Clark, 1994), 180–202. For a creatively radical (yet to my mind implausible) recent attempt to expand the number of texts employing prosopopoeia in Romans by suggesting that Paul re-presents the words of his opponents, see Douglas A. Campbell, *The Deliverance of God: An Apocalyptic Re-Reading of Justification in Paul* (Grand Rapids: Eerdmans, 2009), esp. pp. 532–3.

[56] When I was presenting a paper, "When Jesus Speaks in the Old Testament: A Theodramatic Proposal," at the SBL national conference in Baltimore (November 2013), a recent dissertation that touches on the use of *prosopopoeia* as an OT reading strategy for the author of Hebrews was brought to my attention: Brian C. Small, "The Characterization of Jesus in the Book of Hebrews" (Ph.D. diss., Baylor University, 2012), see esp. pp. 188–92, 208–10, 262–72. Since my book was already drafted in its entirety independent of engagement with Small, I felt it best to maintain this independence. So I do not interact with his dissertation in any of my own exegeses, but I want to alert the reader to his work.

[57] For additional ancient theoretical descriptions, see the sources given on ancient Homeric interpretation by Dachs, *Die λύσις ἐκ τοῦ προσώπου*, esp. pp. 8–11. For other methodological statements, see Irenaeus, *Epid.* 49–50; Origen, *Comm. Rom.* 2. 11. 2; *Philoc.* 7. 1–2. For further discussion, see Bates, *The Hermeneutics of the Apostolic Proclamation*, 215–19.

are put forward as participating in dialogue [prosōpa de ta dialegomena pleiō parapheronta]. (36. 1–2)[58]

Several things should be noted. Above all, it is clear that *distinct divine persons* (*prosōpa*) are construed by Justin as participating in dialogue (*dialegomena*) with one another, as reflected in the text, via the divine inspiring agent—the *Logos*—and all this back in the time when the Old Testament was written.

On the Term "Prosopological Exegesis." First, Justin identifies the inspiring agent—here construed as the *Logos*—that speaks through the *prosōpon*, the person or character; hence *prosopological exegesis.*[59] In recognizing that the *Logos* is not the only or even the usual name for this inspiring agent, we might compare this with Tertullian's statement given previously, "for there is *the Spirit* himself who makes the statement" (*Prax.* 11). The critical thing to realize is that the divine inspiring agent was felt to be the most primal speaker and that this agent spoke through the human prophet in the semblance of other persons—frequently as the Father and the Son. We shall see in due course that Justin is by no means the first Christian reader to interpret in this fashion, although he does provide the most forthright explanation of his method and rationale, and he may have been the first Christian to reify the prosopological technique as a self-conscious reading strategy.

Prosopological Exegesis and Time. Second, the inspired speech is not chronologically constrained to the time in which it was delivered by the prophet, but as Justin indicates, "he speaks as one announcing in advance things which are about to happen." So, when Justin identifies an in-character speech when reading the ancient Jewish Scripture, he believes that the dramatic setting of the speech becomes the reference point for establishing the tenses for the speech, so that the future character can refer to the past, present, or future with respect to his or her future dramatic setting.[60] Just as a buoy rises and sinks with the fluctuating level of a lake, so also the tenses "float" forward or "sink" backward in time for the ancient reader with reference to the temporal setting of the theodrama that the reader has identified.

Thus, for Justin, as he reads the book of Isaiah, the Christ, whose advent is in the distant future, might speak in the past tense to God the Father about his suffering on the cross, and appropriately so, because the tense is established by reference to the chronological location of the speech within the divine drama,

---

[58] With regard to Justin, all Greek texts are cited per Marcovich, PTS 38/47, while translations remain my own unless otherwise noted.

[59] The term "prosopological exegesis" is not an emic first-order term used by ancient practitioners, but rather an etic modern designation. The use of a contemporary etic term is justified since there was not a consistent nomenclature used to describe this reading technique in antiquity, although this reading practice was theoretically discussed as a distinctive phenomenon by ancient practitioners (for ancient descriptions, see n. 57 in this chapter).

[60] See Justin, *Dial.* 114. 1; *1 Apol.* 42. 1–2; cf. Irenaeus, *Epid.* 67; Tertullian, *Marc.* 3. 5. 2–3.

not by reference to the time of Isaiah the prophet. For example, for Justin, the future Christ can speak in *the past tense* saying, "I set my back for whippings and my cheeks for beatings; indeed, my face did not turn away from the shame of spittings" (*1 Apol.* 38. 2 citing Isa. 50: 6), because through the ancient prophet the future Christ is delivering this speech from a time after the passion, and he is looking back on his past suffering. Thus, tense is bound up with setting, and the proper identification of the specific setting of the in-character divine dialogue that our various ancient Christian readers have identified is critical.

Three Settings within the Theodrama

Now that we have had the opportunity to explore the theoretical framework of person-centered interpretation as presented in the ancient sources themselves, I would like to draw some of the threads together and present an explanatory model to add precision to the ongoing discussion.

The Prophetic Setting. The earliest Christians believed that ancient prophets, such as David or Isaiah, could speak in the character of God the Father, Christ the Son, and others. We might call this horizon of the time and the circumstances of the prophet in ancient Israel "the prophetic setting." The prophet, however, they believed, could slip into a role (*prosōpon*, hereafter usually prosopon except when transliterating) and perform a speech or dialogue that has already come to pass, is presently happening, or will occur in the future, whether on earth or in the heavens. The speech is functionally *a script* authored by the Holy Spirit, as in the final analysis it is the Spirit who supplies the words to the prophet, because these words have been, are, or will become a reality when performed.

The Theodramatic Setting. Because this reading strategy is metaphorically rooted in the world of ancient theater, I call the visionary landscape in which the prophet was felt to perform these roles the *theodrama*.[61] Accordingly, the

---

[61] If the question is posed, What is the exact ontological status of the theodrama for earliest Christian interpreters?, it is difficult to formulate a precise and definitive answer. On the one hand, the term "theodrama" itself is merely my own neologism (although the drama metaphor is encouraged by the ancient sources—see Bates, *The Hermeneutics of the Apostolic Proclamation*, 192–4), selected to describe the way in which a prophet was believed to speak from the person of someone else, much as an actor would adopt a role in ancient theater. On the other hand, ancient Christian readers certainly believed that the prophets had experienced genuine visions that had prompted them to take on these various *personae*. So, in this way the ontological status of the theodramatic world is that of an oracular experience. In sum, we probably should not believe that ancient readers had a firm, reified concept of what I term the "theodrama." Yet I contend that we should affirm that they assigned a visionary-level of reality to certain prophetic discourses, and that this visionary-level of reality is congenial to the concrete description of the theodrama that I have given here, making it an appropriate modern (etic) shorthand term to describe succinctly the visionary scene ancient interpreters felt that a prophet could really inhabit.

time at which the speech is delivered from within the narrative world of the "divine play" itself is "the theodramatic setting." If David was read as performing a speech in the character of the Christ (i.e. the prophetic setting is David's own time), and the character of the Christ is speaking from the cross, then the crucifixion is the present-tense theodramatic setting. But the Christ may speak about things past, present, or future with regard to that theodramatic setting, perhaps speaking in the past tense about a previous moment of consolation that the Father gave in his earthly life, or perhaps in the future tense about a moment of anticipated celebration on the other side of the grave.

In addition to taking on a prosopon, for early Christian readers, seemingly, the prophet could also watch a theodramatic scene as an external observer, not entering into a speaking role himself, but nonetheless observing and overhearing the prosopa as they perform. Thus, to be precise, although I often use the terms interchangeably, I consider theodramatic interpretation a larger category in which an ancient reader invokes an assumed theodrama as an explanation of a text, and prosopological exegesis to be a subset of it, in which the interpreter believes the prophet has entered into a character-role and is speaking or being addressed as that person. Most of my interest in this book is prosopological exegesis in the early church rather than theodramatic interpretation more generally, although I hope that in time others will join me in exploring more fully both the former and the latter in the New Testament and beyond.

The Actualized Setting. Finally, "the actualized setting" is the moment at which the theodrama is truly performed, not by the prophet-actor but by the person(s) the prophet was representing in the theodrama. That is, for example, the actualized setting is when the incarnate Christ actually speaks from the cross, bringing to pass that which the prophet anticipated in his theodramatic performance. Note that because the theodramatic setting is chronologically unrestrained (past, present, or future) with respect to the prophetic setting, the actualized setting is likewise unrestrained. In this way the whole chronological spectrum of the divine economy may be involved in any given prophetic utterance.

So, applying this new vocabulary to a specific example by returning to Justin's prosopological exegesis of Isa. 50: 6, "I set my back for whippings and my cheeks for beatings; indeed, my face did not turn away from the shame of spittings" (*1 Apol.* 38. 2), we might analyze Justin's interpretation as follows. Since Isaiah would have been construed by Justin as the human author of the oracle, the "prophetic setting" is during the lifetime of Isaiah. Yet the "theodramatic setting" is sometime after the crisis of the cross, because the Christ is here taken as speaking to the Father in the past tense (aorist) about what he suffered on the cross, as if these events have already been accomplished. So Justin most likely located the theodramatic setting after the crucifixion and exaltation, during the time when the Christ is seated at the right hand of the

Father. From that position the Christ is reminiscing with the Father about that climactic earlier moment of grim testing. Finally, the "actualized setting" is the time when the theodramatic speech was really performed, the moment when the Christ solemnly reflected using the words, "I set my back for whippings," with God the Father during his session at the right hand. For Justin, these words have already been actualized, the Christ has been seated at the right hand and has already had this specific conversation with the Father. Thus, in this particular case, the prophetic setting, the theodramatic setting, and the actualized setting are now all in the past from Justin's vantage point, but we shall see different temporal alignments throughout this book.

From Prosopological Exegesis to Established Trinitarian Dogma

Now that the basic contours of this ancient theodramatic reading technique have been drawn, perhaps the gap in New Testament and early Christian scholarship with regard to how this interpretative strategy contributed to the origins and growth of the doctrine of the Trinity can be better appreciated. In short, prosopological exegesis demanded that the interpreter identify a speaking character or person (Greek: *prosōpon*; Latin: *persona*) and/or a personal addressee, and early Christian interpreters frequently assigned persons that are not explicitly mentioned in the scriptural passage at hand as an explanatory move.

This was critical to the emergence of the doctrine of the Trinity, because after the first two centuries of the common era it would largely be presumed, albeit often tacitly and certainly not uniformly, primarily on the basis of theodramatic readings of the Old Testament, readings also present in the earliest strata of Christian literature, that the Father, Son, and Spirit are distinct *persons* (*prosōpa*; *personae*).[62] Or at least that *person*, however

---

[62] The use of the term *prosōpa* as a way of differentiating within God's oneness was certainly not uniform nor was it precise in the third century. Indeed, it is fair to suggest that it was the Monarchian crisis itself that compelled the early church to reflect more precisely on the quality of individuality of the divine persons presupposed by prosopological exegesis, to extract the *prosopa* metaphor embedded in the exegetical technique, and to generalize toward individual divine persons (see further n. 63 in this chapter). For example, Callistus (d. 223), a Monarchian, reportedly objected to emerging orthodoxy by asserting "one God" necessarily implies that God is a single *prosopon*, and thus it is nonsensical ditheism to speak of the Father and the Son as one God (Hippolytus, *Haer.* 9. 12)—all of which implies that his opponents were affirming at least two divine *prosopa* could appropriately be called "one God." Likewise the Sabellians also did not prefer to speak of multiple divine *prosopa*, or if they did so it was to assert that they appeared in a transitory modalist fashion. The development and deployment of Trinitarian nomenclature is nonlinear, geographically convoluted, and exceedingly complex. Even in the wake of the Council of Nicaea, Marcellus, Bishop of Ancrya, could still declare that God is a single *prosopon*—although the promulgation of this theology contributed toward his removal from ecclesial office in 336. For a helpful overview of the main movements, see Anatolios, *Retrieving Nicaea*, 15–27, while the reader should consult the standard works listed in n. 3 in this chapter for more details.

imprecisely that concept may have been understood, was a divinely authorized metaphor that could suitably parse God's oneness.[63] The Greek word *prosō-pon*, which in the classical era usually meant face or mask, had come by New Testament times to be a standard term, generally speaking, for referring to personal presence or the whole person.[64]

When we speak of "persons" in this study, the reader must beware of the danger of anachronistically foisting contemporary notions of the person onto the ancient texts, especially since most modern Westerners tend to focus on the person as the center of individual psychological consciousness or as determined by social role-playing. In contrast first-century ancient Mediterranean ideas of the person were collectivist and strongly group-embedded, based primarily on gender, geographic origin, the nobility or baseness of family lineage, upbringing, and accomplishments.[65] Persons in antiquity nonetheless were capable of exercising personal will, had idiosyncratic affections, and were known as unique, distinct individuals, much as is the case today, so the ancient and contemporary differences should not be overdrawn.

On a related note, we must be equally cautious in affirming that even ancient "person" language (when properly retrieved by us today) is nonetheless still a metaphor, much like "Father" or "Mother" when speaking about God, albeit for those who take Scripture as authoritative, "person" is a God-granted and hence divinely approved metaphor. And as Augustine (whose sentiments are echoed by many contemporary theologians) is quick to remind us, the would-be theologian must always bear in mind that all such metaphors are an accommodation to our creaturely limitations, and as such they do not directly capture God's ultimate reality.[66] Rather they are signposts that guide

---

[63] The persons of the Trinity are already clearly described as prosopa from within theodramatic exegesis by Justin Martyr (e.g. *1 Apol.* 37. 1–39. 1; 49. 1–4; *Dial.* 36. 6; 88. 8), but this mode of reading and its "person" assumptions about God can be traced back into the NT itself, including Paul, our earliest extant Christian author, as this book as a whole seeks to demonstrate. Apart from Tertullian (who used the Latin term *persona*), the first author to extract the term *prosōpon* from prosopological exegesis and use it in the abstract to discuss plurality within the Godhead appears to be Hippolytus (d. 235) in *Noet.* 7, 11, 14.

[64] For evidence, see the standard Greek dictionary that covers the NT era, BDAG, *s.v.* πρόσωπον, defs. 1b and 2. E.g., for the whole person, see 2 Cor. 1: 11; *1 Clem.* 1. 1; 47. 6; for personal presence, see 1 Cor. 13: 12; 2 Cor. 10: 1; Acts 25: 16. The typical comprehensive term for the whole person in the NT era was *anthrōpos* ("human being"). The use of *prosōpon* as personal presence is common, but for the whole person it less common although still adequately attested.

[65] For a convincing reconstruction using ancient sources of how the "person" was conceptualized in the Greco-Roman world of the first century, see Bruce J. Malina and Jerome H. Neyrey, *Portraits of Paul: An Archaelogy of Ancient Personality* (Louisville, Ky.: Westminster John Knox, 1996), 10–33.

[66] Much of Augustine's *De Trinitate* is concerned to show that God has accommodated our creaturely weakness by giving perceptible signs (e.g. scriptural metaphors about God, with the incarnate Christ as the ultimate sign) that point beyond themselves to God's ultimate reality. For instance, in his introduction Augustine programmatically states, "It was therefore to purify the human spirit of such falsehoods [e.g. that God is dazzlingly white or fiery red in physical

us along a path of ascent to an ever truer knowledge of God. As Augustine puts it, "The divine scriptures then are in the habit of making something like children's toys out of the things that occur in creation, by which to entice our sickly gaze and get us step by step to seek as best we can the things that are above and forsake the things that are below."[67] Thus, in this study when we speak of divine persons as revealed through scriptural interpretation, the *quality* of personhood envisioned is necessarily metaphorically determined. That is, the fullness or flatness of the portraitures of the divine persons is controlled at the most basic level by the descriptions in the scriptural texts themselves. Divinely revealed metaphorical language about God is, then, a necessary and indispensable vehicle that assists us in coming to as true a conception of God as our human finitude permits.[68]

In time the term *prosōpon* would come to be augmented by Origen and later Fathers with the alternative *hypostasis* ("discrete individual being") as a conceptual tool for parsing God's oneness,[69] in part because *prosōpon* and especially its rough Latin equivalent, *persona*, were perceived as connoting the surface appearance or external presentation of a person, and hence were deemed more susceptible to modalism,[70] whereas *hypostasis* stressed the underlying reality.

---

appearance] that holy scripture, adapting itself to babes, did not shun any words, proper to any kind of thing whatever, that might nourish our understanding and enable it to rise up to the sublimities of divine things" (*Trin*. 1. 1 [§2]; trans. Hill). As such, we do not generally have direct access to God's ultimate reality in scriptural descriptions of God, only metaphors about God that mediate truths about God. As one example of a contemporary warning about the dangers of pressing the metaphor of "person" too far in considering the inner reality of the Trinity, see Karl Rahner, *The Trinity* (trans. Joseph Donceel; New York: Seabury, 1974), 103–15.

[67] Augustine, *Trin*. 1.1 [§2]; trans. Hill.

[68] For Augustine, as we increasingly catch a vision of God's triune reality (through the guidance of signs), our sickly gaze becomes healthier, and we find ourselves recrafted into a triune idiom, so that these divinely authorized metaphors become our primary source of self-meaning (see the epilogue to *Trin*. 15 [§§50–1]).

[69] See Origen, *Comm. Jo*. 2. 75; 10. 246; *Cels*. 8. 12; for additional references see PGL *s.v.* ὑπόστασις def. II.B. In a tantalizing remark, Marcellus of Ancyra, *On the Holy Church* 9, relates that the second-century gnostic Valentinus was actually the first to devise the notion of three *hypostaseis* in his lost work titled *On the Three Natures* (*Peri tōn triōn physeōn*). (I owe this observation to personal correspondence with my good friend and colleague Eric Rowe.) Rowe and I both agree, however, that even if we were to grant that Valentinus was indeed the first to mention three *hypostaseis*, it is exceptionally unlikely in light of the extant witness to Valentinian Gnosticism that Valentinus would have used three *hypostaseis* specifically to differentiate the one most high God. For Marcellus's text and some brief remarks, see Bentley Layton, *The Gnostic Scriptures: A New Translation with Annotations and Introductions* (ABRL; New York: Doubleday, 1987), 233. For a succinct discussion of Origen's use of *hypostasis* language, see Behr, *The Way to Nicaea*, 184–7 (esp. 184 n. 67 regarding Origen and the Valentinians).

[70] Briefly, the modalists argued that God was an non-differentiable single principle that could nonetheless appear as Father during one era of human history, Son in another, and Spirit in still another, but not all three at once.

Nevertheless it is vital to realize, as this book as a whole seeks to show, that this augmentation, inasmuch as it sought to add precision to the previously established person metaphor, was primarily a reaffirmation and extension along the "person" trajectory already embedded in and fixed by prosopological exegesis as it was practiced in the New Testament and early church. Semantic overlaps and disjunctures between *prosōpon, persona, hypostasis,* the closely related Latin term *substantia* ("essence" or "substance"), and the Greek word *ousia* ("substance" or "being") add a further layer of cloudy complexity to the waters of Trinitarian discourse in the third and fourth centuries.[71] At the Council of Nicaea (325) the only begotten Son was declared *homoousios* ("of the same essence" or "consubstantial") with the Father. Meanwhile the relationship of the Spirit to the Father would be clarified at Constantinople (381), where it was affirmed that the Holy Spirit proceeds from the Father and is worshiped and glorified along with the Father and the Son. The procession of the Spirit would later be modified in the Creed, primarily in the Western church, to include procession not just from the Father but also from the Son by adding the *filioque* clause ("and the Son"), all of which would become a cankerous sore-spot between the East and the West.

The practical result of all of this semantic wrangling was the consolidating neo-Nicene formulation—the One God is "one substance" or "one essence" (*mia ousia; una substantia; una essentia*) in which three fully divine "discrete individual beings" or true "persons" (*hypostaseis; prosōpa; personae*) subsist, with each person differing from the others only in how the divine substance is possessed—the Father without cause, the Son as eternally begotten by the Father, and the Spirit through procession from the Father (and the Son). Since our focus in this book is restricted to the crucial initial phase, more specifically to the Trinitarian and Christological implications of prosopological exegesis in the first two centuries of the church, it is critical to recognize that the Trinitarian story told herein is not complete. Rather, prosopological exegesis informed emerging metaphysical models of unity and distinction with respect to God, and these together resulted in the full-orbed Trinitarianism of the third and fourth centuries and beyond.

So, in speaking of the "birth of the Trinity" I do not want to suggest that real and complex theological issues were not still under intense negotiation and vital development in the third and fourth centuries (and beyond). Nor am

---

[71] The degree to which the Cappadocian Fathers innovated in moving *hypostasis* from an initial alignment along the *ousia* ("essence" or "substance") axis of meaning to the *prosōpon* ("person") axis while arguing for a self-emptying *philanthrōpia* ("love for the other") as a constitutive, fundamental divine attribute is a question still debated by scholarship. At the fountainhead of the discussion, see John D. Zizioulas, *Being as Communion: Studies in Personhood and the Church* (Crestwood, NY: St Vladimir's Seminary Press, 1985), esp. pp. 27–41. Zizioulas's impact on recent Trinitarian theology has been enormous—see Grenz, *Rediscovering the Triune God,* 131–47.

I claiming that nomenclature to express the Trinity had attained stability—anyone who is even remotely acquainted with the literature will immediately recognize that, on the contrary, nothing could be further from the truth. Yet, I do want to assert in a forceful way that the die had been cast long prior—in the first two centuries of the Christian era—because "God" had already been read dialogically and prosopologically in the ancient Jewish Scripture, and hence the foundational conceptual decision to privilege the "person" meta-phor in considering internal distinctions within the one God had already been made via scriptural interpretation. Even if a minority might desire to retrench (the Monarchians and the like), and many would dispute how to best express the inherited person metaphor in light of the scriptural testimony to the interrelatedness of Father, Son, and Spirit, the prosopological interpretative precedent had already shown to the satisfaction of most of the early church that the one God could successfully be read in the ancient Jewish Scripture as multiple "persons." So the Trinity emerged conceptually to a large degree through interpretative reading of the Old Testament, especially through a specific technique, prosopological exegesis.

* * *

When these person-centered readings of the Old Testament in the New Testament and the early Christian literature are examined collectively, we find that they are like windows into the divine story as perceived by the emerging church, helping us to catch small glimpses into the interior rela-tionship between Father, Son, and divine Inspiring Agent—frequently al-though not exclusively identified as the Spirit. Yet, when these small glimpses are connected and joined, we find that we have a surprisingly robust portrait of the manner in which the interior divine life was understood by the earliest church, not a static portrait, but an unfolding story of mutual esteem, voiced praise, collaborative strategizing, and self-sacrificial love.

In summary, although there are three other ways in which the emergence of the doctrine of the Trinity has been traced by scholarship, a fourth way, the approach via continuity in prosopological exegesis of the Old Testament, has been widely neglected for the earliest strata by scholars of the New Testament and early Christianity. Nonetheless, it has a clear ancient prominence and pedigree that suggests it is a central strand in need of recovery—indeed, as the remaining chapters seek to demonstrate, it is not too large a thing to say that theodramatic interpretation within a messianic movement in late Second Temple Judaism was foundational to the birth of the Trinity.

2

Divine Dialogues from the Dawn of Time

Theodramatic scriptural interpretations provide snapshots of the relationship between divine persons as envisioned by the earliest Christian readers of Scripture, and when stitched together, these individual pictures form a panorama of the interior divine life. The first set of snapshots we will examine are those conversations that the earliest Christians construed as pertaining to the dawn of time. Upon occasion, these dialogues look even further back, if you will, to *the time before time*—before the stars, the sun, and the moon were set in place.

If it is indeed the case, as I am seeking to demonstrate, that Trinitarian dogma arose in essential ways via a particular person-centered way of reading the Jewish Scripture in the earliest church, then perhaps we should not be surprised to find Jesus himself depicted as engaging repeatedly in this practice. Indeed, although my overall thesis in this book does not depend upon it, it is reasonable to suppose (as a testable hypothesis) that this is not just a portrayal by the Gospel writers, but that the historical Jesus did in fact engage in theodramatic readings of his Scripture. For not only did many of his contemporaries, both pagan and Jewish, undertake "solution-by-person" to solve riddles in inspired texts,[1] evidence from reception history also contributes to the calculus of probability in favor of the historical Jesus' own usage.

THE HISTORICALLY PLAUSIBLE JESUS

Given the white-hot controversy surrounding the topic, it would be much safer to bypass the question of the historical Jesus altogether. Yet, since we

---

[1] For evidence, see Carl Andresen, "Zur Entstehung und Geschichte des trinitarischen Personbegriffes," *ZNW* 52 (1961): 1–39 esp. 12–18; supplements to Andresen can be found in Michael Slusser, "The Exegetical Roots of Trinitarian Theology," *TS* 49 (1988): 461–76 esp. 468–70; and Matthew W. Bates, *The Hermeneutics of the Apostolic Proclamation: The Center of Paul's Method of Scriptural Interpretation* (Waco, Tex.: Baylor University Press, 2012), Chs. 4 and 5.

will be dealing with a number of Gospel texts throughout this book in which Jesus is depicted as interpreting Scripture, and because the question of the historical Jesus' self-understanding with respect to the texts he interprets is both fascinating and potentially theologically momentous, I cannot bear to leave it aside. Yet, how might one determine whether or not the Gospel renderings in question have historical value? The tendency in some quarters to regard the canonical Gospels merely as myths does not stand up to sober-minded comparative analysis of ancient genres—nearly all contemporary scholars of the Hellenistic era agree that the Gospels are generically comparable to Greco-Roman biography and historiography, and as such they intend, unlike myths, to make referential historical truth claims, even if the value of the claims is variously assessed.[2]

There are essentially two methodologies current in historical Jesus studies, atomistic and holistic.[3] In the *atomistic approach* the historian is comparable to an entomologist, collecting individual specimen, and examining the properties of each specimen *according to predetermined rules* to decide whether it has the properties of a beetle or a spider, and classing it accordingly. Similarly, practitioners of the atomistic approach seek to separate the "authentic historical Jesus" from the "Jesus created by the early church" by applying established methodologies (e.g. form criticism, redaction criticism) and criteria (e.g. embarrassment, multiple attestation) to individual sayings or actions recorded in the Gospels. If these discrete sayings or actions "pass the test" in the eyes of the historian when evaluated in (relative) isolation from one another, they can be attributed to the historical Jesus and are allowed by that historian to contribute to a composite portrait of Jesus' life. Those who use this sort of method include John D. Crossan and one of my mentors, John P. Meier, whose portraits of the historical Jesus differ wildly.[4] In my judgment, however, recent studies have effectively demonstrated numerous epistemological weaknesses in this atomistic approach—such as, positivist assumptions bound up with a modernist worldview, inability to deal sufficiently with innovation and singularity in history, a lack of regard for human intentionality, and dubious conjectures about how the Gospel material was transmitted before it was written down—and indeed there are definite signs that due to these insufficiencies the

---

[2] For a lucid synthesis of this scholarship, see David E. Aune, *The New Testament in Its Literary Environment* (Library of Early Christianity 8; Philadelphia: Westminster, 1987), 17–157.

[3] For this division of the discipline, see Donald L. Denton, Jr., *Historiography and Hermeneutics in Jesus Studies: An Examination of the Work of John Dominic Crossan and Ben F. Meyer* (JSNTSup 262; New York: T&T Clark, 2004). The explanatory metaphors, however, are my own.

[4] John D. Crossan, *The Historical Jesus: The Life of a Mediterranean Jewish Peasant* (San Francisco: HarperSanFrancisco, 1991), esp. pp. xxvii–xxxiv; John P. Meier, *A Marginal Jew* (4 vols.; ABRL; New York: Doubleday, 1991–2009), i. 167–95, gives widely accepted criteria for those who adopt an atomistic approach for historical Jesus studies.

once-pervasive atomistic approach is now in rapid decline, even among ardent former practitioners.[5]

Thus, siding with the most recent scholarship, I hold that judgment about the historicity of any given episode in Jesus' life or in the Gospels can be rendered only when using a *holistic approach*. Here the historian is more like a scientist who examines the concrete details of the data while exercising a healthy caution toward the dominant scientific paradigms and categories explaining that data, actively considering new hypotheses as the work progresses. The historian is keenly aware that perhaps the predetermined classification systems and tools used for data collection might be skewing the results, indeed, there must even be an appropriate self-suspicion: "Am I only finding results that confirm my current worldview because that is more convenient for me?" Rather than trying to build a picture of the historical Jesus using short, isolated, discrete sayings and actions that are prejudged by modern standards before being allowed to "count," it attempts to build from the top down, using large-scale hypotheses that are subsequently tested and verified against the details of the data (including both the text's prior history and reception history), while also emphasizing the importance of unique human agency in history. This more sound holistic methodological foundation for historical Jesus studies has been advanced by Ben F. Meyer and supplemented by N. T. Wright and others.[6]

Obviously, since I cannot put forward a full-scale holistic theory of the historical Jesus here—I would need a separate book—I must limit myself in what follows to showing how the various Gospel writers *portray Jesus*, remarking on *historical plausibility* when appropriate, but without making definitive judgments about historicity. And even though I do not find the atomistic approach convincing, it does sometimes give a historical minimum that nearly everyone can agree upon, so I will occasionally make use of its tools in that fashion.

So regardless of how the present reader discerns matters of Jesus and history, there is still much to gain by incorporating evidence of Jesus as a reader of the Scripture as portrayed in the Gospels into this study. For those who are uncertain precisely when and where in these complex texts we are hearing the voice of the historical Jesus as opposed to that of the early church,

---

[5] See Gerd Theissen and Dagmar Winter, *The Quest for the Plausible Jesus: The Question of Criteria* (trans. M. Eugene Boring; Louisville, Ky.: Westminster John Knox, 2002); Chris Keith and Anthony LeDonne (eds.), *Jesus, Criteria, and the Demise of Authenticity* (London: T&T Clark, 2012). For a chastening assessment of the method by a leading former practitioner, see Dale C. Allison, Jr., *Constructing Jesus: Memory, Imagination, and History* (Grand Rapids: Baker Academic, 2010), pp. x, 435–62.

[6] Ben Meyer, *Reality and Illusion in New Testament Scholarship* (Collegeville, Minn.: Michael Glazier, 1994); N. T. Wright, *The New Testament and the People of God* (Minneapolis: Fortress, 1991), 31–144.

still *these texts indisputably show how the early church portrayed Jesus' self-understanding as he read his ancient Scripture.* For those, such as this present author, who find the depictions of Jesus in the Gospels to be largely historically plausible (even if the historiography is artistically sophisticated—more like a Monet rendering than a photograph, especially in John), then the study has additional significance inasmuch as the historical Jesus' own self-understanding—potentially including his (growing?) sense of his own divinity—was directly and decisively impacted by his person-centered reading of his ancient Jewish Scripture. In either case, our goal, to discern to what degree prosopological exegesis contributed to the birth of the Trinity, can be reached.

We begin with an enigmatic episode where Jesus himself is portrayed as arriving at a solution-by-person when interpreting the Scripture—a reading that ultimately, I would contend, has profound Christological and Trinitarian implications. This passage is found in Matthew, Mark, and Luke and is widely regarded by scholars of the historical Jesus—even those prone to skepticism—as a plausible portrayal of a real episode of controversy in the life of Jesus.

A CONVERSATION ABOUT PREEXISTENT BEGOTTENNESS—PSALM 110

In all three synoptic accounts the episode I would like to discuss is situated in a sequence of attempts by the enemies of Jesus to trap him in his words and to discredit him through public shaming. When they prove unable to snare Jesus, he turns the tables on them by issuing a riddle that appears on the surface as if designed simply to catch them, but which—I shall argue—also has a much deeper purpose:

> And answering Jesus said to them (while teaching in the temple): How is it that the scribes are saying that the Christ is the son of David? David himself said while speaking by means of the Holy Spirit, "The Lord said to my Lord, 'Sit at my right hand until I place your enemies as a footstool for your feet'" [Ps. 109: 1 LXX]. David himself calls him "Lord," and so how is he his son? And the large crowd was listening to him delightedly.   (Mark 12: 35–7; cf. Matt. 22: 41–6; Luke 20: 41–4)

In order for Jesus to turn the tables on his enemies effectively, he presents an interpretative conundrum to them that is based on a careful, person-centered reading of Psalm 109 LXX (that is, Ps. 110 in contemporary English translations). Jesus, as he is portrayed, has seemingly noticed a puzzle in the text of the psalm that he seeks to tease out. The psalm is headed by the superscription, "A psalm of David," and then opens with the words, "The Lord said to my Lord." Clearly the first "Lord" in the text (LXX: *kyrios*; MT: *YHWH*) would be understood by any ancient reader to be the most high God, that is Yahweh. Not only is this unambiguously certain in the Hebrew version since the consonants *YHWH* are given, even in the more equivocal Greek translation of the Old Testament, the Septuagint (LXX), this first "Lord" (*kyrios*) is the one who ultimately delegates rule to the other Lord. However, the second "Lord" in the text is identified as "my Lord" (LXX: *kyrios mou*; MT: *ʾădōnî*) which must be a different *person* than the most high God, Yahweh, since Yahweh is directly *addressing* this individual with specific words. Yet why would this second person be called *my* Lord? God is directly addressing someone, speaking to someone else in the first person, but who?

A glance at the surrounding context does much to show that Jesus' scriptural interpretation, with his "Lord said to my Lord," is anything but innocuous. Although modern readers may not feel the tugging undertow of this bold exegetical claim, Jesus' enemies certainly did. In fact, these words form a capstone to a series of controversial teachings in which Jesus repeatedly makes claims that his enemies see as inappropriate, perhaps even blasphemous. That these controversial moments are more subtle than is sometimes recognized can be shown by paying careful attention to Jesus' words in two episodes that lead up to this one, and they are of assistance as we consider Jesus' person-centered interpretation of this psalm. These two preliminary episodes ostensibly involve controversy over taxes and marriage, but the discerning reader may find something more seditious.

The Subversive Context

Caesar and Image Bearing. When asked whether or not taxes should be paid to the Romans, Mark reports that Jesus responds with regard to the procured coin, "Whose is this *image* and inscription?" and "Render the things of Caesar to Caesar and of God to God" (12: 16–17). Contrary to popular Christian understandings of this passage, this is absolutely *not* a blanket affirmation that taxes should unquestionably be paid to the government. Rather Jesus has forced his opponents to ponder what ultimately belongs *to Caesar* (whose representational *image* appears on the coin)—who is at best a frequently misguided steward of the things of God but at worst a blasphemous idolater who is ripe for judgment—and what truly belongs *to God*, who is the source and ultimate owner of everything, and to make their decision about "rendering" taxes and all else accordingly.

Are they also encouraged to consider, although the invitation is almost inscrutably veiled, what it might mean for something, like a mute relief on a coin *to bear the image of Caesar*?—and by analogical extension, what it might mean for something, or better, in Jewish theology for someone, *to bear the image of God*, since humans are made in God's image (Gen. 1: 26–7)? After all this bearing-the-image-of-God business was quite literally immediately in view on the coin itself, since on the specific denarius in question the image of the emperor Tiberius was surrounded by words that make a claim to divine sonship: "Augustus Tiberius Caesar, Son of the Divine Augustus."[7] In favor of this bearing-the-image interpretative view, it should be noted that Jesus himself places the stress on Caesar's image, so Jesus may be subtly hinting at traditional Jewish criticisms of images (idols)—that they are unable to represent God because they are deaf, dumb, and mute (e.g. Ps. 135: 15–18; Isa. 44: 9–20)—thereby implying that only a living, breathing, made-in-the-image-of-God human can truly represent God. Is it perhaps suggested that only a human that is functioning entirely as God intended, only the Son of Man—a title that suggests "the paradigmatically human one" but is further invested with meaning through Daniel 7: 13–14 and elsewhere—can *fully image* God?[8] We are left uncertain, although Jesus' use of hidden transcripts elsewhere as a means of subversive criticism and the intense animosity generated by Jesus' teachings in general, with the crucifixion less than a week later, should, perhaps, leave us in less doubt.[9] Clearly his contemporaries felt Jesus was in the habit of saying terribly inappropriate things.

The God of the Living Dead. Jesus' interpretative boldness extends to his conversation with the Sadducees about the resurrection (Mark 12: 18–27). The Sadducees did not believe in the resurrection and attempted to trap Jesus with a puzzle about the incongruities caused by the notion of a future resurrection-age in light of the special problem posed by a woman who had married multiple husbands in this age. Jesus, as he is portrayed, turns to the Scripture to show them their error. When God appeared to Moses, God does *not* identify himself by saying "I *was* the God of Abraham, Isaac, and Jacob," using what we would call the *past tense* with reference to the long-dead Abraham, Isaac, and Jacob; rather he says, "I *am* the God of Abraham, the God of Isaac, and the God of Jacob" (citing Exod. 3: 6). That is, he spoke to Moses of them in the implied

---

[7] Regarding the image and the exact textual inscription on the denarius issued by Tiberius, see N. T. Wright, *Paul and the Faithfulness of God* (2 vols. in 4 parts; Minneapolis: Fortress, 2013), i. 1. 336.

[8] It is at least worth noting that one of our first Christian interpreters of this passage, Tertullian, *Marc.* 4. 38. 3, sees this humans-in-the-image-of-God theology at work in the "render unto Caesar" saying. Tertullian argues that Jesus was hereby trying to teach that "man must be given back to his Creator, in whose image and likeness and name and metal he was stamped into shape." Even earlier the Apologists had used this text to show that Christians were taught by Jesus himself to be law-abiding citizens—e.g. Justin Martyr (*1 Apol.* 17. 1–2), Tatian (4. 1), and perhaps Theophilus (*Autol.* 3. 14, although Rom. 13: 7–8 and 1 Tim. 2: 1–2 are directly in view).

[9] On Jesus' use of "hidden transcripts" as a mode of resistance, see the papers collected in part one of Richard Horsley (ed.), *Hidden Transcripts and the Arts of Resistance: Applying the Work of James C. Scott to Jesus and Paul* (Semeia Studies 48; Atlanta: Society of Biblical Literature, 2004); Richard Horsley, *Jesus and the Powers: Conflict, Covenant, and Hope of the Poor* (Minneapolis: Fortress, 2011), 155–78; Matthew W. Bates, "Cryptic Codes and a Violent King: A New Proposal for Matthew 11:12 and Luke 16:16–18," *CBQ* 75 (2013): 74–93.

present tense,[10] because (so Jesus infers from a careful construal of the implied tense used in the Scripture), the patriarchs, although dead by human standards, were still very much alive to God during the time of Moses, living in God's presence both then and by implication still in his own day. As Jesus climactically states, "He is not the God of the dead, but of the living" (Mark 12: 27), foreshadowing his own anticipated resurrection-life beyond the horizon of temporal death. Again we find a provocative yet tacit allusion to his future vindication and exaltation to divine glory.

Psalm 110 as a Triune Theodramatic Conversation

As Mark paints the picture, after Jesus is interrogated by a scribe regarding which command is most important, Jesus' opponents do not dare to ask him any more questions, and Jesus, with a nimble repartee, pivots to offense, asking a question about the cogency of current scribal opinions regarding the coming of the Messiah—obviously a topic of paramount importance to Jesus—in light of Psalm 109: 1 LXX ("The Lord said to my Lord, 'Sit at my right hand'"). Moreover, on the basis of the passages just examined, we might suspect that just as in the preceding passages in Mark, this saying might also have an understated bite in which Jesus craftily vexes his enemies by making veiled claims. And indeed, what at first appears only to be a surface-level puzzle designed to stump his enemies has a subversive undercurrent flowing below the surface of the water. For Jesus states that this passage pertains to *the Christ* as the son of David (12: 35), and inasmuch as Jesus has accepted the title *the messiah* or *the Christ*, then, here Jesus is portrayed as questioning his enemies about the manner in which Psalm 109: 1 LXX pertains *to his very self.*

And although New Testament and historical-Jesus scholarship famously underwent a lengthy phase in which it was popular to deny that Jesus viewed himself as the Son of Man, or alternatively as the messiah, this edifice is rapidly disintegrating, and a new consensus is beginning to emerge that the historical Jesus must have viewed himself as some sort of elevated figure, at the very least as a climactic eschatological prophet, and quite plausibly as something

---

[10] I speak of the implied tense because ancient Hebrew does not have a tense system that corresponds in a straightforward way to English tenses. Moreover, typically in Hebrew the subject (here: "I") and predicate nominative (here: "the God of your Fathers") are directly juxtaposed without an intervening equative verb, so the English translator must supply the appropriate verb tense from context. In this case it is self-evident (and not seriously disputed by scholarship) that the present tense is implied in the Hebrew, "I [am] the God of your Fathers," all of which is confirmed and made explicit in the ancient Greek translations of the text, "I *am* the God of your Fathers" (*egō eimi ho theos tou patros sou*), on which the Gospel writers would in all likelihood have depended.

much more. [11] Granted that there were a variety of messianic views current in Jesus' day, by far the most widely attested is the royal-Davidic type, and my own assessment is that the historical Jesus and his followers most likely regarded Jesus as the Davidic *messias designatus*—the individual selected and anointed by God as Davidic messiah but as of yet lacking a throne from which to rule.[12] Since within the confines of this book I cannot argue for such a view, only point to others who have to my mind persuasively demonstrated its sweet reasonableness, in what follows I will simply assume that it is at least plausible that the historical Jesus had determined that he was the *messias designatus*, the chosen Christ awaiting his enthronement.[13] In any case, it is indubitably clear (and not really disputed) that the synoptic writers retrospectively understood Jesus to be the Davidic messiah, however imprecisely defined, so at the very least we can affirm that they are portraying him as such. So even for those who remain cautious about the historical Jesus' own messianic claims, much can still be gained in the following discussion at the level of the Christology of the synoptic Evangelists.

[11] The non-eschatological Jesus is associated especially with Bultmann, Funk, Crossan, Borg, and the Jesus Seminar, but these views have generally been abandoned in favor of a decisively eschatological Jesus by a large and diverse cross-section of recent scholars (including Catholics, Jews, liberal Protestants, conservative Protestants, and independents). For surveys of the history of scholarship on the historical Jesus, see James D. G. Dunn, *Jesus Remembered* (Grand Rapids: Eerdmans, 2003), 17–97; N. T. Wright, *Jesus and the Victory of God* (Minneapolis: Fortress, 1996), 3–124.

[12] On the variety, as is well known, there is some evidence that the community responsible for the production of the Dead Sea Scrolls was anticipating two messiahs, one royal Davidic and one priestly (e.g. 1QS 9. 10–11; CD 7. 18–20; 12. 23; 1QSa 2. 11–20). Regarding the variegated messianic expectations in the Second Temple period but the preponderance of a royal Davidic hope, see John J. Collins, *The Scepter and the Star: Messianism in Light of the Dead Sea Scrolls* (2nd edn.; Grand Rapids: Eerdmans, 2010); Andrew Chester, "Jewish Messianic Expectations and Mediatorial Figures and Pauline Christology," in Martin Hengel and Ulrich Heckel (eds.), *Paulus und das antike Judentum* (WUNT 58; Tübingen: Mohr [Siebeck], 1991), 17–89. For an authoritative recent discussion of Messiah language, see Matthew V. Novenson, *Christ among the Messiahs: Christ Language in Paul and Messiah Language in Ancient Judaism* (Oxford: Oxford University Press, 2012). Novenson argues that in our earliest extant Christian literature the term "Christ" as applied to Jesus functioned as an honorific title.

[13] See Luke 1: 32–3; Matt. 19: 28; 25: 31; there is further discussion in Ch. 6. It should be noted that David was remembered as a *messias designatus*, having been selected by God and anointed as a youth (1 Sam. 16: 13) but not installed as king until around age 30, after Saul's suicide (2 Sam. 2: 4; 5: 3–5). So David himself could have served as a model around which a *messias designatus* self-conception could have coagulated for Jesus. On Jesus' self-identification as a climactic prophet and ultimately the *messias designatus*, see Allison, *Constructing Jesus*, 279–93; on Jesus as an eschatological prophet and the royal messiah, see Wright, *Jesus*, 147–97, 477–539; John P. Meier, "From Elijah-Like Prophet to Royal Davidic Messiah," in James D. G. Dunn et al. (eds.), *Jesus: A Colloquium in the Holy Land* (New York: Continuum, 2001), 45–83; Craig S. Keener, *The Historical Jesus of the Gospels* (Grand Rapids: Eerdmans, 2009), 238–67. Yet Dunn, *Jesus Remembered*, 647–66, and esp. 706, still represents some scholars when he opines that Jesus viewed himself as an eschatological prophet, but that he saw the messianic designation as "more of a hindrance than a help."

Now we get to the heart of the person-centered strategy employed by Jesus as portrayed. He has, as was common within late Second Temple Judaism, construed the Davidic psalm title as a claim of Davidic *authorship*. So for Jesus, David as the inspired author is speaking "by means of *the Holy Spirit*" (*en tō pneumati tō hagiō*—Mark 12: 36) and has called this second Lord, "my Lord." Furthermore, so it would seem Jesus reasons, the figure addressed as "my Lord" must be exalted indeed since he is, among other things, invited to sit down at the right hand of Yahweh. The mighty king David has called this person in the psalm "my Lord," and God has invited this person to participate in the divine rule. *Jesus (as portrayed by the synoptic writers) has in effect exegetically construed himself as the person, the "my Lord," addressed by God (the Father) in the text.* That Jesus has taken himself as the referent here is made emphatic by his subsequent reapplication of Psalm 109: 1 LXX, conflated with Daniel 7: 13–14, in his trial before the Jewish leadership: "Again the high priest questioned him saying, 'Are you the Christ, the son of the Blessed One'? 'I am,' Jesus said, 'And you will see the Son of Man sitting at the right hand of power and coming with the clouds of heaven'" (Mark 14: 61–2; cf. Matt. 26: 63–4; Luke 22: 67–70).

The best explanation is that Jesus, as he is portrayed in Mark 12: 35–7, is interpreting Psalm 109: 1 LXX prosopologically, pointing out a conundrum in the text and then encouraging the audience to identify the speaker and the addressee correctly. More precisely, Jesus seems to believe that the Holy Spirit had inspired David to slip as an actor into what we might term "a theodramatic vision" and from within that visionary world to make a speech in the character (*prosōpon*) of someone else.[14] As such, the Spirit is really speaking the words through David ("David himself said while speaking *by means of the Holy Spirit*"—Mark 12: 36), so the Spirit is supplying the script. For Jesus, the role in the theodrama that David adopts here is GOD, and God's theodramatic addressee is a person David himself calls "my Lord." We might paraphrase Mark's depiction of Jesus' reading and the persons assigned to the words thus:

DAVID *Himself* (reporting the setting): The Lord [God] said to my Lord,
David in the prosopon of GOD (*spoken to* MY LORD, THE CHRIST): Sit at my
   right hand, O Christ, Lord of David, until I make your enemies a footstool
   for your feet.   (Ps. 109: 1 LXX)

And what sort of assumptions and theological implications does such a reading involve? Although we shall have more to say about how this psalm speaks of appointment to a special heavenly office and of final eschatological vindication (Ch. 6), here I want to focus on the way it in all probability was

---

[14] On the ontology of the theodramatic world, see n. 61 in Ch. 1.

construed by Jesus, as he is portrayed, as speaking of his own preexistence and divine begottenness.

Preexistence and Prosopological Exegesis

By preexistence I intend *real or personal preexistence* as a distinct being, person, or hypostasis—which is not to be confused with the rather trivial and less substantive notion of *ideal preexistence*, foreordained existence only in the mind of God. Nor with *eschatological preexistence*, the belief that the earliest Christians, because they were so convinced after Easter Sunday and the subsequent ascension that Jesus was now alive in heaven, fabricated the idea of preexistence in order to provide a counterbalance to Jesus' after-death existence with God—as is alleged by some scholars.[15]

Prosopological exegesis on its own does not necessarily entail anything more than ideal preexistence, as the theodramatic characters invoked can exist simply in the mind of God at the time of the prophetic utterance, only to come subsequently into ordinary human existence prior to the future actualization of the utterance.[16] Yet, with regard to Jesus, real preexistence is demonstrably probable for early Christian theodramatic readers due to two interrelated factors involving time sequencing. (1) Sometimes not just the delivery of the theodramatic speech by the prophet (in the prophetic setting) but the realization of the theodramatic speech (in the actualized setting) is felt by the early Christian reader to have occurred prior to the appearance of the earthly Jesus.[17] (2) The complex tense shifts between past, present, and future settings within the dialogues themselves with respect to the prophetic, theodramatic, and actualized setting as it pertains to Christ's role frequently do not permit a merely idealized foreordination.[18] In short, as will be shown

---

[15] For these categorical distinctions and an outline of the relevant scholarship, see Douglas McCready, *He Came Down from Heaven: The Preexistence of Christ and the Christian Faith* (Downers Grove, Ill.: InterVarsity, 2005), 15–19.

[16] For an example in which prosopological exegesis entails only ideal preexistence, observe how Paul has assigned "the apostles" as the "our" of the "O Lord, who has believed our audible message" (Isa. 53: 1 in Rom. 10: 16) as discussed in Bates, *The Hermeneutics of the Apostolic Proclamation*, 255–69.

[17] For example, the theodramatic prophetic speech of David, "A body you prepared for me" (Heb. 10: 5), is felt to have been actualized just as Christ was entering into the world, that is, the pre-incarnate Jesus Christ is thanking God the Father for the body God has crafted for him. See "A Body You Have Prepared for Me" in Ch. 3.

[18] For example, as I will seek to show later in this chapter, for many early Christian readers of Ps. 2: 7 the prophetic setting of the dialogue is in the *past* at the time of David, but the *present-tense* theodramatic setting is the post-resurrection enthronement of Jesus, and at this time the Christ reports a *previous* occasion during which he was addressed by God (the Father) in the *distant past*, at which time God also announced actions still in the *future* for the enthroned Christ. Similar examples are adduced in subsequent chapters.

throughout this book, for early Christian readers the Christ as speaker or addressee often rises above ordinary time categories in his theodramatic dialogues, speaking in and about events before, during, and after the life of the historical Jesus, implying not just real preexistence, but also a certain timeless transcendence.

The issue of preexistence in the Synoptics, let alone the historical Jesus' own view of the matter, is obviously very controversial—and here I cannot fully engage in the terms of the debate or even summarize the vast literature, but only say a few words. On the one hand, in agreement with much New Testament scholarship produced over the last century, the preexistence of Jesus in the Synoptic Gospels is flatly denied in a recent book by Yarbro Collins and Collins.[19] On the other hand, a number of recent studies attempt to show that the synoptic writers affirm the preexistence of Jesus, the most important of which is Simon Gathercole's *The Preexistent Son*, which both summarizes and surpasses all previous efforts.[20]

In this scholarly discussion of preexistence in the Synoptic Gospels, the Old Testament citation that I treat in what follows has not generally loomed large.[21] For example, in *How Jesus Became God*, Bart Ehrman argues that the historical Jesus never intimated his own preexistence or divinity, and Ehrman reads Psalm 109 LXX as if it is addressed merely to the ancient king of Israel; but he does not grapple with the synoptic Jesus' own interpretation (as portrayed) of this

---

[19] Adela Yarbro Collins and John J. Collins, *King and Messiah as Son of God: Divine, Human, and Angelic Messianic Figures in Biblical and Related Literature* (Grand Rapids: Eerdmans, 2008), 123–48, esp. the blunt statement, "The Synoptic Gospels do not portray Jesus as preexistent" (p. 209).

[20] Simon J. Gathercole, *The Preexistent Son: Recovering the Christologies of Matthew, Mark, and Luke* (Grand Rapids: Eerdmans, 2006). While sharing with Gathercole an affirmation of Christologies of preexistence in the earliest church, and finding much of his evidence highly persuasive, I do not unilaterally endorse what he regards as his central contribution—that is, I think his argument for preexistence from the "I have come" sayings in the Synoptics is somewhat weak in light of the standard prophetic interpretation (cf. the critical remarks by Yarbro Collins and Collins, *King and Messiah*, 123–6). Undoubtedly, however, the "I have come" sayings do show at the very least that Jesus was an extraordinarily special and climactic prophet. So it is problematic to use Gathercole's possible misstep with regard to the "I have come" sayings as an excuse to disregard the rest of the frequently convincing evidence that he does present—as Yarbro Collins and Collins seemingly do. With regard to Mark 12: 35–7 on Ps. 110, Gathercole comes to similar conclusions (pp. 236–8) regarding how this text was being read and its implications for preexistence as are reached in this study, in agreement with among others, Johannes Schreiber, *Die Markuspassion: Eine redaktionsgeschichtliche Untersuchung* (BZNW 68; Berlin: de Gruyter, 1993), 210–59 esp. 238–40.

[21] An important exception is the stimulating study of Aquila H. I. Lee, *From Messiah to Preexistent Son: Jesus' Self-Consciousness and Early Christian Exegesis of Messianic Psalms* (WUNT 192; Tübingen: Mohr [Siebeck], 2005), which treats the potential of Ps. 2: 7 and Ps. 110: 1 for Jesus' preexistence and messianic self-consciousness extensively. Lee's study is still recent, so undoubtedly its results are still being weighed by scholarship, but he certainly gives much to ponder. I find that where we overlap, our conclusions are often (although not always) complementary, even though our angle of approach is quite different.

important passage in the Gospels.[22] I contend that this neglected evidence must be integrated, especially when considered in light of the new theodramatic model for which I am advocating. In short, the synoptic Jesus' reading of Psalm 110: 1 here, and of other scriptural passages elsewhere, strongly suggests that he saw the Christ (ultimately understood as his very self) and the most High God as *divine persons* having a conversation set sometime *after* the dawn of time in the theodramatic world—surely at the time of the Christ's enthronement—in which matters *before* the dawn of time were discussed. It is no accident that Psalm 110 stood at the center of Christological reflection in the earliest church—Jesus' own exegesis, as portrayed by the Evangelists, urges it.

From the Womb, before the Dawn, I Begot You

How is it that the portrait of Jesus drawn by the synoptic writers suggests that Jesus saw himself as a preexistent divine person in conversational fellowship with the most high God at the dawn of time in his reading of Psalm 110: 1? Jesus believes that David, by the agency of the Holy Spirit, spoke in the person of God, who in turn was addressing the person of the Christ. Since the *prophetic setting* for David is some one thousand years before Jesus' birth, Jesus is portrayed as believing that he preexisted to such a degree that God (the Father) could speak to him in the theodramatic world at that time. And even more critically for our purposes, the specific words spoken in the theodramatic dialogue itself suggest that the Christ existed with the Father even earlier—before time itself began.

Since Jesus has covertly signaled that he is the "my Lord"—the person addressed by God the Father with the words, "Sit at my right hand until I make your enemies a footstool for your feet," we can make a strong case on the basis of analogous readings by his contemporaries that Jesus as he is portrayed (and I would argue the historical Jesus himself) could have plausibly understood the words that follow in the psalm to be addressed likewise to himself—and these words are startling. In the next verse in the psalm, an unidentified speaker talks about God in the third person while addressing this second Lord, saying, "The Lord [God] will send forth your rod of power from Zion," and it appears that David qua David is the speaker given the pattern in verses 1 and 4, with David thereafter appearing in the guise of God (the Father) who speaks to this second Lord. So we might summarize a plausible early Christian reading as follows:

---

[22] Bart D. Ehrman, *How Jesus Became God: The Exaltation of a Jewish Preacher from Galilee* (New York: HarperOne, 2014), 78, 124–8. Historically speaking, Ehrman's analysis in this regard is methodologically weak inasmuch as it stresses diachronic origins over synchronic context vis-à-vis the import of Ps. 110: 1 (109: 1 LXX) for the synoptic Jesus' self-understanding.

DAVID Himself (reporting the theodramatic setting to "my Lord"): The Lord God will send forth your rod of power, O my Lord, from Zion.   (Ps. 109: 2 LXX)

David in the prosopon of GOD (spoken to *MY LORD, THE CHRIST*): Rule in the midst of your enemies! With you is the sovereign authority on the day of your power in the midst of the bright splendors of the holy ones; from the womb, *before the dawn-bearing morning star appeared, I begot you.*   (Ps. 109: 2–3 LXX)

Since Jesus' reading of Psalm 109: 1 LXX, as portrayed by the Evangelists, strongly suggests that Jesus has construed himself as the Lord whom God addresses in the psalm, it is fair to assert (especially given the evidence from the Dead Sea Scrolls manuscript 11Q13 to be presented momentarily) that we, as Gospel readers, are being invited by the Evangelists to consider that Jesus had also determined that verses 2–3 were equally directed at him. Jesus, after all, is asking his audience to puzzle out a riddle about the meaning of Ps. 109: 1 LXX, and it is dubious to suggest that the audience is not being encouraged by Jesus (as portrayed) to think about the context and details of the psalm as a whole in working toward a solution to the riddle.[23]

So, Jesus has cited the first verse of Psalm 109 LXX in such a way that the listener is invited by the Evangelist to consider—and note the Trinitarian implications—that this psalm pertains to a theodramatic conversation scripted by the *Holy Spirit* between *the Christ* and *God* via David, and shockingly *Jesus has identified himself as this Christ* even though Jesus himself was not yet born at the time of David. In fact, as this divine conversation continues, which for Jesus as he is portrayed as an interpreter finds a theodramatic setting sometime *after* the dawn of time (surely at the anticipated future enthronement),[24] we learn via the speech in Psalm 109: 3 LXX that "*before* the dawn-bearing morning star"—that is, before the dawn of time itself in creation—that the

---

[23] For those engaged in scriptural instruction and disputation in the late Second Temple period of Jesus—and the context in Mark 12: 35–7 (cf. 12: 28) is precisely a scribal dispute—it is generally agreed by biblical scholars that quoting one verse of a psalm would have been sufficient to evoke many of the details of the whole psalm. Indeed, the cogency of the debates in the Mishnah and the collections of Haggadah frequently depend on such an ability. This one-part-generates-the-whole thesis for the exegesis of NT authors is argued for throughout the classic by C. H. Dodd, *According to the Scriptures: The Sub-Structure of New Testament Theology* (New York: Scribner's, 1953). Note especially Dodd's concluding remarks that specific quotes by NT authors serve "as pointers to the whole context" (p. 126). If "context" is properly nuanced, this part of Dodd's thesis has by and large been affirmed by subsequent scholarship. In fact it is demanded by the widely endorsed "echoes" method of Richard Hays, *Echoes of Scripture in the Letters of Paul* (New Haven: Yale University Press, 1989). For a recent statement of how the OT context should be evaluated in early Christian interpretation, see Greg K. Beale, *Handbook on the New Testament Use of the Old Testament: Exegesis and Interpretation* (Grand Rapids: Baker Academic, 2012), 41–54.

[24] On the theodramatic setting as the time of the future enthronement, see "The Coronation of the Son" in Ch. 6. At this future enthronement it is stated that the rod of power of this "my Lord" will be sent forth sometime in the even more distant future.

Christ was begotten by God ("I begot you"—*exegennēsa se*), and furthermore, that somehow this begetting had been (or would be) "from the womb" (*ek gastros*).[25] The language is metaphorical yet specific—this Lord is said to be begotten, not created or made, and the phrase "from the womb, before the dawn-bearing morning star [appeared]" suggested to many early Christian readers that God had foreordained that the messiah's birth "from the womb" was to transpire in an unusual fashion and that God was giving a prophetic hint accordingly—all of which would be fulfilled when the messiah would be born "from the womb" of a virgin.[26]

Selected in Advance—Priest and Messiah

After this discussion of begetting, the psalm continues, and once again it would seem that David himself speaks and then steps into the role of God addressing the "my Lord" whom Jesus identifies as "the Christ":

DAVID *Himself* (reporting the theodramatic setting of an earlier past-tense speech to the "my Lord"): The Lord [God] swore and will not change his mind,

---

[25] The Masoretic Text (i.e. the Hebrew consonantal text with the medieval vowel-pointing and accentuation) which forms the basis for most English translations of Ps. 110: 3 (= Ps. 109: 3 LXX) is famously difficult. A literal translation of the MT yields: "Your people [will be] willing on the day of your power, in holy attire; from the womb of the dawn, unto you [is] the dew of your youth." However, the Masoretic vowel pointing is unlikely to reflect how this was being read in Jesus' era, as the other ancient manuscript traditions make clear. For instance, on the strength of comparison with Ps. 2: 7, where we find the same Hebrew consonants, as well as the LXX evidence from Ps. 109: 3 itself, it is much more likely that the consonants were originally read as a qal perfect verb *yĕlidtîkā* ("I have begotten you") rather than as a possessive noun *yaldûtêkā* ("your youth"). Thus, the prosopological reading I am proposing for the Greek text corresponds closely to the most likely reading of the Hebrew consonantal text in the time of Jesus, even if this reading departs from the later MT vocalization. Several others have seen Ps. 109: 3 LXX as evidence for the preexistence of the "my Lord" who is addressed by God—see discussion in Lee, *From Messiah to Preexistent Son*, 111–14, 225–38. My concern here is to give a plausible reconstruction regarding how this psalm was being read toward the end of the Second Temple era by Jesus and his contemporaries, not with the origin or compositional history of the psalm. For a more thorough discussion of the latter, see Yarbro Collins and Collins, *King and Messiah*, 15–19; Frank-Lothar Hossfeld and Erich Zenger, *Psalms* (trans. Linda M. Maloney; vols. ii–iii of a projected 3 vols.; Hermeneia; Minneapolis: Fortress, 2005–), iii. 139–54.

[26] See e.g. Justin, *Dial.* 83. 4–84. 1; cf. 63. 3; Tertullian, *Marc.* 5. 9. 7–8; Irenaeus, *Epid.* 51 (in this last text the "from the womb" is with regard to Isa. 49: 5–6 but the broader context (cf. *Epid.* 48, 53) makes it clear that Ps. 109: 3 LXX and the virgin birth are also in view). Even though we have no such indication in the earliest Christian readings of Ps. 109: 3 LXX, so such a supposition is quite speculative, it is also plausible that the "from the womb" language could have been taken by theodramatic readers as an extension of the metaphor for preexistent begetting by God rather than as a hint about the incarnational virgin birth. Under this reading, God, who transcends male–female categories would then metaphorically perform the male role of begetting and the female role of bringing forth from the womb, and all of this before the creation of the world.

David in the prosopon of GOD (spoken to **MY LORD, THE CHRIST**): You are a priest forever according to the order of Melchizedek. (Ps. 109: 4 LXX)

For at least one early Christian—the author of Hebrews—this theodramatic speech-segment in which the Father addresses the Son in Psalm 109: 4 describes the moment when the preexistent Christ receives, before the dawn of time, his eternal priesthood in the order of Melchizedek by virtue of an oath sworn by God himself (Heb. 5: 5–6; 7: 21)—a topic we shall revisit toward the end of the book. So there is a precedent in the earliest church for supposing the Evangelists are implying that the historical Jesus would have read the psalm in this fashion as well.

The notion that God made certain other things before the creation of the physical world was quite common in Second Temple and early rabbinic Judaism—including wisdom, the heavenly throne, the Torah, the garden of Eden, Gehenna, the temple, and intriguingly, *the name of the Messiah*.[27] For example, Psalm 72: 17, which contains a litany of prayer-requests for the king, was understood to announce that the Messiah's name had been selected by God in advance: "Let his name be forever (*lĕ ʿôlām*), let his name flourish before the sun (*lipnê-šemeš*), let them bless themselves in him, let all the nations call him blessed." Similarly in the "similitudes" of *1 Enoch*, a text written contemporaneously to the life of the historical Jesus, we find that Enoch observes the moment at which the Son of Man is given his name, which is described as "even before the sun and constellations were created" (48. 1–3 here 48. 3).[28] Yet since the moment for this Son of Man's role as "a light of the nations" and object of worship has not yet come, for the present time this Son of Man has merely been "chosen and hidden" in God's presence (*1 En.* 48. 4–6). Early Greek-speaking Christian interpreters such as Justin Martyr would be quick to pick up on the notion that the name of this ideal king (and hence, for Justin, his identity as Jesus) was preselected by God, proving that "Christ existed before the sun" and moreover, that his name would endure forever.[29] As the Septuagint puts it, "His name persists *before* the sun" (*pro tou hēliou diamenei to onoma autou*—Ps. 71: 17 LXX).

The argument that we are not just invited by the Gospel writers to consider that Jesus engaged in prosopological exegesis of Psalm 110, but that it is plausible that the historical Jesus did in fact read in this fashion, can,

---

[27] See the primary source texts collected in James L. Kugel, *Traditions of the Bible: A Guide to the Bible as It Was at the Start of the Common Era* (Cambridge, Mass.: Harvard University Press, 1998), 44–5, 54–60, such as *b.Pesaḥim* 54a; *2 En.* 25. 3–4; *4 Ezra* 3: 6; *Targum Neophyti* Gen. 3: 24; *Targum Ps-Jonathan* Gen. 2: 8.

[28] Cf. *1 En.* 62. 7; trans. Nickelsburg and VanderKam.

[29] Justin, *Dial.* 64. 5; cf. 34. 6; 64. 6; 121. 1; Irenaeus, *Epid.* 43. Cf. the closely related idea of the visitation of the "rising from on high" in Luke 1: 78 (see Gathercole, *The Preexistent Son*, 238–42).

I would contend, be greatly enhanced by examining the way in which this psalm was interpreted by other Jews and Christians that read this text before, with, and in the wake of Jesus' own reading. A few words, however, need to be said about this method, especially the legitimacy of using later interpretations to evaluate earlier ones.

HISTORICAL PROBABILITY, RECEPTION HISTORY, AND INTERTEXTUALITY

Since all historical reconstruction involves extrapolations from an incomplete data set, we must work both forward *and backward* in time with respect to the event to fill in the historical gap. If we are trying to reconstruct the interior meaning of any ordinary historical event, let's say Lincoln's assassination, we do not ignore what happened afterward, Booth's attempt to flee, as irrelevant in reconstructing what happened before he approached Lincoln's box in the theater and pulled the trigger. His flight afterward is important in reconstructing the meaning of the prior events, because his subsequent rendezvous with others shows his participation in a broader plot and helps cast light on his previous activities and his pro-South motives. Turning a blind eye to what follows only impoverishes the historical reconstruction of what had transpired earlier—and for the serious historian, completely ignoring subsequent events in reconstructing the meaning of an earlier event could ultimately lead to wildly irresponsible and unlikely hypotheses with respect to the earlier event. Also upon occasion there is simply a lack of information available to the historian regarding what happened prior to a specific event, but what happened later is well attested by ancient literary and material sources, so the most reliable way of reconstructing the event will be to work almost entirely backward. All of this is fairly easy to recognize with respect to an ordinary historical event, but has not always been accepted in the emotionally charged field of Christian origins.

Thus, contrary to the heavy-handed developmentalism deployed by a previous era of historical-critical scholarship on early Christology, where it was falsely judged, in my estimation, that later data should generally not be considered at all when reconstructing the meaning of earlier texts, because the risk of importing later ideas back into earlier texts was deemed too great,[30] it should increasingly be recognized—and I think that it is—that the quest for

---

[30] James D. G. Dunn, *Christology in the Making: A New Testament Inquiry into the Origins of the Doctrine of the Incarnation* (2nd edn.; Grand Rapids: Eerdmans, 1989), 13, is typical of many when he states, "We must attempt the exceedingly difficult task of shutting out the voices of the early Fathers . . . in case they drown out the earlier voices . . ." (cf. also p. 33).

"what we can say an author may have intended once any and every possibility of taint from later developments is removed" is by no means equivalent to "what we can say an author most probably intended." Why? Because the correct identification of the alleged later taint *as later taint* and its removal is highly conjectural. It may be that the alleged later contamination is in fact an indigenous seminal development that simply shares significant continuity with the more robust attestation of the idea in slightly later sources, so that its removal actually decreases the likelihood of an accurate historical reconstruction.

The influential developmental Christology of James Dunn is a paradigmatic example of this quixotic quest for the pristine wellspring of Christian origins.[31] However, in my judgment, for the reason just outlined (failure to integrate reception history successfully) among other problems, Dunn's quest for purity comes at the expense of historical probability. There are ultimately a number of problems at the level of method—and much the same could be said for others who adopt similar backward-movement-of-Christology schemes.[32]

In other words, "the indisputably developmentally pure historical reconstruction" is often quite different from "the most likely historical reconstruction"—and throughout its modern history, scholarship on Christian origins has

---

[31] In his *Christology in the Making*, Dunn's basic line of reasoning, applied repeatedly, is thus: (1) The Christ's preexistence is not indubitably present in relevant pre-Christian Jewish or Hellenistic sources (that is, the sources indisputably untainted by later Christian ideas). (2) Therefore, for any early Christian text that could possibly entail preexistence, any competing explanation is to be strongly preferred. (3) In examining possible early Christian instantiations, specific passages are first given a competing explanation in relative isolation from consideration of the cumulative evidence, and only then the cumulative results are considered. Dunn's conclusion (see his summary on pp. 251–8)? A developmental rise in Christology can be traced in the NT itself from low in our earliest sources (Jesus is neither preexistent nor God's Son) to high in our later sources (Jesus as the preexistent and incarnate Son of God). See n. 32 in this chapter for a critique of these three points.

[32] Regarding the three-part method in Dunn's *Christology in the Making* (see n. 31 in this chapter), in response to (1), most scholars, even those sympathetic to his overall backward-development scheme, have concluded against Dunn that preexistence is present in Paul's letters (e.g. Ehrman, *How Jesus Became God*, 252–62—see however my n. 25 in Ch. 1). And if Jesus is already regarded as the preexistent Son in our earliest extant Christian sources, then it is difficult to argue that this idea gradually developed. Regarding (2), with his individual examples Dunn merely shows that a competing explanation is sometimes possible, but he consistently falls short of demonstrating probability. With respect to (3), as part of a dialectical process the cumulative evidence should be weighed *while* assessing possible individual instantiations (not just afterwards), and the cumulative evidence absolutely must be considered when drawing conclusions about overall probability. That is, for example with regard to Paul, our earliest extant source, when a possible instance of preexistence is read on its own (e.g. Rom. 1: 3, 8: 3, 10: 6–8, 15: 3; 1 Cor. 8: 6, 10: 4, 15: 45–7; 2 Cor. 4: 13, 5: 21, 8: 9; Gal. 4: 4; Phil. 2: 6–8; Col. 1: 15–20), Dunn does perhaps show that it is possible that Paul does not hold to preexistence in a couple of the specific passages in question, but when all the evidence is considered *together* (as it must be), then the non-preexistence conclusion is radically unwarranted. In addition to these methodological problems, I also think Dunn misinterprets and/or ignores evidence in the early strata (the pre-Pauline tradition, Paul's Letters, Q material, Mark, and Hebrews) that contravenes his developmental scheme, especially the evidence from prosopological exegesis, as I seek to show in my own analysis.

generally failed to make this distinction or has claimed to be giving us the latter when it was really giving us a highly speculative version of the former. Yet the responsible historian is compelled to aim for what is most probable while assessing all the evidence, not merely for what is indubitably pristine—that is, early reception history, weighted appropriately, must be included in the calculus when evaluating the intended meanings of an ancient text.[33] The irony is that in spinning stories of Christian dogmatic development, scholarship has by and large significantly *overvalued* the evidence of the hypothetical pre-history and redactional layers that we do not actually possess (and about which there is lack of scholarly agreement), but has *undervalued* the non-hypothetical coeval and subsequent Christian texts that we do actually have. This is not a drumbeat for uncritically back-reading later ideas into earlier texts, nor is it a rejection of source, form, and redaction criticism, but it is a call for methodological rebalancing by incorporating early reception history into our historical-critical toolbox.

Accordingly the method that I employ to contextualize New Testament interpretations of the Old Testament by utilizing Second Temple Jewish resources and the early Fathers of the church is best termed *diachronic intertextuality*—that is, analysis of the redeployment of the same *text* by multiple authors through the course of time. This method uses *pre-texts*, *co-texts*, and *post-texts* in order to argue toward a probable meaning for any given *text*. What I call early Christian *co-texts* (coeval interpretations of the same OT passage as in the *text*) and *post-texts* (received interpretations of the OT passage via the *text* in the early Fathers) are particularly vital for illuminating New Testament interpretations of the Old Testament, because they have been and continue to be neglected. Yet, I submit, given the indisputable evidence that early Christians frequently borrowed one another's scriptural

---

[33] If we have learned nothing else from contemporary hermeneutics, surely we have learned that textual meaning is a complex affair, involving author, reader, textual artifact, implied author and reader, intended or unintended resonance with other cultural artifacts, sociohistoric reading location, the real contemporary reader, reading communities, and other factors (potentially including divine intention). Even to speak, as I do here, of appropriately prioritizing "intended meanings" runs a certain risk. For example, W. K. Wimsatt and Monroe D. Beardsley, "The Intentional Fallacy," in William K. Wimsatt, *The Verbal Icon: Studies in the Meaning of Poetry* (Lexington: University of Kentucky Press, 1954), 3–18, have famously argued that we should not link meaning to authorial intention because we do not have sufficient psychological access to any given author's mental state. However, in my judgment the so-called "intentional fallacy" of Wimsatt and Beardsley is itself shot through with problems, especially that a given author's intended meanings are to be sought not in the external mind of the author, but as encoded in the text itself, to which we do have access. Modern historians ideally should attempt to decode any given ancient author's intentions (as embedded in the textual artifact the author produced) by acquiring a broad acquaintance with not just the author and the author's extant literary corpus, but with all of that culture's social, material, and linguistic artifacts (including reception history). For discussion, see Ben F. Meyer, *Critical Realism and the New Testament* (Allison Park, Penn.: Pickwick, 1989), 15–55.

interpretations, *Wirkungsgeschichte* ("history of effects") is certainly one of the most crucial horizons for assessing the most probable intended meaning for any given intertextual engagement in the earliest church, but especially for first or inaugural engagements with the Old Testament in our extant Christian literature in light of the dearth of other critical controls.[34] I have also developed various criteria to assist in detecting prosopological exegesis in the New Testament.[35] Yet, in order to make this study approachable for a non-specialized audience, I have opted not to make the deployment of the method overt throughout the course of this book, even though it is operating in the background. The reader who desires greater clarification regarding the cogency and utility of this method is free to explore my fuller, more technical articulation and explicit exemplification elsewhere.[36]

OTHER PERSON-CENTERED INTERPRETATIONS OF PSALM 110

Psalm 110 and Melchizedek

The most crucial pre-Christian interpretation of Psalm 110 ("The Lord said to my Lord, 'Sit at my right hand'") can be found in a manuscript discovered at the Dead Sea, 11Q13,[37] in which the author interpreted Genesis 14: 18–20,

---

[34] On the need for a recovered emphasis on reception history, see Markus Bockmuehl, *Seeing the Word: Refocusing New Testament Study* (Grand Rapids: Baker Academic, 2006), esp. pp. 64–8, 161–88. Since there is definitive evidence that early Christian exegetes frequently borrowed OT interpretations from one another, the widespread failure in the academy to use reception history as a critical control in the study of how NT authors use the OT especially is troubling. But perhaps attitudes are beginning to change. For example, no mention of the need to use reception history was made in the procedure outlined by Greg K. Beale and D. A. Carson (eds.), *Commentary on the New Testament Use of the Old Testament* (Grand Rapids: Baker Academic, 2007), pp. xxiv–xxvi. However, in the more recent treatment by Beale, *Handbook*, 51–2, 122, it is helpfully recommended that students make recourse to post-NT Christian resources in thinking about what NT authors may have intended in using the OT.

[35] The basic criteria for detecting prosopological exegesis in the NT as given and explained in Bates, *The Hermeneutics of the Apostolic Proclamation*, 219–20, are: (1) speech or dialogue, (2) nontriviality of person, (3) the primacy of introductory formulas or markers, and (4) similar prosopological exegesis in co-texts, post-texts, and inter-texts.

[36] On *diachronic intertextuality*, see Matthew W. Bates, "Beyond Hays's *Echoes of Scripture in the Letters of Paul*: A Proposed Diachronic Intertextuality with Romans 10:16 as a Test-Case," in Christopher D. Stanley (ed.), *Paul and Scripture: Extending the Conversation* (Early Christianity and Its Literature 9; Atlanta: SBL, 2012), 263–92. This diachronic intertextual method is spelled out in much the same fashion in Bates, *The Hermeneutics of the Apostolic Proclamation*, 44–56.

[37] Consider also *T.Job* 33. 3 and Rabbi Akiba's interpretation of Dan. 7: 9–14 as reflected in *b. Sanhedrin* 38b, which was probably impacted by his exegesis of Ps. 110, in which one throne belongs to God and one to the Davidic messiah. For discussion of the pre-Christian and later rabbinic evidence, see David M. Hay, *Glory at the Right Hand: Psalm 110 in Early Christianity*

the puzzling passage about the priest Melchizedek, in light of Psalm 110, and then applied that interpretation to make a pesher-exposition of a variety of thematically related passages.[38] Critically for our purposes, just as Jesus (as portrayed), was urgently seeking to discern the addressee to whom God speaks, so also the author of 11Q13, with the latter determining that Melchizedek is the one to whom God speaks throughout the psalm.[39] Moreover, the author of 11Q13 believed that Melchizedek (construed as a powerful heavenly warrior, likely an archangel) rules in the divine assembly, will execute divine vengeance, will return to the heavenly heights, and will offer atonement for the sons of light. Throughout 11Q13, Melchizedek is occasionally referred to as God (*ʾēl* or *ʾĕlôhîm*) or his name is substituted in place of the divine name YHWH in the author's exegesis. For example, for Isaiah 61: 2 we find "the year of the grace of Melchizedek" rather than "the year of the grace of YHWH" and Melchizedek is probably referred to by the author as "your God" in his exegesis of Isaiah 52: 7. So Melchizedek was at the very least viewed as the divine representative par excellence by the author of 11Q13, if not something more. And most critically he was understood as *the addressee to whom God speaks in Psalm 110*, all of which greatly enhances the historical probability that Jesus may in fact have used prosopological exegesis to determine that God was addressing him as the Christ in his interpretation of the same psalm—that is, there is a precedent within contemporaneous Judaism for something closely akin to this type of reading.

Christian Theodramatic Readings of Psalm 110

Vital corroborating testimony indicating that the Gospel writers intend us to construe the synoptic Jesus' interpretation of Psalm 110 in the theodramatic fashion described, and indeed that it might be plausible for the historical Jesus himself, can also be found in subsequent interpretations of this passage in the earliest church. Here I focus on the basic evidence that the earliest Christians

---

(SBLMS 18; Nashville: Abingdon, 1973), 21–33; some supplemental material is presented in Donald Juel, *Messianic Exegesis: Christological Interpretation of the Old Testament in Early Christianity* (Philadelphia: Fortress, 1988), 137–9.

[38] In numerous manuscripts from the Dead Sea Scrolls, one frequently finds a short citation of the scripture followed by an interpretative gloss signaled by a form of the word "pesher." The citations and pesher-explanations can be thematically linked or can exist as a running commentary on a specific book.

[39] For evidence that the author of 11Q13 believed Melchizedek to be the addressee in Ps. 110, see my more detailed treatment in Matthew W. Bates, "Beyond *Stichwort*: A Narrative Approach to Isa 52,7 in Romans 10,15 and 11Q Melchizedek (11Q13)," *RB* 116 (2009): 387–414, here 390–4. Although it may be a related phenomenon, I do not regard the first-person speeches in 1QHymns (i.e. 1Q Hoyadoth) (etc.) to be prosopological exegeses since the first-person voice is not predominately concerned with scriptural exposition.

read Psalm 110: 1 (109: 1 LXX) prosopologically and how they attest that this implies the preexistence of Jesus as he conversed with God (the Father).[40] I will reserve a fuller discussion of how early Christian interpreters discerned a dialogue between the Father and the Son about the Son's coronation and conquest in this psalm until Chapter 6.

Accordingly, the author of Acts asserts that the words, "Sit at my right hand" were not appropriate to David, implying that although they were uttered by David, David was speaking prosopologically as a prophet in the guise of God the Father to Jesus at his ascension long before the earthly Jesus of Nazareth was born (Acts 2: 33–5).[41] Justin Martyr is explicit and emphatic in affirming that the words of Psalm 109 LXX were spoken not about Hezekiah, as some of his Jewish opponents think, but rather they reflect a divine dialogue in which David, during the time in which the Christ only preexisted, spoke in the person of God to the yet-to-be-revealed Christ.[42] Ps-Barnabas believes that David in his prophetic capacity knew that future skeptics would call the Messiah merely the Son of David as opposed to the Son of God, and thus that David addressed him in Psalm 109: 1 LXX as "my Lord" to signify that he is necessarily more than his own scion.[43] Yet in addition to Ps-Barnabas the words of Psalm 109: 1 LXX are explicitly affirmed to be addressed by God to the preexistent Jesus (as the subsequently-to-be-revealed Christ) by Clement of Rome and Irenaeus, and were probably understood similarly by Melito of Sardis and Theophilus of Antioch.[44] To the degree the early church reveals its interpretative posture with respect to Psalm 109 LXX, coeval and subsequent testimony to a theodramatic reading along the lines

---

[40] Regarding preexistence and theodrama for Ps. 109: 3 LXX ("from the womb, before the dawn-bearing morning star appeared, I begot you"), see nn. 25 and 26 in this chapter.

[41] For evidence that Acts 2: 33–5 involves prosopological exegesis, see the fuller treatment in Ch. 6.

[42] Justin, *Dial.* 83; cf. 63. 3; 76. 7; *1 Apol.* 45. 2–4.

[43] *Barn.* 12. 10; cf. related ideas in Ps-Clementine, *Hom.* 18. 13; Clement of Alexandria, *Str.* 6. 15. In fact, Ps-Barnabas views Isa. 45: 1 as a first-person speech of God, who is speaking to a person he identifies as "my messiah, the Lord" (*ō Christō mou, kyriō*)—a person whose right hand God holds. That is, Ps-Barnabas takes this additional text as a speech between God and the Son of God *(Barn.* 12. 11; cf. Irenaeus, *Epid.* 49), a reading that the MT and most LXX manuscripts disallow inasmuch as this "my messiah" is explicitly identified not as "the Lord" but as Cyrus, the ancient Persian king. This deviant reading can be explained because there is only an iota of difference (quite literally!) between the Greek word for Lord, *kyrios*, and Cyrus's name, *kyros*. Moreover, it is likely that here and in other places Ps-Barnabas relies not on full biblical manuscripts as would be found in a continuous scroll, but on extract collections (frequently called *testimonia*), and these often give textual readings that deviate from the mainline manuscript tradition. For discussion of the viability of such a reading, see the subsection "Absolute Blocks" in Ch. 7.

[44] *1 Clem.* 36. 5; Irenaeus, *Epid.* 48–9 (cf. 85); *Haer.* 2. 28. 7 (cf. 3. 10. 5); Melito, *Pascha* 82; *Frag.* 15; Theophilus, *Autol.* 2. 10. For an excellent survey of the Christian reception history of Ps. 110, see Hay, *Glory*, 34–51—although to my mind Hay is not sufficiently attuned to the person-centered reading strategy that drives the scriptural exegesis in much of this reception history.

I have suggested for the synoptic Jesus is consistent and cohesive, all of which is powerful testimony in favor of the prosopological reading I have advanced for Psalm 109 LXX in Mark 12: 35–7.

* * *

In sum, Mark and the other synoptic writers portray Jesus as engaging in a startling prosopological reading of Psalm 110 (Ps. 109 LXX), indicating that Jesus, at least as he is described by the Evangelists, believed that the preexistent Christ—of whom Jesus himself was the human embodiment—was begotten by God and brought forth from the womb before the dawn of the first morning, also telling of his eternal priesthood and his future role as a powerful ruler. We shall have more to say about theodramatic exegesis of Psalm 110 and the emergence of these twin roles—priest and conquering king—as the book unfolds. If this hypothesis is correct, then note the Trinitarian implications. At the very least we are encouraged by the Gospel writers to believe *Jesus* would have deduced via scriptural exegesis that *God (the Father)* via a script authored by the *Holy Spirit* had spoken directly to him after the dawn of time about his origin before time began. Although we must remain uncertain, the interpretation of Psalm 110 in the Dead Sea Scrolls and the early church shows that it is at least plausible that this portrayal by the Gospel writers is faithful to the historical Jesus. Now, we will continue to explore the way in which person-centered divine conversations illuminate the interior of the divine life at the beginning of time.

A REPORTED SPEECH ON DIVINE BEGOTTENNESS—PSALM 2:5–9

The first text that we have explored in detail—Psalm 110 as interpreted in Mark 12: 35–7—gives a snapshot of the manner in which the earliest Christians, including Jesus himself, arrived at a solution-by-person in interpreting their Scripture. A thematically similar second text, Psalm 2, was also read theodramatically in the earliest church.

Psalm 2 contains several unmarked dialogical shifts, all of which made it ripe fruit for early Christian theodramatic interpretative plucking, but there is some disagreement over the boundary of those shifts between the ancient Hebrew and the ancient Greek manuscript traditions (the MT and the LXX respectively).[45] The most critical dialogical switches for our purposes are found

---

[45] For example, in Ps. 2: 3 the kings of the earth speak, exhorting one another, and in 2: 4–5 we hear that the Lord God laughs, scoffs, and speaks to them. Then, in the MT of 2: 6 God speaks the words, "I have consecrated my king upon Zion, my holy mountain." But in the LXX of 2: 6, the identity of the speaker cannot be God since God is referred to in the third person, but rather the speaker is *an otherwise unintroduced "I" whom God establishes as king.* We can infer

in Psalm 2: 5–9 LXX. Note how many times the speaker and the addressee change in this short passage:

> Then he [God] will speak to them in his wrath and in his anger he will trouble them. But I was established as king by him upon Zion, his holy mountain, by heralding forth the decree of the Lord [God]. The Lord [God] said to me, "You are my Son, today I have begotten you. Ask of me and I will give you the nations [as] your inheritance and the ends of the earth [as] your possession. You will rule them with an iron scepter; as a clay pot you will shatter them." (Ps. 2: 5–9 LXX)

The lens and angle from which this divine conversation is viewed is slightly different than in Psalm 110, although the emphasis on preexistence and divine begottenness remains.

The Baptism as Affirming a Previous Conversation

As portrayed by the Evangelists, when Jesus was baptized in the Jordan by John, the heavens were opened, the Holy Spirit descended upon Jesus in the form of a dove, and a voice came from heaven, saying: "You are my Son, the beloved one, with you I am well pleased" (Mark 1: 11; Luke 3: 22; Western text of Matt. 3: 17) or less directly, "This is my Son, the beloved one, with whom I am well pleased" (Matt. 3: 17).[46] The allusion to Psalm 2: 7 LXX is quite obvious—it is widely recognized by current biblical scholarship—not least because the allusion is made emphatic in some portions of the textual tradition and the early reception history, which turn the words into a direct quote of Psalm 2: 7 LXX: "You are my Son, today I have begotten you."[47]

---

on the basis of 2: 2 that this must be the Lord's anointed one (the messiah) who is now speaking. This anointed one says, "I was established as king by him upon Zion, his holy mountain" (Ps. 2: 6 LXX). Yet, in 2: 7 for the MT an unannounced shift in the speaker occurs, and we now find agreement between the MT and the LXX inasmuch as the speaker is no longer God, but it is this "I" whom the Lord God addresses. Thus, despite the complexity, both the MT and the LXX ultimately agree as to the speaker and addressee by the time the critical reported speech occurs, "The Lord [God] said to me, 'You are my Son'" (Ps. 2: 7).

[46] In order to avoid unnecessary repetition, in the main I will discuss only the baptism while asserting that the same basic argument could be made vis-à-vis Ps. 2: 7 at the transfiguration (Matt. 17: 5; Mark 9: 7; Luke 9: 35).

[47] For example, "You are my Son, today I have begotten you," is attested in the Western text of Luke 3: 22; Justin, *Dial.* 88. 8; 103. 6. Cf. the so-called Gospel of the Ebionites as reported in Epiphanius, *Pan.* 30. 13. 7–8, which has the heavenly voice make two separate statements, "You are my Son, the beloved one, with you I am well pleased" and "Today I have begotten you." Even more fascinating is the free rendering of the words that Jerome attests for *The Gospel of the Hebrews* (Jerome, *Comm. Isa.* 4 per Wilhelm Schneemelcher [ed.], *New Testament Apocrypha* [trans. R. McL. Wilson; rev. edn.; Louisville, Ky.: Westminster John Knox, 1991], i. 177): "My Son, in all the prophets was I waiting for thee that thou shouldest come and I might rest in thee. For thou art my rest; thou art my first-begotten Son that reignest for ever." There is a further allusion to

Yet, what the bulk of biblical scholarship misses is that, unless we are to suggest their exegeses were idiosyncratic vis-à-vis the rest of the earliest church, the Gospel writers would have sought the meaning of this allusion by reflecting on Psalm 2: 7 through a person-centered exegetical process.[48] More specifically, previous New Testament scholarship pertaining to this allusion at the baptism and transfiguration has tended to see it merely as a *direct* speech made by God to Jesus that evokes Psalm 2: 7 in accordance with the surface narrative in the Gospels, but has neglected an absolutely crucial datum.[49] As will be shown, for the earliest Christians Psalm 2: 7 was consistently regarded not merely as a direct speech made by the Father to the Son, but rather it was taken as *a speech within a speech that was originally spoken by the Son*, who was reporting the words the *Father had spoken to him at an earlier time*, all of which has critical implications for how Christology and Trinitarian dogma developed.

Jesus, Scriptural Interpretation, and Identity Formation

Is it possible that we are being invited by the Evangelists to consider that Jesus, in the wake of the baptism, would have sought to clarify his own true identity through a deductive person-centered exegetical reflection on Psalm 2: 7?[50]

Isa. 42: 1 in the baptismal words (cf. also Gen. 22: 2), on which see the subsequent discussion. Although this conclusion is increasingly coming into disfavor, several scholars, especially of the past generation, rejected the idea of an allusion to Ps. 2: 7 in the earliest layer of traditions about the baptism/transfiguration on the basis of a speculative reconstruction of the pre-history of the Synoptic tradition—e.g. see W. D. Davies and Dale C. Allison, Jr., *A Critical and Exegetical Commentary on the Gospel According to Saint Matthew* (3 vols.; ICC; Edinburgh: T&T Clark, 1988–97), i. 337–9.

[48]   Although he does not approach Ps. 2: 7 from a prosopological angle, nor does he stress the reported nature of the Father's speech to the Son, Lee, *From Messiah to Preexistent Son*, 166–78, 278, makes a particularly thoughtful attempt to reconstruct how the words of Ps. 2: 7 could have impacted Jesus' self-consciousness of his preexistent status as Son of God.

[49]   In fact, none of the critical commentaries on the Synoptic Gospels that I consulted (I checked about twenty commentaries although my search was by no means exhaustive), nor any of the several major works on Christology that I examined identified *the reported* rather than the direct nature of the "You are my Son" speech in the psalm as significant for understanding its refraction in the Synoptics for the portrayal of Jesus' own self-understanding. However, as will be shown— and I believe that this helps demonstrate the necessity of retaining *Wirkungsgeschichte* as a historical-critical horizon in assessing the author's intended meaning(s)—unlike modern scholarship, non-synoptic early Christian authors were very much attuned to its reported dimension, enhancing the likelihood of this for the synoptic authors as well. This is missed even by those who are particularly concerned to include a discussion of reception history, e.g. Ulrich Luz, *Matthew* (trans. James E. Crouch; 3 vols.; Hermeneia; Minneapolis: Fortress, 2001–7), i. 143–6.

[50]   The basic historicity of the baptism of Jesus by John in the Jordan is almost universally affirmed by scholars due to the criterion of embarrassment. It is extraordinarily unlikely that the earliest Christians would have freely created such a scene—in which a well-known and revered religious figure such as John the Baptist takes the lead over Jesus in baptizing. Moreover, since John's baptism is explicitly purposed toward repentance and the forgiveness of sins, and because Jesus was regarded as sinless in the early church, early Christians might have felt chagrined at

That is, in light of other factors that undoubtedly weighed even more heavily, such as Jesus' intimate relationship to his Abba-Father in prayer and perhaps a more mystical connection,[51] could it be that prosopological meditation on Psalm 2: 7 might have resulted in a growing self-realization that he was the person-centered solution to a scriptural riddle? Although the Evangelists have not left any definite statements that could firmly substantiate the matter one way or another, one possible reconstruction of Jesus' logic, as portrayed, would be:

GOD (speaking to JESUS at the baptism): You are my Son . . .

JESUS (thinking to HIMSELF): Those are the words that the person—the "me"—in the second psalm *reported* that the Father had spoken *previously* to him. Seemingly, God is hereby indicating that I correspond to the "me," the addressee. But exactly who is this addressee according to the psalm?

JESUS (thinking to HIMSELF): During the time of David, this addressee was able to report a previous conversation between God and himself, "The Lord God said to *me*, 'You are my *Son*, today I have *begotten* you,'" so this "me" was begotten as Son *before* the time of the speech if David is able to report it in this fashion.

Although the precise reconstruction of Jesus' internal logical as I have sketched it here must remain nothing more than a matter of speculation, that Jesus himself had made some sort of begotten-Son deduction in connection with his own scriptural meditations is a plausible historical proposal.

There are three considerations that make a scripture-based begotten-Son deduction a reasonable proposal as at least a minor factor in Jesus of Nazareth's developing awareness of his special filial relationship to the God of Israel. First, since Jesus is portrayed as receiving this "You are my Son . . ." message from heaven *twice*—once at the baptism and then again at the transfiguration—the suggestion that we are invited by the Evangelists to suppose that Jesus *meditated repeatedly* on the scriptural underpinnings of these words throughout the years of his active ministry is substantially enhanced. In other words, the Evangelists urgently press us toward the conclusion that when the earliest church remembered Jesus, above all they remembered that his self-identity was bound up with this

Jesus' baptism, since it could be construed as a self-admission of sin and of his need for cleansing. Thus, the embarrassment is double, making the historicity of the general episode extraordinarily firm. Of course, the historical worth of some of the details within the episode, including the precise words spoken from heaven, are not so easily assessed. In rendering judgment contemporary interpreters will inevitably fall back on atomistic criteria or holistic macro-hypotheses as discussed at the outset of this chapter.

[51] Jesus' strange fondness for addressing God as "Abba" has been widely noted. For critical discussion of Jesus' special relationship to God as Father, see Marianne Meye Thompson, *The Promise of the Father: Jesus and God in the New Testament* (Louisville, Ky.: Westminster John Knox, 2000). A more mystical intimacy between Jesus and God the Father is perhaps intimated in Luke's portrayal of the boy Jesus at the temple. Jesus responds to his mother's complaint, "*Your father* [Joseph] and I have been anxiously searching for you," with the sharply pointed question, "Did you not know that it was necessary for me to be in *my Father's* house?" (Luke 2: 48–9).

scripturally informed "You are my Son" conviction. So even if some today are disinclined to accept the precise historical details of the words spoken and the happenings at the baptism and transfiguration, it would nonetheless be historically hazardous, apart from compelling evidence to the contrary, to suggest that the basic tenor of the historical Jesus' overall convictions were substantially misremembered on this point.

Second, although this proposed solution-by-person logic might seem overly complex or alien to the synoptic Jesus on first inspection, it also must be pointed out that Jesus is portrayed as undertaking a very similar exegesis of Psalm 110 in Mark 12: 35–7 and parallels, as was demonstrated at the beginning of this chapter. And a number of additional examples for Jesus will be provided in subsequent chapters, so the process of deductive scriptural reasoning itself is reasonable to suppose for the historical Jesus.

Consider also that although the exegetical logic is somewhat cumbersome to explain, it would be a rather simple move for the historical Jesus if he was accustomed to seeking a solution-by-person in the inspired text. Jesus need not to have mastered Greco-Roman rhetorical theory or even to have been consciously aware of what we have termed prosopological exegesis as a distinctive reading strategy.[52] Jesus need only to have believed that David, under the inspiring influence of the Holy Spirit (cf. Mark 12: 36), was capable of taking on a different *persona* when speaking as a prophet. Accordingly, here, the words are not David's alone, but the words of the preexistent Christ as the preexistent Christ reports an earlier conversation that he had with God the Father about his begottenness and Sonship. In my opinion, the truly astounding thing here is not the exegetical logic Jesus may have used vis-à-vis Psalm 2—even if it is currently underappreciated by scholarship solution-by-person was nonetheless a common enough technique—but the radical conclusion to which the reading possibly helped bring Jesus as he is hereby portrayed, that he preexisted in some fashion as the Son of God, begotten in the far-distant past.[53]

---

[52] When assessing whether or not an ancient reader could have been cognizant of "prosopological exegesis," it must be remembered that we are speaking of an awareness that aligns with assumptions and methods congenial to ancient emic descriptions of this reading practice, not with etic modern nomenclature—see nn. 59 and 61 in Ch. 1.

[53] If any reader doubts that a real and sane (as best as that can be measured) historical person could seriously believe himself to be preexistent, a pivotal figure in divine–human affairs, the messiah, or even divine, then I would gently encourage the reader to spend a little time reviewing the documented evidence, for there have been countless such individuals throughout history who have believed such things, including a number of Jesus' immediate Jewish contemporaries. For a compact discussion of numerous real-life examples, see Allison, *Constructing Jesus*, 253–63. Regarding Jewish royal messianic claimants roughly contemporaneous with the historical Jesus, see Josephus, *Ant.* 17. 271–2, *B.J.* 2. 56, Acts 5: 37 (Judas son of Hezekiah); *Ant.* 17. 273–6 (Simon); *Ant.* 17. 278–85 (Athronges); *Ant.* 20. 169–71, *B.J.* 2. 261–3, Acts 21: 38 ("the Egyptian false-prophet"); *B.J.* 2. 433–4 (Menahem); *B.J.* 2. 652–3, 5. 309, 5. 530–3, 7. 29–36 (Simon bar Giora), *j.Ta'anit* 4.8 68d (Bar Kochba). For a convenient treatment of these primary sources, see

Now for the third consideration. It might be tempting and quite easy to brush off this reconstruction of the synoptic Jesus' prosopological interpretative logic with respect to Psalm 2: 7 as nothing more than a fanciful scholarly hypothesis if it were not for the reception history of Psalm 2: 7 in the earliest church. As the subsequent sections seek to show, coeval and slightly later authors such as the author of Hebrews, Clement of Rome, Justin Martyr, Irenaeus, Tertullian, Origen, and the author of Acts (arguably), all agree that this is precisely how Psalm 2: 7 is to be understood—as reflecting conversation between the preexistent Christ and the Father. And hermeneutical continuity in scriptural interpretation between the historical Jesus, the synoptic writers, and the early church is prima facie historically more likely than discontinuity.

Although biblical critics of the last several centuries, in their rush to divorce themselves from traditional ecclesial readings and to reassess "the original meaning" have frequently failed to appreciate this truth, the value of subsequent interpretation is not that it merely gives quaint anecdotal evidence for how the later church understood the earlier tradition, but rather, it is one of the *absolutely essential* horizons for reconstructing the most likely original meaning. All thoughtful historical reconstruction involves making extrapolations from an incomplete data set by working forward, backward, and around an event to grip it—much like curved tongs are used to grab a slippery carrot out of a salad bowl.

A Reported Theodrama within a Theodrama

I want to show that Psalm 2: 7 LXX was read prosopologically as pertaining to a conversation about divine begottenness between God the Father and the Son by a wide variety of early Christians, with the prophet David alternating between narration and role performance. As such, for the earliest Christians, the primary theodramatic setting of this conversation is at the Son's enthronement ("I was established as king"), but within the conversation there is *reported speech* which finds a second theodramatic setting before the dawn of time (the Son says, "The Lord God said to me, 'You are my Son, today I have begotten you'"), and it is the reported dimension of the speech that above all else has not been noted sufficiently by previous scholarship.[54] In other words, the primary theodrama looks back to an earlier moment in the theodrama. In

---

Richard A. Horsley and John S. Hanson, *Bandits, Prophets, and Messiahs: Popular Movements at the Time of Jesus* (San Francisco: HarperSanFrancisco, 1985). On Jesus of Nazareth himself, see Josephus, *Ant.* 18. 63–4; 20. 200, although unfortunately the first passage almost certainly contains interpolations (see Meier, *A Marginal Jew*, i. 56–88).

[54] See my remarks in n. 49 in this chapter. As I seek to demonstrate, early Christian readers were carefully attuned to the reported nature of the speech in Ps. 2: 7, as well as to the theological implications.

support of this claim, we will look at a number of early Christian readings of Psalm 2: 5–9 LXX shortly, but as a proleptic summary, the shifts characteristic of early Christian readings are:

Dᴀᴠɪᴅ *himself*: Then he [God] will speak to them in his wrath and in his anger he will trouble them.

David in the prosopon of Tʜᴇ Sᴏɴ (providing the occasion for the direct speech in theodramatic setting "B"): But I was established as king by him upon Zion, his holy mountain, by heralding forth the decree of the Lord [God].[55]

David in the prosopon of Tʜᴇ Sᴏɴ (continuing): The Lord [God] said to me . . . [begin REPORTED SPEECH]

REPORTED SPEECH (with Tʜᴇ Sᴏɴ reporting a previous dialogue between Gᴏᴅ ᴛʜᴇ Fᴀᴛʜᴇʀ *and* Hɪᴍsᴇʟf that occurred in theodramatic setting "A"): You are my Son, today I have begotten you. Ask of me and I will give you the nations as your inheritance and the ends of the earth as your possession. You will rule them with an iron scepter; as a clay pot you will shatter them.

Ultimately in Psalm 2: 7–9 it is the one who is declared to be the Son who is speaking, *reporting* the direct speech of the Lord God—that is, Psalm 2: 7–9 is *a speech within a speech* in the psalm. It is *the Son* who says, "The Lord God said to me, 'You are my Son, today I have begotten you'" (Ps. 2: 7 LXX), and any event reported necessarily occurred earlier than the report itself.

A Reported Conversation—Reception History

There is abundant evidence that the earliest Christians were aware that the words spoken by the Father to the Son are in reality *reported speech spoken at a much earlier time*—all of which, I suggest, has important implications for Christology and the rise of Trinitarian dogma, namely that Jesus was not thought to have been adopted as God's Son but was exegetically construed as preexisting his own earthly life as the Son. Thus, my claim that the synoptic Evangelists invite us to read the "You are my Son" statement (derived from

---

[55] The masculine singular active participle *diangellōn*, best rendered literally, "by heralding forth" or perhaps "when promulgating," has an unclear subject. It could be the Lord (God), but this is very unlikely because we would expect "his decree" (*to prostagma autou*), rather than "the decree of the Lord" (*to prostagma kyriou*) in light of the possessive phrase in the preceding clause, "his holy mountain" (*oros to hagion autou*). It could also be a generic herald not mentioned in the text, so that this is best rendered by the English passive—"when the decree of the Lord was promulgated"—but a referent internal to the text itself is more probable. So it is best to take the "I," that is, the one ultimately declared to be the Son, as the speaker. In the MT the imperfect first-person verb (*'ăsappĕrâ*—"I will recount") makes it explicit that the "I" is speaking, enhancing the plausibility of this solution for the Septuagint. Origen, *Comm. Jo.* 6. 196, concurs as he declares that the words of Ps. 2: 6 were spoken by David "in the person of Christ."

Psalm 2: 7) prosopologically in the baptism and transfiguration, finds solid support in the like-minded interpretations of this text by other authors in the first- and second-century church.

The author of Hebrews is difficult to date with precision, but is probably pre–70 CE and is at the latest just prior to 96 CE (since it is generally agreed that Clement of Rome used Hebrews), so he is roughly contemporaneous with the Synoptic Gospel writers. Moreover, the author of Hebrews frequently solves puzzles in the scriptural text by assigning various prosopa as speakers and addressees. For example, in attempting to show the superiority of the Son to any mere human priest, the author cites Psalm 2: 7 in the following way: "In this manner also the Christ did not honor himself to become high priest, but rather [he was honored by] the one who said to him: 'You are my Son, today I have begotten you'" (Heb. 5: 5).[56] Thus, the Christ as the Son is taken as the theodramatic addressee to whom God speaks, exactly as I have proposed for Jesus as portrayed by the synoptic Evangelists. Furthermore, God does not speak in this way to mere angels, but only to the Son, as the author reminds us by another citation of Psalm 2: 7 in Hebrews 1: 5, while adding the absolutely critical qualification that these words and others—"I will be his Father, and he will be my Son" (2 Sam. 7: 14 LXX in Heb. 1: 5)—were spoken to the Son by the Father *not* at the occasion of his resurrection or enthronement, but at or prior to the time when God commanded his angels, "Let all the angels of God worship him" (Heb. 1: 6 citing LXX Deut. 32: 43/Ps. 96: 7). That is, at or prior to *the incarnation*, as the author further explains through his introductory formula, "*and again when God brings his firstborn into the world*" (*hotan de palin eisagagē ton prōtotokon eis tēn oikoumenēn*—Heb. 1: 6).[57] So the

---

[56] Observe the intimate connection between Ps. 2: 7 LXX and a text that we have already shown pertains to a preexistent divine conversation, Ps. 109: 4 LXX (in Heb. 5: 5–6), all of which suggests that these two texts were mutually interpretative for the author of Hebrews.

[57] On the concurrency in temporal aspect between Heb. 1: 5 and 1: 6 forged by the words introducing the citation "and again when God brings," see the helpful analysis of Gareth L. Cockerill, *The Epistle to the Hebrews* (NICNT; Grand Rapids: Eerdmans, 2012), 104. Yet even while granting that the incarnational interpretation is grammatically unobjectionable, a number of recent commentators (e.g. Ellingworth, Lane, and also Cockerill) have nonetheless argued that enthronement in heaven rather than the incarnation is in view in Heb. 1: 6, but I believe this is to conflate the two distinct theodramatic settings (i.e. the enthronement and the moment at or prior to the incarnation). Although enthronement alone is possible, it is lexically quite improbable granted the normal range of meaning of *oikoumenē* as the ordinary human "inhabited world" exclusive of the divine sphere—see BDAG *s.v.* οἰκουμένη def. 1. If an atypical meaning "heavenly realm" is to be attributed here, a heavy burden of proof is necessary, and this burden has not been met by these commentators. The probability in favor of the ordinary human "inhabited world" meaning doubles when weighed in light of the only other occurrence of *oikoumenē* within Hebrews itself, where the future world is described as "the inhabited world that is to come" (*tēn oikoumenēn tēn mellousan*—Heb. 2: 5). It is not plausible that the author of Hebrews would qualify this second instantiation of *oikoumenē* as "the inhabited world *that is to come*" if the first instantiation was to be understood as anything different than the present-tense ordinary human world—as is correctly noted by Harold W. Attridge, *The Epistle to the Hebrews*

hypothesis that the Gospel writers saw two theodramatic settings in Psalm 2: 6–9 finds support here, with the author of Hebrews affirming that the words "You are my Son, today I have begotten you" (Ps. 2: 7) were first spoken by David in the person of the Father to the Son at or before the incarnation, only subsequently to be reported by the Son at some later time. This suggests that the author of Hebrews saw two distinct theodramatic settings as operative. The prophetic setting is during the time of David, who spoke in the person of the Son at the time of the Son's enthronement, when the Son, who had previously been designated high priest (Heb. 5: 6 citing Ps. 109: 4 LXX), was installed as high priest (cf. Heb. 6: 20) in theodramatic setting "B." Yet while speaking in character, the Son is looking back even further in time and reporting a prior conversation that occurred at or before the moment of incarnation in theodramatic setting "A." All this undergirds the idea that early Christian exegesis of Psalm 2: 7 was felt to entail Jesus Christ's preexistence.

Likewise Clement of Rome, who is probably only slightly later than Matthew and Luke, declares that the Master spoke Psalm 2: 7–8 to the Son (*1 Clem.* 36. 4), and in context it is likely that he means that the Father spoke to the preexistent Jesus as the Christ via David, not to the earthly or the enthroned Jesus, much as in Hebrews.

Justin reports that the voice from heaven spoke, "the words which had also been uttered by David, when he, *in the person (hōs apo prosōpou) of Christ* spoke what was later to be said to Christ by the Father, 'You are my Son, today I have begotten you.'"[58] Observe that Justin regards the words of the psalm to be spoken by David *in the prosopon of the preexistent Christ* as the preexistent Christ *reports indirectly* the words of God the Father—it is identified as *reported speech* exactly as I have argued for Jesus as depicted in Mark and our other early Christian authors.

In short, early Christian authors consistently determined that David spoke in the person of the Son, and that the Son was thereby *reporting* the speech of God (the Father), who had previously addressed him as Son with these particular words—and in so doing, these authors have exegetically presupposed that God the Father and Christ the Son are *distinct persons (prosōpa)* who were capable within the bounds of the divine economy of having a dialogue with one another via the prophet David some 1,000 years before the advent of the Christ in the flesh. As Irenaeus puts it:

> Since David says, "The Lord says to me" [Ps. 2: 7], it is necessary to affirm that it is *not* David nor any other one of the prophets, *who speaks from himself*—for it is

(Hermeneia; Minneapolis: Fortress, 1989), 55–6 and Gathercole, *The Preexistent Son*, 34, among others. It should also be observed that the author unambiguously exegetes along incarnational lines in Heb. 10: 5–10, so the possibility of an incarnational interpretation in 1: 5–6 is further strengthened.

[58] Justin, *Dial.* 88. 8; trans. Falls.

not man who utters prophecies—but [that] the Spirit of God, *conforming himself to the person concerned*, spoke in the prophets, producing words sometimes from the Christ and at other times from the Father.[59]

Irenaeus confirms that early Christians firmly recognized that Psalm 2: 7 was *reported speech* ("David says, 'The Lord says'"), and that such a recognition was deemed essential for proper interpretation. When a prophet spoke in this way, the prophet via the Spirit was, as Irenaeus puts it, "*conforming himself to the person concerned*" and speaking "from the Christ" or "from the Father"— that is, taking on a theodramatic role. In fact, not only could David speak in the guise of the Father and the Christ, these divine conversation partners were able to speak about events that occurred before David himself was born— indeed, about things that happened at or before the dawn of time.

Thus, we see that there is a plethora of coeval and subsequent passages that show that Psalm 2: 7–8 was understood prosopologically in the earliest church, with the crucial words first spoken not at the enthronement (theodramatic setting "B"), but at some earlier time (theodramatic setting "A").[60] On what legitimate historical basis, then, can it be demonstrated as more probable that the synoptic writers intended anything otherwise? These twin theodramatic settings are arguably present even in a very early text that at first blush might be felt to indicate the opposite.

PROMISE AND PERSON—ACTS 13: 32–5

A sophisticated example of theodramatic interpretation can be found in Paul's speech at Pisidian Antioch. A careful reading of this text pays rich dividends:

What God promised the fathers he has fulfilled for our children, having raised Jesus, as it is written in the second psalm: "You are my Son, today I have begotten you" [Ps. 2: 7 LXX]. Moreover, that God raised him from the dead no

---

[59] Irenaeus, *Epid.* 49, capitalization and emphasis mine.

[60] In support of this consensus, see also Origen, *Comm. Jo.* 13. 5; Tertullian, *Marc.* 3. 20. 3; 4. 22. 9. An interesting yet idiosyncratic prosopological interpretation of Ps. 2: 7 (which remains only a subtext and is not explicitly invoked) is given by the infamous second-century interpreter Marcion, who denied that the creator god of the OT was truly the most high God, affirming instead that Jesus Christ (who only appeared to have a material human body) had come as an ambassador to reveal this previously hidden most high God. Accordingly, Tertullian, who sought to refute Marcion's interpretation, reports in *Marc.* 4. 22. 1 that Marcion construed the words spoken from heaven at the transfiguration, "This is my beloved Son, listen to him" (cf. Mark 9: 7), as uttered by the formerly unknown most high God rather than the creator god of the OT. According to Marcion the most high God was trying to signal with his "listen to *him*," that one should listen *only to Jesus* as the true ambassador of the most high God, and emphatically *not* to Moses and Elijah, who belong solely to the inferior creator god's dispensation. For more on gnostic prosopological exegesis, see Ch. 7.

longer destined to turn to decay, he stated in this manner: "I will grant to
you the faithful decrees of David" [Isa. 55: 3 LXX], because he also said in a
different psalm: "You will not permit your Holy One to see decay" [Ps. 15: 10
LXX].   (Acts 13: 32–5)

The author of Acts goes on to say that David died and experienced decay,
but that the one whom God raised up, Jesus, did not (13: 36–7), all of which
greatly weakens the standard typological explanation of Hays and others,
because the point is specifically that David's experience was *incommensurable*
with the words spoken by the psalmist, but Jesus Christ's was not.[61] We will
have more to say about the manner in which the author has read these
additional texts from Isaiah and the Psalter in a moment. First I want to
focus on the citation of Psalm 2: 7.

Psalm 2: 7 in Acts 13: 32–3

The critical thing to recognize is that despite initial appearances to the contrary,
Paul is probably *not* portrayed as citing Psalm 2: 7 in support of the notion that
Jesus was raised, but rather as specific evidence that, "What God promised the
fathers he has fulfilled for our children,"[62] with only the subsequent quotes as
intended to support the reality of the resurrection of the Son. Paul is depicted as
undergirding the two parts of his single assertion separately and in order, as if

---

[61] On the relationship between Acts 2: 22–36; 13: 32–5; Heb. 1: 5, 5: 5; and other passages, see
the section "The Coronation of the Son" in Ch. 6. A typological explanation demands *iconic
mimesis*, that is, that the events compared participate in a common image. Yet the point in Acts
13: 36–7 is precisely that David himself *cannot* supply the image because the words do not
correspond to David's own experiences. On the necessity of iconic mimesis for what has
traditionally been termed "typology," see Frances M. Young, *Biblical Exegesis and the Formation
of Christian Culture* (Peabody, Mass.: Hendrickson, 2002), 192–201; Bates, *The Hermeneutics of
the Apostolic Proclamation*, 133–8.

[62] Contemporary English translations mask serious text-critical difficulties in Acts 13: 33. The
Greek text preferred by the 27th edition of Nestle-Aland, the Greek edition used by nearly all
modern English translations, reads *tois teknois [autōn] hēmin* ("for their children, for us"), but
this is only very weakly attested in the ancient manuscripts. The best Greek manuscripts read *tois
teknois hēmōn* ("for our children"). Many scholars find this nonsensical since it seems to exclude
the present horizon of fulfillment, and they prefer to suggest an error in Luke's own grammar or
an early scribal corruption in which *hēmin* ("for us") was intended, but *hēmōn* ("our") was
written into the text. I find concern over Luke's systematic consistency to be an inadequate
criterion here (in part because it is so hyperactively detected and woodenly applied), especially
given the overwhelming external evidence in favor of *tois teknois hēmōn* ("for our children").
Therefore, I side with the ancient manuscripts over against the majority of contemporary
scholars. In agreement with my textual decision, see Mikeal C. Parsons and Martin M. Culy,
Acts: A Handbook on the Greek Text (Waco, Tex.: Baylor University Press, 2003), 261. For
further discussion, see Bruce M. Metzger, *A Textual Commentary on the Greek New Testament*
(2nd edn.; New York: United Bible Societies, 1994), 362.

the one statement were in reality two separate propositions. I submit that the logic of Paul's speech at this juncture works like this:

> *Proposition 1*: "What God promised the fathers he has fulfilled for our children,"
>
> *Proposition 2*: "having raised Jesus,"
>
> *Evidence for Proposition 1 only*: "as it is written in the second psalm: 'You are my Son, today I have begotten you.'" (Ps. 2: 7 LXX)
>
> *Evidence for Proposition 2*: "Moreover, that God raised him from the dead no longer destined to turn to decay, he stated in this manner . . ." (citations from LXX Isa. 55: 3 and Ps. 15: 10 follow)

This reconstruction of the logic of Paul's speech is made probable by two observations when considered together. First, in the initial phase of Paul's speech, *the promise* that a savior will come from David's seed (*sperma*) takes center-stage (see Acts 13: 22–4). Since this promise of a Davidic offspring is the only promise mentioned in the speech, the initial Davidic promise rather than the resurrection is the natural antecedent for the Psalm 2: 7 quote, as its introduction makes clear, "what God *promised the fathers*."[63]

Second, that the citation of Psalm 2: 7 pertains to the initial promise concerning David's seed only, not to the resurrection, is made emphatic by the introduction to the quotation that follows immediately upon the heels of the citation of Psalm 2: 7, that is, the introduction to Isaiah 55: 3 LXX, which reads, "*Moreover, that* he raised him from the dead . . . is stated in this manner." The "moreover that" (*hoti de*) is best taken as pointing to a minor shift in topic to resurrection in Paul's presentation of the evidence—implying that the preceding quote, Psalm 2: 7 LXX, *was not directly aimed at the topic of resurrection*, but that the quotations that follow will be—Isaiah 55: 3 LXX and Psalm 15: 10 LXX.[64] Thus, Psalm 2: 7 is quoted as evidence that the promise made to the fathers concerning the provision of a Davidic offspring has truly

---

[63] This proposal makes much better sense in my judgment than the suggestion of F. F. Bruce, *The Acts of the Apostles: The Greek Text with Introduction and Commentary* (3rd edn.; Grand Rapids: Eerdmans, 1990), 309, and C. K. Barrett, *A Critical and Exegetical Commentary on the Acts of the Apostles* (2 vols.; ICC; London: T&T Clark, 1994–8), i. 645, that here the verb *anastēsas* means "bringing [Jesus] on the stage of history" (Barrett's phrase) rather than its customary meaning vis-à-vis Jesus of raising from the dead. Barrett's suggestion is of course possible if certain texts are read with no resurrection connotation (cf. Acts 3: 22, 26; 7: 37), but is demonstrably not probable in light of the customary use of this verb and its cognates in Luke-Acts with reference to Jesus (e.g. Luke 24: 7, 46; Acts 2: 24, 32; 10: 41; 13: 34; 17: 3, 31). Furthermore, the verse that immediately follows, Acts 13: 34, emphatically refers to resurrection using the same verb ("he raised [*anestēsen*] him from the dead") as in 13: 33, making it extraordinarily unlikely that Acts 13: 33 does not also refer to Jesus' resurrection.

[64] The author of Luke–Acts uses this exact "moreover that" (*hoti de*) construction in only one other place, Luke 20: 37, where it also signals a minor topical shift that functions to show that a specific belief is warranted in light of scriptural evidence, just as I am arguing it does in Acts 13: 34. Cf. Gal. 3: 11 for a semantically comparable usage.

been fulfilled, not in support of the adoption of Jesus as messiah at the time of the resurrection or the enthronement.[65]

Isaiah 55: 3 and Psalm 16: 10 in Acts 13: 34–5

As an additional new proposal for other scholars to consider, I want to suggest that the linking of Isaiah 55: 3 LXX and Psalm 16: 10 (15: 10 LXX), the next texts in the chain in Acts 13: 34–5, involves an intricate series of prosopological maneuvers that merits more attention:

> Moreover, that God raised him from the dead no longer destined to turn to decay, he stated in this manner: "I will grant to you the faithful decrees of David" [Isa. 55: 3 LXX], because he also said in a different psalm: "You will not permit your Holy One to see decay" [Ps. 15: 10 LXX].   (Acts 13: 34–5)

Regarding the first text cited, Isaiah 55: 3 LXX, which, in order to provide context, I cite along with vv. 4–5, note how many shifts in speaker and addressee are present:

> "*I* will grant to *you* [*plural*] the faithful decrees [*I* promised] to David. 4 See, *I* have given *him* as evidence to the nations, as a ruler and commander to the nations." 5 "Nations that were not acquainted with *you* [*singular*] will call upon *you*, and peoples who did not know *you* will flee to *you* for refuge, for the sake of *your God*, the Holy One of Israel, because he has glorified *you*."   (Isa. 55: 3–5 LXX)

Isaiah 55: 3 LXX is the verse quoted by the author of Acts, but I submit that this verse has been interpreted by our author using solution-by-person applied to Isaiah 55: 3–5. The author of Acts identifies several characters: God the Father ("I") is speaking to a group of people—"you" (plural)—about the actualization of the Davidic promise via a *third* person ("him") who will serve as "proof" (*martyrion*) to the nations, since this third person has been provided as "a ruler and commander to the nations" (55: 4).

However, intriguingly, notice that beginning at Isaiah 55: 5 the "you" addressed changes from the plural to the singular, and that God is now referred

---

[65] It has become standard to suggest that Acts 13: 32–3 supports the idea that for the earliest Christians, Jesus became the messiah or "Son of God" only at the resurrection, not preexisting as such, all of which is tantamount to adoptionism (even if that specific word is sometimes deliberately avoided by modern interpreters because of its heterodox overtones). E.g. Richard I. Pervo, *Acts: A Commentary* (Hermeneia; Minneapolis: Fortress, 2009), 338–9; Joseph A. Fitzmyer, *The Acts of the Apostles: A New Translation with Introduction and Commentary* (AB 31; New York: Doubleday, 1998), 516–17; Ehrman, *How Jesus Became God*, 225–6. Yet in view of the prosopological reading employed by the earliest Christians (in conjunction with the additional evidence from context and the Greek syntax already presented), I do not think adoptionism can be demonstrated as probable here. For discussion, see the section "Non-Adoptionist Christology" in this chapter.

to in the third person whereas previously God was the first-person speaker. At Isaiah 55: 5 the conversation partners have shifted. *God is no longer speaking to a group, but someone else is speaking to an individual.* The reader must undertake solution-by-person to provide suitable identifications.[66]

I suggest that it is most likely that the author of Acts used solution-by-person in interpreting Isaiah 55: 3–5 in response to these radical shifts in speaker and addressee in the text, so that the collective "you" of Isaiah 55: 3, the people of God, is now identified as the first-person speaker in Isaiah 55: 5, who is talking to a new individual, saying: "Nations that were not acquainted with *you* [singular] will call upon you, and peoples who did not know you will flee to you for refuge, for the sake of your God, the Holy One of Israel, because he has glorified you" (Isa. 55: 5 LXX).

We might summarize this complex prosopological maneuvering by suggesting that Paul's speech seems to presuppose the assignments of the following prosopa as the author's solution for reading Isaiah 55: 3–5 LXX:

GOD (speaking to CORPORATE ISRAEL): I will grant to *you* [plural] the faithful decrees I promised to David. See, I have given **him** [i.e. the one who stands as a fulfillment to those faithful decrees, the Davidic seed] as evidence to the nations, as a ruler and commander to the nations.   (Isa. 55: 3–4 LXX)

CORPORATE ISRAEL (now speaking directly to the *"HIM"* just mentioned, that is to the Davidic seed): Nations that were not acquainted with *you* [singular] will call upon *you*, and peoples who did not know *you* will flee to you for refuge, for the sake of your God, the Holy One of Israel, because he has glorified *you*.   (Isa. 55: 5 LXX)

If this reconstruction is correct, then the follow-up which Paul is portrayed as making to his Isaianic assertion, "I will grant *you* [plural] the faithful decrees I promised to David" (Isa. 55: 3 LXX) in his speech in Acts 13: 34 makes lucid sense, inasmuch as the singular "**him**" mentioned in the subsequent Isaianic verse (Isa. 55: 4 LXX), the one about whom it is prophesied that he will be glorified by God in due course, the Davidic scion identified here as Jesus Christ, is the real aim, albeit his identity is momentarily transumed by the author of Acts.[67] He is the one who stands as a fulfillment to the faithful decrees God promised to David.

Thus when we find that Paul is depicted as continuing, "because God also said in a different psalm: 'You will not permit your Holy One to see decay'" (Ps. 15: 10 LXX), there is continuity between the "**him**" transumed in the near context of the first citation and the reference to the "Holy One" in the second, so that the same person, the Davidic heir, the Christ, has been identified

---

[66] Cf. Tertullian, *Marc.* 3. 20. 5–7.

[67] On the transumption and the reconstitution of scriptural contexts in citation, see Hays, *Echoes of Scripture*, 20–4. The application is my own.

as the referent in both cases by the author of Acts when the transumption is reconstituted.[68]

Prosopological Exegesis in Acts 13: 32–5

In sum, in the chain of three citations in Acts 13: 32–5, the combination of the second and third citation serves as the collective warrant to the assertion that God raised Jesus, with Paul portrayed as identifying Jesus as the prosopon addressed by the people as "you" in Isaiah 55: 5 LXX, that is, the "him" mentioned in Isaiah 55: 4 LXX, as well as taking Jesus as the Holy One who will not see decay in Psalm 15: 10 LXX. Meanwhile, in the first citation in Acts 13: 33 the words, "You are my Son, today I have begotten you" do *not* refer to the adoption of Jesus at the time of his resurrection or heavenly enthronement, but are given as evidence that long ago God had made a promise to the Jewish forefathers concerning a Davidic offspring. I suggest, therefore, that in the absence of evidence to the contrary, that interpretative continuity between the author of Acts and the other early Christian interpreters of Psalm 2: 7 LXX is probable, and so it is most likely that Psalm 2: 7 LXX was regarded by the author of Acts as the reported speech of David, who was deemed to be speaking prosopologically as a prophet from the person of his own future offspring, the Christ.

NON-ADOPTIONIST CHRISTOLOGY

Regarding early Christian interpretations of Psalm 2: 7, there is a corollary implication that is of utmost importance for Christology and the development of Trinitarian dogma. Any reported dialogue must have occurred *earlier* than the report itself. If I say to my wife, "Kent told me, 'We need to get our families together for a barbeque,'" then it is necessarily the case that my discussion with Kent occurred prior to my conversation with my wife. We have the same situation here. That is, along with all the other early Christian readers surveyed above, the author of Acts had most likely determined that in Psalm 2 David had spoken prophetically from the prosopon of his own future offspring, the messiah, from within theodramatic setting "B" (the enthronement of the Son), at which time this Davidic scion had reported a *prior conversation* with God (the Father) concerning his divine begottenness, a dialogue that had occurred sometime *earlier* in theodramatic setting "A": "You are my Son, today I have

---

[68] Note the presence of the Greek word *hosios* ("pertaining to the divine") in both Isa. 55: 3 LXX and Ps. 15: 10 LXX as a *Stichwort* that provides a natural linguistic connection between the two citations.

begotten you." This speech of the Lord God to the Son was regarded as having been uttered *prior to* the moment when the Son was established as king, because the latter is said to be the occasion for the reported speech (cf. Ps. 2: 6). Indeed for early Christian readers this prophetic stepping-into-character by David had happened a myriad of years before the theodrama was actualized with the resurrection or heavenly enthronement of Jesus. Although certainty is elusive in any historical reconstruction, this proposal has the merit of hermeneutical congruence with other readings of Psalm 2: 7 LXX in the earliest church as already examined above, so I would contend it is the most likely scenario.

Failure to observe that the earliest church, when the matter is discussed, consistently identified *the indirect, reported nature* of the speech in Psalm 2: 7 has contributed to what I would regard as a faulty conclusion by some biblical scholars regarding the development of Christology. Primarily on the basis of reconstructions for how Psalm 2: 7 fits into the life-setting of the early church, some specialists working on early Christology have determined that the Christology of the nascent church was originally adoptionist, especially in light of various ancient Near Eastern sources that indicate that the king upon his coronation was adopted as a son of the most high God, a son of a patron god, or a son of the gods.[69] Indeed, it must be affirmed that the idea of divine adoption itself is not implausible for the New Testament era because the reigning Roman emperor was sometimes called a "son of god" (*divi filius*) once his (usually adoptive) father was posthumously declared a god by decree of the Senate.[70] So, the problem is not that son-of-god adoption is alien to the larger cultural milieu. Rather, the difficulty is that the New Testament and other early sources do not adequately support this specific model with respect to Jesus and the God of Israel. Nevertheless, in light of this broader cultural environment, it is suggested by those that adhere to this adoptionist model that for the very earliest Christians, Jesus did not preexist as God's Son, nor was he deemed God's Son from before the dawn of time, but he became God's Son when, after or in conjunction with his resurrection, he was adopted and enthroned at the right hand. As such "Son of God" was originally a messianic title with no grounding in preexistent reality. At a later date, as dogma developed, according to these scholars, the original timing of the adoption was pushed backward, so that Jesus was then asserted to have been adopted by God at the moment of his baptism. Still later, as Christology

---

[69] See esp. Yarbro Collins and Collins, *King and Messiah*, 10–15, 117, 127.

[70] Usually this "son of God" decree was officially given only after the death of the emperor-Father, as was the case with Octavian and Tiberius. However, as the *divi filius* assertion became increasingly common, more brazen individuals laid claim to the title after adoption but before the death of the emperor-Father (e.g. Nero made this claim prior to the death of Claudius). See Michael Peppard, *The Son of God in the Roman World: Divine Sonship in Its Social and Political Context* (New York: Oxford University Press, 2011), 46–7, 77–80.

progressed in the expanding church, Jesus was subsequently identified as God's *preexistent* and *eternally* begotten Son.[71]

Without denying the royal overtones and the ancient Near Eastern background of kingly adoption in the original *Sitz im Leben* of Psalm 2, we must at the same time beware of the danger of stressing putative origins and the general cultural environment (including emperor divinization) over explicit contemporaneous early Christian readings of this text.[72] The fact is that the *very earliest strata* of Christian literature that we possess or can even reliably reconstruct—e.g. Paul's letters and the pre-Pauline tradition that can sometimes be detected therein—never speak of Jesus' adoption and insists that Jesus preexisted as the Son.[73]

---

[71] For this basic reconstruction of the development of Christology, see Dunn, *Christology in the Making*, esp. pp. 33–6, 46–60, 251–8; Yarbro Collins and Collins, *King and Messiah*, esp. pp. 204–13; Ehrman, *How Jesus Became God*, esp. pp. 236–82; Peppard, *The Son of God*, 14–28, esp. 132–6. These scholars are synthesizing an older view—e.g. see Barnabas Lindars, *New Testament Apologetic: The Doctrinal Significance of the Old Testament Quotations* (Philadelphia: Westminster, 1961), 139–44; John H. Hayes, "The Resurrection as Enthronement and the Earliest Church Christology," *Int.* 22 (1968): 333–45.

[72] This is the misstep, in my judgment, made by Peppard, *The Son of God*. Peppard does successfully show that adoption did not entail low social status in antiquity, but if adoptionist Christology is illusory in the NT, then this is a red herring when applied. Peppard argues that Mark is mimicking (and hence subverting) Roman imperial ideology in the baptismal scene by presenting Jesus rather than the emperor as the adoptive Son of God, but I disagree with his conclusions for the following reasons. (1) Peppard downplays the OT background to the words spoken by God during the baptism (pp. 93–8), but I find this illegitimate. We have indisputable evidence that Mark frequently drew upon OT sources and imagery. Rikk E. Watts, "Mark," in Greg K. Beale and D. A. Carson (eds.), *Commentary on the New Testament Use of the Old Testament* (Grand Rapids: Baker Academic, 2007), 111–249, here 111, counts sixty-nine OT references or allusions. But we do not have any definitive evidence that Mark was countering imperial adoptive *divi filius* claims, making Peppard's move historically improbable. (2) Peppard gives no unambiguous evidence that Jesus is regarded as the *adopted* Son of God in Mark or elsewhere in the NT (it is telling that the earliest firm evidence for an adoptionist Christology that Peppard can produce pertains to Theodotus, who was active in the late second century [p. 147]). Much of Peppard's evidence (some of which overreaches regardless, pp. 123–31) could equally be explained within the category of *non-adoptive* Sonship and election. (3) Peppard occasionally uses comparative religion in questionable ways to further his adoptive thesis—e.g. directly equating *genius/numen* in the Roman context with the Spirit in the Jewish–Christian (p. 114). (4) Peppard fails to take into account the *reported* dimension of Ps. 2:7 as read in the early church and the weight of probability in favor of a metaphor concerning natural procreation over adoption ("Today I have begotten you"—*egō sēmeron gegennēka se*—cf. Ps. 109:3 LXX). (5) Peppard (pp. 19–21, 133–40) essentially accepts the backward-development Christological scheme of Dunn, but there are serious problems with Dunn's method and results (see nn. 31 and 32 in this chapter).

[73] On texts indicating preexistence in Paul, see n. 32 in this chapter; the pre-Pauline tradition can be discerned in Rom. 1:3–4; Phil. 2:6–11; for a compact discussion, see Larry W. Hurtado, *Lord Jesus Christ: Devotion to Jesus in Earliest Christianity* (Grand Rapids: Eerdmans, 2003), 118–26. If adoption was truly a critical Christological category in the earliest church, why is it that the people of God are said to be adopted in a number of texts (e.g. Rom. 8:15, 23; 9:4; Gal. 4:5; Eph. 1:5), but such is never said of Jesus Christ? Peppard, *The Son of God*, 139–40, asserts that such adoptive evidence is in fact present as a mixed-metaphor in the *prōtotokos* (literally "first born") of Rom. 8:29 with respect to Jesus Christ, but it is telling that he is not able to offer any evidence that would *uniquely* favor adoption over the more common category of

If non-adoptionist preexistence is demonstrably probable in the very earliest stratum—and I believe that it is—then it becomes quite absurd to argue that such ideas gradually developed.[74] Additionally adoptionist Christology, inasmuch as it relies on Psalm 2: 7–9 (which is invariably the linchpin of the adoptionist reconstruction) is quite implausible given the person-centered reading strategy that the earliest church expressly employed, because the speech, "You are my Son, today I have begotten you," was read as occurring *before* the enthronement, at which time the Son subsequently *reported* these previously spoken words. As evidenced above and as will be discussed further in Chapter 6 with respect to the enthronement, the earliest church, at least to the degree it reveals its interpretative posture, consistently attests that these words were spoken between the Father and the Son in the time before time began.[75]

WITH "YOU" I AM WELL PLEASED—ISAIAH 42: 1

We have examined the function of Psalm 2: 7 LXX as part of the words spoken from the heavens at Jesus' baptism ("You are my Son, the beloved one, with you I am well pleased"), but most scholars concur that there is at least one other allusion in these words. God is the speaker in Isaiah 42: 1 LXX, and he describes Israel as "my chosen one" (*ho eklektos mou*) saying, "my soul has welcomed him."

God continues speaking in Isaiah 42: 1 LXX, "I have put my spirit upon him, he will bring justice to the nations," so there is a conceptual link in this Isaianic text to the way in which the Spirit comes to rest upon a designated, approved person and the baptismal scene. The allusion is even more explicit in Luke's depiction of the transfiguration (9: 35), where the language "chosen one" (*ho eklelegmenos*) appears. We will have occasion to revisit Isaiah 42: 1–9 in Chapter 3, but note well how conducive this passage is to a prosopological interpretation, with God the Father speaking about the servant in the third

---

natural birth. In other words, just because *prōtotokos* can entail adoption in the NT era (a point I do not dispute) when very specific signals indicate that the term is being mobilized beyond its ordinary usage, this does not demonstrate probability in a given instantiation granted the rarity of this application.

[74] See "Incarnation and Enthronement—Romans 1: 3–4" and "The Coronation of the Son" in Ch. 6.

[75] In the Arian controversy of the fourth century all the principle parties agreed that the Son was begotten *before creation* (as in the prosopological exegeses explored in this chapter), but Arius did not agree that the Son was *eternally* begotten, famously declaring, "before he [the Son] was begotten or created or defined or established, he was not" (Arius's *Letter to Eusebius of Nicomedia* 5; trans. Rusch). Thus, the Nicene Creed is a clarifying further development in asserting the Father as the *eternal* cause of the Son rather than merely as the cause prior to the creation of the rest of the cosmos.

person in 42: 1–4, but inexplicably in 42: 5–7 God begins to address an unintroduced, mysterious figure in the second person as "you." The reader must supply the identity of this "you," seeking to explain what character is now being addressed by the Lord God. In short, the person-centered interpretative process reflected in the allusion to Isaiah 42: 1 at the baptism is very much akin to what I have suggested for Psalm 2: 7, reinforcing the theodramatic interpretation that has been proposed.

* * *

So in the prosopological exegesis of Psalm 2: 5–9 in the earliest church we learn that Jesus as the Christ is preexistent and begotten by the most high God, although unlike in Psalm 109: 3 LXX, nothing here is said about the manner in which the Son was brought forth "from the womb." Likewise the time signals in the two texts are different—although not incompatible—with Psalm 109: 3 LXX locating the begetting before the morning star that heralds the dawn and Psalm 2: 7 LXX declaring the begetting as happening "today," with the "today" being sometime prior to the theodramatic setting of Christ's enthronement. Thus it is best to conclude that for most early Christian readers, these two speeches when understood in light of one another would have been taken as referring to conversations after time began about *one and the same act of preincarnational begetting*. Indeed, we find that LXX Psalm 2 and Psalm 109 are made to be mutually informing by a number of early Christians (e.g. Heb. 5: 5–6; *1 Clem.* 36. 4–5; Irenaeus, *Epid.* 49), and these psalms, as will be discussed further in Chapter 6, also were judged to be pertinent to the enthronement, as well as to the final consummation.

LET "US": DIVINE PLURALITY IN CREATION

The issue of divine plurality via the first-person plurals in Genesis (e.g. "Let *us* make man in *our* image"—1: 26; cf. 2: 18 LXX; 3: 22; 11: 4, 7) has been much discussed from almost every conceivable angle, including the binitarian or Trinitarian possibilities.[76] And no matter what the most likely ancient Near Eastern background to these proclamations might be, whether the "royal we," the address of the chief God to his divine council, or the proclamation of the most high God to his angelic servants (favored by most contemporary commentators as well as Philo), or a statement of divine self-deliberation, it is extraordinarily clear that the earliest Christians frequently used a solution-by-person strategy to arrive at binitarian or proto-Trinitarian conclusions—even

---

[76] Discussion and bibliography can be found in any standard critical commentary at Genesis 1: 26—e.g. Claus Westermann, *Genesis* (trans. John J. Scullion; 3 vols.; Minneapolis: Augsburg, 1984–6), i. 144–5.

if such conclusions are now, as Gordon Wenham concludes, universally rejected by modern biblical scholarship,[77] at least, I would qualify, modern biblical scholarship inasmuch as it is exclusively rooted in the historical-grammatical method of interpretation.

The Literal Sense of Scripture

I will be brief. As this book as a whole seeks to demonstrate, in addition to these "let us" passages from Genesis, a large number of other texts in the Old Testament involve conversations between the Lord God and characters that are unintroduced yet enigmatically described. And as we seek to determine the meaning of these passages by reading in context, we must think carefully about precisely what we mean by the "literal sense" of the Scripture and how we establish the acceptable horizon or context against which the literal sense can be fixed. Today when a student of the Bible offers the plea, "Shouldn't we just take this literally?," it is presumed that the literal sense of Scripture is something simple and obvious, but studies of how the meaning of the "literal sense" and related ideas such as the "historical sense," "original sense," and "narrative sense" have shifted through time and culture show that nothing could be further from the truth.[78] As Brevard Childs puts it, in our contemporary historical-critical interpretative environment that focuses on original intention, "The literal sense of the text no longer functions to preserve fixed literary parameters," but rather, "the literal sense dissolves before

---

[77] Gordon J. Wenham, *Genesis* (2 vols.; WBC 1–2; Dallas: Word, 1987–94), i. 27–8.

[78] "The 'literal sense,'" as David Dawson wryly notes, "has often been thought of as an inherent quality of a literary text that gives it a specific and invariant character," but in reality it is communally determined (*Allegorical Readers and Cultural Revision in Ancient Alexandria* [Berkeley: University of California Press, 1992], 7–8). On the "plain sense" or the *sensus literalis*, see Raymond E. Brown and Sandra M. Schneiders, "Hermeneutics," in Raymond E. Brown, Joseph A. Fitzmyer, and Roland E. Murphy (eds.), *The New Jerome Biblical Commentary* (Englewood Cliffs, NJ: Prentice-Hall, 1990), 1146–65 esp. §§9–29; Hans Frei, *The Eclipse of Biblical Narrative: A Study in Eighteenth and Nineteenth Century Hermeneutics* (New Haven: Yale University Press, 1974); Brevard S. Childs, "The *Sensus Literalis* of Scripture: An Ancient and Modern Problem," in Herbert Donner, Robert Hanhart, and Rudolf Smend (eds.), *Beiträge zur Alttestamentlichen Theologie: Festschrift für Walther Zimmerli zum 70. Geburtstag* (Göttingen: Vandenhoeck & Ruprecht, 1977), 80–93; Paul R. Noble, "The 'Sensus Literalis': Jowett, Childs, and Barr," *JTS* NS 44 (1993): 1–23; Margaret M. Mitchell, "Patristic Rhetoric on Allegory: Origen and Eustathius Put 1 Samuel 28 on Trial," *JR* 85 (2005): 414–45. Mitchell shows that the "literal sense" was hotly contested even in antiquity. Meanwhile Childs and Frei are in basic agreement that before the modern era the "literal sense" did not entail a separation between the "historical sense" and the "narratival sense." However, with the rise of modernity (esp. with Spinoza), the "literal" or "true" meaning of a text was increasingly sought in the "original sense" and happenings outside the text. That is, the literal meaning of a text became bound up with its ability to testify to things external to the world created by the text itself, and the "narratival sense" was marginalized as the horizon for the literal. See Ch. 7 for further discussion.

the hypothetical reconstructions of the original situations on whose recovery correct interpretation allegedly depends."[79] The result is that broader literary contexts—and the fullest literary context is the entire canon for those who affirm divine authorship of the whole Scripture—are denigrated for many modern historical-critical readers when searching for the "literal" meaning, while instead the literal meaning is sought *outside the text* in historical reconstructions of how this text points at what (purportedly) *really* happened.

Trinitarian Reading and Authorial Intention

The earliest Christians assigned suitable characters to the first-person plural speeches in Genesis by reading the Old Testament through the lens of the early Christian apostolic proclamation. For instance, Ps-Barnabas finds in Genesis 1: 26 a speech from Father to Son, "For the scripture speaks about us when *God [the Father] says to the Son*, 'Let us make man according to our likeness and our image'" (6. 12; cf. 5. 5). Likewise, Irenaeus affirms, "It is clear that here *the Father addresses the Son*."[80] Moreover, Justin Martyr believes that it can be proven that Genesis 1: 26–7 refers numerically to more than one divine person because later, in Genesis 3: 22, the text says, "Adam has become as *one of us*," proving that the referent is at least two persons.[81] Intriguingly, the second-century apologist Theophilus of Antioch strikes a slightly different but related chord when he says, "God said, 'Let us make,' to no one other than his own Logos and his own Sophia."[82]

When members of the earliest church determined that these "let us" passages in the Old Testament reflected a discourse between the Lord God and his Son as the words were supplied by the Spirit, it was not as if such divine dialogues were unprecedented in the Old Testament—on the contrary, we have seen abundant evidence for such dialogues already. Regarding dialogue about the role of the Son in creation, for instance, the author of Hebrews sees the Son as the "Lord" addressed in Psalm 101: 26 LXX: "At the beginning you, O Lord, founded the earth; and the heavens are the work of your hands" (1: 10). Moreover, if, as the earliest Christians firmly believed, God orchestrates a vast divine economy, including all events past, present, and future, encompassing both the heavenly and the earthly spheres, as well as the manner in which various events came to be inscripturated, then the supposition that God the Father, Christ the Son, and the Holy Spirit might

---

[79] Childs, "The *'Sensus Literalis'* of Scripture," 90.   [80] Irenaeus, *Epid.* 55.
[81] Justin, *Dial.* 62. 1–3, here 62. 3 citing Gen. 3: 22 LXX (*Adam gegonen hōs heis ex hēmōn*).
[82] Theophilus, *Autol.* 2. 18; cf. 2. 10–11, 20, and esp. his explanation in 2. 22.

appear as speaking characters at the beginning of the drama takes on a whole new level of plausibility.

On the raw level of "original" human intention, it certainly does not seem likely that the first authors (or the later canonical editors) of Genesis were trying to give us hints about a plurality in the Godhead, but is it possible that as the writers were carried along by the inspiring Spirit, they spoke better than they knew? Christopher Seitz invites us, helpfully I think, to consider the issue in this way:

> For the purpose of introduction, consider an alternative way of thinking about the Trinity in the Old Testament. Here it would be held that certain expressions in the literal sense—beginning, light, word, first of ways, wisdom, son—themselves could not refer univocally to a single referent. That is, the literal sense of the Old Testament had a historically determined meaning at one level—it made sense to an audience in time and space within Israel's ancient referentiality—but pointed as well to a further reference. This sense of multiple reference does not evacuate the historicity of the witness nor the meaningfulness and intelligibility of the economic activity of One God. Rather, it evolves from an awareness that the subject matter being vouchsafed is richer than a single intentionality in time can measure. If this is so, a history-of-religion account of the economic life of God can only get one so far, and indeed, it could misunderstand the character of the literal sense and how it is to be appreciated.[83]

Could it be that we should seek the literal meaning not simply on the horizon of human authorial intention, treating the Bible as an ordinary human production, but more importantly on the level of divine authorial intention? Although the notion of the *sensus plenior* (the fuller sense not clearly intended by the human author but nonetheless intended by God) has not been popular, Seitz's proposal comes close to it, and perhaps it is time to resurrect it, albeit in a slightly transformed (hopefully glorified) fashion. If God has arranged a comprehensive divine economy, including external events throughout human history, as well the process of Scripture formation, and if God has crafted the ancient Jewish Scripture according to an open-ended master plot that craves denouement and recapitulative closure beyond the horizon of the Old Testament itself, then this larger, richer metatextual horizon, I would argue, should be regarded as not the only but certainly the most vital backdrop for the "literal sense" against which we ought to read. I will have more to say about this in the final chapter.

Regardless of precisely what hermeneutic is adopted by the modern reader, at this juncture the important thing is to recognize that reading the Old Testament text for a solution via person was so characteristic of the early

---

[83] Christopher R. Seitz, "The Trinity in the Old Testament," in Gilles Emery and Matthew Levering (eds.), *The Oxford Handbook of The Trinity* (New York: Oxford University Press, 2011), 28–39, here 29.

church that its theology is ultimately inseparable from the technique, even if many contemporary readers will find this or that particular deployment of the technique in the earliest church strains credulity.

* * *

Prosopological exegesis casts light on the way the early church conceptualized God at or before the dawn of time. As the earliest Christians sought to solve puzzles in texts, they assigned various characters as speaker or addressee in order to discern the meaning of the text. Jesus himself is portrayed as engaging in a person-centered reading of Psalm 110, presuming that he, as the "Lord" addressed in the text, had previously been told by God the Father that he was begotten from the womb before the appearance of the morning star. Similarly, although the point has not been fully appreciated in biblical and theological scholarship, Psalm 2: 7 was read by the earliest Christians as a *reported speech* in which the Son tells of a prior dialogue with the Father, at which time the Father told him, "You are my Son, today I have begotten you." This act of begetting was not regarded as occurring at the time of the enthronement or the resurrection, as those favoring an adoptionist Christology have argued—this is to conflate the two distinct theodramatic settings. Rather it was taken as occurring sometime much earlier, most likely before the dawn of time in accordance with Psalm 109: 3 LXX. Additionally, the nascent church frequently construed the "let us" passages of Genesis to refer in a binitarian or Trinitarian sense to a conversation between divine persons.

Far from being an oddity, such a solution-by-person was a common technique that was encouraged by, indeed sometimes virtually demanded by, the appearance of unannounced speakers or addressees that frequently appear in the Old Testament text. It must be stressed that the person-centered puzzles in the Old Testament are genuine riddles that urgently plead for a satisfying solution. The earliest church offered a triune key to these interpretative locks—a triune key that was thoroughly grounded in a detailed reading of the Old Testament texts in question. The notion of divine *persons* in fellowship from before the dawn of time emerges to a significant degree from the matrix of prosopological readings of the Old Testament.

3

Theodramatic Stratagems—The Son's Mission

In the previous chapter Trinitarian dialogues pertaining to the dawn of time were described, dialogues that reflect on the begottenness of the Son before time began. Yet early Christian readers discerned in the ancient Jewish Scripture many other conversations in which the Spirit spoke in the semblance of the Father and the Son. In this chapter we will look at examples of early Christian interpretation of the Old Testament that are no less animated and alluring, those pertaining to interior dialogue between divine persons about the incarnation, preparation, and earthly mission of the Son. In it we will find that the earliest Christians found conversations in which the Father provides a suitable body for the Son, the Father tells the Son that he will send a special messenger to make ready the Son's arrival, and the Father and the Son discuss strategy. While the plan is being carried out, however, the Son expresses concern to the Father that the selected stratagems are proving futile even while continuing to trust the Father. In response, the Father comforts the Son with a bold message of hope—the fulfilled plan will be even more glorious than the Son has yet realized. When the Old Testament was read by the earliest Christians, the one God, the God of Israel, was being dialogically read into human history as differentiable persons.

CONVERSATIONS ABOUT THE INCARNATIONAL MISSION

A Body You Have Prepared for Me

The author of Hebrews seeks to show that Jesus, as the great high priest, made the singular offering of his own body and blood, and in so doing brought the sacrificial system of the Old Testament period to its appropriate *telos*—its fulfilling completion and temporal end. This conclusion was reached, at least in part, through a person-centered scriptural interpretation that pertains to a conversation between the Son and the Father about the incarnation.[1]

The author of Hebrews (10: 5) introduces his citation of Psalm 39: 7–9 LXX (= Ps. 40: 6–8) by declaring, "Therefore, *when he* [Jesus Christ] *comes into the world*, he says" (*Dio eiserchomenos eis ton kosmon legei*).[2] By means of the tense combinations the author of Hebrews has fixed for us the theodramatic temporal setting of this Old Testament speech.[3] For the author of Hebrews, although the prophetic setting for this utterance was during the time of David, the Holy Spirit is not time-bound, and the Spirit can establish a different setting for the divine speech uttered through David as the prophet takes on various roles.[4] Thus, in this text, the Spirit is perceived to be speaking from the person of Jesus Christ, and the Christ is speaking to the Father when Jesus came into the world, that is, at the moment of incarnation, in these words: "Sacrifice and offering you did not desire, but a body you prepared for me" (Heb. 10: 5 citing a deviant form of Ps. 39: 7 LXX). Making the dialogue explicit, we might paraphrase:

JESUS CHRIST (speaking to GOD [THE FATHER]): Sacrifice and offering *you*, O my Father, did not desire, but a body you prepared for *me*, that is for *me*, your Son.

The phrase "but a body you prepared for me" (*sōma de katērtisō moi*) that is central to the incarnational interpretation supplied by the author of Hebrews for this divine conversation is textually difficult. The MT (i.e. the Hebrew text) reads instead, "ears you have dug out for me" (*'oznayîm kārîtā lî*) while the LXX (i.e. the Greek Old Testament) gives, "ears you have prepared for me" (*ōtia de katērtisō moi*).[5]

---

[1] Anthony T. Hanson, *Jesus Christ in the Old Testament* (London: SPCK, 1965), 140, proposed that the author of Hebrews found prophetic dialogue between the Father and the Son in a number of places, including Heb. 10: 5–9.

[2] It is possible that the Greek verb *legei* could intend a generic reference to scripture as the subject ("it [the scripture] says"), but the nearest referent, *eiserchomenos* ("the one coming into the world"), is more likely, and the identification of the speaker as Jesus Christ is made virtually certain by the subsequent exposition in Heb. 10: 8–10.

[3] A present participle with a present-tense verb of speech usually signals simultaneity. See Daniel B. Wallace, *Greek Grammar Beyond the Basics: An Exegetical Syntax of the New Testament* (Grand Rapids: Zondervan, 1996), 625, for a category description.

[4] The author of all OT utterances is ultimately the Spirit for the author of Hebrews—cf. Heb. 3: 7 where the citation is introduced with the formula: "As the Holy Spirit says."

[5] Most other scholars think—and I concur—that the deviant textual form of the Septuagint used by the author of Hebrews is an interpretive paraphrase of the obscure Hebrew rather than a textual corruption (probably, for the Greek translator, with ears representing the whole person as obedient to the voice of God). See discussion in Harold W. Attridge, *The Epistle to the Hebrews: A Commentary on the Epistle to the Hebrews* (Hermeneia; Minneapolis: Fortress, 1989), 274; Paul Ellingworth, *The Epistle to the Hebrews: A Commentary on the Greek Text* (NIGTC; Grand Rapids: Eerdmans, 1993), 500.

Note well that from the theodramatic setting (when the Son is brought incarnationally into the world) the Son speaks of the body as having *already been prepared in the past* (aorist tense), that is, before the Son is brought into the world, revealing two things: (1) the Father's intense involvement in the incarnational plan—the Father had planned for this flesh-forming event long before its arrival, and (2) the Father's active, loving concern for the Son in providing a suitable human body. This is not a distant Father God who stands aloof from an ongoing role in divine and human affairs, but a Father who oversees the unfolding of the divine plan, showing special concern for the enfleshment of his Son at this critical juncture in salvation history.

As the Son's speech continues, we learn more about the attitude of the Son as he speaks to his Father:

THE SON (speaking to GOD): You did not delight in whole burnt offerings and sin offerings. Then I said, "Here I am, I have come"—just as is written in the scroll about me—"in order to do your will, O God." (Heb. 10: 6–7 citing Ps. 39: 7–9 LXX)

Here the Son tells the Father that he recognizes that the Father was not ultimately pleased with the physical animal sacrifices of Israel's *cultus*, but rather that all of this was purposed toward the Father's supreme will for the Son, namely, that *the gift of the incarnational body* that the Father had given the Son *would freely be offered back* by the Son to the Father. That the Son recognized that this was the Father's ultimate will—the regifting of his human body—is expressly stated by the author of Hebrews, as he explains, "By the will of the Father we have been sanctified through the singular offering of *the body* of Jesus Christ" (10: 10). In this Old Testament dialogue between Father and Son, prosopologically interpreted, we find a certain divine mutuality and grace-filled symmetry: The Father *initiates* the gracious gift-giving with the presentation of the incarnational body to the Son, yet the Son *consummates* the gift-giving by offering this very same body back to the Father as an act of willing obedience to him, recognizing that this is what the Father ultimately desires.

He Has Established Me as a Solid Rock

Writing in the early second century, the author of the *Epistle of Barnabas* was convinced that the flesh of Jesus is essential to the salvation of humanity—a docetic Jesus who only appeared to have a physical body simply would not do. For Ps-Barnabas, our Lord Jesus submitted to the destruction of his flesh so that we might receive forgiveness of sins by the sprinkling of his blood (5. 1). Moreover, his appearance in bodily form to sinners gave them the opportunity to be saved by gazing on him, since he had revealed himself as God's Son

(5. 9–10). For Ps-Barnabas, Jesus himself speaks theodramatically via the Psalter to God the Father about his future incarnation, saying, "And in what manner shall I appear before the Lord my God and shall I be glorified?" (*Barn.* 6. 15 citing a deviant form of Ps. 41: 3 LXX), a text that for Ps-Barnabas speaks of the intense longing of the Son for fellowship with the Father, much as the doe yearns for water.

Indeed, for Ps-Barnabas, Jesus has been revealed as the mighty stone that crushes and also as the chosen, precious capstone;[6] yet this, for our author, does not mean that the Christian hope is placed in a mere stone. Rather, it is connected to the well-crafted flesh Jesus was given by God the Father at the incarnation. As Ps-Barnabas puts it, the prophet Isaiah speaks about Christ as a stone: "Because the Lord [God] has established his [Christ's] flesh in a strong fashion" (6. 3). As evidence Ps-Barnabas gives a citation that depends on a prosopological reading of Isaiah 50: 7 in which he has determined the Christ speaks:

THE CHRIST (to the AUDIENCE): And he [God] established me as a firm rock.
   (*Barn.* 6. 3 citing Isa. 50: 7)

The change from self-action in the LXX ("I have set my face") to the God-oriented action in *Barnabas* ("And he established me") is difficult to explain—perhaps it is a free rendering or the *testimonia* source on which Ps-Barnabas relied was corrupt—but nonetheless Ps-Barnabas sees Isaiah 50: 7 as a first-person speech in which Jesus, speaking *after* the gift of the body had already been given ("he established"—past tense), yet still anticipating the future cross, states that God has already given him flesh capable of withstanding the necessary suffering in order to fulfill his God-given mission (cf. *Barn.* 5. 14). Along the same lines Irenaeus indicates that the immediately preceding verse, Isaiah 50: 6, is a first-person speech spoken by "the Word himself," that is, by Jesus Christ as the preexistent *Logos*, although his citation stops shy of the rock phrase (*Epid.* 68).

Writing toward the end of the second century, Melito of Sardis was perhaps also familiar with this tradition since he attributes the next line in Isaiah 50: 8, to the newly risen Christ, who "arose from the dead and cried out these words, 'Who contends with me? Let him take a stand against me!'" (*Pascha* 101; cf. Irenaeus, *Epid.* 88). Having endured suffering in his flesh, Jesus, for Melito, has defeated death itself and has bound the strong man (cf. Mark 3: 27)! So, for several early Christian authors, Jesus was not just given flesh by God the Father, but the Father in his loving-kindness toward the Son gifted him with *flesh* imbued with stone-like (although obviously not special superhuman) strength in order to assist him in enduring the suffering that would come.

---

[6] On Jesus as the capstone or cornerstone, see *Barn.* 6. 2; cf. Dan. 2. 44–5; Isa. 28: 16; Ps. 118: 22–3; Matt. 21: 42–5; Mark 12: 10–11; Luke 20: 17–18; Acts 4: 11; Rom. 9: 32–3; 1 Pet. 2: 4–8.

DIALOGUE ABOUT THE ENVOY

For the nascent church, not only did the preexistent Son and the Father converse about the incarnation via the Spirit, they also discussed how the world might be made ready to receive the Son once he did take on human flesh. The stratagem selected by the Father and the Son, as discerned by the emerging church, was the use of a prophetic ambassador, through whom the Spirit could clear the way. For the synoptic Evangelists, the Spirit speaking in the guise of the Father announces his intention to use a prophetic ambassador quite clearly. Mark states, "Look, I will send my messenger ahead of you, who will prepare your way" (1: 2),[7] while Matthew and Luke present Jesus himself as the one reporting these words, adding: "your way *before you*" (Matt. 11: 10; Luke 7: 27). In other words, this is another possible example of the historical Jesus engaging in prosopological exegesis in seeking to understand his own self-identity, and the authenticity of this "Q" saying is very rarely doubted by scholars.[8]

In the Old Testament context in Malachi, the prophet is speaking on behalf of God (Yahweh) to the general populace, comprised of people who have been questioning God's justice. God via Malachi makes it emphatically clear that his justice will be demonstrated through divine visitation. God states:

> Behold, I will send my messenger, and he will superintend the path *ahead of my personal presence* [*pro prosōpou mou*]; suddenly the Lord [*kyrios*; MT: *hā'ādôn*] whom you seek will come to the temple. And the messenger of the covenant whom you want—behold, he is coming, says the Lord Almighty [*kyrios pantokratōr*; MT: *YHWH ṣĕbā'ôt*]. And who will endure the day of his arrival? Or who will be able to bear his appearance? (Mal. 3: 1–2 LXX)

This passage promises that after a forerunning messenger, there will be a divine visitation from the Lord Almighty himself, who will come suddenly to the temple. Indeed, the anticipated messenger of the covenant—probably identical to the forerunner—is certainly coming.[9] And although the people who are clamoring for justice are eagerly awaiting this messenger's arrival, when he comes it will be dreadful for many, because he will serve as a radical agent of burning purification (Mal. 3: 2–3).

---

[7] Mark 1: 2 cites Mal. 3: 1 (perhaps via Exod. 23: 20 LXX), although Mark attributes the words to Isaiah, presumably per the citation of Isa. 40: 3 in Mark 1: 3.

[8] E.g. even the notoriously radical John D. Crossan, *The Historical Jesus: The Life of a Mediterranean Peasant* (San Francisco: HarperSanFrancisco, 1991), 236, places this multi-attested saying (cf. *Gospel of Thomas* 78) in the first stratum ("2Q" is his classification for the earliest apocalyptic Jesus material, see p. 429).

[9] See the outstanding discussion of this complex composite citation in Mark 1: 2–3 by Rikk E. Watts, "Mark," in Greg K. Beale and D. A. Carson (eds.), *Commentary on the New Testament Use of the Old Testament* (Grand Rapids: Baker Academic, 2007), 111–249, here 113–20.

In light of this, we might paraphrase the most likely person-centered interpretation of Malachi 3: 1 by Mark, and indeed by Jesus himself as depicted in Matthew and Luke, as follows:

GOD (to the CHRIST): Look, *I, God*, will send *John the Baptist, my messenger*, ahead of *you*, **my personal presence**, so that he will prepare the path before *you*.   (Mark 1: 2 citing Mal. 3: 1 LXX)

Indeed, this synoptic-based paraphrase is almost precisely the interpretation given by Irenaeus, who takes the Father as the speaker, the Lord Jesus Christ (as the Son) as the one addressed and heralded, and John the Baptist as the forerunner.[10] Here, even though the prosopological assumptions of a conversation between divine persons (God and the "you" that God describes as "my prosopon") are relatively straightforward in this text, nonetheless the dialogical features of the Old Testament text are not highlighted by modern commentators, perhaps because the citation is clearly aimed by Jesus and the Evangelists at the unveiling of John the Baptist as the messenger, who is further identified as the anticipated Elijah on the basis of a closely related text in Malachi 4: 5 ("Behold, I will send you the prophet Elijah before the great and terrible day of Yahweh comes"),[11] and most of the interpretative energy gets channeled in that direction.[12]

Early High Christology

Yet, when we press the issue, this passage reveals an important assumed Old Testament conversation between God and the "you," the one God describes as "my prosopon," that is, the person Jesus is portrayed as identifying as his very self (Matt. 11: 10; Luke 7: 27). Namely, for Jesus as depicted by Matthew and Luke, prior to the appearance of this "you," God had maintained a discourse

---

[10] Irenaeus, *Haer*. 3. 10. 5; cf. 3. 9. 1–2. That Jesus is the "Lord" heralded by John has already been clarified explicitly in *Haer*. 3. 10. 1; indeed, Irenaeus insists that Isa. 40: 3–5 proves that "there is, therefore, one and the same God, the Father of our Lord" (trans. Unger). Moreover, immediately after discussing Isa. 40: 3 in *Haer*. 3. 10. 5 the "Lord Jesus" is acknowledged to be the addressee to whom God the Father speaks in Ps. 110: 1, showing that this line of thought has in all likelihood been adopted for the citation of Isa. 40: 3 which directly precedes it.

[11] See Mark 6: 15; 9: 11; Matt. 11: 14; 17: 10–12; Luke 1: 17; cf. John 1: 21–5.

[12] For exceptions who are more carefully attuned to the person-related shifts in the OT, see the scholarship reviewed by Simon J. Gathercole, *The Preexistent Son: Recovering the Christologies of Matthew, Mark, and Luke* (Grand Rapids: Eerdmans, 2006), 250–1. Gathercole himself is aware that a prophetic dialogue is probably in view, and he helpfully lists a few others who have read Mark 1: 2–3 in this fashion, among whom Rainer Kampling, *Israel unter dem Anspruch des Messias: Studien zur Israelthematik im Markusevangelium* (Stuttgart: Katholisches Bibelwerk, 1992), 39–40, is the most forceful and provocative, saying that before the advent of the earthly Jesus, God "in conversation with his Son" speaks about things that Mark knows to have already occurred in a "prologue in Heaven."

with this "you" about a fitting way for him to be unveiled to the awaiting world—in other words, this is yet another example of early high Christology—what I prefer to call a Christology of Divine Persons. Read in this fashion, Malachi 3: 1 does not just reveal the Baptist, but is also a consoling announcement by God the Father *designed to reassure the Son*, because the Father hereby announces to the Son that the world will be appropriately prepared for the Son's arrival: "Look, *I, the Father*, will send *John the Baptist, my messenger*, ahead of *you, my personal presence, my Son*, so that he will prepare the path before *you*." God does not callously shove an unwilling Son to the earth—he carefully arranges things (cf. Gal. 4: 4) by raising up a prophet, Elijah turned John the Baptist, that can suitably ready the people.

Even if the theodramatic background has not been in view for most biblical scholars, that is not to say that recent scholarship has been unaware of the early high Christology presupposed by Mark in the Isaiah prophecy which follows on the heels of the Malachi citation. And the results are perhaps equally arresting. The citation by Mark of Isaiah reads: "A voice of one crying out in the wilderness, 'Prepare the way of the Lord, make straight his paths!'" (Mark 1: 3 citing Isa. 40: 3 LXX).[13] As is well known, Mark and the other Evangelists have cited the Septuagintal form of the Isaiah text, "Prepare the way of the Lord [*kyrios*]," intending Jesus as the Lord, while the Masoretic Text preserves the specific divine name for the God of Israel, "Prepare the way of *YHWH*."[14] In other words, in Mark's application of this citation, the Lord Jesus has been substituted for Yahweh.

Moreover, it is very clear that often this conflation of Jesus and Yahweh via Old Testament citation is quite intentional in the early church, which is very suggestive as many others agree, for how New Testament and other early Christian authors invite us to conceptualize the relationship between the Father and the Son.[15] It would seem that the Evangelists and other Christians felt quite comfortable conflating Jesus and Yahweh via Old Testament citation, both here and elsewhere, as if Jesus is coterminous with Yahweh. Or perhaps,

---

[13] The textual form of the citation of Isa. 40: 3 in Matt. 3: 3 and Luke 3: 4 is identical to Mark 1: 3. John 1: 23 gives only a slight variation. However Luke extends the quotation until it reaches the triumphant conclusion, "and all flesh will see the salvation of God" (Luke 3: 6).

[14] Although Mark and the other synoptic Evangelists front this "wilderness" and "preparation" passage from Isa. 40: 3, the community living at Qumran was even more preoccupied with it —in fact, their whole *raison d'être* is perhaps best explained by asserting that they had gathered in the desert near the shore of the Dead Sea in order to prepare for the ultimate eschatological coming of Israel's God, just as their community charter states (1QS 8. 14; 9. 19–20; cf. 4Q176 frgs. 1–2. i. 4–9).

[15] For example, Watts, "Mark," 120, concludes by affirming, "the striking identification of Jesus (1: 1) with Yahweh's coming (1: 2–3) can hardly be missed" and "Whatever else, for Mark Israel's Lord is, in some mysterious and unparalleled sense, present in Jesus." For a convenient collection of much of the evidence, see Richard Bauckham, *Jesus and the God of Israel: God Crucified and Other Studies on the New Testament's Christology of Divine Identity* (Milton Keynes: Paternoster, 2008), 186–9, 219–21.

as Richard Bauckham would prefer to put it, we find here a Christology of Divine Identity, for the early church spoke as if Jesus possessed the personal identity of Yahweh.[16] Yet I still presently prefer the fourth-century Nicene language that has come to dominate traditional Christian theology—that the Father and the Son are *homoousios*, sharing the same essence or substance, which unlike Bauckham's proposal does not focus on personal identity established through time, but distinct persons subsisting in the same essence inside and outside of time.[17]

SENT TO EFFECT GOOD NEWS

On Messengers and Messiahs

The arrival of a messenger who would prepare for the eschatological presence of God was not an idea unique to the early Christians—we also find this notion in a fascinating interpretation of Isaiah 52: 7 in the Dead Sea Scrolls in 11Q13 (11Q Melchizedek), a document that has already captured our attention in Chapter 2. Isaiah 52: 7 describes "a messenger who announces peace" further describing him as "a messenger of good who announces salvation." Moreover, this messenger declares to Zion, "Your God reigns!" (MT) or perhaps "Your God is king!"[18] The author of 11Q13 explains that the messenger in Isaiah 52: 7 is to be identified as "the anointed one of the Spirit" (*māšîaḥ hārûaḥ*) and is further to be identified with an anointed one, a messiah, whose coming is mentioned in Daniel.

Here we have a difficulty, however, because there are in fact two anointed ones, two messiahs, mentioned in Daniel and the intended referent is uncertain. Most scholars have identified the intended referent as the anointed one, the prince of Daniel 9: 25 ("until an anointed one [*māšîaḥ*], a prince [*nāgîd*], it is seven weeks"), who will appear after seven weeks of years, that is forty-nine years. Yet, as I have argued elsewhere, in agreement with Émile Puech, it is equally plausible (probably more) that the second anointed one, the messiah

---

[16] See Bauckham, *Jesus*, 3–7, and his remarks about Mark 1: 1–3 (p. 265).

[17] In speaking of Bauckham's notion of identity established through time, I refer to his "personal identity" theoretical framework, as best as I can discern his model. It should be noted, however, that elsewhere (Bauckham, *Jesus*, 251–2) he speaks of the "Today I have begotten you" of Ps. 2: 7 for the author of Hebrews as the "eternal today of divine eternity," appealing to the Hellenistic idea that true divinity is "unoriginated" or "self-originated." I remain uncertain how to reconcile his overall "personal identity" model with this more specific statement.

[18] The Hebrew consonantal text reads *mlk 'lhyk*, and within this phrase the word *mlk* could have been vocalized either as a noun *melek* ("king") or a verb *mālak* ("reigns").

of 9: 26 is intended,[19] whose demise is described in association with the sixty-ninth week, "An anointed one shall be cut off, and he shall be no more" (*yikkārēt māšîaḥ wĕ'ên lô*), which, because he appears near the end of the unfolding chronological sequence, makes this anointed messenger a truly eschatological figure for the author of 11Q13.

This messenger would announce the good news of the beginning of Melchizedek's eschatological reign to the sons of light (those living at Qumran), while a climactic atoning liberation was anticipated by the Qumran covenanters at the seventieth week (= 490 years; = 10 Jubilees). What is truly captivating about this interpretation for our purposes is that since Isaiah 61: 1–2 is self-evidently a first-person speech, *this messianic messenger* is implicitly identified in 11Q13 via an allusive citation as *the speaker of Isaiah 61: 2*, whose duty is "to comfort the mourners" (*lĕnaḥēm ha'ōblîm*),[20] which the author interprets further as "to instruct them in all the ages of the world."

Intriguingly, another text from Qumran, 4Q521, usually called 4Q Messianic Apocalypse, describes the messiah of God while invoking the language of Isaiah 61: 1, saying: "For the heavens and the earth shall listen to his [God's] Messiah.... He [God? or God's Messiah?] shall heal the critically wounded, He shall revive the dead, 'He shall send good news to the afflicted' (Isa. 61: 1), He shall satisfy the poor, He shall lead the uprooted, and the hungry he shall enrich..."[21] Now, it is not clear in 4Q521 precisely who is envisioned as carrying out these actions—such as sending "good news to the afflicted"—whether it is God alone, or as John Collins has at least to my mind persuasively argued, God through the agency of his messiah, but either way the actions are anticipated in conjunction with the messianic era.[22] Moreover, even if the Qumran community stood a bit outside the mainstream, these specific activities—healing, reviving the dead, sending good news to the poor—are uncannily similar to the very activities Jesus describes as transpiring around himself when Jesus is asked by John the Baptist whether or not Jesus is "the

---

[19] The likelihood of a reference to Dan. 9: 25 in 11Q Melchizedek was first proposed by Joseph. A. Fitzmyer, "Further Light on Melchizedek," *JBL* 86 (1967): 25–41, now reprinted in Joseph A. Fitzmyer, *The Semitic Background of the New Testament* (Grand Rapids: Eerdmans, 1997), 245–67, here 265–6. The equal likelihood of Dan. 9: 26 is noted by Émile Puech, "Notes sur la manuscrit de XIQMelchîsédeq," *RevQ* 12/48 (1987): 483–513, here 499. For a fuller bibliography and discussion, see Matthew W. Bates, "Beyond *Stichwort*: A Narrative Approach to Isa 52,7 in Romans 10,15 and 11Q Melchizedek (11Q13)," *RB* 116 (2009): 387–414, here 400–2.

[20] The manuscript is fragmentary here and the reading of all but the first letter of the second word, *ha'ōblîm*, must be conjectured. The MT reads slightly differently: "To comfort all of the afflicted" (*lĕnaḥēm kol-'ăbēlîm*).

[21] 4Q521 frg. 2; trans. Michael Wise et al. in Donald W. Parry and Emanuel Tov (eds.), *The Dead Sea Scrolls Reader* (6 vols.; Leiden: Brill, 2004–5), vi. 161.

[22] John J. Collins, "A Herald of Good Tidings: Isaiah 61:1–3 and Its Actualization in the Dead Sea Scrolls," in Craig A. Evans and Shemaryahu Talmon (eds.), *The Quest for Context and Meaning: Studies in Biblical Intertextuality in Honor of James A. Sanders* (BIS 28; Leiden: Brill, 1997), 225–40.

coming one." Jesus replies to John, "The blind receive sight, the lame walk, lepers are cleansed and the deaf hear, the dead are raised, and the poor receive good news; blessed is the one who does not fall away on account of me" (Luke 7: 22–3; cf. Matt. 11: 5–6).

Enacting the Messianic Script—Luke 4: 16–21

So, when in Luke 4: 18–19 we find Jesus reading this same passage, Isaiah 61: 1–2, and then announcing, "Today this scripture has been fulfilled in your hearing" (4: 21), we have a plausible basis for suspecting that this Second Temple Jew, at least as he is portrayed by Luke (although converging lines of evidence point to the essential historicity of this episode),[23] was not speaking of a *generic* fulfillment, as if Jesus believed that Isaiah was speaking merely *about him*, but rather of a *prosopological* fulfillment because Isaiah was construed as speaking *in the dramatic character of the Christ*. In other words, Jesus believed that the Spirit had inspired Isaiah to step into a future theodramatic role and from this provisional platform in the divine economy, to perform a speech in the character (*prosōpon*) of the anointed herald of God—a herald that had not yet been revealed at the time of Isaiah, but who preexisted (at the very least) to the degree that he could make an appearance on the theodramatic stage in advance of his future role on the earthly (actualized) stage.

In this way, Jesus, not long after the Spirit had descended upon him at the Jordan, unrolls the scroll from the prophet Isaiah, finds the appropriate place, and with all eyes riveted upon him begins to read:

> The Spirit of the Lord is upon *me*, on account of which he anointed *me* to announce good news to the poor; he sent *me* to proclaim release for the prisoners and recovery of sight for the blind, to send forth the oppressed with pardon, to proclaim the favored year of the Lord.   (Luke 4: 18–19 citing Isa. 61: 1–2)[24]

Although the words of Isaiah 61: 1–2 are not a divine conversation between the Father and the Son, a theodramatic reading technique is employed, and there are implications for the interior relationship between divine persons.

---

[23] See recent discussions in Michael F. Bird, *Are You the One Who Is To Come? The Historical Jesus and the Messianic Question* (Grand Rapids: Baker Academic, 2009), 98–104; Dale C. Allison, Jr., *Constructing Jesus: Memory, Imagination, and History* (Grand Rapids: Baker Academic, 2010), 263–6.

[24] There are several minor differences between the Isaianic text and Jesus' citation in Luke. For instance, Isa. 61: 1–2 LXX has "to heal those crushed in heart," which Luke omits, while citing instead "to send forth the oppressed with pardon" (cf. Isa. 58: 6 LXX).

Isaiah 61: 1–2 is taken as a dramatic speech that the *Son* makes to an unspecified audience, in which the *Son* speaks about the anointing by the *Spirit* of the *Lord (God the Father)* which he has just received as part-and-parcel of his task of proclaiming a special season of divine favor issued by the *Lord (God the Father)*.

We find that the Son has been moved into a special state of ritual purity and empowerment by the fortifying power of the Spirit and that this Spirit is described as God's Spirit; thus, it is with the aid of the Spirit and God the Father that the Son embarks on his central mission—to proclaim boldly by word and deed that the concrete rule of God is breaking into the world in a markedly new way. His words are a *performative utterance*—he is actualizing, seemingly, what hitherto was spoken by Isaiah in the role (*prosōpon*) of the Christ in the divine drama, but now this scene, scripted long ago as part of the great theodrama, has now been brought to life, incarnated, as the part has been played out by the appropriate flesh-and-blood divine person (*prosōpon*) in such a manner that Jesus can declare, "Today this scripture is fulfilled in your hearing."

Confirmation that Luke intends to portray Jesus as reading prosopologically in the manner just described is significantly bolstered by evidence from the early Fathers. For if the Fathers used a person-centered reading strategy to take the words of Isaiah 61: 1–2 as the voice of the future Christ speaking from the theodramatic stage, then we have better grounds—apart from any evidence to the contrary—for positing that at the very least Luke, and plausibly the historical Jesus himself, would have made the same basic interpretative move. And we find that the early Fathers are consistent in construing Jesus' reading of Isaiah as a theodramatic performative utterance. For example, Irenaeus introduces the citation of Isaiah 61: 1–2 by saying, "as he [Jesus] Himself says of Himself, by Isaias," indicating that Jesus was the speaker of the original Isaianic text that was subsequently performed in Luke 4: 18.[25] Likewise, Origen affirms that the Christ was in Isaiah as these words were spoken, avowing that these and many like-minded words in the Psalter were spoken "in the person of Christ," while Tertullian says much the same.[26] Meanwhile, writing considerably earlier, Ps-Barnabas reads Isaiah 61: 1–2 as a dramatic speech of the to-be-revealed-in-the-future Christ, and, provocatively, he has made this move as the final link in a chain of three servant texts from Isaiah (see *Barn.* 14. 7–9), all of which he has interpreted prosopologically. In fact, these servant texts merit further exploration.

---

[25] Irenaeus, *Epid.* 53.   [26] Origen, *Comm. Jo.* 6. 196; Tertullian, *Prax.* 11.

CONVERSATIONS BETWEEN THE SERVANT-SON
AND THE FATHER

The three Isaianic texts cited by Ps-Barnabas as part of this chain, Isaiah 42: 6–7, 49: 6–7, and the text we have already treated, 61: 1–2, were in fact all definitive for the mission of the Son in early Christian interpretation. Ps-Barnabas was by no means alone in the early church in reading these texts as divine dialogues—some of the New Testament authors did as well. So teasing out of the person-centered reading strategy in this *catena* does much to illuminate how the early church conceptualized the relationship between the divine persons that would eventually come to be termed the Trinity. This was done by assimilating the anointed Isaianic messenger of 61: 1–2 to the enigmatic servant mentioned elsewhere in Isaiah through thematic linkage and prosopological exegesis.

I Have Given You as a Covenant—Isaiah 42: 1–9

Ps-Barnabas identifies the speaker of the first citation as God the Father and the addressee as the Son by asserting that the citation shows "how the Father commanded him [Jesus the Son] to prepare a holy people for himself," when he had brought us out of darkness (14. 6). In order to prove that the Father (the "I" in the text) verbally commissioned the Son (the "you" in the text) with this task, Ps-Barnabas notes that Isaiah says:

> I, the Lord your God, called you in righteousness, and I will seize your hand and empower you. I gave you to be a covenant for people, a light for nations, to open the eyes of the blind and to lead the shackled out from their shackles and those sitting in darkness from prison.   (*Barn.* 14. 7 citing Isa. 42: 6–7 LXX)

A solution-by-person for Isaiah 42: 6–7 was utilized here and elsewhere in the early Christian literature not because of some perverse and intractable desire to find Jesus Christ in every nook and cranny of the Jewish Scripture, but because the surrounding context in Isaiah itself contains enigmatic shifts in speaker and addressee that any sensitive reader will find perplexing.

   In Isaiah 42: 1–4 an unidentified speaker—but almost certainly God (the Father) on the basis of 42: 5—is speaking about a special servant.[27] The audience to whom God is speaking is never identified in the Masoretic Text, although it appears to be the people as a whole, since the servant is presented

---

[27] Irenaeus, *Haer.* 3. 11. 6, likewise identifies God (the Father) as the speaker of Isa. 42: 1–4 while also affirming that the Servant-Son is the main subject of this portion of Isaiah's oracle but not the addressee, all of which accords with the reconstruction of the prosopological assignments and switches posited in what follows.

to the audience with the words, "Behold, my servant" (42: 1). This servant is also called by God "my chosen one in whom I delight" (42: 1),[28] and despite this servant's relatively unassuming role (42: 2–3), in a faithful and unfaltering fashion he will "bring justice to the nations" (42: 1) and "establish justice on earth" (42: 4), a task above all appropriate for a king.

Yet, in 42: 6–7 there are three subtle person-related shifts that require an explanation. First, the servant is no longer referenced in the third person and, second, the addressee—"you" in the singular—suddenly becomes explicit. God is definitely still the first-person speaker (the "I"), but ancient readers, who were attuned to dialogical shifts, would assign a suitable new addressee as they deemed appropriate. Third, when God speaks in 42: 8–9, the addressee has certainly changed again because the "you" is now plural.

The Overarching Prosopological Solution. The solution of Ps-Barnabas and other early Christians, such as Justin Martyr and probably the author of Matthew's Gospel, was first of all to seek the identity of the addressee within the bounds of the text itself—a sensible thing to do. They inferred that God had now turned from speaking *to the people as a whole* about the servant (Isa. 42: 1–4) to address *the servant himself* (with Isa. 42: 5 as a preamble and in 42: 6–7 directly),[29] after which God turned once again to address *the entire people* (Isa. 42: 8–9), all of which can be summarized thus:

GOD (speaking to THE PEOPLE as a whole): [Here is] my servant {Jacob}, whom I will assist, my chosen one {Israel} in whom I delight; I put my Spirit upon him; he will bring forth justice for the nations . . .   (Isa. 42: 1 LXX)[30]

---

[28] Unlike Isa. 42: 1 in the MT, the LXX identifies the servant specifically as Jacob/Israel (cf. Isa. 41: 8; 49: 3). Yet early Christian readers of the LXX still identified the servant as Jesus Christ (see n. 30 in this chapter).

[29] Isaiah 42: 5, when cited in isolation, is not marked in the early Christian literature as prosopologically addressed by God to the Servant or the Son (see Theophilus, *Autol.* 2. 35; Irenaeus, *Haer.* 5. 12. 2), so it is perhaps best to reconstruct the most likely early Christian reading of it as a preamble that God (the Father) speaks to a more general audience before turning specifically to address the Servant-Son in 42: 6–7.

[30] In these three extracts from Isa. 42: 1–9 I have followed the LXX, the preferred version of the earliest Christians, rather than the MT—except I have placed Jacob/Israel in curly brackets to indicate that these explanatory names are not present in several noteworthy ancient manuscript traditions. For example, the MT (and hence most English translations) mentions only the servant in 42: 1 without further identifying the servant as Jacob/Israel (although see Isa. 41: 8; 49: 3 MT) while adding "Behold" (*hēn*) at the outset. Diverse important ancient witnesses follow suit, both Jewish (e.g. 1QIsaᵃ; *Targum Isaiah* 42: 1; Theodotion) and Christian (Matt. 12: 18; Irenaeus, *Haer.* 3. 11. 6). The LXX, however, explicitly identifies the servant specifically as Jacob/Israel. Yet even this identification, when present, did not deter early Christian readers of the LXX from further identifying the servant as Jesus Christ, since, as Justin Martyr mentions, this servant is said to execute judgment on the earth, which is a kingly role, and therefore this was not felt to fit the character description of Jacob/Israel in the rest of Scripture (*Dial.* 123. 8; 135. 1–3; cf. Eusebius, *Dem. ev.* 376). For the earliest Christians the purposes for which God had called Israel had devolved onto the Son—see discussion of Isa. 49: 1–12 later in this chapter.

GOD (now speaking to THE SERVANT): I, the Lord God, have called you in
   righteousness.... I have given you to be a covenant for people, to be a light
   for nations, to open the eyes of the blind, to lead the shackled out from their
   shackles and those sitting in darkness from prison.   (Isa. 42: 6–7 LXX)[31]
GOD (now speaking to THE PEOPLE as a whole again): I am the Lord God.
   This is my name. I will not give my glory to another.... Old matters, look,
   they have come about, and new things which I will announce are revealed to
   you even before they arise.   (Isa. 42: 8–9 LXX)

Additionally, I would posit that these character-assignments made sense to
various early Christian interpreters because: (1) God is introducing the servant
to the people, so the servant is put forward as dramatically present ("My
servant" or "Here is my servant"); (2) the description of the servant's tasks
described in *the third person* in 42: 1–4 seems to match the tasks specified for
the second-person addressee in 42: 6–7. Specifically in 42: 6–7 the words of God
to the servant are quite readily construed as giving *the method* by which the
servant will establish justice—namely "I gave you in order that you might be a
covenant for people, a light for nations," as well as giving the anticipated
effects of the deployment of the method—the healing of the blind and the
liberation of captives.

   In this manner Isaiah 42: 1–9 was a critical text for the early Christians,
since 42: 1–4 describes the mission of the Servant-Son, while the Father was
even found in 42: 6–7 to have spoken directly to the Son about his mission,
clarifying the method by which he would accomplish it. Reflection on it
provides ample fare for those interested in the interior relationship between
the Father and the Son in the early church, especially as it pertains to shared
knowledge of the Son's task.

   The Servant-Son as the Covenant. In 42: 6–7 God the Father sends his Son to
the earth precisely as a Servant, but he is quick to tell the Servant-Son about
the virtuous nature of his call: "I have called you in righteousness." The Father
explains to the Son that he will not be abandoned, but that he will be with him,
"I will take hold of your hand," and that the Son will be divinely empowered by
him for the mission, "I will strengthen you" (LXX), or that he will be divinely
safeguarded, "I will protect you" (MT). The mission as the Father describes it
to the Son is unassumingly humble, but it will ultimately result in something
terrifyingly marvelous—"I have given you to be a covenant for people." Here
the Servant-Son is expressly told by the Father the ultimate stratagem, the
master-stroke of the divine plan—that *he himself is to be the covenant*, which
for early Christian readers signaled that the covenant would be in the Servant-

---

[31] Note the tense difference between the MT ("I will give"—imperfect, best translated as
future) and the LXX ("I have given"—aorist, best translated as past).

Son's blood.[32] This daring maneuver would result in something quite unanticipated. Thus, the Father here announces to the Servant-Son that he will be, "a light to the nations"—a beacon drawing the Gentiles. The Apostle Paul will later term all of this the great cosmic mystery—that the Gentiles are to be fully welcomed by the Father through the Son into the one people of God via a new covenant (see Rom. 11: 25–7; cf. Eph. 3: 1–6; Gal. 4: 24–7; 1 Cor. 11: 25; 2 Cor. 3: 6).

The Servant in Matthew 12: 18–21. Thus, when we find Matthew citing Isaiah 42: 1–4, we are invited to consider that he sees this as a description of the Servant-Son's mission—and that Matthew was aware that the Father had spoken in Isaiah 42: 5–7 to his Servant-Son directly, detailing the new covenant and the Gentile in-gathering. This must remain speculation however, because Matthew cites not the divine conversation itself (Isa. 42: 5–7), but its introduction (Isa. 42: 1–4), in which the Servant is presented by God to the people:[33]

> Here is my servant whom I have chosen, my beloved, with whom I am delighted; I will put my Spirit on him, and he will proclaim justice to the nations. He will not quarrel or cry out; nor will anyone hear his voice in the broad streets; a crushed reed he will not break and a smoldering wick he will not extinguish, until he brings forth righteousness for victory. And nations will hope in his name.   (Matt. 12: 18–21)

In context, Matthew sees Jesus' *healing of the sick* as evidence of the Servant-Son's Spirit-empowered compassion to the oppressed (cf. Matt. 12: 13, 22)—"a bruised reed he will not break and a smoldering wick he will not snuff out."[34] Meanwhile Jesus' *withdrawal from the crowds* and warning to those he healed *to keep his identity a secret* was felt to corroborate with the Servant's unpretentious humility (cf. Matt. 12: 15–16)—"he will not wrangle or cry out, nor will anyone hear his voice in the broad streets." In the broader context of Matthew's Gospel, obviously, themes central to Isaiah 42: 1–4 such as the *establishment of kingly justice* ("until he brings forth righteousness for victory") and *the ingathering of the nations* ("nations will hope in his name") were important vis-à-vis Jesus as well, with both motifs, for example,

---

[32] See *Barn.* 14. 5–7; cf. 4. 8; Justin, *Dial.* 122. 3–6; on the covenant in blood more generally apart from specific connections to Isa. 42: 6–7, see Matt. 26: 28; Mark 14: 24; Luke 22: 20; 1 Cor. 11: 25; Heb. 9: 20; 10: 29; 12: 24; 13: 20.

[33] The speculation that Matthew made a prosopological assignment when reading Isa. 42: 1–4 is further encouraged by the probable allusion to Isa. 42: 1 in the baptism and transfiguration (Matt. 3: 17; 17: 5)—see "With 'You' I Am Well Pleased—Isaiah 42: 1" in Ch. 2.

[34] Irenaeus, *Haer.* 4. 20. 10, takes "a bruised reed he will not break and a smoldering wick he will not snuff out" (Isa. 42: 3) as signaling not only Jesus' own mildness and tranquility, but also that of the kingdom he has established. Meanwhile Tertullian, *Marc.* 4. 23. 8, also finds the gentleness of Christ prophesied in Isa. 42: 2–3, adding in *Marc.* 3. 17. 4 that the bruised reed refers to flagging Jewish faith, but the burning flax to the rekindled faith of the Gentiles.

coinciding in the parable of the sheep and the goats (see esp. Matt. 25: 31–2; cf. also 28: 18–20).[35]

The Servant-Son and Monotheism. We have already noted the manner in which the person-centered interpretation of Isaiah 42: 1 was vital to early Christian understandings of the baptism/transfiguration of Jesus (see Ch. 2), where the Father borrows the language of the oracle when speaking to the Son via the Old Testament text. In addition to the dialogical switches between Isaiah 42: 1–4 and 42: 5–7, there is yet another shift at Isaiah 42: 8–9, and there we find God (the Father) emphatically declaring to the people as a whole that he will give his glory to no one else.

Thus, in the midst of a passage, Isaiah 42: 1–9, that irrepressibly urges monotheism, we find without any sense of contradiction that the one God was dialogically read in the earliest church as the Father and the Servant-Son. And this is by no means an isolated occurrence—on the contrary, the inclusion of the Lord Jesus Christ on the divine side of the equation in citations of the Old Testament is inordinately common in earliest Christianity.[36] For example, with regard to this very text, Isaiah 42: 1–9, Justin Martyr heavily underscores the theme of Gentile inclusion in his interpretation,[37] while noticing that Isaiah 49: 8–9 indicates that God is *not* ultimately willing to share his glory with any other *but nonetheless* that this divine conversation implies that the Servant must be construed as sharing in that glory (see *Dial.* 65)—implying that the Servant-Son is necessarily, therefore, a distinct divine person along with the Father.

So, after determining on the basis of a careful reading of the details of the oracle itself that God was the speaker and the servant the addressee, it would seem early Christians applied a kerygmatic hermeneutic (i.e. an interpretative method centered on the proclamation of Jesus Christ) that married their experience of the reality of the Christ-event (i.e. his incarnation, life, death for sins, resurrection, and ascension to the right hand) with the Old Testament

---

[35] On Isa 42: 1–4 as announcing the ingathering of the nations in Christ, the king, see also Justin, *Dial.* 135. 1–3. It is also remotely possible that another instance of prosopological interpretation is preserved by Matthew, who explains Jesus' proclivity for teaching in parables as a fulfillment of that which was spoken *through* the prophet: "I will open my mouth in parables, I will utter things hidden from the foundation [of the cosmos]" (Matt. 13: 35 citing a deviant form of Ps. 77: 2 LXX). The "of the cosmos" is quite uncertain textually. Given Matthew's fondness for a hermeneutic of types, however, it is more likely that here Matthew has seen the earlier psalmist as establishing a type or pattern of teaching "in parables" that Jesus fulfills. For the contrary opinion that Matthew sees this as a speech by the preexistent Christ, see Gathercole, *The Preexistent Son*, 264–6.

[36] On the early church's use of OT texts that are housed in intensely monotheistic contexts as it pertains to Jesus' divinity, see Rom. 10: 13 (Joel 2: 32); Rom. 14: 11 and Phil. 2: 10–11 (Isa. 45: 23); 1 Cor. 1: 31 and 2 Cor. 10: 17 (Jer. 9: 24); 1 Cor. 2: 16 (Isa. 40: 13); 1 Cor. 10: 22 (Deut. 32: 21); 1 Thess. 3: 13 (Zech. 14: 5); 2 Thess. 1: 7, 12 (Isa. 66: 5, 15); 2 Thess. 1: 9 (Isa. 2: 10, 19, 21). My list depends on Bauckham, *Jesus*, 191–7, who also provides an excellent succinct discussion.

[37] See Justin, *Dial.* 26. 2; 122. 3; 123. 8–9; 135. 2–3.

prophecies, identifying this as an advance theatrical performance, in which Isaiah, full of the Spirit, had spoken in the character (*prosōpon*) of God the Father to the prosopon of the Servant, Jesus the Son. This kerygmatic hermeneutic undoubtedly was facilitated by other Isaianic descriptions of this servant as one who suffers on behalf of others, bearing their sins—"and the Lord has *laid on him the sin of us all*" (Isa. 53: 6)—much as we find in the earliest statements in the church about how the Christ-story relates to the ancient prophecies. For example, the kerygmatic protocreed of 1 Corinthians 15: 3–5 stresses that Jesus "died *for our sins in accordance with the scriptures,*" correlating external event with scriptural interpretation. The role of the apostolic proclamation in early Christian hermeneutics will be addressed more fully in Chapter 7.

Servant-Israel Returns, Gentiles Welcomed—Isaiah 49: 1–12

The next passage in the chain that Ps-Barnabas has interpreted prosopologically is—at least to my mind—even more illuminating than the preceding example. The dialogical maneuvering that prompted a solution-by-person in Isaiah 42: 1–9 was quite subtle; in contrast, the tectonic slippage in persons in Isaiah 49: 1–12 screams for interpretative attention. Although the oracle is made intensely complex because of the presence of numerous reported speeches, the basic situation can be sketched as follows.[38]

In Isaiah 49: 1–4 the speaker reports *a prior conversation*, when the Lord God had told him, "You are my servant, Israel," so at an earlier time the speaker had accepted the designation Servant-Israel from God, and the addressee to whom the speaker is talking is expressly geographically distant peoples. Yet in 49: 5, as the speech continues, the Servant begins to speak *about Israel and Jacob in the third person*, making it difficult to affirm that the present speaker still accepts in an unqualified sense the title Servant-Israel that he had initially been given by God—especially since the speaker has "now" received a new message from God. In 49: 7 and following the Lord God speaks again, and the addressee is not named; his identity must be inferred on the basis of the description of the addressee and the words spoken to him, but the Servant is the most natural referent.

Since all the reported speeches must have occurred *earlier* than the speeches themselves, we can reconstruct the chronological order in which the speeches occurred within the theodramatic world. Accordingly, I have reordered them so that they follow the chronological theodramatic sequence. In Isaiah 49: 1–12

---

[38] For a different reconstruction of how the dialogical shifts work in Isa. 49: 1–9, see Hanson, *Jesus Christ in the Old Testament*, 150.

there are in fact eight theodramatic speeches in total and the details of each speech reveal something new as the Servant and God converse.

*Speech 1 (*reported in *Speech 5)*:

GOD (addressing himself to THE SERVANT in the *more remote* past with respect to the theodramatic setting of *Speech 5*): You are my servant, Israel, and in you I will be glorified.   (Isa. 49: 3 LXX)

In this first speech the Lord God, Yahweh in the Masoretic Text, dubs some otherwise unintroduced and unidentified individual—the "you" is singular— as Israel, my servant, with the purpose that this designation will result in God's increased glory. This does not appear to be the moment at which this servant came into existence, but rather the assigning of the title is connected with the summoning of this servant to a task, as the next speech makes clear. God had spoken similarly about Israel through Moses to Pharaoh, "The Lord says this, 'Israel is my firstborn son'; now I say to you, 'Send forth my people in order that they might worship me'" (Exod. 4: 22–3 LXX). Overlapping themes are present—Israel's sonship and Israel's purpose of worshipping/glorifying God.

In light of the alterations in persons and the themes in Isaiah 49: 1–12, early Christians would, of course, ultimately identify this servant as Jesus, the Christ, the Son. The triune implications are startling: Through the Spirit via Isaiah, God the Father spoke to Jesus the Son *giving him in advance Israel's vocation*—Jesus was told by the Father to live out the purpose for which God had called the nation of Israel.

We see refractions of this tradition in, for instance, Matthew's description of Jesus' flight to Egypt and return, which is said to fulfill the oracle, "Out of Egypt I called my Son" (Matt. 2: 15 citing Hos. 11: 1). The implication for Matthew is that Jesus is now living out *in nuce* the mission that God had given to Israel. However, the nation of Israel, collectively speaking, was felt to have failed to enact sufficiently the mission of glorifying God, as the wider context in Hosea makes clear: "When Israel was a child, I loved him, and out of Egypt I called my son. The more I called them, the more they went from me; they were sacrificing to the Baals and were burning incense to idols" (11: 1–2). Matthew hereby appears to be asserting that Jesus as the true Israel will succeed in carrying out the divine mission precisely where corporate Israel was not able to succeed—compare the temptations in Matthew 4: 1–11. In the same vein, early Christian's would read Isaiah 49: 1–12 as announcing that the vocation of corporate Israel (or a remnant thereof) had devolved onto the Son.

Speech 2 (reported in *Speech 5*):

THE SERVANT (replying to GOD in the *more remote* past with respect to the theodramatic setting of *Speech 5*): I have labored in vain, and I have given my strength for uselessness and nothingness; for this reason my verdict is with the Lord, my labor is in the presence of my God.   (Isa. 49: 4 LXX)

The second speech is the servant's reply to the first speech. Although this individual has been designated by God as God's special servant, Israel, and called to a hitherto undefined task, the labor spent on the task has seemed entirely fruitless to the servant. Yet the servant acknowledges that God alone must remain the judge of the merit of his work.

This speech within a speech was important for the earliest Christians because it helped them fix the theodramatic setting. Although uttered long ago by the Spirit through Isaiah, the Spirit was capable of selecting a dramatic setting far in the future, so that a window is cut into the future by the dramatic dialogue. That is, to use a cinematic analogy, early Christians felt that these dramatic speeches could give a sneak preview of a later scene in the divine drama. Here it becomes clear that for early Christian interpreters this speech is set after the servant has tried to implement the mission, but after having made the attempt, the servant now feels that his method has been entirely ineffectual, that he has spent his strength to no avail. Yet the servant realizes that God is the judge of all such efforts, and that his method may be vindicated in the end. This suggested to early Christian readers—I would argue on the basis of evidence to be given shortly—that the theodramatic setting of this second speech was after the inauguration of the earthly Jesus' public mission, but before his resurrection.

Speech 3 (reported in *Speech 6*):
GOD (addressing THE SERVANT in the *recent* past with respect to the theodramatic setting of *Speech 5*): It is a great thing for you to be called my servant to raise up the tribes of Jacob and to turn back the scattered of Israel. Behold, I have established you to be a light for nations, in order that you might be for salvation unto the end of the earth.   (Isa. 49: 6 LXX)[39]

This third speech (along with the fifth) is critical to the whole sequence, for now we discover that the servant received new information, transforming his discouraged sense of futility to a purpose-filled hope, when he was directly addressed by God. The servant learned—and this point is critical—that although he was initially designated as Servant-Israel by God, *his identity is not precisely coterminous with Israel,* because his mission is "to raise up the tribes of Jacob" and "to turn back the scattered of Israel." One might suggest that he is a representative of Israel par excellence. Although undoubtedly this task is

---

[39] There are some noteworthy textual matters pertaining to Isa. 49: 6. First, the role of the servant in effecting salvation is more emphatic in the LXX ("in order that *you* might be for salvation unto the end of the earth") than in the MT ("that my salvation might be unto the end of the earth"). Second, some LXX manuscripts include "to be a covenant for people" among the servant's appointed tasks (cf. Isa. 42: 6; 49: 8), although this is not supported by the MT, Targum Isaiah, or 1QIsaᵃ. Third, the Hebrew tradition reads, "it is not too small a thing" rather than the LXX rendering "it is a great thing," so the MT emphasizes to a higher degree the grandeur of the second task (regarding the nations) in comparison to the first (regarding Israel).

truly great, God says that this alone, as splendid as it might be, would not be sufficient for this outstanding servant. The ultimate mission is even more astoundingly marvelous: to be "a light for nations," so that through the servant, God's salvation can reach "unto the end of the earth." Vitally, the servant has learned all this *before* making his speeches to the distant peoples.

Speech 4:

GOD (addressing PEOPLE WHO ARE GEOGRAPHICALLY DISTANT): Hear me O islands! Pay attention O nations! {After a long time it shall be established, says the Lord}.   (Isa. 49: 1a LXX)

Now the principle audience for the prophetic setting is indicated—the nations, those far away from Israel. The Septuagint, which I have followed since we are trying to reconstruct plausible early Christian readings, attributes these lines to the Lord (God), as God serves as a master-of-ceremonies of sorts, summoning the nations to listen to *Speeches 5* and *6*, the words spoken by the servant. The Septuagint also adds the enigmatic and intriguing qualifying note, that the theodramatic performance expressed in *Speeches 5* and *6* will only be established after a long duration of time. The Masoretic Text (as well as 1QIsaᵃ) leaves the identity of the speaker of these opening lines ambivalent—the Lord God could be the speaker as in the Septuagint (and the Isaiah Targum) or it could be the servant himself directly addressing distant people groups.[40] To make all this clear, I have marked the additions unique to the Septuagint in curly brackets. Regardless, the meaning of the surrounding speeches and the principle dialogical shifts are not affected since both the Septuagint and the Masoretic Text agree as to the audience, and in both it is also evident that the servant is the speaker of 49: 1b–4 immediately thereafter.

Speech 5:

The SERVANT (addressing PEOPLE WHO ARE GEOGRAPHICALLY DISTANT): From the womb of my mother he [God] called my name; he made my mouth like a sharp sword and he hid me under the shelter of his hand; he made me like a chosen arrow and he sheltered me in his quiver. And he said to me . . . [*Speech 1* is reported]. But I said . . . [*Speech 2* is reported]. (Isa. 49:1b–4 LXX)

---

[40] There are no overt markers in the MT or 1QIsaᵃ that would indicate a dialogical shift in the first-person speaker between Isa. 49: 1a and 49: 1b, although this on its own is not incontrovertible evidence that no switch is intended. Tantalizingly, in 49: 1a of the Isaiah Targum, the Lord (God) says, "Attend to my Memra, O islands, and hearken, you kingdoms from afar" (49: 1a), seemingly inviting us to consider that the servant and the Memra are coterminous in 49: 1b–4, but then in 49: 5 the servant says "the Memra of God has become my help," which compels us to conclude that Memra is not the servant here after all (trans. Chilton). It is clear nonetheless that as in the Septuagint the Lord (God) is the speaker of 49: 1a in the Isaiah Targum rather than the servant.

By the time we arrive at the fifth speech, in terms of the theodramatic chronology, God and the servant have already had a lively exchange. Yet we obtain essential new information from this speech about the prior relationship between God and the servant. As was inferred earlier, it is now confirmed—this servant was known by name by God long before he was designated "Israel" and also before this Israel-designation was redefined so that the Servant could restore Israel and extend salvation to the nations. Indeed, although God knew him, God kept his identity hidden, shrouded in long shadows, until he was called forth "from the womb" (Isa. 49: 1 LXX; cf. Ps. 109: 3 LXX). This, as we shall see, was important evidence that helped lead some early Christians to identify Jesus, the one who had come forth from the womb under such unusual circumstances, as the Servant in this passage. Of course, the identity of the addressee to whom the Servant speaks as distant peoples—Gentiles—was enormously crucial to the construal of the whole in the early church.

Speech 6:

THE SERVANT (continuing *Speech 5* but addressing PEOPLE WHO ARE GEOGRAPH-ICALLY DISTANT in light of the changed circumstances due to *Speech 3*): And now thus says the Lord [God], who formed me from the womb to be his very own servant, to gather Jacob and Israel; indeed I will be gathered unto him and I will be glorified in the presence of the Lord [God] and my God will be my strength. And he said to me . . . [*Speech 3* is reported].   (Isa. 49: 5–6 LXX)

In conjunction with *Speech 3*, this sixth discourse compels any sensitive reader to seek for an adequate person that could have been designated by God as "my servant, Israel" (49: 3) yet God could later have declared this same person to be a servant *unto Israel* since the servant will "gather Jacob and Israel." It might be inferred that it is the disobedience of corporate Israel in failing to carry out fully their God-glorifying mission for the sake of self and of the nations that has made it necessary for this singularly outstanding servant to rescue a remnant within corporate Israel[41]—and as if that were not enough, to bring salvation to the nations as well.

Moreover, on the basis of *Speech 5*, this person must necessarily have existed prior to his designation as "my servant, Israel." Prosopologically

---

[41] See the rebukes issued to collective Israel for its failure in the near context in Isaiah. For example, "I know that you are hardened, and your neck is an iron sinew and your forehead bronze" (Isa. 48: 4 LXX); "You have neither known nor understood; from the very beginning I have not opened your ears, for I knew that you would certainly act unfaithfully; you were called lawless even from the womb!" (Isa. 48: 8 LXX)—cf. Tertullian, *Marc.* 3. 6. 6 on Isa. 42: 19. On the whole topic of the failure of corporate Israel to carry out its mission and the raising up of the Isaianic servant to fulfill that mission in response, see the insightful analysis of Rikk E. Watts, "Consolation or Confrontation? Isaiah 40–55 and the Delay of the New Exodus," *TynBul* 44 (1990): 31–59; Brevard Childs, *Isaiah* (OTL; Louisville, Ky.: Westminster John Knox, 2001), 385.

attuned early Christian readers did not have trouble finding a suitable candidate. And in light of all the clues in the preceding speeches, they were able to determine a theodramatic setting for the speeches during the earthly ministry of Jesus, yet before his resurrection/glorification. As Irenaeus says, speaking with reference to this text, Isaiah 49: 5–6, here we learn

> that the Son of God pre-existed, that the Father spoke with Him, and caused Him to be revealed to men before his birth; and then that it was necessary for Him to be begotten, a man amongst men; and that the same God himself fashions Him from the womb . . . . That the Son calls Himself the servant of the Father, because of His obedience to the Father, for also among men every son is a servant of his father.[42]

Like Irenaeus, Justin Martyr also expressly states that Isaiah 49: 5–6 contains a conversation between the Father and the Son, indicating that God uses this particular dialogue to announce Gentile inclusion in the plan of salvation.[43] Ps-Barnabas finds a Father–Son dialogue much as Irenaeus and Justin (see *Barn.* 14. 8; cf. 14. 6), with the author of Acts alone, perhaps, moving in a quite different direction than our other early Christian witnesses.[44] The vital point is that *Speech 6* (which reports *Speech 3*) was read by most early Christians as evidence that the Servant must not be exactly identical to Israel since he has a mission to restore Israel—thus solution-by-person deduced a divine dialogue between the Father and the Servant-Son in which the Father restores the Son's hope by tacitly affirming the effectiveness of the Son's method, asserting that the result will not only be the restoration of a remnant of Israel, but also Gentile inclusion.

Speech 7:
GOD (speaking to one "abhorred by the nations"—we are invited to infer on the basis of *Speech 3* that this person is THE SERVANT): Thus says the Lord,

---

[42] Irenaeus, *Epid.* 51.

[43] Justin, *Dial.* 121. 4; cf. Tertullian, *Marc.* 3. 20. 4–5.

[44] The author of Acts does not appear to regard Isa. 49: 6 as the words of the Father to the Son, since Paul and Barnabas in Acts 13: 47 are portrayed as finding justification for the apostolic mission to the Gentiles via Isa. 49: 6—as if the Isaianic oracle contained words directed straight at future Christian ambassadors, such as follows: "I [the Father] have made you [apostles] a light for the nations, that you [apostles] may bring salvation to the ends of the earth." It remains possible, however, that the hermeneutical logic of the author of Acts is more complex than we can see on the surface, taking these as the words of the Father to the Son, which are then made applicable as words to apostles inasmuch as apostles carry on the work of the Son. The plausibility of this supposition is enhanced since the "you" is singular in the Greek, so it is unlikely that the plural "you [apostles]" would have directly been inferred by the author of Acts, despite surface appearances. In view of the strong evidence elsewhere in the early church for reading Isa. 49: 5–6 as containing a dialogue between divine persons, the Father–Son dialogical possibility should not be lightly dismissed here for the author of Acts, especially in light of Paul's application of Isa. 49: 8 in 2 Cor. 6: 2 (see the subsequent discussion under *"Speech 8"*), even if such a reconstruction is quite speculative.

{the God of Israel, who rescued you: "Consecrate the one who considers cheap his own soul}, who is abhorred by the nations, by the slaves of rulers; kings shall see him, and rulers shall arise and pay homage to him on account of the Lord [God], because the Holy One of Israel is faithful and I have chosen you." (Isa. 49: 7 LXX)

We now find the Servant strangely silent as the spotlight falls on a new speaker, God, who is addressing someone. The speech is prefaced in the Septuagint with the words, "Thus says the Lord, the God of Israel, who rescued *you*," so the character addressed, the "you" (singular) is someone who has been, or, prophetically speaking, will be, saved from a trial or difficulty by God. The identity of this character can be further deduced—and indeed in the Masoretic Text it must be deduced since the prefatory remarks are lacking—through his description: one "abhorred by the nations."[45] Since the servant has just finished speaking to God, it is most likely that now the servant is the "you" being addressed by God, and this conclusion would only have been reinforced for ancient readers by thematic similarities with other servant passages in Isaiah, in which the servant, the royal response to him, and his homage are depicted in very similar terms:

Behold, my servant will understand, he will be lifted up, and he will be exceedingly glorified; just as many will be astonished at *you*—your appearance will be so lacking in glory as a human—so many nations will marvel over him and kings will shut their mouths, because those who were not informed about him will see and those who had not heard will understand. (Isa. 52: 13–15 LXX)[46]

---

[45] The MT has some crucial differences from the LXX for Isa. 49: 7. A typical English translation based on the MT runs as follows: "Thus says the LORD, the Redeemer of Israel and his Holy One, to one deeply despised, abhorred by the nations, the slave of rulers, 'Kings shall see and stand up, princes, and they shall prostrate themselves, because of the LORD, who is faithful, the Holy One of Israel, who has chosen you'" (*NRSV*). Thus, the MT calls God "the redeemer and Holy One of Israel" but lacks the prefacing remarks *by God*, in which we are told that the "you" has been rescued by God. Also, the MT is devoid of the command to "Consecrate the one who considers cheap his own soul," instead giving a character description of the addressee, "one deeply despised," all of which I have sought to signal by placing the LXX's prefacing remarks in curly brackets. Also in the MT the addressee is the "slave of rulers" whereas in the LXX in all probability it is the nations that are described as "slaves of rulers" rather than the addressee. Finally, the LXX makes it emphatically clear that God is the speaker by ending with "and *I* have chosen you" rather than the "who has chosen you" as in the MT. Despite these differences, both the LXX and MT concur about the truly vital things for a dialogical analysis—that the Lord God is the speaker and that the addressee, the "you," is one who is "abhorred by the nations"—all of which leads to the inference with respect to both traditions that the addressee is the servant.

[46] In the MT, Isa. 52: 13–15 is entirely a third-person description of events transpiring around the servant, whereas in the LXX and 1QIsaᵃ the third-person description is blended with a direct second-person address to the servant (as in my translation). Accordingly, Tertullian, who relies on the Greek OT even though he writes in Latin, explicitly says that Isa. 52: 14 is spoken by the Father to the Son (*Marc.* 3. 17. 1). Unfortunately, Paul in Rom. 15: 21 cites only the latter bit of the third-person portion, Isa. 52: 15 (in support of the Gentile mission), so it is difficult to surmise whether

Early Christian readers saw God as announcing to the Servant-Son the culmination of his method and mission in Isa. 49: 7, 52: 13–15, and related servant texts. As the Servant-Son pursued the ordained plan of the Father to its self-negating end, living as true Israel—as a voluntary suffering servant to the nations—in order to bring glory to God the Father, the Servant would come to be despised, hated, and rejected. Yet, in the final analysis, the kings and rulers would find themselves paying homage to the glorified Servant-Son. But how would this reversal in the fortune of the Servant-Son come about?

Speech 8:

GOD (speaking to "you" [singular]—we are invited to infer that it is the same "you"—*THE SERVANT*—as in *Speech 3* and in *Speech 7*): Thus says Lord [God]: At a favorable time I heard you [singular] and on a day of salvation I helped you; I gave you to be a covenant for nations, in order to establish the land and to claim a share of the wilderness, saying to those who are in shackles, "Come out," and to those who are in darkness, "Be seen" .... Behold they are coming from afar, some from the north, some from the west, others from the land of the Persians. (Isa. 49: 8–12 LXX)

In *Speech 8* the mission of the Servant-Son is again clarified, and one might hypothesize that early Christian readers discovered herein that the Son would cry out to the Father for deliverance, the Father would hear, and the Son's plea would be answered by the Father—as it states, "on a day of salvation I helped you." The Father has made the Servant to be a covenant, effecting a season of remittance, return, and the release of captives through his blood (cf. Isa. 42: 6).

Although it is a quite speculative additional new proposal that I invite other scholars to consider, it is just possible that Paul deploys the theodramatic logic suggested above when he cites Isaiah 49: 8 in 2 Corinthians 6: 1–2:[47]

> Now as co-laborers [with God through Christ] we are exhorting you [plural] not to receive the grace of God in an empty manner. For [God] says, "At a favorable time I heard you [singular] and on a day of salvation I helped you" [Isa. 49: 8 LXX]. Behold, now is the favorable time! Behold, now is the day of salvation!

Paul's reasoning process, perhaps, works thus: Isaiah in the prosopon of God the Father spoke to his Servant-Son, Jesus Christ, from a post-resurrection

---

or not he prosopologically read the preceding verse, 52: 14, as a second-person address to the Servant-Son or rather took the whole as a third-person description, but the former is certainly more probable given the proximity of Paul's citations, generally considered, to the Septuagint.

[47] In fact, because I was not confident that Paul employed prosopological exegesis in 2 Cor. 6: 2, I did not treat this passage in Ch. 5 of my earlier book, *The Hermeneutics of the Apostolic Proclamation*. However, I am increasingly inclined toward this view. Hanson, *Jesus Christ in the Old Testament*, 147–52, argues extensively in favor of "prophetic dialogue" for Paul in 2 Cor. 6: 2, believing Paul applies this text "to us Christians, but to us as in Christ," seeing Christ as a corporate representative in a quasi-typological application here.

theodramatic setting, reflecting on the past moment of decisive rescue from death.[48] Thus Paul reads Isaiah 49: 8 in this fashion:

GOD (speaking to THE SERVANT-SON): At a favorable time, O my Son, you cried out to me for rescue and I heard you, and on a day of salvation—the day I rescued you from death—I helped you.

Then Paul makes his application: As co-laborers with God, Paul's mission team is speaking in precisely the same way that God spoke to the Servant-Son. That is, they are making an appeal to the Corinthians, directly described as "you" (plural) by Paul, and the Corinthians are those in need of exactly the sort of rescue-from-death that the "you" (singular), the Servant-Son, needed in Isaiah itself.[49] Making the substitutions, Paul accordingly applies the text:

"WE," PAUL AND HIS TEAM *in behalf of* GOD (speaking to "YOU," THE CORINTHIANS): At a favorable time, right now, God, on whose behalf we are speaking will hear you, O Corinthians, if you cry out for rescue—and on a day of salvation, right now, he will help you by supplying that much-needed rescue, just as he rescued his Servant-Son Jesus.

In support of this interpretation it should be noted that this makes excellent contextual sense within 2 Corinthians 5: 18–6: 2, as it is the substitutionary offering of the Son that makes human reconciliation to God possible, that is, if the reconciling offer is accepted. If indeed this is a convincing reconstruction of Paul's logic, it becomes more plausible that a similar hermeneutic might be operative for Isaiah 49: 6 in Acts 13: 47.[50]

Regardless of whether or not Paul has read Isaiah 49: 8 in the manner suggested, the language of Isaiah 49: 8–9 is noticeably similar to that of Isaiah 61: 1–2—the passage read by Jesus in the synagogue at Nazareth—inasmuch as both pertain to a favorable time of rescue by God in which prisoners are released. It is not surprising, then, to find that Isaiah 61: 1–2 was interpreted prosopologically as a speech by the Son in the earliest church by Ps-Barnabas (see *Barn.* 14. 9) and quite plausibly by Jesus himself

---

[48] Modest additional support for a prosopological reading of Isa. 49: 8 by Paul can be found in a *co-text* in Justin, *Dial.* 122. 5. Although Justin does not explicitly mark the Christ as the theodramatic addressee in Isa. 49: 8 ("I have given *you* to be *a covenant* for nations"), he implicitly does signal it through his subsequent questions to Trypho, saying, "Who is *the covenant* of God? Is it not *the Christ*?" Justin thereby shows that he has taken the "you" of Isa. 49: 8 as the Christ, while God (the Father) is the speaker, just as I have proposed for Paul. This is subsequently reaffirmed as Justin adds a prosopological interpretation of Ps. 2: 7–8 in further support of his reading of Isa. 49: 6.

[49] On the basis of the immediately prior context, Paul and his team most likely see themselves as co-laboring with God specifically through Christ: "Therefore we are ambassadors in behalf of Christ, *as if God were exhorting you through us.* We plead with you in behalf of Christ: 'Be reconciled to God'" (2 Cor. 5: 20).

[50] See the previous discussion in this section under "*Speech 6.*"

as portrayed in Luke 4: 18–19. And now our discussion of the dialogue between the Servant-Son and the Father that began with Isaiah 61: 1–2 in Luke 4: 18–19 has come full circle.

The Speeches in Isaiah 49: 1–12. In sum, the lengthy sequence of speeches in Isaiah 49: 1–12 was understood in the earliest church to consist of *a series of speeches and reported speeches in which the Father converses with the Servant-Son.* In this dialogue the Father shows his love for the Son and unveils his bold mission. God (the Father) will attain glory for himself through the self-abasing humiliation of the Servant-Son. The Servant-Son takes up this vocation willingly, as an obedient Son, but nearly despairs because the mission and its method seem too futile; yet at the same time the Son expresses trust, knowing that the Father alone can judge the fruit obtained. At this low point for the Son, the Father shows special personal concern for the Son, announcing to him that his mission will be wildly successful. Not only will he, as true Servant-Israel, fulfill the mission of disobedient Israel, he will also restore a portion of disobedient Israel along with the Gentiles. This will be accomplished, God announces to his Servant-Son, by the Servant-Son himself becoming the covenant, that is, the covenant will be in his blood. And that covenant will effect a favorable season of grace during which the oppressed captives, those bound by sin, will obtain release.

Concerning Himself or Somebody Else?—Acts 8: 26–40

I have been arguing throughout this book that even when the church was first budding forth, Christians used a solution-by-person reading technique that is in direct continuity with those later Fathers who definitively framed the doctrine of the Trinity—to such a degree that it is not inappropriate to speak of the exercise of this reading strategy by the earliest Christians as necessary for the birth of the Trinity. Often we, as contemporary readers of these ancient sources, can show only that it is probable that something akin to prosopological exegesis has been deployed. However, there are particularly instructive moments where the theodramatic rationale bubbles to the surface, and one possible New Testament example of this can be found in Philip's encounter with the Ethiopian eunuch in Acts 8: 26–40, who is reading from the scroll of the prophet Isaiah about an enigmatic suffering figure.

As described by the author of Acts, Philip is prompted by the Spirit to take the road from Jerusalem to Gaza. Upon hearing the eunuch read aloud from Isaiah as the eunuch journeys in his chariot, Philip is further prodded by the Spirit to run alongside. Then Philip listens as the eunuch reads the pregnant passage: "As a sheep led to its slaughter and as a lamb before a shearer is silent, in this manner he does not open his mouth; in his humiliation his justice was taken away. Who can describe his generation?—because his life is taken away from the earth" (Acts 8: 32–3 citing Isa. 53: 7–8 LXX). As the eunuch wrestles with the meaning of the passage, he asks Philip a singularly provocative question: "I beseech you, *concerning whom* is the prophet speaking, concerning himself or concerning someone else?" (*deomai sou, peri tinos ho prophētēs legei touto; peri heautou ē peri heterou tinos—*Acts 8: 34). To the contemporary reader unaware of ancient theodramatic reading strategies—and this includes all the recent biblical commentators on Acts that I surveyed[51]—the eunuch's question is understood as giving a choice between two separate and distinct referents, determining that for the eunuch the passage in Isaiah 53 refers either to Isaiah the prophet or to someone else. However, if this is the correct way to construe the eunuch's question, then one aspect of the question remains worrisome. What would possibly lead the eunuch to think that Isaiah might be speaking *about himself*, as the ultimate referent in this passage?—especially since it would be quite unusual for the prophet (although not entirely unprecedented), if truly speaking about himself to use the third person, as is done in Isaiah 53, rather than the first person. There is precious little in the book of Isaiah itself that might cause a reader, ancient or modern, to take Isaiah the prophet as the ultimate referent for Isaiah 53 (although a few moderns have, perhaps under the influence of the suggestion in Acts!) and C. K. Barrett states that there is no ancient precedent whatsoever for such a reading.[52]

Theodramatic Reading in Acts 8: 32–4. Yet if the contemporary reader is aware of ancient theodramatic reading strategies, then there is, I suggest, a more reasonable possibility.[53] Could it be that the eunuch (as portrayed) is not so much giving a choice between two separate and distinct referents, but is instead asking Philip if Isaiah is speaking from the horizon of the prophetic setting ("concerning himself") or if Isaiah is speaking about a future character that

---

[51] Among the commentators I surveyed, the remarks of Richard I. Pervo, *Acts: A Commentary* (Hermeneia; Minneapolis: Fortress, 2009), 226, come the closest to my proposed solution: "This [the Eunuch's query] is evidently an ancient way of raising the question of whether prophetic texts apply primarily to their own times or to later eras." But Pervo stops shy of suggesting the Eunuch's deployment of prosopological exegesis or the primacy of a theodramatic frame of reference.

[52] Perhaps the first-person speeches of the servant (e.g. Isa. 49: 5; 50: 4) could possibly have led an ancient reader to the conclusion that Isaiah was speaking purely about himself. Yet there is no evidence, at least according to Barrett, that any ancient reader did draw this conclusion, which considerably weakens this supposition—see C. K. Barrett, *A Critical and Exegetical Commentary on the Acts of the Apostles* (2 vols.; ICC; London: T&T Clark, 1994–98), i. 431.

[53] Marie-Josèphe Rondeau, *Les Commentaires patristiques du Psautier (3e–5e siècles)* (2 vols.; Orientalia Christiana Analecta 220; Rome: Institutum Studiorum Orientalium, 1982–5), ii. 21, suggests that the Eunuch is engaging in prosopological exegesis. However the suggestion I further develop in this paragraph remains my own—namely, that the Eunuch is first of all concerned to identify whether the setting is "ordinary prophetic" (concerning Isaiah) or "theodramatic" (concerning a prosopon speaking from an alternative setting in the divine drama), since this would also determine precisely who is intended by Isaiah as the speaker.

Isaiah has observed within the theodrama ("concerning someone else")? Thus construed, the eunuch is asking whether the prophet Isaiah is speaking about things seen from the vantage point of his own person in the more typical prophetic fashion or if the prophet Isaiah is *describing a theodramatic sequence* that Isaiah has seen played out by an alternative prosopon. Thus read, the eunuch's question pertains more to the setting of the words—ordinary prophetic versus theodramatic—than to the exact referent, because the setting is more primal and hence determines the referent.

Evidence from Reception History. Precisely these type of theodramatic interpretative concerns vis-à-vis the eunuch's question were noted by Athanasius, who remarks that we must show special concern for properly identifying the time (*kairon*), the subject matter (*pragma*), and the person (*prosōpon*) when interpreting, declaring that in this regard we must strive to be like the Ethiopian eunuch, "For," Athanasius states, the Eunuch was afraid that, "taking the reading in the wrong person (*para prosōpon*), he would err from the sound understanding."[54] Notice that Athanasius believes the eunuch was particularly concerned with theodramatic matters of first import—the time, subject matter, and especially the correct identification of the true speaking prosopon.

In weighing the intention of the eunuch's question, "concerning himself or concerning someone else?" in Acts, it should certainly be noted that it is possible that the author of the Gospel of John read Isaiah 53: 1 in John 12: 38 in a theodramatic fashion, and the warrant given by the fourth Evangelist is suggestive: "Isaiah said these things because he saw his glory and he spoke *concerning him* [*peri autou*]" (John 12: 41). Meanwhile, a contemporary of the author of Acts, Clement of Rome (*c.*96 CE), clearly reads Isaiah 53 in a theodramatic manner. He introduces the Isaiah 53 citation by saying, "the Lord Jesus Christ did not come with pretentious pomp or arrogance, though he could have, but humbly, just as the Holy Spirit had said in speaking *concerning him* [*peri autou*]" (16. 2). Any lingering doubt we might have that Clement intends a theodramatic reading of Isaiah 53 is quickly released when we observe that he follows it with an explicit prosopological construal of Psalm 21 LXX, prefaced with the words, "he [Jesus] himself says," and followed by the quotation, "I am a worm and not a man, a disgrace to humanity and an object of hatred to the people," showing the in-character nature of both readings. A number of second-century authors follow suit with similar interpretations of Isaiah 53.[55] In short, especially given the congruence of this interpretation with this evidence from

---

[54] Athanasius, *C. Ar.* 1. 54 as cited by Michael Slusser, "The Exegetical Roots of Trinitarian Theology," *TS* 49 (1988): 461–76, here 465.

[55] For direct comments on Philip, the Eunuch, and Isa. 53, see Irenaeus, *Haer.* 3. 12. 8; 4. 23. 2; on Isa. 53 more generally, see esp. Justin, *1 Apol.* 50. 2–11; *Dial.* 13. 2–9; Irenaeus, *Epid.* 69–70; Melito, *Pascha* 64.

reception history, I think this theodramatic proposal for Isaiah 53: 7–8 in Acts 8: 30–5 makes much better sense than the standard interpretation now current in biblical scholarship.

Theodrama and Scriptural Interpretation. Another question asked by the eunuch is also insightful. Philip had asked the eunuch, "Do you understand what you are reading?," to which the eunuch responds with a counter-question, "How can I understand," the eunuch replies, "unless someone *guides* me?" (Acts 8: 30–1). The counter-question asked by the eunuch also unveils the degree to which scriptural interpretation was bound up with the kerygma ("proclaimed gospel") in earliest Christianity. For the early church, not least for the author of Luke–Acts, it was felt that the ancient Jewish Scripture could not be fully comprehended apart from the guidance of the proclaimed word about Jesus as the Christ, but the kerygma itself was judged to contain the principles that could unlock the "mind" of not just the interpreter, but of the Scripture itself, since the Scripture manifests a divinely given inner unity, a "mind," a *dianoia* or *nous*.[56] Accordingly, Philip, beginning with this very passage from Isaiah expounds the good news about Jesus.

If indeed, as has been proposed, the eunuch's queries and Philip's response indicate that we should regard them as believing that Isaiah was reporting the observed theodramatic performance of the Servant-Son in Isaiah 53, then the mission of the Son was even more specifically understood as one of vicarious suffering in order to bear the sins of others (Isa. 53: 4–6, 12; cf. Matt. 8: 17; Luke 22: 37; 1 Pet. 2: 21–5). Although the Servant-Son's life would be taken away from the earth (Isa. 53: 8), as the eunuch has read, even in death God would vindicate the Son, so that he might once again see, be filled with understanding, and enjoy a rich inheritance (Isa. 53: 11–12).

* * *

For the earliest Christians, much is revealed about the interior personal dynamics of the One God as the Spirit speaks in the theodramatic character of the Father, who explains the divine plan to the Son, including his receipt of a body and his need for flint-like resolve in taking up the vocation of the suffering servant. Despite the overwhelming despair that the Son feels at the apparent futility of the mission, he casts his trust upon the Father. The Servant-Son is consoled by the Father as he discovers that he himself will

---

[56] On the "mind" of the Scripture in early Christianity, see Robert Grant, *The Letter and the Spirit* (New York: Macmillan, 1957), 125–6; Frances M. Young, *Biblical Exegesis and the Formation of Christian Culture* (Peabody, Mass.: Hendrickson, 2002), 29–45 esp. 34–6; Frances M. Young, "The 'Mind' of the Scripture: Theological Readings of the Bible in the Fathers," *International Journal of Systematic Theology* 7 (2005): 126–41. On the "mind" of the Scripture in Luke-Acts specifically, see Matthew W. Bates, "Closed-Minded Hermeneutics? A Proposed Alternative Translation for Luke 24:45," *JBL* (2010): 537–57 esp. 555–7.

bring back a remnant of faithless Israel as well as the Gentiles, and in so doing he will offer the body that the Father had gifted him back to the Father by becoming a covenantal sacrificial offering to the Father.

In this chapter we have focused on the way the early Christians read certain prophetic dialogues that were felt to unveil the large-scale plans of the Father and the Son. Even more intimate and emotionally charged words, however, were discovered to have been spoken between the Father and the Son through the Spirit as the dreadfully glorious center of the plan transpired—the crucifixion.

4

Cross-Shaped Conversations

As the earliest Christians pored over the ancient Jewish Scripture—the Christian Old Testament—and the divine dialogues contained therein, they learned much about the Son's begottenness before creation, his incarnation, and about the grand strategy by which the Servant-Son would fulfil the mission his Father had ordained. Yet the gruesome trial of the cross—the cruel, black melting-pot in which the Son would be tested and refined—released a new layer of conversational depth. The face of the triune God, who reveals himself as the God willing to suffer on our behalf, is revealed afresh through the passionate words of the divine persons who together bring the theodrama to its climax at the crucifixion.

THE STORM CLOUDS GATHER

As Jesus has increasingly come under public scrutiny, the rising tide of opposition has frequently lapped at his feet, but he has not yet been swept away by the foaming waters. Jesus, however, according to the Gospel writers, does not get sucked in by a dangerous rip tide against his will; on the contrary, he resolutely sets his face toward Jerusalem (Luke 9: 51), even though he has concluded that the cross awaits him there (Mark 8: 31; 9: 30–1; 10: 33–4; and parallels). He deliberately leaps from the shore, knowing full well that in light of his vocation as the suffering Servant-Son that it is only by allowing the water to enter his mouth and overwhelm his lungs—by drowning in the God-hatred—that he will finally be able to drain the sea of intense evil that is swirling around Israel and the nations.

They Hated Me Without Reason

The Pharisees and Herodians are depicted as plotting against Jesus' life practically from the beginning of his public ministry (Mark 3: 6; John 5: 18), and although the hostility relentlessly increases with time (Matt. 12: 14; Luke 18: 31–3; John 7: 19–25; 8: 37–40), a breaking point is not reached in the Synoptic Gospels until Jesus performs his confrontational yet cryptic actions in the temple (Mark 11: 15–29 and parallels). Meanwhile, in the Gospel of John it is the stir caused by his raising of Lazarus that finally brings the full weight of institutional violence against him (11: 53). We should not be surprised, then, to learn that the earliest Christians identified divine conversations between the Father and the Son in the Old Testament in connection with these surging waves of evil *even before* the ultimate passion of the cross. The general sentiment is captured by John's rendering of Jesus' person-centered reading of the Psalter as part of his farewell discourse after the Last Supper. John depicts Jesus as warning his disciples that they can expect to experience the same violent hatred that he is feeling, saying:

> Remember the saying which I spoke to you, "A servant is not greater than his lord." If they persecuted me, also they will persecute you.... Now they have seen and have hated both me and my Father. But this has happened in order to fulfill the saying that is written in their law, "*They hated me without reason [emisēsan me dōrean].*" (John 15: 20–5 citing Ps. 68: 5 LXX [cf. Ps. 34: 19 LXX])[1]

That is, long ago David theodramatically performed in the prosopon of the Christ a script that is just now being actualized in the passion week, "They hated *me* without reason." As a first piece of evidence that the Christ was consistently regarded as the speaker of Psalm 68 LXX in the earliest church, consider Matthew 27: 34 and parallels,[2] where Jesus is offered "wine mixed with gall," which corresponds to Psalm 68: 22 LXX, "and they gave [*me*] gall for *my* food and brought *me* sour wine for *my* thirst." Since the first-person speaker of Psalm 68 LXX calls the gall "*my* food" and identifies the sour wine as offered to slake "*my* thirst," the application of Psalm 68 LXX to Jesus as part of the crucifixion scene necessitates a reading of Psalm 68 LXX that identifies the Christ (now revealed as Jesus) as the true speaker of the psalm, even if this attribution is not made overt by the Evangelists and other early Christians.[3] Furthermore, in another citation of Psalm 68 LXX found in Romans 11: 9–10, even though Paul attributes the words to David, Paul also, arguably, identifies

---

[1] In light of another direct reference to Ps. 68 LXX in John 2: 17 (to be discussed in the next subsection) and the high frequency with which this particular psalm was cited in the earliest church, it is highly likely that Jesus' citation is drawn from Ps. 68: 5 LXX, although the exact same phrase can also be found in Ps. 34: 19 LXX.

[2] Cf. Matt. 27: 48; Mark 15: 23, 36; Luke 23: 36; John 19: 28–9; *Barn.* 7. 3; *Sib. Or.* 1. 367; 6. 25; 8. 303. On the gall/vinegar/sour-wine tradition in the early church more broadly, consider Irenaeus, *Haer.* 3. 19. 2; 4. 33. 12; 4. 35. 3; *Epid.* 82. For a fascinating poetic refraction of this tradition, see Melito of Sardis, *Pascha*, 79–80, 93.

[3] Origen, *Cels.* 2. 37, directly identifies Christ as the speaker. Tertullian is likewise explicit, saying, "the Spirit Himself of Christ was already singing, saying . . . 'They put into my drink gall, and in my thirst they slaked me with vinegar'" (*Adv. Jud.* 10. 4 [cf. 13. 10–11]; trans. ANF).

the enthroned Christ as the ultimate speaker of the psalm. In this interesting text, the Christ, speaking in parallel with the Father, calls down an imprecatory curse on his Jewish compatriots for their unbelief—an imprecation ultimately aimed at a temporary hardening to stimulate salvation—saying, "May their table be for a trap and for a snare and for a stumbling block and for a retribution unto them, may their eyes be darkened lest they see and may their backs continually be bent" (Rom. 11: 9–10).[4]

The words Jesus cites from Psalm 68: 5 LXX in John 15: 25, "They hated me without reason," should not be regarded as merely typological—as if Jesus is hereby portrayed as asserting that his life experiences followed a pattern established by David's sufferings.[5] On the contrary, there is virtually no evidence that the earliest church found special significance in David's specific moments of suffering so that they were regarded as paradigmatic, as is required for a so-called "typology." On the contrary, given the consistent construal of the words of Psalm 68 LXX as spoken from the person of the Christ in the earliest church,[6] it is far more likely that Jesus is being portrayed by the Evangelist as having undertaken a performative prosopological reading—and in so doing there is an affirmation that the Spirit spoke through David in the person of the Christ long ago in the theodrama, but that the theodrama has been actualized in the present by Jesus. As such, for the earliest Christians, the psalmist speaking in the character (*prosōpon*) of the Christ utters this lament and plea:

THE CHRIST (speaking to GOD): Save me, O God, because waters encroached as far as my soul. I was stuck in the slime of the deep, and there is no foothold; I came to the depths of the sea, and a windstorm capsized me. I toiled, crying out; my throat grew hoarse. My eyes failed from hoping in my God. *Those who hate me without reason* [cf. John 15: 25] multiplied more than the hairs of my head; my enemies, those who persecuted me unjustly, were strengthened. I had to repay that which I had not wrongfully acquired. O God, you knew my folly [*aphrosynēn*], and my mistakes [*plēmmeleiai*] were not hidden from you. Let not those who steadfastly hold to you be put to shame because of me, O Lord, Lord of hosts.   (Ps. 68: 2–7a LXX)

If the Christ is taken to be the theodramatic speaker of the psalm, then we find first of all that Jesus' words to his disciples in John 15: 25 are lucid—he is the

---

[4] For a full discussion, see Matthew W. Bates, *The Hermeneutics of the Apostolic Proclamation: The Center of Paul's Method of Scriptural Interpretation* (Waco, Tex.: Baylor University Press, 2012), 275–85.

[5] The typological explanation is favored by the vast majority of biblical commentators—e.g. Andreas J. Köstenberger, "John," in Greg K. Beale and D. A. Carson (eds.), *Commentary on the New Testament Use of the Old Testament* (Grand Rapids: Baker Academic, 2007), 415–512, here 495.

[6] Jesus Christ is taken to be the speaker of Ps. 68 LXX by a diverse array of ancient authors—see subsequent discussion.

first-person actor who has directly experienced the life-threatening crisis described in the psalm, albeit the event is recounted with poetic and metaphorical language. He has chosen the path of self-abnegation with all its apparent folly (*aphrosynē*), futility, and even mistakes (*plēmmeleiai*);[7] he has wearied himself while crying out to God, waiting for him to turn the wheel of history, to bring forth the kingdom in all its glory. In the meantime, enemies have multiplied until they outnumber the hairs of his head, and they are accusing him falsely. Jesus is desperately casting his hope on the Father while instructing his disciples, so that they will not "be put to shame" when Jesus' hour of darkness ineluctably arrives. As such, *the very moment* of Jesus' speech in John 15: 25 is a *realization of the theodrama*, a fusion of the prophetic window that gazes upon the actors in the divine drama with the actualization of that play in the real-time of space and of human history. Thus, when Jesus says, "They hated me without reason" (John 15: 25), it is a *performative utterance*, an incarnation of the already scripted theodrama, an immediate fulfillment of the ancient Scripture, much as when he reads the Isaiah scroll in Luke 4: 18–19.

Zeal for Your House Will Consume Me

Jesus' controversial temple action is full of mystery. His basic activity, however, is straightforward enough, although the precise depictions of it by the Evangelists contain some differences: Jesus entered the temple, overturned the tables of the moneychangers and those selling pigeons for sacrifice. The sharpest variance in portrayals is, famously, that the synoptic Evangelists report that this happened soon after Jesus had descended the Mount of Olives at the start of his final week of ministry, but the Gospel of John places it close to the beginning of Jesus' public career (2: 13–22). The synoptic writers have Jesus explain his actions by a citation from the Scripture, "*'My house shall be called a house of prayer for all the nations,'* but you have made it a den of bandits."[8] Although we do not want to preclude the possibility that Jesus, at

---

[7] However the "folly" (*aphrosynē*) and "mistakes" (*plēmmeleiai*), or more literally, the "moments of disharmony," of the speaker of Ps. 68 LXX were construed by the earliest church, they were not considered sinful actions that precluded identifying Jesus Christ as the speaker. It is probably best to assume they were regarded as statements of Christ's full humanity as he wrestled with the seeming futility of his mission, much as self-deprecating statements such as "I am a worm and not a man" (Ps. 21: 7 LXX) that were also assigned to the prosopon of the Christ—e.g. Justin, *Dial.* 101. 2–3. It is noteworthy, however, that in his otherwise rather full exposition of Ps. 21 LXX, Justin includes but does not really explain how it is that Jesus Christ could be the speaker of the difficult line in Ps. 21: 2 LXX, "the words of my transgressions are far away from my salvation" (*Dial.* 99. 1–2).

[8] Mark 11: 17; cf. Matt. 21: 13; Luke 19: 46. The citation is from Isa. 56: 7, while there is also an allusion to Jer. 7: 11.

least as he has been portrayed here, has deliberately conflated his identity with that of the Lord (God) in his interpretation of Isaiah 56: 7,[9] this is not a clear case of prosopological exegesis.

The citation in John, however, is a different matter. In John it is reported that Jesus' disciples, after seeing Jesus' striking table-overturning spectacle, remembered that the scripture states, "*Zeal for your house will devour me*" (2: 17 citing Ps. 68: 10 LXX).[10] I would suggest the psalm was being read by the author of John thus:

THE CHRIST (speaking to GOD): Zeal for *your* house, *O God my Father*, has devoured me, *your Son, the Christ.*

This, "Zeal for your house will devour me," is a modified citation from Psalm 68 LXX, the same psalm that was just discussed with regard to John 15: 25, and which was consistently given a prosopological interpretation in the earliest church. Origen's fascinating interpretation is apropos:

> However, we must know that Psalm 68, which contains the statement, "The zeal of your house has devoured me," and a little later, "They gave me gall for my food, and in my thirst gave me vinegar to drink," both having been recorded in the Gospels, is spoken from the *person of Christ* [*ek prosōpou legesthai tou Christou*], indicating *no change* in the *person of the speaker* [*oudemian emphainonta tou legontos prosōpou metabolēn*].[11]

Origen goes on to declare that his gnostic opponent Heracleon has made a faulty prosopological interpretation of Psalm 68: 10 LXX in John 2: 17. This shows that person-centered interpretations of the Old Testament were common in the early church among not only the orthodox but also the heterodox, a point that will be taken up more fully in the discussion in Chapter 7 of what makes for a viable prosopological reading.

Thus, for the disciples as portrayed by John, the Spirit had uttered these words through David in the person of the preexistent Christ, who is speaking here to the Father, "Zeal for *your* house, *O God my Father*, has devoured me, *your Son, the Christ.*" Yet, these pregnant words, along with the shift from the past tense in the Septuagint ("has devoured me") to the future tense in John ("will devour me") can only be fully appreciated against the larger backdrop of the significance of Jesus' temple exploit, holistically viewed.

---

[9] In the MT it is YHWH who speaks Isa. 56: 7 and accordingly the "Lord" who speaks in the LXX is manifestly the Lord (God), not any other.

[10] The LXX is in the past tense ("Because zeal for your house has consumed me") whereas John 2: 17 gives the future tense ("Zeal for your house will consume me"), on which see my subsequent remarks.

[11] Origen, *Comm. Jo.* 10. 222; Greek text in Blanc, SC 157; trans. Heine, FOTC (slightly modified).

The Meaning of Jesus' Temple Action. In Mark and Matthew, Jesus' action is closely aligned with Jesus' withering of a fig tree. Yet in Mark the temple act is sandwiched between the cursing and the withering (11: 11–21), whereas Matthew's cursing and withering of the fig tree follow the temple action and the withering is instantaneous (Matt. 21: 18–19). The fig tree is cursed and withered because it has no fruit, and the implication seems to be that the temple is likewise failing to "bear fruit" and is therefore destined to suffer the same withered fate—all of which is made quite explicit by Jesus when he announces the forthcoming destruction of the temple in the Olivet Discourse (Matt. 24; Mark 13; Luke 21). So, Jesus is at the very least enacting a parable of destruction with his radical temple actions.[12] One might surmise further, however, on the basis of Mark's use of Malachi (see Mark 1: 2 as discussed in Ch. 3) that Mark sees Jesus as the personal presence of God, who has "suddenly come to the temple," but has found the temple to be full of unrighteousness—hence, judgment is coming. Moreover, Mark adds several interesting details that the other Evangelists neglect, reporting that Jesus visited the temple on the previous evening, making this action premeditated (Mark 11: 11) and also that Jesus "would not allow anyone to carry anything through the temple" (Mark 11: 16).

Any reasonable account recognizes that Jesus' temple action is directed toward enhanced Gentile participation in the worship of God ("a house of prayer *for all the nations*"), quite plausibly because the merchants had set up operation in the court of the Gentiles within the temple precincts. Pushing further, however, N. T. Wright has seen this as evidence that Jesus did not merely want *to cleanse* the temple's economic and worship system, but rather that he was deliberately and provocatively attempting *to stop all sacrifice in the temple*—if only for several hours—in order to announce symbolically to anyone with "ears to hear" that the temple's sacrificial system should now be regarded as fulfilled, and hence, the sacrifices should permanently stop. That is, the animal sacrifices were now to be regarded as pointlessly redundant in light of the sacrificial offering he was about to make of his own body—indeed he and his followers should be regarded as the true temple.[13]

There is at least some evidence for such a view in the Gospels. In particular the Evangelists indicate that Jesus had come to see his own body as the true temple, the physical space in which the most high God—the God so

---

[12] Increasingly (and correctly in my judgment) scholarship has come to regard Jesus' temple actions as deeply symbolic, although the precise meaning of the symbolism remains a matter of dispute. For example, E. P. Sanders, *Jesus and Judaism* (London: SCM, 1985), 61–76, believes Jesus is enacting a parable of destruction. Meanwhile, Craig A. Evans, "Jesus' Action in the Temple: Cleansing or Portent of Destruction?," in Bruce Chilton and Craig A. Evans (eds.), *Jesus in Context: Temple, Purity, and Restoration* (AGJU 39; Leiden: Brill, 1997), 395–439, here 434, declares that the "cleansing idea is too firmly entrenched in the tradition to be so easily set aside."

[13] Wright, *Jesus and the Victory of God* (Minneapolis: Fortress, 1996), 413–28.

marvelously exalted that even the highest heavens cannot contain him (cf. 1 Kgs. 8: 27)—had chosen to dwell in a special way. Note the charges ultimately brought against Jesus: "We heard him say, 'I will destroy this handcrafted temple and in three days will build another, not handcrafted'" (Mark 14: 58), or "This man said, 'I am able to destroy the temple of God and build it in three days'" (Matt. 26: 61)—as well as the taunting words spoken by the crowds, "You who are going to destroy the temple and build it in three days, save yourself!" (Matt. 27: 40).

Jesus Houses the Glory. It is in this context—Jesus as the true temple—that we find this interesting person-centered interpretation in the Gospel of John. John alone adds three further details: (1) Jesus himself had made a whip for the very purpose of driving out the moneychangers (aligning with the premeditation we find in Mark), (2) Jesus also drove out oxen and sheep and poured out the coins of the moneychangers (which adds support to the idea that he was trying to disrupt all forms of animal sacrifice), and (3) Jesus had told those selling pigeons, "Take these away! You will not make my Father's house a marketplace!" (John 2: 16). Beyond this, however, John has already made the motif of divine indwelling central in his Gospel prologue by affirming that Jesus houses the divine *glory* (*doxa*) much like the *tabernacle* (*skēnē*), the precursor to the temple, had done in ancient Israel—"The Word became flesh and *tabernacled* (*eskēnōsen*) among us, and we have seen his *glory* (*doxan*)" (1: 14). Yet this theme is foregrounded all the more in the wake of the temple action, when Jesus tells his opponents, "Destroy this temple, and in three days I will raise it up."[14] Just in case we do not get the point, the Evangelist makes it crystalline: "He was speaking about *the temple of his body*" (John 2: 21). Here Jesus knows with certainty that his *own body* is the true house of the Father, the real locus of divine glory.[15]

The Consumed Body-House. The Evangelist has hereby invited us to consider: if Jesus feels such extraordinary zeal for his Father's soon-to-be-disregarded "house" (the Herodian temple), so much so that his zeal consumes him and he is driven to use a whip in its defense, then how much more the boundless zeal that he must feel for the true "house" of God, his own physical body? When, therefore, Jesus in John's Gospel *voluntarily* releases his body

---

[14] Jesus says here that he will raise himself, while the tradition is nearly uniform both in John and elsewhere that it is the Father who raises Jesus (John 2: 22; 21: 14; Acts 2: 24; 1 Cor. 6: 14). We frequently find in John an overlap in operations among the divine persons—what the later Fathers would call *perichōrēsis*, the mutual interpenetration and operation of the divine persons (cf. John 5: 21, 6: 39–40).

[15] Harold W. Attridge, "Giving Voice to Jesus: Use of the Psalms in the New Testament," in Harold W. Attridge and Margot E. Fassler (eds.), *Psalms in Community: Jewish and Christian Textual, Liturgical, and Artistic Traditions* (SBLSymS 25; Atlanta: SBL, 2003), 101–12, here 105, describes well the manner in which Jesus is portrayed as inhabiting the first-person speech of Ps. 68: 10 LXX, saying, "John's Jesus claims to become the temple, the place where God is present to his people. To realize that mission consumes his life."

back to the Father on the cross by giving up his spirit (John 19: 30; cf. Mark 15: 37), we are compelled by way of John's typically delicious irony to see that *zeal for God's "house"* quite literally has *consumed Jesus*, since his zeal has led him to cast his own body, the true house of God, into the insatiable, gaping maw of death for the sake of the Father. In this way, the disciples will find in the final moments of the passion in the Gospel of John that the original *past* tense statement ("Zeal for your house *has consumed* me"—Ps. 68: 10 LXX) that John reports in the *future* tense ("Zeal for your house *will consume* me") did indeed apply at the time of the temple action to Jesus' *future*, a future that has now arrived in the actualized theodrama, as his body has now been devoured by death and the tomb.

The disciples will also discover, however, that one cannot out-give the Father. The Son's gift of the "house," that is, the temple, his body, is accepted by the Father, but a renewed, even more glorified body is given back to the Son at the resurrection. Thus, it is only after Jesus was raised that his disciples would remember his words and would believe "the scripture *and* the word which Jesus had spoken" (John 2: 22). That is, they would find that Jesus had offered a theodramatic performative utterance as the first-person speaker of Psalm 68: 10 LXX, since Jesus' temple words and actions portended his *future* fate: "Zeal for your house *will* consume me" (John 2: 17).

CROSS-SHAPED CONVERSATIONS

For the earliest Christians, the closest and most pathos-filled exchanges between the Father and the Son as facilitated by the inspiring Spirit in the Old Testament pertain to the agony of the cross.

The Son as a Substitutionary Sacrifice for the Father

If the plaintive cry of the Christ ultimately speaks the words of Psalm 68: 10 LXX, "Zeal for your house will consume me," for the disciples in the Gospel of John, then the fitting counterpart is found in Paul's letter to the Romans, which contains the next part of the verse. This portion of the psalm, accordingly, was read by the earliest Christians as spoken by the Christ to God the Father:

THE CHRIST (speaking to GOD THE FATHER): Do not let those who wait for you be put to shame because of me O Lord, O Lord of hosts; do not let those who seek you become dishonored because of me O God of Israel; because for your sake I bore insult; dishonor covered my face; I became alienated from my brothers, a stranger to the sons of my mother; *because zeal for your house consumed me* [cf. John 2: 17] *and the insults of those who were insulting you fell on me* [cf. Rom. 15: 3].   (Ps. 68: 7–10 LXX)

That is, John begins with Psalm 68: 10a, "Zeal for your house will consume me" (2: 17) while Paul by a happy coincidence finishes with Psalm 68: 10b: "the insults of those who have insulted you have fallen on me" (Rom. 15: 3). Paul prefaces the citation with an affirmation, "*For even the Christ did not please himself,* but just as it is written, 'The insults of those who insulted you fell upon me,'" which fixes the Christ as the probable speaker.[16]

As always in prosopological exegesis of the Old Testament, the inspiring agent supplies the words to the ancient prophet—here, David—who then steps as an actor into the divine drama. As such, the prophet is chronologically unrestrained—he may speak about events far in the past, in the present, or in the distant future. Moreover, ancient Christian interpreters sometimes looked to the tense used in the speech as a clue to the setting for the speech.[17] From the perspective of the divine dialogue partners, the moment of the speech would be their present, but in their present, they could converse about events in their own past, present, or future, all of which would be reflected in the tenses used.

Thus, for instance, in this case for Paul, David is speaking in the person of the Christ from a setting in which the Christ is already enthroned at the right hand of the Father, and the Christ is speaking retrospectively to the Father about his experiences on the cross. Thus, although both the cross and the enthronement are future events with respect to David, for the role that David is playing here as the Christ in the theodrama, the enthronement of the Christ is the present event and the cross is in the past, so the words are appropriately in the past tense, and we might paraphrase the words the Christ speaks thus:

---

[16] Anthony T. Hanson, *Jesus Christ in the Old Testament* (London: SPCK, 1965), 154, also finds "prophetic dialogue" between the Son and the Father reflected in Rom. 15: 3–4, a proposal I accept while offering an alternative explanation for how it transpired. A few scholars argue that Christ is not the speaker at all for Paul, but rather that Paul is merely asserting that the Christ and the psalmist suffered analogously—e.g. Dietrich-Alex Koch, *Die Schrift als Zeuge des Evangeliums: Untersuchungen zur Verwendung und zum Verständnis der Schrift bei Paulus* (BHT 69; Tübingen: Mohr [Siebeck], 1986), 325; Scott J. Hafemann, "Eschatology and Ethics: The Future of Israel and the Nations in Romans 15:1–13," *TynBul* (2000): 161–92 esp. 164. Yet, if Paul did not take the Christ as the speaker, then his interpretation was idiosyncratic, and individualism is not as probable as exegetical consistency in the early church. Also, Paul's use of the titular form "the Christ" emphasizes office over personal identity, and the use of the titular form makes more sense for the prosopological rather than analogical explanation. The majority, correctly in my opinion, identify the Christ as the speaker, although the majority have not correctly identified the prosopological method that allowed this move for Paul, preferring a typological explanation—see Bates, *The Hermeneutics of the Apostolic Proclamation*, 240–55.

[17] E.g. Justin, *1 Apol.* 36. 1–3; *Dial.* 114. 2; Irenaeus, *Epid.* 67; Tertullian, *Marc.* 3. 5. 2; see my discussion of the *perfectum propheticum* in Bates, *The Hermeneutics of the Apostolic Proclamation*, 201–2.

THE CHRIST (to GOD THE FATHER): The insults of those who insulted *you*, O *God my Father*, they fell upon *me*, *your Son*, when *I* suffered on the cross.

Paul has quoted Psalm 68: 10 LXX in order to exhort his audience to imitate Jesus Christ in their dealings with one another. More specifically, these words are pointedly directed at "the strong" (the group less concerned with main-taining traditional Jewish customs) who have a tendency to despise "the weak" (those more concerned with maintaining such customs), encouraging the strong to be more concerned with edifying the weak than with pleasing their own selves. Yet, Paul's desire to guide the behavior of the weak and the strong with regard to matters of food and drink leads to a succulent feast of another sort for those interested in learning about the interior relationship between the Father, the Son, and the Spirit. The Spirit supplies the words by which the Son addresses the Father, so the Spirit's involvement is intimate although behind-the-scenes, with all three persons of the Trinity cooperating.[18]

We discover that for Paul, the Father was directly insulted by the taunting words and deeds of those, both Gentile and Jew, who gathered around Jesus at the crucifixion. The hatred spewed forth was ultimately aimed at God the Father, although it landed on the Son. We can suppose that Paul has in mind the mocking actions such as we find in the Gospels—spitting, the feigned homage, the crown of thorns, the bludgeoning of the head, the notice reading "King of the Jews," the purple robe—as well as the insulting words: "Hail! King of the Jews!," "Prophesy! Who hit you?," "He saved others but he cannot save himself!," "Let him come down now from the cross and we will believe in him." In Paul's person-centered reading of Psalm 68, he finds Jesus to be indicating to the Father that those malice-filled deeds and words were ultim-ately directed at the Father; yet Jesus as the willing Son stands as a *substitute* in the place of the Father (cf. "for *your sake* I bore insults"—Ps. 68: 8 LXX), voluntarily bearing the taunts. And the insults aimed at the Father did indeed come crashing down on Jesus, as his body was crushed by the overwhelming weight of the God-hatred vomited forth at the crucifixion.

We discover an important truth. For Paul, here Jesus suffered not so much because of his love for humanity, his love for us—although no doubt that was also felt to give some impetus[19]—but rather he suffered gladly primarily *in*

---

[18] On the Trinitarian dimensions of Paul's thought, see Francis Watson, "The Triune Divine Identity: Reflection on Pauline God Language, in Disagreement with J. D. G. Dunn," *JSNT* 80 (2000): 99–124. See also Michael J. Gorman, *Inhabiting the Cruciform God: Kenosis, Justification, and Theosis in Paul's Narrative Soteriology* (Grand Rapids: Eerdmans, 2009), 105–25. On the role of all three persons in Paul's vision of salvation, compare Ben C. Blackwell, *Christosis: Pauline Soteriology in Light of Deification in Irenaeus and Cyril of Alexandria* (WUNT 314; Tübingen: Mohr [Siebeck], 2011), 243–5.

[19] Characteristically, Paul speaks more of God's (i.e. the Father's) love for us (Rom. 1: 7; 2 Cor. 13: 11, 14; 1 Thess. 1: 4) or God's love for us expressed through Jesus (Rom. 5: 8; 8: 39; 2 Thess. 2: 16) than of Jesus' direct love for us—although see e.g. Rom. 8: 35; Gal. 2: 20.

order to spare his Father, to take the insults that would have otherwise landed upon the Father, and to shoulder them himself in place of his Father. Thus considered, Jesus the Son is not just a substitutionary sacrifice that atones sins for the sake of humanity (Rom. 3: 25), but a substitutionary sacrifice *for the sake of the Father*, a sacrifice that absorbs and deflects the vehement God-hatred of the world, so that God the Father is shielded from its malignant and poisonous force. Since John is undoubtedly speaking the truth when he presents Jesus as saying, "No one has greater love than this, to lay down his life for his friends" (15: 13), I do not believe that a more powerful statement of the Son's self-giving love *for the Father* can be found in the earliest church than the one unveiled in Paul's person-centered interpretation of Psalm 68: 10 LXX in Romans 15: 3.

I Stretched Out My Hands over You

Although Paul may stress the Son's selfless love for the Father more than the Son's care for humanity in his prosopological interpretation in Romans 15: 3, other early Christian readers of the Old Testament would find evidence of the Son's tender affection for callous humanity, as the Son never ceased to woo humanity even in his darkest moments of agony on the cross. On the basis of the surrounding context (see Isa. 65: 7), the Hebrew text and the principle Greek manuscript traditions identify *God (the Father)* as the speaker of these words from Isaiah:

> I became visible to those who were not seeking me; I was found by those who were not inquiring after me. I said, "Behold, [here] I am," to the nation that did not call my name. I stretched out my hands for the whole day toward a disobedient and disputatious people, those who were not walking on the true path but after their own sins.   (Isa. 65: 1–2 LXX)

Yet this did not prevent a significant number of early Christians, probably due to reliance on an extract or so-called *testimonia* source, from reading these words as *spoken by the Christ*, who was found to be speaking in the first instance to the Gentiles—those who had not been seeking a messiah—and in the second to the Jews—those who had been urgently seeking the messiah yet who, they felt, had by and large failed to call upon him when he had ultimately appeared.[20]

Accordingly, Ps-Barnabas takes the Christ as the speaker of Isaiah 65: 2, who is heralding forth from the cross to the Jews: "All day long I have stretched out my hands toward a disobedient and disputatious people who

---

[20] A brilliant and convincing treatment of the function and extent of *testimonia* in the early church is given by Martin C. Albl, *"And Scripture Cannot Be Broken": The Form and Function of the Early Christian* Testimonia *Collections* (SupNovT 96; Leiden: Brill, 1999), who locates Isa. 65: 2 as part of an extract collection focused on Jewish hardening (p. 243).

oppose my righteous way" (*Barn.* 12. 4). Meanwhile, Justin Martyr in *1 Apology* 49 makes a similar interpretation, arguing that Isaiah 65: 1–2 was spoken in character ("as from the *prosōpon* of Christ himself"), with one especially interesting change. For Justin the Christ said "all day long I have stretched out my hands" as he spread forth his hands *not* in a beckoning posture *towards* (*pros*) the Jewish people, as Barnabas and the rest of the mainline tradition of the Greek Scripture suggest, but rather the Christ uttered this in agony with wrists pierced, as his weary arms were willingly held wide-open *over* (*epi*) the people as he hung from the cross—"I stretched out my hands *over* a disobedient and disputatious people."[21] Likewise, another second-century Father, Irenaeus, identifies the Son of God as the speaker of Isaiah 65: 1–2 rather than God the Father (*Haer.* 3. 6. 1; cf. *Epid.* 79; 92), and several other early Christians might be added as well.[22] Yet, the tradition of reading Isaiah 65: 1–2 prosopologically as spoken from the person of the Christ, as strong as that tradition might be, was not totally uniform or consistent. For instance, our earliest source, the Apostle Paul in Romans 10: 20–1 does not read Isaiah 65: 1–2 as spoken from the character of the Christ, even though he does identify Isaiah 65: 1 as directed at the Gentiles but 65: 2 at the Jews, much as we see in these slightly later Christian readings.[23]

THEODRAMATIC INTERPRETATIONS OF PSALM 22

Of all the theodramatic interpretations of the ancient Jewish Scripture in the earliest church that we have thus far encountered, the reading of Psalm 21 LXX (= Ps. 22 in most English translations) as the words of the Christ takes a certain pride of place as the example par excellence due to its richness and pervasive influence, beginning with the words of Jesus as reported in the canonical Gospels. Yet, much confusion has been perpetuated (and continues to linger) by the multitudinous biblical and theological interpreters who believe that this psalm had primarily typological significance in the early church—as if the church believed that Jesus' experience was simply an imitative echo of the

---

[21] Justin, *1 Apol.* 49. 3; cf. *1 Apol.* 35. 3; 38. 1; *Dial.* 24. 3; 97. 2; 114. 2. On Justin's complex engagement with *testimonia* sources vis-à-vis Isa. 65: 1–2, see Oskar Skarsaune, *The Proof from Prophecy: A Study in Justin Martyr's Proof-Text Tradition: Text-Type, Provenance, Theological Profile* (SupNovT 56; Leiden: Brill, 1987), 65–7.

[22] See also Hippolytus, *Noet.* 12; Origen, *Comm. Jo.* 6. 196; *Comm. Rom.* 8. 6. 11.

[23] I have proposed elsewhere (Bates, *The Hermeneutics of the Apostolic Proclamation*, 269–75) that Paul's interpretation of Isa. 65: 1–2 in Rom. 10: 20–1 should be termed "trito-prosopon exegesis" since it is not strictly prosopological exegesis, but does pick up on very subtle third-person shifts in the source. This is an instance in which Hanson, *Jesus and the Old Testament*, 45–6, has overreached in positing Christ as the speaker for Paul.

suffering of David or of the generic psalmist. Contrary to the proposal of Richard Hays, among others, the earliest church did not read this psalm as if it was really about David at the first level, but secondarily about Jesus at a second deeper level as he fulfilled the Davidic pattern of suffering while serving as a symbol of corporate Israel.[24] There is little evidence that the earliest Christians had much (if any) interest in this first level, and that is the principle mistake in how the significance of Psalm 21 LXX and other psalms featuring a righteous sufferer has been assessed for the earliest Christians by scholarship. On the contrary, the earliest church did not believe that this psalm was really about David's (or corporate Israel's) suffering because they believed that David's significance here was his prophetic capacity—that he was a willing and able prophet who had taken on a character, and thus he had spoken in the prosopon of the future Christ—that is, the future Christ for David, but the already-having-arrived Christ for the earliest Christians.

The quantity of material illustrating how this particular psalm, Psalm 21 LXX, was read *with the Christ as the speaker* in the earliest church is so overwhelmingly vast—Justin Martyr alone devotes ten chapters of his *Dialogue with Trypho* (chs. 97–106) to its interpretation—that only a few of the highlights can be given. The remainder of this chapter will be concerned with the words of anguish in Psalm 22, while the next chapter will begin by tracing the movement to praise in this same psalm.

My God, Why Have You Forsaken Me?

The heart-rending words with which Psalm 21 LXX begins—"My God, my God, why have you forsaken me?"—have attracted boundless theological attention. Since Jesus reportedly gave voice to these words while suspended from the cross (Mark 15: 34; Matt. 27: 46), at the storm-center of theological interest is the idea that the Father could have temporarily forsaken or abandoned the Son, and all the theological possibilities, problems, and implications that this terrifying God-abandonment might entail. For theologians, if the Father did forsake the Son—and the Greek verb in question, *enkataleipō* (Hebrew = *āzab*; Aramaic = *šābaq*), means to leave behind, abandon, and desert, and thus it implies active and intentional movement away from—then why did the Father abandon the Son at his moment of greatest need? Was it a final, ultimate test of the Son's resolve? A gnawingly excruciating but necessary self-emptying for the Son? Could it be that the holy and pure Father—and this

---

[24] See Richard B. Hays, "Christ Prays the Psalms: Israel's Psalter as Matrix of Early Christology," *The Conversion of the Imagination* (Grand Rapids: Eerdmans, 2005), 101–18. For a fuller discussion of typology and Hays's model, see Bates, *The Hermeneutics of the Apostolic Proclamation*, 133–48, 249–51, and 340–1.

seems to be the most pervasive understanding among both professional theologians and Christians in the pew today—could not bear to gaze upon the Son as he carried the ugly sin of the world on his shoulders? And what are the implications of all of this for divine suffering and impassability, not just for the Son, but for the Father and the Spirit as well?

In What Sense Was Jesus Forsaken? This moment of "godforsakenness" looms especially large for Jürgen Moltmann in his *The Crucified God*, who reads this as a genuine, radical separation between the Father and the Son in which God, therefore, forsakes his very self.[25] For Moltmann this separation, however, is what above all allows for intersubjective relationship between the divine persons, in which God the Father can suffer pain along with the Son, and hence, along with all of creation, since the incarnate Son is a real participant in creation. As such, for Moltmann, God is neither impassible nor immutable, but rather God the Father suffers along with his suffering creation, and this changes God. It is the cross that allows all the painful, sordid, and sad history of humanity to enter into God's own self-life, so it becomes part of God's ongoing history.

Yet, all these theological musings assume—rather than demonstrate as probable—that the Father really did (ontologically) leave the Son, but other solutions must be considered. Richard Bauckham sagely observes that much of the theological literature devoted to this psalm has lacked an adequate exegetical grounding,[26] and I would add that scholarly interfacing with the reception of this psalm in first- and second-century Christianity has also been too slight. Much of the interpretive hand-wringing stems, in my opinion, from a failure to distinguish clearly between different types of abandonment. Among other meanings, the forsakenness could potentially involve: (1) *abandonment unto death* (God's failure to rescue Jesus to prevent his death); (2) *temporary real abandonment when dying* (God truly absent to Jesus during the death-process); (3) *perceived abandonment when dying* (Jesus genuinely believing in God's absence despite God's real presence); (4) *despairingly felt and expressed but not truly perceived abandonment when dying* (Jesus cries out at his feelings of abandonment but does not truly believe that God has forsaken him); and (5) *abandonment in death* (God's failure to rescue Jesus once he has died).

Some of the options are not really reasonable suppositions for the Evangelists' intentions. For instance, any notion of God's abandonment of Jesus in death (option 5) is subsequently disproven on the narrative level within the Gospels by the empty tomb and resurrection appearances. In fact, like option

---

[25] Jürgen Moltmann, *The Crucified God: The Cross of Christ as the Foundation and Criticism of Christian Theology* (trans. R. A. Wilson and John Bowden; New York: Harper & Row, 1974), 145–53.

[26] Richard Bauckham, *Jesus and the God of Israel: God Crucified and Other Studies on the New Testament's Christology of Divine Identity* (Milton Keynes: Paternoster, 2008), 254.

5, on a literary level option 3 is quite implausible as Jesus' intended meaning because the Evangelists consistently and repeatedly portray Jesus as having foreknowledge of rescue after death,[27] so it is not cogent to suggest that the Evangelists expect us to read the cry without any awareness of Jesus' confident expectation of rescue. Moreover, John describes Jesus as firmly anticipating that his disciples will abandon him at the crucifixion, but nonetheless Jesus reports that he will not be alone, "because the Father is with me" (John 16: 32), all of which directly contradicts option 2, Moltmann's assumed solution, the notion that the earliest Christians believed that the Father had really forsaken the Son.

The options can also be combined. For instance, I contend that the Son truly had been abandoned *unto* death by the Father (option 1), and he expressed feelings of despair at abandonment unto death accordingly even though he knew that *the Father had not really* (ontologically) *left him* when he was dying (option 4).

Divine Abandonment and Theodramatic Performance. Perhaps there is a more precise way of speaking about all of this in continuity with the earliest church's prosopological reading of this psalm. Might it be that Jesus was above all *consciously stepping into* what we have termed *a theodramatic vision*, uttering the first lines of a well-known, perhaps even a long-rehearsed script? And could it be that Jesus knew that the divine playwright, the Spirit who had supplied the words in advance to David (cf. Justin, *Dial.* 34. 1), had authored not a tragedy but a comedy because he knew that the script of the entire psalm itself called for *a sequence of despair and trust followed by rescue and praise*? Accordingly, Jesus knew that although the Father had really abandoned him unto death, he also recognized that he had not really left him, and he trusted in the midst of his suffering, expecting rescue after the grave, rescue which he anticipated would culminate in praise.[28]

Hence, for the earliest church and very plausibly for Jesus himself, the forsakenness is not about the inability of the holy Father to gaze upon the sin-laden Jesus (a theme totally alien to the text itself) or about a cataclysmic gulf opening up between the Father and the Son that thereby permits inter-subjective relationality—contra Moltmann. Rather, this is about inhabiting a script, about theodramatic performative utterance, as the Son actualizes the words the Spirit had given David in ages past, as he spoke from the prosopon (character) of the Christ as the Christ addresses the Father.

---

[27] Matt. 16: 21; 17: 23; 20: 19; Mark 8: 31; Luke 9: 22; 13: 32; 17: 24–5; 18: 33; John 2: 19.

[28] Bauckham, *Jesus*, 255, points out that there are a large number of allusions to Ps. 22 found in the passion story *prior to* Jesus' justly famous words, "My God, my God, why have you forsaken me?," and he correctly notes that these anticipatory allusions compel the sensitive reader to see the synoptic Jesus as invoking the whole narrative sequence of the psalm rather than just its opening line. In Ch. 5 I will provide evidence that the earliest church did show awareness of the narrative progression of the psalm toward ultimate rescue.

That Jesus as portrayed is not just mechanically reciting the words, but has deeply internalized them personally, is indicated by his use of Aramaic rather than Hebrew, inasmuch as the former probably represents his own natural idiom but the latter would be expected if he were publicly reading. As such, as the Evangelists describe it, the Son truly is *abandoned unto death*, and cries out "Why?" in the face of the felt futility, but even while hurling forth these words of despair in his moment of deepest darkness, he knows the playwright—the Spirit—and he is aware of the conclusion to the script.

The Mocked Worm

In support of the proposed theodramatic reading of Psalm 21 LXX in the earliest church, including plausibly the historical Jesus' own reading of this psalm, we must consider above all that there are a large number of instances, as it is the burden of this book to show, where the Gospel writers—and indeed Jesus himself as depicted by the Evangelists—undertake solution-by-person as a reading strategy, making this reasonable here as well.

As the psalm unfolds, the speaker of the psalm states, "All who saw me mocked at me; they talked with their lips; they wagged their heads: 'He hoped in the Lord! Let him rescue him! Let him save him, since he wants him!'" (21: 8–9 LXX). Thus, two of the Gospel writers, Matthew and Luke, report that after Jesus began performing the script by uttering the first words of the psalm, "My God, my God, why have you forsaken me?," the expected cohort of additional cast members, the villains, appeared on the world stage at the appropriate time to play their part by actualizing the theodramatic script, echoing the actions and language of the psalm.[29] As Luke states, "And the people stood by, watching; but the leaders sneered at him, saying, 'He saved others; let him save himself if he is the Christ of God, the chosen one!'" (23: 35). Matthew is similar, recording that they said: "He trusts in God; let God rescue him now, if he wants him!" (27: 43).

I would argue that what is implicit in the reading of Psalm 21: 8–9 LXX by Matthew and Luke, the prosopological technique, is made explicit by their

---

[29] On matters of historicity versus expansive theological composition in the early church with respect to Ps. 22 and the Passion Narrative, see Raymond E. Brown, *The Death of the Messiah: A Commentary on the Passion Narratives in the Four Gospels* (2 vols.; ABRL; New York: Doubleday, 1994), ii. 953–8; ii. 988–9; ii. 994–6; ii. 1072–4; esp. ii. 1083–8 on the cry of dereliction. Generally speaking, Brown acknowledges that the similar details found in both the Passion Narrative and Ps. 22 are historically plausible for a generic trial culminating in crucifixion from this time period, while also recognizing that a process of creative reflection on the theological significance of Jesus' passion in light of Ps. 22 itself in the early church may have super-enhanced the correspondences in the Gospel depictions. On the question of the historical Jesus, literary depiction, and method, see my remarks in Ch. 2.

contemporary, Clement of Rome, who was convinced that the Holy Spirit had allowed the prophet David to speak these words from the person of the Christ, indicating such by the introductory words, "And again he himself [the Christ] says".[30]

THE CHRIST (speaking to GOD THE FATHER):   I am a worm and not a man, a disgrace to humans and despised by people. All those who saw me sneered at me, they talked with their lips, they wagged their heads: "He hoped in the Lord! Let him rescue him! Let him save him, since he wants him." (*1 Clem.* 16. 15–16 citing Ps. 21: 7–9 LXX)

Not only does Clement report that the Christ spoke the words of the psalm, we also find *reported speech*, as the Christ, who is clearly deemed to be speaking sometime *after* the moment of mockery, tells God the Father about the taunting words that certain others had spoken to him earlier: "He hoped in the Lord, let him deliver him; let him save him since he desires him"—the basic script that Matthew and Luke found to have already been performed by the mocking crowds. Justin Martyr's reading is much like Clement's, emphasizing that these words were spoken via "the prophetic Spirit" (*to prophētikon pneuma*) and "from the person of the Christ" (*apo prosōpou tou Christou*—*1 Apol.* 38. 1), as the Christ reports through an in-character speech the words of his tormentors (*1 Apol.* 38. 6). Thus, we are invited to see that the theodramatic performance that the incarnate Christ has initiated with his words, "My God, my God, why have you forsaken me?," has been confirmed as a true *performative utterance* by the Evangelists, as other actors have joined the stage, bringing the script to life as they fill it with a tauntingly cruel God-hatred.

An Enacted Mystical Parable

Justin Martyr is typical of the earliest church as a whole in that he reads the entirety of Psalm 21 LXX as not merely *about* the Christ (*Dial.* 97. 4; 99. 1),[31] but also as *spoken from his character*, as he is understood to be the first-person speaker (*Dial.* 98. 1). As Justin himself puts it, "the whole psalm . . . was spoken *about* Christ" (*Holon oun ton psalmon . . . eis ton Christon eirēmenon*), yet the

---

[30] That Clement intends the Lord Christ via the Spirit as the speaker of this text is made evident in the surrounding context. The nearest referent is the first-person speaker of Isa. 53, the servant, identified as Jesus Christ (via the Holy Spirit, see *1 Clem.* 16. 2). Also the words that follow the citation of this psalm give an exhortation to imitate the Lord Christ's humility (16. 17), obviously implying that the Christ has been construed as the speaker.

[31] On Justin's reading of Ps. 22 (21 LXX), see above all Judith M. Lieu, "Justin Martyr and the Transformation of Psalm 22," in Charlotte Hempel and Judith M. Lieu (eds.), *Biblical Traditions in Transmission: Essays in Honour of Michael A. Knibb* (Leiden: Brill, 2006), 195–211.

words, "O God, my God, attend to me, why have you forsaken me?," do not simply refer to Christ but are spoken *by him* as a script to be performed, because, "This spoke in advance *what was to be spoken by Christ*" (*touto anōthen proeipen hoper hypo Christou emelle legesthai*), for when he was crucified he said, 'O God, O God, why have you forsaken me?'" (*Dial.* 99. 1).

Indeed, the whole psalm was felt by Justin to be a screenplay designed for later performance, not just the first line alone, because Justin says that the next lines of the psalm describe "the very things Jesus would do in the future" (*auta hōsper ha poiein emelle*). For Justin, for example, the next portion of the psalm reads: "The words of my salvation are far distant from my transgressions; my God, *I shall cry out to you* by day and you will not listen, by night, and it is *not for lack of understanding in me*." Justin interprets, pointing out that Jesus went to the Mount of Olives to pray with his disciples, *crying out to God*, even though Jesus *did not lack understanding*, that is he had definite knowledge that God's will for him was to drink the cup down to its dregs and to walk the road of the cross, which is why Jesus ultimately said, "Not as I desire, but as you will" (*Dial.* 99. 2). Justin continues to explain the entire psalm in this fashion, presuming that the psalm is not just about Christ, but was spoken from the person of the Christ to function for the people of God as "a teaching and advance announcement" (*didaskalia kai proangelia*—*Dial.* 105. 1).

In fact, more specifically, Justin says that here David speaks "about the passion and the cross in *a mystical parable*" (*en parabolē mystēriōdei*—*Dial.* 97. 3), by which Justin does not mean a parable as a homey analogy—for instance, comparing the final judgment to a harvest—such as we find on the lips of Jesus in the Gospels; rather, as Willis Shotwell, who surveys all of the occurrences of *parabolē* ("parable") in Justin's corpus, puts it: for Justin a parable "is something hidden in the Scripture that can be brought to light by proper interpretation."[32] That is to say, for Justin a parable is a divinely implanted scriptural riddle that can be unraveled only by thoughtful exegesis. As such, Justin understands David to have spoken these words in the character of the Christ, yet Jesus as the come-in-the-flesh Christ enacts the already scripted divine drama on the world-stage.

---

[32] Willis A. Shotwell, *The Biblical Exegesis of Justin Martyr* (London: SPCK, 1965), 17. On *parabolē* in Justin's corpus see, e.g. Justin, *Dial.* 36. 2; 52. 1; 77. 4; 78. 10; 90. 2; 97. 3; 113. 6; 114. 2; 115. 1; 123. 8. Likewise, Robert Grant, *The Letter and the Spirit* (New York: Macmillan, 1957), 134, describes *parabolē* as "equivalent to prefiguration" for Justin and others, by which he means that a *parabolē* is a pattern or sequence from the past that finds a reenacting fulfillment in the future (cf. Heb. 9: 9; 11: 19; *Barn.* 6. 10; 17. 2; Melito, *Pascha* 35; 40–2). As such, Justin understands David to have spoken these words in the person of the Christ, yet Jesus of Nazareth as the Christ-come-in-the-flesh performs the words.

A Script Inhabited—Other Cruciform Details

There are a host of additional details in Psalm 21 LXX which are either conducive to a prosopological reading or are overtly announced as spoken from the person of the Christ in the earliest church, in which the words of the psalm are not merely *about* things that would happen to the future Christ, but are a script spoken and performed by the Christ and others.

For instance, in a first-person speech, the psalmist reports, "they divided my clothes among themselves, and for my garment they cast lots" (Ps. 21: 19 LXX). This detail is enacted in the crucifixion scene as reported by all three synoptic Evangelists (Mark 15: 24; Matt. 27: 35; Luke 23: 34), while it is both enacted and said to be a fulfillment of this very scripture in John 19: 24.[33] That the Christ was the true speaker of these words about casting lots and dividing garments is further acknowledged by Justin Martyr,[34] along with numerous other details that connect with the passion narratives in the Gospels, since Justin interprets the whole psalm as spoken from the character of the Christ— e.g. "they pierced my hands and my feet" or "my tongue is stuck fast in my throat."[35]

Other Fathers, such as Irenaeus, Ps-Barnabas, and Tertullian apply the words of Psalm 21 LXX to the crucifixion. For example, Irenaeus self-evidently construes some of the same phrases from the psalm that appear in Justin (and others) as spoken by Christ, even if he has not made the prosopological designation overt.[36] For instance, he repeats the words about piercing and being surrounded by evildoers that we have already discussed, while also

---

[33] Among the fourfold Gospels, John 19: 23–4 alone stresses the different fate of the majority of the garments (*ta himatia*), which were divided and shared by the soldiers, in contrast with the singular seamless garment (*chitōn araphos*) over which lots were cast (although cf. Irenaeus, *Epid.* 80). In reflecting on Jesus' passion, John has clearly noticed the shift between the plural and the singular in describing the clothing in the psalm itself, "they divided my garments [plural—*ta himatia mou*] among themselves, and for my garment [singular—*ton himatismon mou*] they cast lots" (Ps. 21: 19 LXX).

[34] For casting lots, see Justin, *1 Apol.* 35. 5; 35. 8; 38. 4; *Dial.* 97. 3; 104. 1–2.

[35] On the piercing, see Justin, *1 Apol.* 35. 5; 35. 7; 38. 4; *Dial.* 104. 1 citing Ps. 21: 17 LXX (cf. John 19: 37 citing Zech. 12: 10). For the tongue stuck fast, see Justin, *Dial.* 102. 5 citing Ps. 21: 16 LXX (cf. John 19: 28). Writing in the Syriac tradition, the author of the extant *Odes of Solomon* (*c.*125 CE) also takes the Christ as the speaker of Ps. 22 through numerous allusions placed on the lips of the Christ (trans. Charlesworth): "And they surrounded me like mad dogs" (28. 14 on Ps. 22: 16), "in vain did they cast lots against me" (28. 18 on Ps. 22: 18), "they divided my spoil though nothing was owed to them" (31. 9 on Ps. 22: 18). Indeed the numerous first-person speeches of the Christ in *Odes* are fertile grounds for further exploration of prosopological exegesis in the early church.

[36] That prosopological exegesis can be intended although not made explicit can be proven by comparing instances where an ancient author carries out the same exegesis of a text in different locations in his corpus, while in one case marking the exegesis as prosopological and in the other case not marking it but presuming the reader can infer the prosopological technique. For example, compare Justin, *Dial.* 42. 2 (marked) with *1 Apol.* 50. 5 (unmarked); Irenaeus, *Epid.* 49 (marked) with 85 (unmarked).

pointing out the suitability of the words, "My heart is become like wax, melting in the midst of my bowels; and they have scattered my bones," as well as "They looked upon me, they parted my garment<s> among them, and for my tunic they cast lots."[37] Meanwhile Ps-Barnabas seizes upon lines from the psalm such as "rescue my soul from the sword" and "an assembly of evildoers have risen up against me," evidently taking them as spoken theo-dramatically from the character of the Christ, even though the prosopological identification is not explicit.[38] Tertullian forthrightly affirms that Christ has spoken about himself in this psalm (e.g. *Marc.* 3. 7. 2; 3. 19. 5).

THE CRY OF DERELICTION AND TRIUNE RELATIONAL HONESTY

In considering the cry of dereliction, "My God, my God, why have you forsaken me?," the earliest Christians did understand that Jesus was aban-doned unto death (allowed to die), but they did not view this "forsakenness" as a genuine separation of Jesus and the Father—that is an improbable scholarly construct with no substantive root in the earliest writings. Rather they dis-covered that Jesus had inhabited a foreordained theodramatic script authored by the Spirit. For the nascent church, the psalmist was speaking in the person of the future Christ, and when Jesus as the true Christ arrived on the scene, he was prepared and willing to incarnate this theodramatic vision. Indeed, as the Son gave voice to the scripted words, those words captured his true emotions perfectly, as the fully human Son was in the process of being abandoned unto death and perhaps even felt himself really (ontologically) forsaken by the Father, even though the Son had confidence that the reality was otherwise, that the Father would, as we shall see in the next chapter, ultimately rescue and vindicate him on the other side of his suffering.

Moving beyond the bounds of historical theology to the constructive theo-logical task, Jesus' words, "My God, my God, why have you forsaken me?," can teach us something significant about the raw, edgy, surprisingly candid intim-acy of expression that is permitted between the divine persons within the Godhead—even if within a constructive or systematic approach, when moving from a consideration of the economic Trinity to the immanent, this "conver-sation" must be treated as an imprecise anthropomorphic (but nonetheless God-given!) metaphor for a higher reality.[39] God the Son's plaintive and

---

[37] Respectively, Irenaeus, *Epid.* 79 citing Ps. 21: 15 LXX and *Epid.* 80 citing Ps. 21: 18–19 LXX.

[38] *Barn.* 5. 13 citing LXX Ps. 21: 21 and 21: 17; cf. *Barn.* 6. 6.

[39] For example, the problem of how to handle anthropomorphic metaphorical language when speaking about God [e.g. *Trin.* 2. 4 (§§17–18)]—and it is indeed a complex issue—undoubtedly

heart-rending speech to the Father is flagrantly honest—it is not accusatory—but it is nonetheless truly anguished, pained, and needful. In describing the relationships among the persons of the Trinity, it is not enough for the church merely to speak of the begotten Son and the sent-forth Spirit. This text reminds us that our constructive descriptions of the interpersonal dynamic between Father, Son, and Spirit must also find a way to foreground such words of gritty relational transparency if they are to take seriously the witness of the dialogue between divine persons as attested in the earliest Christian literature.

helped push Augustine toward his famous psychological analogy for the Trinity. That is, the Trinity is akin to memory, intellect, and the will (see esp. *Trin.* bks. 9–11). For Augustine, creaturely analogies do not capture fully the mystery of the Trinity, which has no perfect earthly analogy, but they do provide the sites and signs through which we can progressively ascend unto a true vision of the mystery—see Khaled Anatolios, *Retrieving Nicaea: The Development and Meaning of Trinitarian Doctrine* (Grand Rapids: Baker Academic, 2011), 241–80.

5

Praise for Rescue

An exploration of the manner in which various Old Testament passages were interpreted as divine conversations in the earliest church is theologically instruct-ive on a number of levels. These divine dialogues are like shafts of heavenly light shooting through the cloudy sky of our earthly sojourn, giving us brief glimpses of how the first generations of Christians understood the interior relationship between the persons that would later be identified as the Trinity. Moreover, as the previous chapters have sought to demonstrate, these conversations stretch chronologically across the canvas of the divine life-together, beginning before time began. In the preceding chapter, we overheard divine speech pertaining to opposition and anguish, cross-filled words—including the words of the Son to the Father as the Son honestly reflected on his abandonment unto death, performing the script of Psalm 21 LXX, which the earliest Christians determined had been authored in advance by the Spirit specifically for him, especially the heart-rending words: "My God, my God, why have you forsaken me?"

Yet abandonment and suffering are certainly not the final words between the Father and the Son in the Scripture, nor even in Psalm 21 LXX. Thus, as the early church read this psalm prosopologically, identifying the Spirit as inspiring David to speak in the character of Christ the Son to God the Father, they detected an inexorable movement toward trust and praise. In fact, they dis-covered in their Scripture, not just in this psalm, but in a number of other places as well, moments where the Son expresses trust in the Father in the midst of crisis (even unto death), while the Son also praises the Father after deliverance.

THE SON SPEAKS TRUST AND PRAISE
TO THE FATHER

I Will Proclaim Your Name

Although Psalm 21 LXX contains words of despair that express a feeling of divine abandonment, the psalmist does remember that his forefathers were rescued when they placed their hope in God and cried out for deliverance (21: 4–6). Additionally, he expresses a personal history of hope in God (21: 10–11), and has confidence in God's ability to rescue (21: 12, 20–2), even though his crisis is as deep as death itself (21: 16). Theodramatically attuned readers in the earliest church noticed that there is a movement from trust in the midst of anguish to anticipated praise in light of achieved rescue in the psalm—this transition actually occurs quite suddenly yet subtly in an unmarked gap in the narrative sequence of the psalm, between verses 22 and 23. Note the clear shift in tone in the psalm as manifested by the speaker:

Psalm 21: 22 LXX (trust while in despair): Save me from the mouth of the lion, and [preserve] my humble station from the horns of one-horned beasts!
[unmarked gap: Rescue is achieved!]
Psalm 21: 23–5 LXX (anticipated praise followed by actual praise): I will tell your name to my brothers; I will sing your praise in the midst of the assembly. You who fear the Lord, praise him! . . . he did not turn his face away from me, and when I cried to him, he heard me.[1]

After the rescue has been accomplished, the psalmist speaks words of praise for God in ever-expanding circles, from family, to the local assembly, to the Jewish people, to the ends of the earth.

The earliest church was by no means unaware of the narrative progression of the psalm, and they were able to fill in the gap by asserting a very specific sort of rescue, resurrection from the dead.[2] Just as they had construed the words of despair as belonging to Jesus via prosopological exegesis, so they also attributed the subsequent words of trust and praise to Jesus. As evidence for how the earliest church read Psalm 21 LXX as containing the words of the Son expressing trust and praise to the Father, consider the following bold

---

[1] Here, assuming the theodramatic solution, the Son says, the Father "did not turn his face away from me" (Ps. 21: 25 LXX), which is precisely the opposite of what is concluded by those who find that the Father could not bear to look upon the sin-laden Son—see "Theodramatic Interpretations of Psalm 22" in Ch. 4.

[2] On the awareness of narrative progression by the Gospel writers, see Richard Bauckham, *Jesus and the God of Israel: God Crucified and Other Studies on the New Testament's Christology of Divine Identity* (Milton Keynes: Paternoster, 2008), 255; Harold W. Attridge, "Giving Voice to Jesus: Use of the Psalms in the New Testament," in Harold W. Attridge and Margot E. Fassler (eds.), *Psalms in Community: Jewish and Christian Textual, Liturgical, and Artistic Traditions* (SBLSymS 25; Atlanta: SBL, 2003), 101–12, here 102. Moreover, Justin, *Dial.* 97–106, proves that Ps. 22 was being read as a whole continuous narrative about Jesus by some in the middle of the second century. Judith M. Lieu, "Justin Martyr and the Transformation of Psalm 22," in Hempel and Lieu (eds.), *Biblical Traditions in Transmission,* 195–211, here 202, gives a cautionary warning about assuming that the cry of dereliction adumbrates the expression of confidence in God at the end of the psalm (due to the relative dearth of reference to Ps. 22: 25–32 in the early church), but I think Lieu is being far too cautious—esp. in light of the broad cross-section of evidence cited below, including Hebrews, Barnabas, and above all Justin, *Dial.* 106. 1 (cf. additionally Tertullian, *Marc.* 3. 22. 6).

interpretative maneuver in Hebrews 2: 11–12, which contains a citation of
Psalm 21: 23 LXX, that is, the verse that immediately follows the unmarked
rescue-is-achieved gap in the psalm:

> For both the one who sanctifies and those who are sanctified are all from one, for
> which reason *he* [*Jesus*] is not ashamed to call them brothers, saying,

JESUS (speaking to GOD THE FATHER): *I* [*Jesus*] will proclaim *your name* [*O
my Father*] to my brothers, in the midst of the congregation [*en mesō
ekklēsias*] *I* will sing *your* praise [Ps. 21: 23 LXX].   (Heb. 2: 11–12)

In context, the author of Hebrews wants to be certain that his audience is
aware of Christ's full humanity, so he stresses common human origin, saying
both Christ the sanctifier and the humans whom he sanctifies are "all from one"
(*ex henos pantes*), which can credibly be translated, "all from one God, the
Father" or perhaps, "all from one spiritual family," since Jesus is not ashamed to
call those who have been sanctified his brothers and sisters. In giving evidence
that Jesus and his human brothers (and sisters) are indeed truly part of one
family, the author of Hebrews simultaneously gives us a window into a divine
dialogue, in which we are privileged to listen in as the Son speaks to the Father.

Thus when the author of Hebrews cites from the second portion of Psalm 21
LXX (the part spoken after the speaker of the psalm has already been delivered),
he does so with an awareness that the Christ, taken as the Son through
prosopological exegesis, is here speaking to the Father after the dramatic rescue,
that is, after the resurrection. Accordingly, from within the dramatic world of
the psalm itself, the speaker is now anticipating praising God in the midst of the
gathered assembly. Thus, the theodramatic temporal setting of praise is fittingly
future as expressed in the psalm itself ("will proclaim"/"will sing your praise")
because these words are spoken just after the rescue but before praise is
publicly rendered. Yet *this future is now present* for the author of Hebrews, as
the exalted Son through the Spirit is expressing praise to the Father in the
gathered assembly, the church (*hē ekklēsia*).

Overflowing Praise in Hebrews 2: 12. In this passage, paraphrasing, we see
the esteem that the Son has for the Father in his intense desire to bring the
Father the praise that is his rightful due: "*I, the Son*, will proclaim your name,
O my Father, to my brothers and sisters; in the midst of the assembly *I* will sing
your praise" (Heb. 2: 12 citing Ps. 21: 23 LXX) Accordingly, we learn at least five
things about how the Son relates to the Father through this theodramatic
appropriation. First, the Son himself, who has been definitively delivered, tells
the Father that he will *testify* to the Father's rescuing power by exalting the name
of the Father—"I will *proclaim your name*." He thus will delight in enhancing
the reputation of God the Father. Second, this testimony is designed to bring
God glory when the human family accepts it—"*to my brothers (and sisters)*."
Third, Jesus will be busy not just testifying, but he himself *will sing the Father's*

praise—"*I* will sing your praise"—showing that it is fitting for one person in the Godhead to praise another. Fourth, this praise will be public—"in the midst of the assembly." Jesus offers it in the midst of the gathered people of God, the assembly, the *ekklēsia*, the church, and the assembly is invited, encouraged, indeed expected to join with Jesus in praising the Father. Fifth, not from the citation itself, but from the narrative sequence of the psalm, we also discover that this assembly, gathered to praise the Father and led by the Son, is open to ever-widening circles of membership, as the whole world—unto the very ends of the earth—is invited to join the chorus of praise.

Psalmic Praise and Reception History. The author of Hebrews, of course, was not alone in detecting the narrative progression of Psalm 21 LXX in the earliest church, that is, in identifying Jesus as leading the people of God in praising the Father after his dramatic rescue from the grave. Ps-Barnabas takes these words as referring to the way in which the Lord Christ comes to the people of God through the Spirit, so that human hearts become a sanctuary of divine indwelling, and the people of God becomes *a holy temple*. In the midst of this holy temple, the Lord Jesus via the Spirit leads the assembly by proclaiming God the Father to the assembly, in accordance with the words of Psalm 21: 23 LXX read prosopologically in conjunction with Psalm 41: 3 LXX, with Jesus speaking directly to the Father much as in Hebrews 2: 12. Ps-Barnabas prefaces the citations, "For the Lord [Jesus] says again," after which he relates:

JESUS (speaking to GOD THE FATHER): And in what fashion shall *I* appear before the Lord my God and shall *I* be glorified?   (*Barn.* 6. 16a citing Ps. 41: 3 LXX)[3]

After this incarnational application, Ps-Barnabas continues by adding, "He says," showing that a new passage is being cited, although the same speaker, Jesus, is envisioned:

JESUS (speaking to GOD THE FATHER): *I* will profess you in the assembly of my brothers, and *I* will sing your praise in the assembly of the saints.   (*Barn.* 6. 16b citing Ps. 21: 23 LXX)[4]

The result for Ps-Barnabas is that the people of God have been fashioned anew as a temple "in the last times" through the indwelling presence of the Father-praising

---

[3] That God is the addressee in Ps. 41: 3 LXX (despite the third-person reference to "the Lord my God") is made explicit in the surrounding context in the psalm—e.g. in Ps. 41: 2 ("you, O God").

[4] As is characteristic for Ps-Barnabas, the scriptural citation of Ps. 21: 23 LXX (cf. Ps. 34: 18 LXX) is periphrastic not exact. The Greek text of *Barn.* 6. 16 reads, *Exomologēsomai soi en ekklēsia adelphōn mou kai psalō soi anameson ekklēsias hagiōn* ("I will profess you in the assembly of my brothers and I will sing about you in the midst of the assembly of saints") whereas the Septuagint attests, *diēgēsomai to onoma sou tois adelphois mou en mesō ekklēsias hymnēsō se* ("I will relate your name to my brothers, in the midst of the assembly I will hymn about you").

Spirit of Jesus. Accordingly, the followers of Jesus are those being led into the true promised land, fulfilling God's original intention for creation (*Barn.* 6. 16–19).

Meanwhile, Justin Martyr also reflects on the rescue-implying gap and on the new movement in Psalm 21 LXX that begins with verse 23, as already identified:

> The rest of the psalm shows that he knew that his Father would grant all his requests, and would raise him from the dead. It also shows that he encouraged all who fear God to praise him . . . and that he stood *in the midst of his brethren*, that is, of the apostles. . . . The psalm finally shows that *he sang the praise of God* while he was with them, which actually happened, according to the *Memoirs* of the Apostles.   (*Dial.* 106. 1; trans. Falls)

Thus, Justin affirms that Jesus' cry of dereliction did not reflect ultimate despair, nor was it a real separation, but Jesus knew that his cry for help would be answered, because the predetermined script (given by the Spirit) that he was performing announced in advance to him what would happen. Furthermore, for Justin, Jesus' anticipated praise of the Father—"I will proclaim your name to my brothers" (Ps. 21: 23 LXX)—was fulfilled when, historically speaking, Jesus was reunited with the apostles after his resurrection and could testify to them about God's rescue. And all of this culminated in Jesus singing the praise of God the Father in the midst of the gathered assembly—probably envisioned by Justin as occurring when Jesus appeared to his eleven gathered apostles in Jerusalem, explaining to them how he fulfilled the Law of Moses, the Prophets, *and the Psalms*, with the latter perhaps implying hymnody.[5]

I Will Put My Trust in Him

The author of Hebrews took Jesus as the ultimate speaker of Psalm 21: 23 LXX. That is, in the psalm the freshly raised Jesus tells his Father about his plan to proclaim and praise him personally, indeed to do so in such a way that many others are invited to participate in the praise in the *ekklēsia* ("assembly" or "church"). Yet, for the author of Hebrews, Jesus was in fact also discovered to be the speaker of a closely related series of texts in Isaiah. A literal translation of the chain of citations as we find them in Hebrews 2: 11–13 runs thus:

---

[5] See Luke 24: 36–49 esp. 24: 44–5. By "*Memoirs* of the Apostles," Justin intends either the canonical Gospels or a harmonized form of them (a precursor to Tatian's *Diatessaron*). There is abundant evidence that Justin knew Matthew and Luke, some that he knew Mark, and various hints that he probably knew John. Luke alone mentions post-resurrection instructions *from the Psalter*, so this is probably the singing event Justin intends (on the Jerusalem gathering, cf. John 20: 19–29). Or possibly it was assumed by Justin that singing would inevitably transpire when Jesus shared a meal with his apostles as in Luke 24: 41–3 and John 21: 12–13. Tertullian, *Marc.* 3. 22. 6, understands the singing of Christ as the praise transpiring "in his name and in his Spirit" in the church.

For both the one who sanctifies and those who are sanctified are all from one, for which reason he [Jesus] is not ashamed to call them brothers, saying, "I will proclaim your name to my brothers, in the midst of the congregation I will sing your praise" [Ps. 21: 23 LXX]. And again, "I will trust in him" [Isa. 8: 17 LXX]. And again, "Behold, [here] I [am] and the children whom God has given me" [Isa. 8: 18 LXX].

That is, immediately after citing Psalm 21: 23 LXX, the author of Hebrews continues in the next verse by claiming that Jesus spoke additionally through Isaiah ("And again"):

JESUS: I will trust in him (*egō esomai pepoithōs ep autō*).   (Heb. 2: 13a citing Isa. 8: 17 LXX)

Moving further into Hebrews 2: 13, the maintenance of the same speaker for yet another Old Testament quote is indicated by a second "And again," but the surprise is that the citation is drawn from the very next line in Isaiah with respect to the previous citation:

JESUS: Behold, here I am and the children [*paidia*] whom God has given me. (Heb. 2: 13b citing Isa. 8: 18 LXX; cf. *Odes Sol.* 31. 4)

There are three mysteries to solve in this complex chain of citations in Hebrews 2: 13. First, why did our author (or his source) split a continuous text in the Old Testament into two parts and treat it as if it is two separate and distinct citations? Directly below I have italicized and placed a vertical line (" | ") to show where the author of Hebrews cleaves what is one continuous text in Isaiah into two quotes:

> Then those who seal up the law so that they might not learn will appear. And one will say, "I will wait for God, who has turned his face away from the house of Jacob, and *I will trust in him*." | "*Behold, here I am and the children whom God has given me*, and they will serve as signs and portents in Israel from the Lord of Hosts, who dwells on Mount Zion."   (Isa. 8: 16–18 LXX)

So, the first enigma pertains to the chopping of what is one text into two distinct citations by the author of Hebrews. Second, why has Jesus been assigned as the theodramatic speaker of Isaiah 8: 17–18 by the author of Hebrews at all? Unlike for Psalm 21 LXX (quoted in Heb. 2: 12), which was read prosopologically in a quite uniform fashion in the early church, the signals that might have triggered such a reading of Isaiah 8: 17–18 for the author of Hebrews in 2: 13 are difficult to discern. And it is precisely this sort of reading which shows that something more than a so-called Davidic typology must be transpiring when Jesus was found to be speaking in the ancient Jewish Scripture, because these are not the words of David, but rather Isaiah.[6]

---

[6] The customary "Davidic typology" explanation of Jesus' OT speeches has become so engrained in scholarship that it is even imported into these verses via 2 Sam. 22: 3 LXX even

I believe that this is yet another occurrence of prosopological exegesis. Third, who are the addressees?

Who Is Addressed? Taking up the last issue first—the identity of the addressees—I would propose that the author of Hebrews determined that Isaiah had slipped into the guise of Jesus the Son, and that the Son was hereby speaking not to the Father, but rather he was issuing *a warning to the theodramatic audience*, the ancient people of God. For the author of Hebrews, the Son asserts that the chosen people of God would observe various portents, the significance of which it was necessary for them to assess properly. In fact, the assignment of the addressee as the ancient people of God is a fairly straightforward inference from definite signals in the broader context ("those who sit in Jerusalem" [Isa. 8: 14] and "the house of Jacob" [Isa. 8: 17]), but the assignment of Jesus as the speaker by the author of Hebrews (or his source) is very enigmatic.

Why Assign Jesus as the Speaker? Now moving to the second puzzle—what textual details in LXX Isaiah might have prompted the author of Hebrews to assign the role of the speaker to the yet-to-be-revealed Jesus? For the author of Hebrews, that Isaiah was speaking in the prosopon of Jesus the Son was suggested, I propose, by some combination of these seven factors:

1. The identity of the speaker lacks a clear referent in the text (*erei*—"he/she/it/one will say"—Isa. 8: 17) so, in any case, an attuned ancient reader would need to work hard to supply a plausible identification by paying strict attention to the surrounding context.

2. It is highly unlikely that the speaker is the Lord (God) because God is spoken of in the third person in the speech ("I will wait for God"; "the children whom God has given me") even though the Lord (God) was the last identified speaker in 8: 11.

3. The same holds for the very closely related speech in Isaiah 12: 2— "Behold God is my savior, my Lord, I will trust in him" (*pepoithōs esomai ep autō*). The Lord God cannot be the speaker there either.

4. Not just *the setting* of the speech is future ("one will say"), but *the actions envisioned in the speech* are future even with respect to the *realized future setting*, as is signaled by the multiple future tenses—"one will say, 'I will wait . . . I will trust . . . they will serve as signs.'" This could have suggested, I believe, to an

though the citation is drawn from Isaiah, and so David is clearly not the speaker. For example, see the otherwise excellent recent commentary by Gareth L. Cockerill, *The Epistle to the Hebrews* (NICNT; Grand Rapids: Eerdmans, 2012), 143–4, who adopts this Davidic-typology position and lists many others who do as well. For the first citation, that the author of Hebrews intends Isa. 8: 17 itself *not* Isa. 8: 17 (cf. also Isa. 12: 2 LXX) as read through the lens of 2 Sam. 22: 3 LXX is made strongly probable by two factors: (1) it is immediately followed by Isa. 8: 18; (2) the author of Hebrews splits Deut. 32: 35–6 in Heb. 10: 30 in a similar fashion, so a split here does not mean different source texts are in view. Hence, importing 2 Sam. 22: 3 LXX in support of a Davidic typology is of doubtful legitimacy.

ancient reader that Isaiah was speaking in the guise of a future character, and that this future character was speaking about activities in the even more distant future with respect to his adopted role. A retrospective consideration by the author of Hebrews of the substantial distance between Isaiah's prophecy and Jesus Christ's advent may have helped him feel assured that Jesus was a plausible speaker.

5. In the slightly more distant literary-theological context this speech is sandwiched between important messianic texts as read in the earliest church. Preceding the speech we find the oracle regarding the sign of Immanuel (Isa. 7: 1–8: 10), which was taken to anticipate the virgin birth (see esp. Matt. 1: 22–3 on Isa. 7: 14). Following the speech there is an announcement of a glorious moment of special favor in the land of Galilee in conjunction with the birth of a child "with authority on his shoulders"—a Davidic son who will be called "Wonderful Counselor, Mighty God, Everlasting Father, Prince of Peace" (Isa. 9: 6; cf. Matt. 4: 13–16).

6. In the near context the instruction in Isaiah 8: 13–14 to treat as holy the Lord (God in Isaiah but probably inclusive of Jesus Christ for our author) lest he be encountered as a stone of stumbling has strong connections in early Christian interpretation to Jesus' own teachings about himself as the rejected stone (Matt. 21: 42–5; Mark 12: 10–11; Luke 20: 17–18; cf. Ps. 117: 22 LXX), especially as that tradition was refracted in multitudinous ways in the early Christian literature.[7] Thus, the inference that Jesus was the prosopological speaker of Isaiah 8: 16–18 could have had a plausible basis in the near context for our author.

7. Finally in the immediate context in Isaiah 8: 16 LXX, the verse just prior to that which the author of Hebrews actually cites, it first states that a group that "seals themselves in order that they might not learn the Law [of Moses]" will be unveiled.[8] This could have been construed in the earliest church as a

---

[7] E.g. Rom. 9: 32–3; Acts 4: 11; 1 Pet. 2: 4–8; *Barn.* 6. 2–4. In fact the topos of Jesus as a stumbling stone was so popular that it almost certainly circulated as a thematic subcollection in extract form—see Martin C. Albl, *"And Scripture Cannot Be Broken": The Form and Function of the Early Christian Testimonia Collections* (SupNovT 96; Leiden: Brill, 1999), 265–85. For evidence that the earliest church generally was aware of the literary context of Isaiah from which this citation in Hebrews is drawn, see J. Ross Wagner, "Faithfulness and Fear, Stumbling and Salvation: Receptions of LXX Isaiah 8:11–18 in the New Testament," in J. Ross Wagner, C. Kavin Rowe, and A. Katherine Grieb (eds.), *The Word Leaps the Gap: Essays on Scripture and Theology in Honor of Richard B. Hays* (Grand Rapids: Eerdmans, 2008), 76–106. Wagner's reflections on Isa. 8: 17–18 in Heb. 2: 12–13 are helpful and in several ways compatible with my own, although he favors taking Jesus as speaking "as the representative voice of the community" (see esp. pp. 98–104, here 102).

[8] The MT reading of Isa. 8: 16 is quite different, "Bind up the testimony; seal up the torah [teaching, law] among my disciples." The LXX stresses the future appearance of a group of people who seal up the torah in order that they, obstinately, might not learn the ways of God. In the MT, Isaiah gives instructions to bind up the torah among his disciples in response to the gross infidelity of his compatriots, who have refused to trust YHWH in the face of the Assyrian crisis (Isa. 8: 5–11) and who instead are consulting mediums and necromancers (Isa. 8: 19). Despite the differences, the underlying idea in both the MT and the LXX involves sealing up the torah.

reference to the rise in prominence of those who would oppose Jesus' more lenient interpretation of the Mosaic law—and it must be remembered that the hatred-unto-death of Jesus by the Pharisees and the teachers of the Law was instigated above all by his flagrant disregard for their brand of legal interpretation (e.g. Mark 3: 6; John 5: 15). In response to this group's action of sealing themselves off from the Law, the unidentified Isaianic speaker is introduced with "and one will say," and then we find the content of this future speech:

> "I will wait for God, who has turned his face away from the house of Jacob, and *I will trust in him.*" | "*Behold, [here] I [am] and the children whom God has given me*, and they will serve as signs and portents in Israel from the Lord of Hosts, who dwells on Mount Zion." (Isa. 8: 17–18 LXX)[9]

The italicized portion is what the author of Hebrews cites. However, curiously, in accordance with where I have placed the vertical line in the citation ("|"), the author of Hebrews splits it into two separate citations divided by the phrase "And again."

Why Was the Citation Split? Having explored a plausible rationale for the prosopological assignment, we are now in a better position to assess the theological significance of this citation from Hebrews 2: 13. Moreover, a reasonable hypothesis for the third enigma, why the author split the text into two distinct citations can be offered: they represent two chronologically discontinuous events in the theodrama for the author of Hebrews as was indicated for the author by the tense shifts. For the author of Hebrews, Isaiah through the agency of the Spirit spoke in the person of the yet-to-appear-on-the-world-stage Jesus Christ (who at the time of David preexisted) about future realities not only with respect to Isaiah, but with respect to the earthly Jesus. But after the decisive act of rescue, the resurrected Christ then speaks in the past tense as he looks back on what has been gained while also announcing future implications.

Reading Text and World Together. We might synthesize by paraphrasing the theodramatic reading in Hebrews 2: 13 and suggesting that the author read Isaiah 8: 16–18 by correlating certain external events with textual events and speeches thus:

> **Event One**: Prior to Jesus' arrival on the earthly scene, a group arises, "those who seal themselves up in order not to learn the Law." (Isa. 8: 16 LXX)

---

[9] As a secondary consideration, this report of God (the Father) turning away his face from a first-person speaker connects thematically to God-forsakenness—the leading idea in Ps. 21 LXX. Perhaps this might explain (at least partly) not only why Ps. 21: 23 LXX and Isa. 8: 17–18 have been linked by the author of Hebrews (or his source), but also the first-person identification of the speaker as Jesus Christ for the latter. That is, if Jesus is the speaker of Ps. 21: 2 LXX ("My God, my God, why have you forsaken me?"), then, our author may have reasoned, why not also these additional words from Isa. 8: 17–18 about God turning away?

Event Two (assumed rather than expressed in the text): The earthly Jesus undergoes intense hostility from this group to such a degree that he perceives his very life to be in acute danger.

Event Three: And this certain "one" will speak (Isa. 8: 17), the fully human Jesus, when he faces deadly animosity from these legally misguided opponents. That is, Jesus will think about his *future* course of action and will say to those around him as a way of affirming his own resolve and theirs:

Speech 1. JESUS (addressing THE PEOPLE OF GOD prior to the crucifixion): I will wait for God, who has turned his face away from the house of Jacob, and *I will trust in him.*   (Isa. 8: 17 LXX)

Event Four (assumed rather than expressed in the text, much as in the "gap" between LXX Ps. 21: 22 and 21: 23): The trust Jesus exercises results in divine rescue on the other side of death.

Event Five: After the rescue Jesus speaks no longer in the future tense because it is not the earthly Jesus who is now speaking; rather, the resurrected Jesus speaks in the *present tense* about this new state of affairs while reflecting in the *past tense* on what was achieved through the act of deliverance:

Speech 2. JESUS (addressing THE PEOPLE OF GOD after the resurrection): *Behold, here I am, and the children whom God has given me . . .*   (Isa. 8: 18 LXX)

Thus, for the author of Hebrews the resurrected Jesus testifies in Isaiah to the people of God that not only is he alive and well after rescue ("Here I am") but also that through the deliverance process the family now contains many children, implying Gentile inclusion, so that Jesus, here pictured as the firstborn brother, can report this to the audience.

Although the formal citation in Hebrews 2: 13 stops with the first half of Isaiah 8: 18, so this next suggestion is necessarily speculative, we might surmise that for the author of Hebrews the resurrected Jesus also speaks of events yet to appear on his own horizon by using the *future tense* as the Old Testament speech continues in the remainder of Isaiah 8: 18.

Speech 2 (continued). JESUS (still addressing THE PEOPLE OF GOD after the resurrection): . . . and they [the children] will serve as signs and portents in Israel from the Lord of Hosts, who dwells on Mount Zion.   (Isa. 8: 18 LXX)

Event Six (Speech 2 is actualized): The "children" are now real-world, living signs.

If this basic reconstruction is accepted, then this final speech, which the resurrected Christ delivers in the future tense, "they will serve as signs," has in fact already occurred for the author of Hebrews (even if he does not cite it), inasmuch as the "children" God has given Jesus are now living proof ("signs and portents") for anyone who has eyes to see that God's family has new boundaries—Jews and Gentiles together as brothers and sisters. In fact, the author of Hebrews can point to the children's common flesh-and-blood humanity as evidence that Jesus, their brother, truly shared in their flesh-and-blood humanity (Heb. 2: 14).[10]

In sum, I have proposed that the prosopological reading strategy deployed by the author of Hebrews in the chain of citations in Hebrews 2: 11–13 follows the same repeated pattern for LXX Psalm 21: 23 and Isaiah 8: 17–18 as individually considered. In both the citations the prophet has been judged to be speaking in the character of the yet-to-be-revealed Jesus. As such, in both texts, individually considered, this stepping into character presupposes that when the theodrama is actualized, then the earthly Jesus will experience a life-threatening crisis; next, Jesus will trust; third, Jesus will be rescued from death via resurrection (presupposed in order to explain genuine gaps in the narrative sequences of both OT source texts); and finally, the resurrected Jesus will have many siblings or many children. In Hebrews 2: 11–13 the exact same person-centered interpretative pattern is found in the citations from the Psalter and from Isaiah.

Yet both LXX Psalm 21: 23 and Isaiah 8: 17–18 in Hebrews 2: 11–13 add something unique and theologically interesting. We discover in the psalm that Jesus himself tells the Father that he will publicly acclaim the Father, heading up the assembly of brothers (and sisters) in singing praise to the Father, showing that the Son's desire is to lead others in glorifying the Father. Meanwhile, the quotation from Isaiah 8: 17–18 is not a dialogue between the Son and the Father, but rather the Son, Jesus during his earthly sojourn, announces to the audience, the people of God, his trust in the Father when experiencing opposition prior to the crucifixion (Isa. 8: 17 LXX). Then the now-raised Jesus announces his own renewed presence, presenting the children God has given to him to the audience as an exhortation (Isa. 8: 18 LXX).

Ps-Barnabas, Justin Martyr, and the author of Hebrews were not alone in identifying conversations in which the Son speaks words of trust and praise to the Father—the Apostle Paul identifies several such moments as well.

I Trusted, therefore I Spoke

In 2 Corinthians 4: 7–15 Paul recounts his ministerial hardships. Yet despite the woes he and his coworkers have faced, Paul nonetheless asserts that the resurrection-life of Jesus is revealed in the mortal bodies of Christians—that is,

---

[10] We might speculate that for the author of Hebrews, who had connections to both the Pauline mission and Italy (see Heb. 13: 23–4), the Gentile-inclusive identity of the children serves as a further sign to those who are snared by an ethnic boast, much as in Rom. 9–11, so that they might see that the expansion of God's family is anticipated in Scripture.

even though Christians are profoundly weak jars of clay, they are privileged to house an unsurpassable divine power. The Christian carries around in his or her earthly body the death of Jesus so that Jesus' life might be at work in carrying out Christian ministry. In support of this point, Paul offers a cryptic and extraordinarily terse scriptural warrant from the Psalter:

> Moreover, since we have the same spirit of faith in accordance with which it stands written, "I believed, therefore I spoke" [Ps. 115: 1 LXX], so also we believe and therefore are speaking, knowing that the one who raised the Lord Jesus also will raise us with Jesus and he will present us together with you.   (2 Cor. 4: 13–14)

Paul says "we" (himself and his missionary team) have the same belief as the speaker of the words, "I believed, therefore I spoke," but who spoke these words? The citation, comprising just three words in the Greek text—*episteusa, dio elalēsa*—derives from Psalms 114–15 LXX, which was probably not two separate psalms but one united psalm in Paul's Greek version of the Scripture, just as in the Hebrew MT and most English translations that are based on the Hebrew today (i.e. Pss. 114–15 LXX = Ps. 116 MT).[11] Why would Paul offer such seemingly flimsy and trivial scriptural support with his words, "I believed, therefore I spoke"?

The traditional view has been that Paul is simply encouraging his audience to imitate the faith of the generic psalmist or David[12]—generally taking *pistis* as "faith" and *pisteuō* as "I believed." Also, the "therefore, I spoke" has been judged in this traditional view to be an exhortation to speak or preach the gospel—a vapid and shallow explanation that in my judgment ultimately falls short. The acceptance of this (frankly insipid!) traditional view has even caused some scholars to conclude that Paul has no awareness of the wider narrative context of the psalm.[13]

A Call To Imitate Christ. Yet, I am convinced, as are an increasing number of other scholars, that the best explanation is that this is not a bland

---

[11] See Frank-Lothar Hossfeld and Erich Zenger, *Psalms* (trans. Linda M. Maloney; vols. ii–iii of a projected 3 vols.; Minneapolis: Fortress, 2011), iii. 220; Hans-Joachim Kraus, *Psalms* (trans. Hilton C. Oswald; 2 vols.; Minneapolis: Augsburg, 1989), ii. 385–6.

[12] Alfred Plummer, *A Critical and Exegetical Commentary on the Second Epistle of St. Paul to the Corinthians* (ICC; Edinburgh: T&T Clark, 1915), 133, believes that Paul cited this text because, "Trust in God inspires us as it did the Psalmist"; Rudolf Bultmann, *The Second Letter to the Corinthians* (trans. Roy A. Harrisville; Minneapolis: Augsburg, 1985), 121; Paul Barnett, *The Second Epistle to the Corinthians* (NICNT; Grand Rapids: Eerdmans, 1997), 241, believes that Paul in quoting this passage is "basing himself on the psalmist's example, but in different circumstances."

[13] C. K. Barrett, *The Second Epistle to the Corinthians* (Peabody, Mass.: Hendrickson, 1997), 142–3, states, "Paul pays no heed to the context, but picks out the two significant words." Meanwhile, Christopher D. Stanley, *Arguing with Scripture: The Rhetoric of Quotations in the Letters of Paul* (London: T&T Clark, 2004), 100, is even more extreme, saying that a competent ancient reader would have determined that "the sense in which he [i.e. Paul] uses the verse is so far removed from the original context as to raise questions about Paul's reliability as an interpreter."

exhortation "to have faith," but rather a precise and inspiring summons to *imitatio Christi*, "to trust," inasmuch as Paul takes these as the words of the Christ:[14]

THE CHRIST (speaking to GOD THE FATHER after his enthronement): I trusted, therefore I spoke.   (2 Cor. 4: 13 citing Ps. 115: 1 LXX)

Indeed, I would go even further than others in claiming that not a typological but a prosopological interpretation is what allows Paul to identify this as a divine conversation—that is, Paul believes that David had slipped into a role that he was acting out in the theodrama, playing the character of the Christ as the Christ speaks to God the Father via a script authored by the Spirit. As such, Paul's interpretation has Trinitarian implications.

Paul takes the Christ as the speaker of Psalms 114–15 LXX and the setting is after the return of the Son to heavenly glory alongside the Father. As such, the exalted Christ is dialoging with the Father, reminiscing about the sequence of events that culminated in his return to glory. Specifically, for Paul in Psalm 115: 1 LXX the exalted Christ tells the Father about his *past experience* of crisis and trust as the Son underwent the passion. The words "I trusted, therefore I spoke" (Ps. 115: 1 LXX) within the narrative world of the psalm point backward in time within the psalm to the crisis unto death described in 114: 3 LXX. The speaker describes the dire nature of his situation in graphic language, "Anguishes of death surrounded me; the dangers of Hades found me; I found affliction and pain." As the speaker felt this crisis as deep as death flow over him, he responded not by wallowing in self-pity, but rather by casting himself on God's mercy, *by trusting*. This action of trusting was then followed *by speaking*, crying out to God for deliverance, as the next verse in the psalm makes clear: "And I called upon the name of the Lord, 'O Lord, rescue my soul'" (Ps. 114: 4 LXX). In support of this identification of the Christ as speaker by Paul, it should be noted that the author of Hebrews also appears to have taken the Christ as the speaker of Psalm 114: 1–9 LXX, inasmuch as his allusion in Hebrews 5: 7 virtually demands such a conclusion.[15]

---

[14] Anthony T. Hanson, *Jesus Christ in the Old Testament* (London: SPCK, 1965), 145–7; Richard B. Hays, "Christ Prays the Psalms: Israel's Psalter as Matrix of Early Christology," *The Conversion of the Imagination: Paul as Interpreter of Israel's Scripture* (Grand Rapids: Eerdmans, 2005), 122–36; Thomas D. Stegman, *The Character of Jesus: The Linchpin to Paul's Argument in 2 Corinthians* (AnBib 158; Rome: Pontifico Istituto Biblico, 2005), 146–68; Kenneth Schenck, "2 Corinthians and the Πίστις Χριστοῦ Debate," *CBQ* 70 (2008): 524–37; and Douglas A. Campbell, *The Deliverance of God: An Apocalyptic Re-Reading of Justification in Paul* (Grand Rapids: Eerdmans, 2009), 914–24. For a fuller exposition of this position, see Matthew W. Bates, *The Hermeneutics of the Apostolic Proclamation: The Center of Paul's Method of Scriptural Interpretation* (Waco, Tex.: Baylor University Press, 2012), 304–25.

[15] Hebrews 5: 7 enjoys a thorough and specific linguistic overlap with Ps. 114: 1–9 LXX, making an intentional allusion virtually certain—see Schenck, "2 Corinthians and the Πίστις Χριστοῦ Debate," 530–2.

In construing David as speaking via Spirit-inspiration in the character of the glorified Christ, who is reminiscing with the Father, Paul has not only given us important Trinitarian information—the Son trusted his Father, even when facing the dangers of Hades, and cried out to the Father for deliverance—he has also effectively encouraged the Corinthians. Paul's point with his "I trusted, therefore I spoke" is not the self-evident truism that the Corinthians should "have faith" and should "preach the gospel," but is much more precise and crisp in advocating the imitation of Christ. Paul's meaning here is best brought out by a paraphrase:

> We have the same attitude of *trust* as is demonstrated by the psalmist—who actually was speaking in character as the Christ—and those words are written as follows: "*I trusted* in God when I was experiencing a deadly crisis, *therefore I spoke* a plea to God for rescue." Because we have this same attitude of trust as the Christ, we also are trusting in God through our ministerial difficulties for the sake of Jesus, and therefore we are speaking our own plea to God for rescue, acknowledging that the same God who raised Jesus Christ the Lord will also raise us with Christ. (2 Cor. 4: 13–14a)

That is to say, Paul is telling his audience that as Christians undergo ministerial hardships that crush, perplex, and virtually kill them, they should respond as Jesus did—that is, they should *trust* throughout the crisis unto death and should *speak* not so much words of missionary proclamation, but rather they should call upon the name of the Lord God as Jesus did—they should cry out for deliverance, "O Lord, rescue my soul!," knowing that the God of resurrection-life can and will rescue them—even though, as was the case for Jesus, that rescue may only come on the other side of the grave.

I Will Profess You among the Nations

Not only does Paul find in Psalms 114–15 LXX a speech in which the Son recounts to the Father various details about his experience of crisis, trust, plea, and rescue, we find that Paul undertakes a similar prosopological reading of Psalm 17 LXX in Romans 15: 9, although the focus shifts in Paul's citation from trust and then outcry in the face of crisis to praise of the Father after deliverance.

In Romans 15: 1–12 Paul encourages "the strong" to show true Christian love to "the weak" by seeking the interest of the other above self-interest, and all of this in imitation of Christ. We have already discussed the Trinitarian implications of Paul's prosopological reading of Psalm 68: 10 LXX in Romans 15: 3 in detail ("The insults of those who insulted you fell upon me"—see Ch. 4). Paul offers a wish-prayer that the disharmonious strong and weak groups will attain to true Christian unity, all of which will result in the glory of

God the Father (Rom. 15: 5–6). Then, Paul plunges deeper into the theme of unified praise as it pertains to Jew and Gentile (15: 7–9a), offering a chain of scriptural citations in support (15: 9–12). When read in connection with the verses that precede it, the first scriptural citation in the *catena* is best explained by positing that Paul has prosopologically interpreted Psalm 17: 50 LXX, theodramatically taking the Christ as the true speaker.[16] Paul exhorts the Romans, saying:

> Therefore accept one another just as the Christ accepted you unto the glory of God. For I declare that the Christ has become a servant of the circumcision for the sake of the fidelity of God in order to secure the promises of the fathers; moreover he has become a servant to the nations for the sake of mercy, in order to glorify God, just as it is written: "For this reason I will profess you among the nations and I will sing your name" [Ps. 17: 50 LXX]. (Rom. 15: 7–9)[17]

Intriguingly, Psalm 17 LXX, the psalm cited here, features virtually the same crisis-unto-death language as Psalms 114–15 LXX, the passage we just examined with regard to Paul's person-centered interpretation of 2 Corinthians 4: 13. For example, the phrase "anguishes of death surrounded me" (*perieschon me ōdines thanatou*) in Psalm 114: 3 LXX corresponds exactly to the lament in Psalm 17: 5 LXX, "anguishes of death surrounded me," while the psalmist also adds, "torrents of lawlessness besieged me; anguishes of Hades encompassed me, snares of death caught hold of me" (17: 5–6; cf. 17: 7, 18–19). That these crisis-unto-death verses were applied in the earliest church to Jesus' death and descent to Hades is not surprising; there is in fact an allusion to Jesus' escape from these very "anguishes of death" in a theodramatic interpretation found in Peter's Pentecost sermon in Acts 2: 24, a passage we will explore further in the next subsection.

If it is granted that the Christ is the prosopologically determined speaker of Psalm 17: 50 LXX for Paul, then Paul's exhortation toward mutual acceptance makes much better sense because it is grounded in a specific, concrete fashion:

---

[16] Among others, the following scholars emphatically front the Christ as the speaker of Ps. 17: 50 LXX in Rom. 15: 9: Hanson, *Jesus Christ and the Old Testament*, 157 ("an utterance of the preexistent Christ"); Ulrich Wilckens, *Der Brief an die Römer* (3 vols.; EKKNT; Neukirchen-Vluyn: Neukirchener, 1978–82), iii. 108 ("der Sprecher Christus selbst gedacht ist"); J. Ross Wagner, *Heralds of the Good News: Paul and Isaiah in Concert in the Letter to the Romans* (SupNovT 101; Leiden: Brill, 2002), 312 ("Paul has read this psalm as the words of the Christ"). For detailed evidence in support of this position, see Bates, *The Hermeneutics of the Apostolic Proclamation*, 289–304.

[17] On the level of Greek syntax, the relationship between Rom. 15: 8 and 15: 9 is notoriously difficult, and in consequence English translations of 15: 9 vary wildly. In basic agreement with J. Ross Wagner, "The Christ, Servant of Jew and Gentile: A Fresh Approach to Romans 15:8–9," *JBL* 116 (1997): 473–85, I take "the nations" (*ta ethnē*) in 15: 9 as an accusative of respect, believing that Paul is carrying forward the phrase "the Christ has become" from 15: 8 as an ellipsis to be supplied by the reader in 15: 9.

THE CHRIST (speaking to GOD THE FATHER after his enthronement): For this reason I will profess you among the nations and I will sing your name.   (Rom. 15: 9 citing Ps. 17: 50 LXX)

Paul asserts that the Christ became a servant of Jews and he also became a servant of the nations (Gentiles)—and he proves it by showing that the Christ himself, through the agency of David and the Spirit, told the Father of his intention to act as a servant to Jew and Gentile by testifying about the Father among the nations and by singing the Father's praise. For Paul, the Son in effect states: "Because I, the Son, as a servant to both Jew and Gentile have been rescued by you, O my Father, from a death-crisis, I will profess you, O my Father, among the nations, I will sing your name."

The Son Leads as Nations Join the Chorus. Paul's train of thought appears to work in this way: Since Israel was called by God (the Father) to mediate the blessing of God to the nations, all of which was to culminate in the praise of God by Jew and Gentile alike (cf. Rom. 15: 10–11), Christ and his Jewish followers fulfill this mediatorial role when the Christ professes and praises the Father among the nations, allowing the nations to join fully in the chorus of praise—and in light of current real-world developments and the scriptural testimony, Paul has determined that this is now happening. These real-world developments include above all the welcoming of the nations, the Gentiles, to join the Jews in the one family of God as confirmed by the gift of the Holy Spirit (see Gal. 3: 1–9; 4: 6; Rom. 8: 14–17; 1 Cor. 12: 1–3, 11–13), as well as the way in which the Spirit of the Lord Christ is inspiring song-filled worship in the earliest church.

The most natural theodramatic setting that Paul would have assigned for the Christ-speech in Romans 15: 9, "For this reason I will profess you among the nations and I will sing your name," is just after the resurrection, much as in the similar citation in Hebrews 2: 12, "I will proclaim your name to my brethren, in the midst of the congregation I will praise you."[18] In Romans 15: 9, however, unlike in Hebrews 2: 12, the post-resurrection setting is in the Father's glory, not in a setting addressing the people of God.

Thus I suggest that Paul hears David speak in Psalm 17: 50 LXX in the prosopon of the newly exalted Christ, as the Christ announces *future* action to the Father, "I *will* profess you, O my Father, among the nations," and "I *will* sing your praise"—that is, the Son tells the Father that he himself will attest and praise the Father and in so doing, as he leads forth, he will be joined by a mighty chorus as both Jew and Gentile take up the refrain.[19] Thus, in the

---

[18] The intimate relationship between Rom. 15: 9 and Heb. 2: 12, with Christ as the speaker in both, is also noted by Attridge, "Giving Voice to Jesus," 111.

[19] See the additional scriptural citations in Rom. 15: 10–12 where Paul undergirds the notion of Jew and Gentile praising God together through a Davidic offspring: "And again it says: 'Rejoice O nations along with his people' [Deut. 32: 43], and again 'Praise the Lord, O all you

theodrama as reconstructed by Paul, the freshly exalted Christ tells the Father that he will continue to praise him in the future, all of which from Paul's real-world vantage point is no longer purely future action for the Son; on the contrary it is presently being actualized through the missionary activities of the early church, not least through Paul's own gospel proclamation. Thus, in Psalm 17: 50 LXX Paul finds the glorified Christ to be announcing future action that has already reached a degree of fulfillment.

A Trinitarian Circle-Song of Praise. As a final thought on Romans 15: 9, we might wonder precisely how in on-the-ground terms Paul would have felt that the Christ was "professing" the Father and "singing" his praise among Jew and Gentile. Functionally speaking, I think it is plausible to suggest that Paul believed that this was being actualized or incarnated in his communities through Spirit-inspired utterance and song in the early Christian assembly (*ekklēsia*)—see especially 1 Corinthians 12–14.[20] That is, the Lord Christ was deemed functionally present through the Holy Spirit when the church gathered, inasmuch as the Spirit is indeed the Spirit of the Christ (Rom. 8: 9–11) or the Spirit of the Lord (2 Cor. 3: 16–17), or the Spirit of Jesus Christ (Phil. 1: 19). Thus, ultimately, the speech of the Son to the Father in Romans 15: 9, "I will profess" and "I will sing," was in all probability brought into reality for Paul as an audible profession and voiced song through the agency of the Holy Spirit at work in the church, much as we saw earlier for *Barnabas* 6. 13–16.[21] The Spirit facilitates the initial speech and its realization while the Spirit also takes on the Son's task of guiding others to glorify the Father.

Accordingly, we would certainly want to affirm that the method of prosopological exegesis employed in the earliest church is congenial to the notion of *perichōrēsis*—the ever-circling mutual interpenetration of divine persons—that would be developed and expressed in the late patristic period. Here, indeed, looking at all the roles through the flow of time as these were (in all likelihood) assigned by Paul: *the Spirit* inspired the *past* prophetic speech of *David* as it is found in Psalm 17: 50 LXX, and in this prophetic speech *Christ the Son* directly addresses *God the Father* in the theodramatic *present*, announcing that *the Son* will lead *other humans* in rendering *future* praise to *the Father*—all of which is actually performed on the world stage when *the Spirit of the Lord Jesus* inspires *Jew and Gentile* in the earliest *church* to sing

nations, and greatly praise him, O all you peoples' [Ps. 116: 1 LXX]. And again Isaiah says: 'The root of Jesse will come, even the one who will rise in order to rule over the nations; the nations will hope upon him [Isa. 11: 10].'" Note, however, that Paul does not interpret 15: 10–12 as spoken from the person of the Christ—contra Hanson, *Jesus Christ in the Old Testament*, 150, and Leander E. Keck, "Christology, Soteriology, and the Praise of God (Romans 15: 7–13)," in R. T. Fortuna and B. R. Gaventa (eds.), *The Conversation Continues: Studies in Paul and John: In Honor of J. Louis Martyn* (Nashville: Abingdon, 1990), 85–97.

[20] On Spirit-inspired singing, see 1 Cor. 14: 15, 26; Acts 16: 25; Col. 3: 16; Eph. 5: 19; James 5: 13.
[21] Cf. Tertullian, *Marc.* 3. 22. 6.

jubilantly to *the Father*. A wealth of cooperative and interpenetrating theodramatic performance indeed!

In Paul's prosopological interpretation of Psalm 17: 50 LXX in Romans 15: 9 the narrative sequence of the whole psalm was critical, much as in Paul's interpretation of Psalm 115: 1 LXX. In fact, both these psalms feature language about the "anguishes of death" from which the speaker, determined to be the Christ by Paul, was rescued by divine intervention. Perhaps we should not be surprised, then, when we discover that in Peter's Pentecost speech, the author of Acts also alludes to Jesus' escape from the "anguishes of death" (Acts 2: 24) while introducing a different psalm that he interprets prosopologically.

The Father at the Right Hand of the Son

One of the most captivating occurrences of prosopological exegesis in the New Testament can be found in Peter's Pentecost sermon. In this speech we find the Christ speaking directly to the Father in the theodrama, and we learn several new things about the interior relationship between Father and Son. The citation of the Psalter in Peter's speech repays careful scrutiny:

> God raised this man Jesus, having loosed him from the anguishes of death, because it was impossible for him to be held by them. For David says concerning him, "I kept seeing the Lord [God] continually before me, for he is at my right hand lest I be shaken; therefore my heart is cheered, and my tongue rejoices; moreover my flesh will even live in hope. Because you will not abandon my soul to Hades, or permit your Holy One to see decay. You have made known to me the paths of life; you will fill me with joy in your presence." (Acts 2: 24–8 citing Ps. 15: 8–11 LXX)

We should note that although Peter avers that "David spoke about him" (*Dauid gar legei eis auton*), that is, about Jesus the Nazarene (cf. 2: 22), Peter goes on to clarify that David was not merely speaking *about* him, but rather this yet-to-be-revealed Jesus was making an in-character speech at the time of David *through David*.[22]

This is indicated by three features of the Pentecost sermon. First, as this text is further explicated in the sermon, Peter is reported as saying that David foresaw the fulfillment of God's promise to him regarding the deliverance from Hades of his own royal offspring, including the lack of physical decay and the bodily resurrection. Notice how the third-person language of Peter correlates to the first-person language of the psalm itself. Peter states, "[David]

---

[22] Contra Attridge, "Giving Voice to Jesus," 101–12, here 104. In addition to the three reasons in favor of the prosopological interpretation I give in the main body, it also appears to me that Attridge has not sufficiently considered that a prophetic in-character speech can be intended but not marked by a special introductory formula, as can be proven through comparison (see n. 36 in Ch. 4 for evidence).

while foreseeing these things, spoke about the resurrection of the Christ, that *he* was neither abandoned to Hades, nor did *his* flesh see corruption" (Acts 2: 31). The way in which Peter picks up the first-person and second-person phraseology from the psalm, "abandoned to Hades" (cf. "*you* will not abandon *my soul* to Hades") and "flesh see decay" (cf. "*you* will not permit *your Holy One* to see decay") demands that he construed the ultimate first-person speaker of the psalm as the Christ and the addressee as God the Father. For David, whose body remains in the tomb, is not an appropriate character for these words, as Peter himself makes emphatically clear (Acts 2: 29), so these words and others ("David did not ascend into the heavens but he himself says . . ."—Acts 2: 34) are not to be thought of as David's alone. The point stressed by the author of Acts is the *significant disjuncture* between the experiences of David and Jesus as the Christ, all of which significantly weakens the typological solution of Hays and others regarding these sort of ancient exegeses, for the latter requires participation in a common image. Second, the same interpretative logic as is found here in Peter's Pentecost sermon is expressed vis-à-vis Psalm 15: 10 LXX in Paul's speech at Pisidian Antioch in Acts 13: 35, which was also interpreted prosopologically, as was discussed earlier (see Ch. 2), reinforcing that conclusion here. Third, Peter affirms that David, "was a prophet" (2: 30),[23] which suggests that the emphasis is on David's future-oriented words not on David's own past experiences as a righteous sufferer, making it even more unlikely that we are invited to see David as speaking for himself as a "type" of the future Christ.

As such for the author of Acts, David, foreseeing these things, is speaking as a prophet in the prosopon of the Davidic messiah, the fruit of his own loins. And through David it is this Christ, the Son, who in turn is speaking about his own *future* resurrection—which indicates that the theodramatic setting for the speech assigned by the author of Acts is prior to the raising of Jesus. More precisely, the theodramatic setting presupposes that the speaker has thus far endured an intense difficulty through the aid of the personal presence of God—the Son "kept seeing" the Father before him,[24] and indeed, the presence of the Father at his right hand will continue to prevent him from "being shaken." Therefore, I suggest the exact theodramatic setting is *during the crisis of the cross, with death looming, but before the resurrection*. This paraphrase indicates how I suggest the author of Acts was prosopologically interpreting the psalm in the Pentecost speech:

[23] On the origin and development of David's prophetic role in Second Temple Judaism and how this impacted the views of the earliest Christians, see Joseph A. Fitzmyer, "David 'Being Therefore a Prophet . . .' (Acts 2: 30)," *CBQ* 34 (1972): 332–9.

[24] I have translated *proorōmēn* in Acts 2: 25 as "*I kept seeing* the Lord [God] before me" because the imperfect tense of the verb is most likely iterative in light of the prepositional qualifier *dia pantos* ("continually").

THE CHRIST (speaking to GOD THE FATHER from the cross): I, the Son, kept seeing the Lord God, my Father, continually before me, for God is at my right hand lest I be shaken; therefore my heart is cheered, and my tongue rejoices; moreover my flesh will even live in hope. Because you, O my Father, will not abandon my soul to Hades, or permit your Holy One to see decay. You have made known to me the paths of life; you, O my Father, will fill me with joy in your presence. (Acts 2: 25–8 citing Ps. 15: 8–11 LXX)

Notice—and this is both vital and fascinating—at this moment of the Son's deepest need, *the Son sees the Father at his own right hand*. That is, the Son is to the left of the Father, metaphorically occupying the royal position in the center. (Although the Son in his humility is not reported as reflecting on this, focusing instead on the Father's readiness to assist him). Moreover, since the Father is in the less-elevated but authoritative station *at the Son's right hand*, the Father is ready to exercise sovereignty *on the Son's behalf*, poised to meet his need speedily by executing the Son's royal command should he so will.

The mutual love and willingness to condescend functionally to serve the other is poignantly evident in this vision of the Father at the right hand of the Son, especially when we consider that very soon the positions will be reversed and the exalted Son will gladly sit down at the right hand of the Father as he is installed as heavenly "Lord" (Acts 2: 34)—all of which is treated in the next chapter. Yet, in this crisis where Hades threatens, because of God the Father's presence at his right hand the Son is not "shaken," knowing that despite the intense pressure of the moment, God the Father has already provided for him. Specifically, the Father has made known to him "the paths of life." Thus, he can have firm confidence in a future rescue from this crisis unto death, knowing that "you, O my Father, will not abandon my soul to Hades," and that "you, O my Father, will not permit your Holy One to see decay." Indeed, the Son tells the Father that he is certain that after he traverses the paths of life that the Father has already shown to him—thus returning to the Father—that there will be a moment of mutual joy-sharing. The Son tells the Father that he knows that the Father will give him the gift of gladness, "You, O my Father, will fill me with joy in your presence" (paraphrasing Ps. 15: 11 LXX in Acts 2: 28), so that the giver and the receiver might celebrate the successful completion of the center of the divine plan together.

* * *

In sum, for the earliest Christians, when an enemy as deep and dark as death lashed out at the Son, they found that he spoke many things to the Father. He does express dismay at his abandonment unto death—"My God, my God, why have you forsaken me?"—yet even this expression is corralled by a Spirit-inspired script that assures the Son that the tragedy is really a comedy. The hero will be rescued, and the rescue will bring many members of the human family to salvation. The Son tells the Father that he will attest the Father's saving power as he leads the human family in worship of the Father: "I will proclaim your name to my brethren, in the midst of the congregation I will praise you" and "For this reason I will profess you among the nations and I will sing your name." For the first Christians, the Son was able to move from feelings of lonely forsakenness to the joy of corporate praise, and all this because the Father *kept* appearing to him *continually*—the Father even appeared at the right hand of the Son. Then, as the Son himself puts it, he *trusted* in the midst of a crisis unto death. The Son knew the Father would "not permit his Holy One to see decay," and so the Son "spoke" a plea to the Father for deliverance. The Son affirmed, "I will trust in him." The Son is truly delivered by the Father—rescued from "Hades" and the "anguishes of death"—with the result that the Son is then able to say, "Here I am and the children whom God has given me." Accordingly, the Son tells the Father that he knows that the Father will grant him a special measure of joy upon his return, "You will fill me with joy in your presence."

6

Triumphant Talks

In the last chapter, we explored how early Christians, when reading their Old Testament, discovered words of praise rendered by the Son to the Father, especially with a view to the rescue achieved after the crucifixion. Indeed, the earliest Christians discovered that as Jesus speaks these words of acclaim, the entire human race is invited to join the resounding chorus, so that God's praise can reach to the ends of the earth. Yet even with these magnificent words of praise, the story is not yet complete. This chapter brings us to the grand finale, as Father, Son, and Spirit—with the Spirit now occasionally appearing as a speaking character in the Spirit's own person—converse together about the coronation of the Son, the final conquest of the enemies of God, the new creation, and the consummation of the ages.

INCARNATION AND ENTHRONEMENT—ROMANS 1: 3–4

Romans 1: 3–4 is a classic and controversial text that pertains to the enthronement of the Son. Although it does not involve a theodramatic reading of the Scripture, a brief discussion is desirable to prepare the way sufficiently for treatment of the theodramatic texts pertaining to the coronation of the Son in the pages that follow. This important passage is widely viewed by other scholars (correctly in my judgment) as preserving pre-Pauline material:[1]

> [the gospel] concerning God's Son, who as it pertains to the flesh came into existence by means of the seed of David; who as it pertains to the Spirit of Holiness was appointed Son-of-God-in-Power by means of the resurrection from among the dead ones—Jesus Christ our Lord.   (Rom. 1: 3–4)

---

[1] In the remainder of this subsection I am summarizing my article: Matthew W. Bates, "A Christology of Incarnation and Enthronement: Romans 1: 3–4 as Unified, Nonadoptionist, and Nonconciliatory," *CBQ* 77 (2015): 107–27. For more details regarding the history of interpretation, exegetical evidence, and christological implications, the full article should be consulted.

Yet it has been popular in the last several generations of biblical scholarship to suggest that what Paul wrote in Romans 1: 3–4 was the result of a very complex process. According to these scholarly hypotheses, a bare pre-Pauline creed-like fragment was altered by multiple communities (Palestinian and then Hellenistic), and perhaps also by Paul himself, before Paul incorporated it into his letter as we find it today.[2] However, not only the complexity of such hypotheses speaks against their likelihood—can anyone really reliably detect three redactional layers in the space of these two laconic verses?—so also does the notion of separate and hermetically sealed early Christian communities. It is better to view Romans 1: 3–4 as containing a unified pre-Pauline protocreed that is theologically centered on twin transitions in the life of the Son of God, *entering* human existence and *being installed* as Son-of-God-in-Power.

Moreover, contrary to those such as Robert Jewett, Bart Ehrman, and others who favor an original adoptionism in this text—that is, the notion that Jesus was declared "with power" to be "Son of God" (purely a messianic title) by his resurrection from the dead, and so adopted as God's son—this is not tenable because the Son is viewed in Romans 1: 3–4 as already the preexistent Son of God.[3] The Son's preexistence is implied in the "who came into being" (*tou genomenou*) of Romans 1: 3, which contrary to most translations should *not* be rendered as "who was born" or "who was descended," implying nothing more than ordinary, natural birth.[4] He was already deemed by Paul as the sent Son of God who descended from heaven prior to the resurrection and enthronement (Rom. 8: 3; Gal. 4: 4; 1 Cor. 15: 47; 2 Cor. 8: 9). So in light of this "who as it pertains to the flesh came into existence" language, is this not also the most

---

[2] For the history of interpretation of Rom. 1: 3–4, especially the story of the development of the redactional hypotheses that have been in favor from Bultmann onwards, see Robert Jewett, "The Redaction and Use of an Early Christian Confession in Romans 1: 3–4," in D. E. Groh and R. Jewett (eds.), *The Living Text: Essays in Honor of Ernest W. Saunders* (Lanham, Md.: University Press of America, 1985), 99–122. For a more thorough history which also includes patristic interpretations, see Joshua W. Jipp, "Ancient, Modern, and Future Interpretations of Romans 1: 3–4: Reception History and Biblical Interpretation," *JTI* (2009): 241–59.

[3] Robert Jewett, *Romans: A Commentary* (Hermeneia; Minneapolis: Fortress, 2007), 103–8; Bart D. Ehrman, *How Jesus Became God: The Exaltation of a Jewish Preacher from Galilee* (New York: HarperOne, 2014), 218–25. It should be noted that Ehrman ultimately prefers the label "exaltation christology" over adoption nomenclature even though he judges the latter to be perfectly accurate (pp. 230–2).

[4] Excluding Rom. 1: 3, Gal. 4: 4, and Phil. 2: 7 because these are the very instantiations under debate, there is only one fairly certain occurrence and one possible (but doubtful) occurrence of *ginomai* as "to reproduce naturally" out of 667 occurrences in the NT (Matt. 21: 19 and John 8: 58 respectively). More typically it means "to come into existence" or "to come about" and stresses *state of being*. On the other hand, there are 97 fairly certain occurrences of *gennaō* as "to reproduce naturally" in the NT. Thus, assuming for the sake of argument that the semantic context in Rom. 1: 3 would equally permit either instantiation if "ordinary human birth" were the primary intention, I judge that *gennaō* is about 50 times more likely to have been selected than *ginomai*. I also conclude that *ginomai* was most likely chosen by the author over *gennaō* because the author desired to emphasize *change in state of being* through the *human birthing process*, so the former was suitable while the latter was not.

reasonable inference for this pre-Pauline fragment that Paul opted to incorporate into his letter (cf. Phil. 2: 6–8)? The parallel between Romans 1: 3 and Galatians 4: 4 is also especially striking. In Romans 1: 3 it is affirmed that inasmuch as it pertains to the flesh, the Son *"came into being by means of the seed of David"* (*genomenou ek spermatos Dauid*). Meanwhile in Galatians 4: 4 Paul similarly states, "But when the fullness of time came, God sent forth his Son, who *came into being by means of a woman"* (*genomenon ek gynaikos*—cf. Phil. 2: 7). The parallel urges us to consider that a woman, Mary, is in view as the seed of David in Romans 1: 3.[5]

Furthermore, upon this occasion of installation in Romans 1: 4, this Jesus was not granted the title "Son of God," a title that the first words of Romans 1: 3 may suggest that he already possessed ("the gospel concerning God's *Son*") before this installation, but rather he was appointed to a new *ruling office* carrying the title (or, better, the informally descriptive quasi-title) of "Son-of-God-in-Power."[6] Compare the similar logic in Romans 15: 12 where Isaiah 11: 10 is cited in support of the notion that "a root of Jesse," that is, a Davidic offspring, will be raised up in order to rule: "one who will arise to rule over nations" (*ho anastamenos archein ethnōn*). In both Romans 1: 4 and in Romans 15: 12 resurrection leads directly to Jesus' sovereign rule.[7]

Why is Romans 1: 3–4 so significant? Because it yields not just the Christology of Paul, the first extant Christian author (who began writing less than twenty years after Jesus' death), but even more importantly it in all likelihood

---

[5] On Mary as the seed of David, cf. Ignatius, *Eph.* 18. 2, 20. 2; Irenaeus, *Haer.* 3. 16. 3; *Epid.* 36.

[6] It is most probable that "Son-of-God-in-Power" was intended as a unified expression—that is, it is a title or informal description of the new office to which the "Son of God" had been appointed at his resurrection (and enthronement), as can be demonstrated by looking at the structural flow of the Greek syntax of Rom. 1: 3–4:

1: 3 Participle
  ek clause
  kata clause
1: 4 Participle + *huiou theou* + *en dynamei*
  kata clause
  ek clause

In assessing probable historical meaning, the scholarly judgment that Jesus was declared "in power" or "with power" to be "Son of God" (e.g. see Ehrman, *How Jesus Became God*, 221–2) falters in part because this disrupts the tight ABBA pattern among the prepositional modifiers in the Greek text. That is, *en dynamei* ("in power") would then need to be placed down below on its own separate line in verse 4 as an adverbial modifier of the participial phrase *tou horisthentos* ("appointed"), but this is less likely structurally than a unified expression "Son-of-God-in-Power." Thus, it is not only linguistic analysis and reception history, but also the structural symmetry in the Greek text that suggests that Rom. 1: 3–4 is not adoptionist.

[7] This clear Davidic reference in Rom. 15: 12 (Jesse is David's Father) is missed by both Jewett, *Romans*, 98, and Ehrman, *How Jesus Became God*, 222, who mistakenly assert that Paul nowhere else shows interest in Jesus' Davidic lineage (cf. also 2 Tim. 2: 8 if deemed genuinely Pauline). On the link between Rom. 1: 3–4 and 15: 12, see especially the helpful treatment by J. R. Daniel Kirk, *Unlocking Romans: Resurrection and the Justification of God* (Grand Rapids: Eerdmans, 2008), 39–55.

bears witness to the pre-Pauline tradition, so it pushes the horizon back even earlier. It shows, I believe, that the earliest Christological layer we can reliably detect already viewed Jesus as preexistent, having come to earth to take on human flesh in the line of David as God's real Son, not just as God's "son" through messianic adoption. A paraphrase of Romans 1: 3–4 can help bring out the compressed theology:[8]

> The gospel concerning the Son of God, who was brought from preexistence into human existence by means of Mary—the seed of David—as it pertains to the flesh, that is, to the fleshly realm that is characterized by human physicality with all its limitations. This Son of God was installed into a new office—Son-of-God-in-Power—as it pertains to the realm dominated by life in the Holy Spirit—by means of his resurrection from among the dead ones. This Son-of-God-in-Power is Jesus Christ our Lord. (Rom. 1: 3–4)

In short, the Christology of both Paul and also of the pre-Pauline tradition in Romans 1: 3–4 and Philippians 2: 6–11 (among other texts) is already as high as anywhere else in the New Testament. These results should be considered in relationship to the theodramatic readings of the Psalter by the author of Acts, the author of Hebrews, and other early Christians.

THE CORONATION OF THE SON

Theodrama and Enthronement in Peter's Pentecost Sermon

The joyful reunion between the Father and the Son was enthusiastically announced by the earliest church in two psalms that we have already discussed in the second chapter—Psalm 2 and Psalm 110—although we have not yet drawn out the full implications. In fact, the earliest Christians detected a conversation between God the Father and the Son that occurred upon the return of the Son to the heavenly sphere, at which time the Father spoke to the Son, exultantly inviting the Son to sit down at his right hand and rule.

The early Christians found that David had prophetically anticipated the enthronement of the Son via a theodrama in which the Father speaks to the Son. For example the author of Acts has Peter in his Pentecost sermon declare that David himself "did not ascend to the heavens" (2: 34), yet nonetheless David said, "The Lord said to my Lord, 'Sit at my right hand until I make your enemies a footstool for your feet'" (Acts 2: 34–5 citing Ps. 109: 1 LXX). Thus, the author of Acts indicates that since David "did not ascend to the

---

[8]   This paraphrase is taken verbatim from Bates, "A Christology of Incarnation and Enthronement," 126–7.

heavens," this "Sit at my right hand" invitation cannot possibly have been addressed to David.

This undercuts the notion that David was identified as the addressee through a typology, since the point is precisely that the words spoken were *not* suitable for David qua David. Rather the words must have been spoken to Jesus, the Christ, who has now "been lifted up to the right hand of God" (2: 33). The implication is as crystalline here as in the interpretation of Psalm 109 LXX in the Gospels, and the same conclusion regarding the preexistent begottenness of the Son is applicable.[9] David in *the original prophetic setting* is felt by the author of Acts to be speaking in the character of the Father to the Son about 1,000 years before the Son would arrive on the earth,[10] so that we might paraphrase:

DAVID *Himself* (reporting the setting): The Lord God said to my Lord,
David in the prosopon of GOD *(spoken to* MY LORD, THE CHRIST*)*: Sit at my right hand, O Christ, Lord of David, my Son, until I make your enemies a footstool for your feet.

Furthermore, *the theodramatic* setting for these words is explicitly given by the author of Acts: The Father (through David) spoke these words at the theodramatic occasion of the Son's ascension and enthronement ("having been lifted up to the right hand of God"—Acts 2: 33), that is, when he was installed as heavenly Lord. This theodramatic event has already found an *actualized setting* in the heavenly realm for Peter so that it is in his immediate past tense (cf. Acts 1: 9), as has been proven by the outpouring of the Spirit at Pentecost. This installation as heavenly Lord is emphatically described by Peter (as portrayed), "Therefore all the house of Israel must know that God has made [*epoiēsen*] this Jesus whom you crucified both Lord and Christ [*kai kyrion auton kai christon*]!" (Acts 2: 36).

From Chosen to Enthroned—A Non-Adoptionist Christology

Hence, despite this "God has made" language with reference to Jesus as "both Lord and Christ" (Acts 2: 36), we should not leap with James Dunn, Bart

---

[9] See Ch. 2, especially the discussion of a heavenly dialogue via Ps. 109: 3 LXX in the section "From the Womb, before the Dawn, I Begot You." The subsequent remarks in this chapter about how LXX Pss. 109 and 2: 6–9 were being read in light of one another in the early church are also relevant.

[10] It is also likely that Jesus' defense in the Synoptic Gospels before the Jewish high priest contains an allusion to Ps. 109: 1 LXX in conjunction with Dan. 7: 13–14, in which he accepts the title "the Christ, the Son of the Blessed One" and he adds, "And you will see the Son of Man sitting at the right hand of power and coming with the clouds of heaven" (Mark 14: 61–2; cf. Matt. 26: 63–4; Luke 22: 69–70). The background imagery favors an enthronement scene.

Ehrman, and others to the conclusion that this text entails or supports a divine adoption of Jesus predicated on the resurrection[11]—especially since the pre-existence of Jesus is most likely assumed via the quotation of Psalm 110 in the immediate context. A much simpler and better evidenced solution lies ready to hand: the text details not God's adoption of a son, but the transition of Jesus from chosen and anointed messiah to fully authoritative king. That is, Peter is portrayed as describing the moment at which Jesus, who preexisted as the Son of God and who in his earthly life was only the *messias designatus* (the one chosen and anointed as king by God but lacking a throne from which to rule) was made both the *Lord* and the *Messiah* by God, that is, he was installed on the heavenly throne at God's right hand as *sovereign* and *king* and has begun to reign. Indeed, this accords quite precisely not only with the enthronement context in Acts 2, but also with the words spoken near the beginning of the Gospel of Luke anticipating this very sequence, "And he will be great and he will be called *Son of the Most High*, and the Lord God *will give him the throne* of his father David" (1: 32), and *then he will rule forever* (1: 33; cf. Matt. 19: 28; 25: 31).[12] In short, I submit that those who favor adoptionism in this text have either not considered or not sufficiently weighed the flexibility in what it means to be "made the Christ." As was the case with the great king David, so I submit with regard to Jesus in Acts 2: 36—an individual can be said to have been "made the Christ" and can properly be called "the Christ" on the basis of the anointing (literally, "the Christ-ing") activity prior to the assumption of full kingly rule, but also upon official assumption of that rule at the time of the enthronement.[13]

To put it yet another way, borrowing the language of Romans 1: 4, the preexistent Son of God has been made Lord and messiah because he is now ensconced at the right hand of God in a new office, an office described as *Son-of-God-in-Power*. This solution also coheres with the prosopological interpretation in Luke 3: 22 and 9: 35 (and parallels) and Acts 13: 32–7 given previously (see Ch. 2), in which Psalm 2: 7 was most likely interpreted by the author *not* as an adoptionist direct speech from the Father to the Son at the time of the enthronement, but as a theodramatic *reported speech* at the time of the

---

[11] See James D. G. Dunn, *Christology in the Making: A New Testament Inquiry into the Origins of the Doctrine of the Incarnation* (2nd edn.; Grand Rapids: Eerdmans, 1989), 35–6, 142–3; Ehrman, *How Jesus Became God*, 227–8.

[12] For more general remarks regarding how Acts 2: 36 relates to Luke's Christological story, see C. Kavin Rowe, *Early Narrative Christology: The LORD in the Gospel of Luke* (Grand Rapids: Baker Academic, 2009), 189–96. Rowe concludes that in Acts 2: 36 the emphasis is epistemological rather than ontological, while nonetheless correctly noting that "In the Lukan narrative, there was not [a time] when Jesus was not κύριος" (p. 195).

[13] In 1 Sam. 16: 12 LXX David is anointed (*chrison*) as the Christ by Samuel, implying he can properly be termed "the Christ" (cf. 1 Sam. 16: 6 LXX) prior to his attainment of royal rule. Compare this with e.g. 2 Sam. 19: 22 LXX, in which David is called "the Christ" subsequent to his enthronement on the basis of his present ruling authority.

enthronement harking back to an *earlier* theodramatic setting. The Son states that the Father had previously said to him, "You are my Son, today I have begotten you." From this position at the right hand, the Son "has received from the Father the promised Spirit," and the Son has thereby poured out the Spirit on his followers, causing them to speak in other languages (Acts 2: 33).[14]

Support for this interpretation also comes from slightly later Christian interpreters, and as was discussed in Chapter 2, these interpretative trajectories are a crucial but neglected historical-critical control in fixing probable meaning. For example, in agreement with the construal of Psalm 109: 1 LXX in Acts, not only does Justin Martyr determine that the theodramatic setting for this speech is after the resurrection, when God the Father led the Christ to heaven (*Dial.* 32. 3; 36. 5; 83. 1–4; *1 Apol.* 45. 1), he also links it to another psalm that other early Christians, such as the author of Hebrews, believed was addressed to the Christ and which describes the time of his enthronement—Psalm 44: 7–8 LXX.

The Holy Spirit as Distinct Speaker—Hebrews 1: 8–9

Justin Martyr in *Dialogue* 56. 14–15 argues that there are passages in the Old Testament where someone is called "God" or "Lord" alongside the Creator of the universe, a fact attested not only in passages such as Genesis 19: 24 (e.g. "*The Lord* rained upon Sodom brimstone and fire *from the Lord* out of heaven") but also by David in Psalm 109: 1 LXX ("The Lord said to my Lord"). Like Justin, Irenaeus (*Epid.* 47) and the author of Hebrews (1: 8–9) believed that two distinct persons are described as God in Psalm 44: 7–8 LXX, in which a coronation is described. Accordingly, the author of Hebrews states:

> But about the Son he says, "Your throne, O God, is forever and ever and the scepter of justice is the scepter of your kingdom. You have loved righteousness and hated lawlessness; on account of this, O God, your God has anointed you with the oil of gladness beyond your companions." (Heb. 1: 8–9 citing Ps. 44: 7–8 LXX)[15]

---

[14] Precisely what is poured out in Acts 2: 33 is "this which you [both] see and hear" (*touto ho hymeis [kai] blepete kai akouete*). The "this" (*touto*), however, is neuter singular, demanding a neuter singular referent, and the obvious referent is "Spirit" (*pneuma*) in the phrase "of the Holy Spirit" (*tou pneumatos tou hagiou*) found in the preceding clause. Thus, it should be noted in passing that this passage would seem to support the procession of the Spirit from both the Father and the Son, although the neglected emphasis on divine persons in dialogue is, as I have been arguing throughout this book, even more significant for a Trinitarian synthesis.

[15] The manuscript evidence for Heb. 1: 8–9 is complex. I take *ho theos* as a vocative twice ("O God"), but the final "your God" (*ho theos sou*) as a third-person identification. This reading demands that the widely attested *sou* (A D Y 0243 0278 33 1739 1881 𝔐 latt sy co) in *rabdos tēs basileias sou* ("scepter of your kingdom") is the correct reading rather than *autou*, even though the latter enjoys some strong early attestation (𝔭⁴⁶ ℵ B). Most scholars agree that *sou* is correct in view of the criterion *lectio difficilior probabilior* and because of its widespread attestation—see

A person designated "God" is directly addressed in the psalm. This person possesses the royal scepter, rules with justice, and most crucially has been anointed by a second person called "your God" in the text. Since the person designated "your God" anoints the other person called "God," and the action is not reflexive, *two persons both called "God"* are necessarily present in the text. Moreover, the verbal action of anointing (*echrisen*), which the one labeled "your God" undertakes and the one termed "God" receives, is closely associated with the noun *Christos* ("Messiah" or "Christ"), which literally means "anointed one." For the early Christians, thus, the one doing the anointing in this text is God the Father and the one on whom the oil is poured is God the Son, the Christ, the anointed one.[16] But note well that this latter reading was not envisioned as a *dialogue between* the Father and the Son, rather the Son, the Christ, is being addressed theodramatically by some unidentified person who is speaking directly to the Son, while this mysterious speaker also describes the relational activities that characterize the Father and the Son.[17]

Who then is this enigmatically unidentified speaker? The author of Hebrews gives no indication whatsoever apart from closing off certain possibilities. For instance, since God (the Father) is certainly the ultimate speaker in the citations in Hebrews 1: 5 and 1: 13, it might be tempting to suggest that he is also the speaker in Hebrews 1: 8–9, but the third-person references to God the Father in 1: 9 itself (he is the "God" in the phrase "your God") make it very unlikely that he would have been construed as the first-person speaker. So God the Father is not the speaker.

Assuming interpretative continuity in the early church, Justin Martyr perhaps offers a little additional help as we consider the most probable reading for the author of Hebrews—and his testimony is particularly tantalizing. Justin affirms David as speaker while asserting that *the Holy Spirit*, probably appearing here as a speaking theodramatic prosopon in the Spirit's own right, is ultimately the one who called this anointed person "God" in addition to the Father.[18] That the Holy Spirit was regarded at least by the time of Justin Martyr (the middle of the second century) as a distinct person capable of

---

Bruce M. Metzger, *A Textual Commentary on the Greek New Testament* (2nd edn.; New York: United Bible Societies, 1994), 592–3.

[16] Cf. Justin, *Dial*. 56. 14; 63. 4; 86. 3; Irenaeus, *Haer*. 3. 6. 1. Irenaeus specifies further that the throne mentioned in the psalm is "of the everlasting kingdom," that the oil of anointing is "the Spirit," and that the companions are "his disciples" (*Epid*. 47).

[17] Regarding direct speech in Heb. 1: 8, the nominative-for-vocative was common in the NT era and is widely accepted here. For the rationale, see Daniel B. Wallace, *Greek Grammar Beyond the Basics: An Exegetical Syntax of the New Testament* (Grand Rapids: Zondervan, 1996), 59.

[18] Justin, *Dial*. 56. 14–15 ("a certain other was called Lord by the Holy Spirit"; "the Holy Spirit calls a certain other God and Lord"); cf. Tertullian, *Prax*. 11. 7, where the Spirit is said to speak "from the third person about the Father and the Son" (*ex tertia persona de patre et filio*). Yet it is also possible that in *Dial*. 56. 14–15 Justin is merely referring to the Spirit as the inspiring secondary agent rather than as the primary speaking agent.

speaking in the theodrama on his own, not just in the guise of another, is fairly clear. For example, in *Dialogue* 36. 6 Justin explains the conversation in Psalm 24 (= Ps. 23 LXX) by affirming, "the Holy Spirit gave answer to them either from the prosopon of the Father *or in his own prosopon*." Thus, for Justin, the Holy Spirit could at least potentially appear as a unique speaking character in the Spirit's own right. When evaluating the cogency of this possibility for the author of Hebrews, we should consider carefully Hebrews 3: 7 ("even as the Holy Spirit says") and 10: 15 ("The Holy Spirit also testifies"), since in these texts the Spirit is put forward as the ultimate speaker of various Old Testament texts, even if it is unclear that the Old Testament texts thereby cited were being interpreted prosopologically.

Irenaeus is more vague in his analysis of Psalm 44: 7–8 LXX, saying merely that "David speaks about the Father and Son," probably indicating that he sees the Spirit as speaking through David, or maybe showing that he does not see David as taking on a character or guise at all in this particular instance, but rather that David appears as his own person in the theodrama, speaking to the character of the Son, since the Son is addressed in the second person.[19] Alternatively, and the difference is only subtle, Irenaeus may take David as simply speaking from his own person in his ordinary prophetic role, uttering forth to the future Christ as he gazes in his mind's eye upon the future theodrama that will come to pass.[20] Certainty is elusive.

Yet, apart from any evidence to the contrary, since early Christians frequently borrowed interpretations from one another, continuity in hermeneutical logic between the author of Hebrews, Justin, and Irenaeus is the most likely historical hypothesis, so it is most sound to posit that the author of Hebrews probably found the Spirit to be speaking via David in the Spirit's own prosopon to the Son about the Father in Psalm 44: 7–8 LXX in Hebrews 1: 8–9.[21] In this fashion it is likely that all three prosopa of what would later come to be termed the Trinity—Father, Son, and inspiring Spirit—were individually and distinctly found to be "God" through a person-centered reading strategy by the author of Hebrews prior to 70 CE.

CONQUEST

As we have already seen, the theodramatic setting at the time of the ascension and enthronement of the Son for the "Sit at my right hand" speech of Psalm

---

[19] Irenaeus, *Epid.* 47.   [20] Cf. Acts 8: 34 as it pertains to Isa. 53 in Ch. 3.
[21] As a possible second example of the Spirit speaking in the Spirit's own prosopon, cf. Heb. 1: 10–12 citing Ps. 101: 26–8 LXX as discussed subsequently in this chapter.

109: 1 LXX in Acts 2: 32–7 is reaffirmed by Justin Martyr and by Irenaeus.[22] However, both Justin and Irenaeus expand on the significance of the speech for the rule of the Son in ways that help us understand, I believe, how other early Christian authors, such as the author of Revelation, found critical information about the final consummation of God's plan in moments of divine dialogue in the ancient Jewish Scripture.

You Will Rule Over Your Enemies

Justin Martyr has determined that Psalm 109: 2 LXX—"The Lord [God the Father] will send forth a scepter of *power* for you [the Son] from Jerusalem, and you will rule over your enemies" (as cited in *1 Apol.* 45. 3)—announced in advance that the Christ would make effective his rule over his enemies by sending out from Jerusalem apostolic heralds who would proclaim everywhere "the *powerful* message" of the good news of Jesus Christ's reign (*1 Apol.* 45. 5). Justin further clarifies the nature of the enemies overwhelmed by this sending forth of the scepter of power. For not only did Jesus' weeping and moaning in Jerusalem (for Justin, obviously on the cross) turn away those who would war against God (*Dial.* 83. 3), but also the sending forth of the scepter of power is in actuality "the message of summoning and of repentance issued to all the nations where *the demons* formerly ruled over the populace" (*Dial.* 83. 4). Thus, for Justin Psalm 109: 2 LXX describes the manner in which the victory over the demons achieved on the cross will ultimately penetrate all the nations. Meanwhile Clement of Rome is more general in his interpretation of Psalm 109: 2 LXX, declaring that the enemies are "those who are wicked and resist the will" of the Son (*1 Clem.* 36. 6).

Even more arresting, however, is Irenaeus's construal of the way in which the divine dialogue in Psalm 109 LXX (= Ps. 110) announces the triumphant reign of the Son over the enemies of God when combined with Psalm 2. Irenaeus explicitly avows that his reading of this text is prosopological, certifying that David did not speak these words from himself, but the Holy Spirit spoke them "while conforming Himself to the person concerned" (*Epid.* 49). For Irenaeus not only does Psalm 109 LXX prove that the Son was before all things, that is, preexistent (see Ch. 2), but also that he even now rules and judges the nations, especially his enemies—kings and other humans who currently hate him and persecute his name. As Irenaeus notes, the psalm speaks of the Son, saying, "he has crushed kings on the day of his wrath" and "he will judge the nations" and "he will crush the heads of many upon

---

[22] The theodramatic setting for Ps. 109: 1 LXX in Heb. 1: 13, *1 Clem.* 36. 5, and *Barn.* 12. 10 is not specified, although an enthronement setting is congenial to all these texts.

the earth."[23] Irenaeus combines the dialogues between the Father and the Son from Psalm 109 LXX with Psalm 2: 7–8 LXX, both read prosopologically, to unravel how the full triumph of the Son will emerge in the future. In support of the notion that the Christ is declared by the Spirit to be Son of God and the king of the nations, Irenaeus quotes Psalm 2: 7–8: "David says thus, 'The Lord said to me, "You are my Son, <today> have I begotten you; ask of me and I will give you the nations for your inheritance and the ends of the earth as a possession"'" (*Epid.* 49). And Irenaeus explains the significance of this quotation from Psalm 2: 7–8 LXX further, and thus we see how he has married its interpretation to Psalm 109: 1 LXX:

> These things were not said to David, for he did not rule over the nations nor over the ends of the earth, but only over the Jews. So it is evident that the promise made to the Anointed, to rule over the ends of the earth, is to the Son of God, whom David himself confesses as his Lord, saying in this way, "The Lord says to my Lord, 'Sit at my right hand,'" and the following, as we have said before. (*Epid.* 49, slightly modifying Behr's translation)

Irenaeus has noted that both LXX Psalm 109 and Psalm 2 contain *reported speech*, in which we hear about what the Father *had previously* told the Son. Furthermore, both psalms speak of the way the Son *will* come to reign over the nations *in the future*, especially over kings or other rulers that seek to oppose God.

In sum, the two psalms were read quite similarly by Irenaeus and others in the earliest church. The *prophetic setting* for both speeches is during the time of David. *Theodramatic setting "B"* is the Son's enthronement at which time the Father speaks (e.g. "Sit at my right hand"; "Rule in the midst of your enemies"; "before the morning-star appeared, I begot you") and at which time *the reports of earlier speeches* are given. The Father's first speeches to the Son occurred sometime earlier than these reports—the reports look backward to a much earlier moment in the theodrama—the time before time, *theodramatic setting "A,"* when things both present with respect to that setting—"today I have begotten you"; "ask of me"; "you are a priest forever in the order of Melchizedek"—and things future—"I will make the nations your inheritance, the ends of the earth your possession"—were discussed by the Father and the Son. Theodramatic settings "B" and "A" have both been actualized, that is, these divine dialogues have already occurred—for example, Jesus stands as the one begotten before time, has been declared an eternal priest in the order of Melchizedek, and has been enthroned at the right hand—but the actions mentioned as future in these dialogues, such as the gift of the nations as an inheritance and the full reign of the Son over his opponents, are still in the process of being brought about. Indeed, this realization helped fuel the

---

[23] Irenaeus, *Epid.* 49; cf. Ps. 109: 5–6 LXX.

apocalyptic visions found in the book of Revelation, as the Son brings ordinary history to a cataclysmic climax.

You Will Rule Them with an Iron Scepter

A plethora of evidence has already been presented for the centrality of theodramatic readings of Psalm 2 to Trinitarian developments in the earliest church. Since it contains *reported speech*, multiple theodramatic settings were discerned by early Christian readers. Accordingly, in early Christian interpretations of this psalm, at the time of the Son's enthronement not only did the Son report that the Father had previously spoken to him about his begetting before time began—"The Lord [God] said to me, 'You are my Son, today I have begotten you'" (Ps. 2: 7 LXX)—the Son also reports that in this prior conversation the future ruling activity that would occur *after* his enthronement was also announced by the Father to him (paraphrasing):

THE FATHER (speaking to THE SON): Ask of me, O my Son, and I, your Father, will give you the nations as your inheritance and the ends of the earth as your possession. You *will rule them with an iron scepter*; you will smash them as a clay pot.   (Ps. 2: 8–9 LXX)

Although not made explicit, a prosopological reading of this passage is presumed in the interpretation given in the Apocalypse's magnificent vision of Jesus Christ's return to earth as a triumphant warrior on a white horse, leading the armies of heaven.[24] This rider, whose name is King of Kings and Lord of Lords, whose name is also Faithful and True, judges and makes war against the beast *and the kings of the earth* and their armies (cf. Ps. 2: 2, 10 LXX), executing judgment by means of the sharp sword that proceeds from his mouth. John then declares, "and he '*will rule them with an iron scepter*,' and he treads the winepress of the fury of the wrath of God Almighty" (Rev. 19: 15) Although John has made a third-person application of Psalm 2: 9 LXX, he has done so by presuming that the Father is the theodramatic speaker of the psalm and the "*You*" addressed in the psalm is Jesus Christ, the Son (cf. Rev. 12: 5).

In anticipation of this climatic scene, John describes the risen Christ as he exhorts the church at Thyatira in language that evokes this imagery from Psalm 2: 9 LXX, yet the text has been reimagined in a kaleidoscopic fashion. The words of the risen Christ show that if the church is able to triumph, to overcome by avoiding the temptations of idolatry and concomitant sexual immorality—then the church will come to participate in the divine triune life in a whole new way.

---

[24] For other applications, consider *Ps. Sol.* 17. 21–5; *Sib. Or.* 8. 248.

Although he does not draw attention to the prosopological maneuvering, Greg Beale fittingly designates the Apocalypse's use of the term "overcome" (*nikaō*) here as ironic, since the initial conquest is achieved through willingness to accept suffering and martyrdom in association with Christ,[25] and it is this initial conquest that allows participation in the final conquest. Accordingly, the words the Father spoke to the Son in the theodrama in Psalm 2 become the words of the Son to the Church:

THE SON (speaking to the CHURCH AT THYATIRA): To the one who conquers and who preserves my works to the end I will give authority over the nations, and he *will rule them with an iron scepter*, he *will smash them like clay pots.*   (Rev. 2: 26–7)

The Trinitarian and ecclesial implications of this prosopological interpretation and application of Psalm 2 are breathtaking, inasmuch as the message spoken in the theodrama before time began by the Father to the Son, spelling out the nature of the Son's future reign, is made by the Son via substitution to be a word addressed to the church for the final eschaton. In effect, *the church* becomes the *primordial theodramatic addressee* to whom the Father speaks, and the authority to reign given by the Father to the Son *devolves onto the eschatological church*, as the church comes to participate fully in the triumphant rule of the Son (cf. 2 Tim. 2: 12; Rev. 5: 10; 20: 6). As envisioned in Revelation 2: 26–7, the triumphant church will take on the ruling and subjecting role (*prosōpon*) of the Son as the theodrama is actualized, and this alongside the Son (cf. Rev. 19: 15)—indeed, all this has been ordained as part of the divine economy before the foundation of the world.

Thus, undertaking a broader theological synthesis, the Son must reign until all his enemies have been placed under his feet (1 Cor. 15: 25 citing Ps. 110: 1), but this reign is accomplished along with the church when the church, like the Son, overcomes by suffering. And this until the final enemy, death itself, having already been defeated at the cross, is utterly vanquished (1 Cor. 15: 26). Hence, the church (as part of the "all things") will be ruling alongside yet in submission to the Son (15: 27), and the Son to the Father, so that "God might be all in all" (15: 28). In fact, as we shall see, not just the author of the Apocalypse but also the author of Hebrews discovers that the Father speaks to the Son about this very process of final consummation, contrasting the eternal nature of the Son with the impermanence of the present created order.

---

[25] See Greg K. Beale, *The Book of Revelation: A Commentary on the Greek Text* (NIGTC; Grand Rapids: Eerdmans, 2001), 269–72.

CONSUMMATION

The author of Hebrews, who is eager to show that the Son is greatly superior to angels, offers a lengthy chain of Old Testament texts in Hebrews 1: 5–14, many of which, the author has determined, involve speeches in which the Son is directly addressed by the Father or someone else. For example, in this chain, as we have already discovered, the Father speaks to the Son about his begottenness before the incarnation (Heb. 1: 5 citing Ps. 2: 7 LXX), the Father speaks to the Son about his enthronement (Heb. 1: 13 citing Ps. 109: 1 LXX), and the Spirit speaks to the Son about the his installation (Heb. 1: 8–9 citing Ps. 44: 7–8 LXX).

They Will Be Changed—You Remain Unchanged

The author of Hebrews also believes that the Son was theodramatically addressed by someone (whose identity is underdetermined) in the Psalter regarding his role in creation, both old and new:

SOMEONE (addressing THE SON): You, O Lord, at the beginning you founded the earth, and the heavens are the works of your hands; they will perish, but you remain; and everything will become old like a garment, and like a cloak you will roll them up, and they will be changed. But you yourself are the same, and your years will not cease.   (Heb. 1: 10–12 citing Ps. 101: 26–8 LXX)

In contradistinction to the angels, who are mere servants of the Lord Christ, creatures subject to endless change, much like wind or flames of fire, the Son is eternal, fundamentally unchanging, and intimately involved in creation. And as in the citation in Hebrew 1: 8–9 examined earlier, although it is clear that the Son is the theodramatic addressee here, it is not certain precisely who is envisioned as speaking to the Son.

Irenaeus, the only other first- or second-century author, to the best of my knowledge, to cite this passage does not identify any speaker other than David qua David and gives no hint as to a possible theodramatic setting (*Haer.* 4. 3. 1). Yet Irenaeus's interpretation is akin to that found in Hebrews, even if he has used it to thwart his second-century gnostic opponents. The gnostics, Irenaeus alleges, claim that if heaven and earth are slated to fade away, then the Old Testament God must be destined to pass away too. And if the Old Testament God is going to fade away, then he must not be the most high God after all. It is implied by this gnostic exegesis that there must be a higher God than this destined-to-pass-away God. Irenaeus chastises the gnostics for their faulty reading, arguing that the "passing away" mentioned by

Paul (e.g. 1 Cor. 7: 31) does not involve God himself, but rather God will remain after this passing away, as will God's true servants. In support, Irenaeus quotes Isaiah 51: 6 as well as the text cited by the author of Hebrews, Psalm 101: 26–8 LXX, although Irenaeus extends the quotation a line further, also noting that the psalm mentions the endurance of the servants of God after the re-creation: "The children of your servants shall continue, and their seed shall be established forever."[26]

Perhaps the exact identity of the speaker of this particular quote, indeed, was not of paramount importance to the author of Hebrews, seeing it as the speech of David inspired by the Holy Spirit and directed at the Son regardless of whether or not David had taken on a distinct character or different *prosopon* when addressing the Son. Thus, given the past-tense references to the first creation and the future-tense pointers to the consummation, the theodramatic setting is probably best construed as identical to the prophetic setting, with this praise-speech delivered to the Son at the time of David— either by the Spirit in his own prosopon, as seems most likely, or by David in his own character.[27] The absolutely essential point for our purposes is that for the author of Hebrews and other members of the early church, in Psalm 101: 26–8 LXX the Son is theodramatically addressed by someone, whomever it might be, as the one who has authored creation and who will consummate it, transcending its fickle mutability.

Throughout this book I have sought to unfold the interior dynamic of the interpersonal relationship between Father, Son, and Spirit as imagined by the earliest church in its scriptural interpretation of divine speeches, addresses, and conversations. Indeed, I have argued that glimpses of the full range of the lived-together divine life can be obtained therein—from before time began until the final consummation. Hence a fuller analysis of this passage, Psalm 101: 26–8, serves as an apt *inclusio*, bringing the descriptive portion of the book full circle, since in it the Son is addressed as a divine person, active in the inaugural moments of creation all the way until the final transformation of creation at the consummation of ordinary history.

Creation and New Creation

At the outset of his exhortative message, the author of Hebrews gives his audience a framework for receiving subsequent teaching from Psalm 101: 26–8 LXX about the Son's role in creation, stating that the universe was created by God *through the agency* of the Son (Heb. 1: 2). Shortly thereafter

---

[26] Irenaeus, *Haer.* 4. 3. 1; trans. ANF (slightly modified).
[27] Compare my previous discussion in this chapter regarding the identity of the speaker in Heb. 1: 8–9 (citing Ps. 44: 7–8 LXX).

we are made privy to the details of precisely how the agency of the Son was actualized. For the author of Hebrews, the speaker of the psalm addresses the Son directly, "You, O Lord, founded the earth (*tēn gēn*) in the beginning (*kat archas*), and the heavens (*hoi ouranoi*) are the works of your hands" (Heb. 1: 10 citing Ps. 101: 26 LXX).

Overlaps in the precise vocabulary used show that we are quite deliberately being invited to hark back to Genesis 1: 1, in which we are told, "In the beginning God made the heavens and the earth" (*en archē epoiēsen ho theos ton ouranon kai tēn gēn*). And the author of Hebrews has determined precisely how it is that God made the heavens via Psalm 101: 26–8 LXX—the Son is told in the psalm, "the heavens are the works of your hands"—as if the Son were a living paintbrush resting in the fingers of the Father, splashing forth the sky and deeper heavenly spheres. And how was the earth created? Again, the Son is reminded via a prayer-speech directed at him, "At the beginning, O Lord, you founded the earth!"—picturing the Son as a dynamic and gigantic hammer in the Father's hands, firmly laying the cornerstone of the earth amidst the swirling watery-chaos. For the author of Hebrews, the theodramatic praise-speech aimed at the Son in Psalm 101: 26–8 LXX confirms that God the Father truly created the universe *through the agency of the Son.*

In his introduction the author of Hebrews guides the reader regarding how to interpret the role of the Son in the first creation, so that when the author quotes Psalm 101: 26–8 LXX, the reader is ready to receive it as a statement of the Son's personal agency. However we are offered no such initial guidance for how to interpret the language this psalm contains regarding the consummation of creation. During the course of the entire book of Hebrews, however, some directives are given. It becomes clear that the first creation will not utterly perish, as if it were fundamentally worthless or evil, but rather it will be radically remade, purifyingly altered, shaken to its very core, so that what remains is of permanent duration and eternal value. The author reminds the reader that when God warned the Israelites at Mount Sinai, the first creation violently trembled. Yet that was trivial compared to the process of intense shaking and refining to be expected in the future:

> At that time [God's] voice shook the earth, but now he has promised, "Yet once more I will shake not only the earth but also the heaven" [Hag. 2: 6]. This, "Yet once more," indicates the removal [*metathesin*] of what is shaken, namely things having been made [*pepoiēmenōn*]—so that things not shaken might remain. Therefore, since we are receiving an unshakable kingdom, let us give thanks, and thus let us worship in a manner pleasing to God, with reverence and awe; for indeed our God is a consuming fire.   (Heb. 12: 26–9)

As the author of Hebrews has poignantly reminded the reader, the theophany at Mount Sinai was terrifying—filled with burning fire, darkness, gloom, power-ful wind, and a trumpet-like voice issuing commands—in fact, the Israelites begged Moses to intercede for fear that they would be destroyed should they directly encounter God himself or even hear his words. Even Moses shuddered with fear! (Heb. 12: 18–21; cf. Exod. 19: 16–20; 20: 18–19; Deut. 9: 19). Yet as intense as God's engagement with creation and his people was at that time, God (the Father) is not finished. God has promised, "Yet once more I will shake not only the earth but also the heaven" (Heb. 12: 26 citing Hag. 2: 6).[28]

Refinement and New Creation. This shaking of the present created order, the decaying first creation, does not entail an annihilation of it, rather the shaking is a sifting process. The valuables are collected—in the immediate Old Testament context this refers to God causing the choice items from among all the nations to enter his temple so that it might be full of glory when God himself returns to it (see Hag. 2: 7). For the author of Hebrews, the impurities are removed, so that the only the unshakable things might remain in this carefully refined creation—things such as the Son, his kingdom, and those that persevere in order to receive it. With respect to the created order, then, God is indeed "a consuming fire" (Heb. 12: 29), a blaze that ruthlessly devours the worthless stubble and impure dross until only pristine purity remains (cf. 1 Cor. 3: 11–13). Although obviously "what remains" in this drastic re-creation emerges from and has continuity with the first creation, this is a purging so fiery and intense that other early Christian authors are compelled to call what emerges a new heavens and a new earth (2 Pet. 3: 13; Rev. 21: 1–2; cf. Isa. 66: 22).

The Son Will Remain. It is in light of this dramatic melting down of the first creation and the forging of a pure new creation that we should read the praise-speech addressed to the Son in the citation of Psalm 101: 26–8 LXX in Hebrews 1: 10–12. As the praise-speech continues, the Son is directly told that his work in the first creation "will perish," although "*you* will remain." In fact, the psalmist emphatically stresses that the first creation is subject to the grinding effects of time, wearing down to a sad and saggy patchwork, "everything will become old like a garment."

In consequence, according to the author of Hebrews the first creation will eventually come into terminal disuse through the deliberate choice of the Son, "and like a cloak *you* will roll them up," that is, the Son is told that he will remove the threadbare first creation, as if it were being rolled up to be stored away in a state of disrepair for some obscure future use. Yet, this obscure future use is in fact the tailoring of a marvelous new garment. The whole first creation is like a beloved but frayed sports jacket, the best strands of which will remain to be woven into a vibrant new tuxedo. In short, the handiworks of the first-creation "will be changed" in a fundamental way—the corrupt material

---

[28] Anthony T. Hanson, *Jesus Christ in the Old Testament* (London: SPCK, 1965), 75–82, takes Jesus Christ as the speaker of these words rather than God (the Father), but produces no forceful evidence in favor of this view.

will be cast aside, but after the sifting is complete the truly incorruptible material will be rewoven and spun anew.

The Son, however, will not be altered in this process along with the first creation, for, contra the much later Arius, he is not a creature but the Son (Heb. 1: 5). He is not the garment but the tailor, the divine personal agent through whom the Father created the universe (Heb. 1: 3). So the psalmist via the Spirit tells him, "But *you yourself* are the same, and your years will not cease." Thus, for the author of Hebrews, Jesus the Son, whose life is indestructible (7: 16) and who does not need to be purified (7: 26–7), is told via the first-person praise-speech in Psalm 101: 26–8 LXX that he is superior to the ephemeral angels, creatures that will grow old and begin to disintegrate along with the rest of creation. The Son as the intermediate personal agent in creation and re-creation is directly addressed, while the Father is the ultimate agent. In this way—"they will perish, but *you, the Son,* remain"—the consummation of God's story is reached, with divine discourse framing the whole, from creation to new creation.

7

Reading God Right

The scriptural interpretations that we have been gathering are like tiles in a mosaic that combine to show the face of the triune God. Each tile has a complex yet separate design of its own, but when collected they form a larger, more glorious image. Due to the boundless number of artistic renditions over the many centuries of history, the triune face of God has become quite familiar—perhaps there is even danger of a tired over-familiarity, especially for those exclusively acquainted with a portrait rendered in the monochrome hues of procession and subordination. It is hoped that the retrieval and restoration of the specific tiles collected in this book have helped in some small way to refresh the Trinitarian visage of God as beheld by the earliest Christians.

The overriding concern in this book has been historical exploration and description. That is, when ancient Christians were reading their Scripture, how were they reading it? Why did they read in this fashion? What are the implications for the manner in which the doctrine of the Trinity emerged as historically considered? While acknowledging that early Christian experiences of Jesus and the Spirit, philosophical developments, and mediatorial categories such as *Logos* and Wisdom were undoubtedly critical for Trinitarian and Christological developments, I have argued that prosopological exegesis of the Old Testament as evidenced in the New Testament and the early church was also of decisive importance, so that it is not inappropriate to speak of its presence in the earliest Christian writings as essential to the birth of the Trinity. Prosopological exegesis enabled the emerging church to read the one God as multiple persons in the ancient Scripture—Father, Son, and inspiring Spirit. It also ultimately gave the metaphor of "person" (*prosōpon; persona*) embedded in its assumptions a privileged status as the premier category for conceptualizing and expressing differentiation within the one God, to such a degree that this language would ultimately become normative for the church in the wake of the fourth-century councils of Nicaea and Constantinople: God is three "persons" (*prosōpa* or *hypostaseis*) subsisting in one divine essence or substance. Furthermore, in considering how Jesus came to be regarded as divine, prosopological exegesis was vital. Not only is prosopological exegesis well attested in the earliest strata of extant Christian literature, it is likely that the historical Jesus himself even used this reading strategy in considering his relationship to the God of Israel, his Abba-Father. In short, when the early church pondered, Who is Jesus?, the answer was fixed to a surprising extent by evaluating who he was in relation to God (the Father) and the Spirit, as they were found to converse with one another in what would come to be termed the Old Testament. Thus I currently find it more appropriate to speak of a Christology of Divine Persons than a Christology of Divine Identity.

Yet despite the historical approach of this book, undoubtedly most readers are interested in the ancient Jewish Scripture (the Old Testament), the New Testament, and the development of Trinitarian dogma not simply as a series of footnotes on dead history, but rather as integral and foundational to the living religious traditions of Judaism, Christianity, and to a lesser degree Islam—traditions that together claim the allegiance of approximately half the population of the world. So this final chapter broaches a topic that is of paramount concern, but which has until now been deliberately neglected: When the earliest Christians interpreted the ancient Jewish Scripture in a theodramatic fashion—assigning various divine persons to explain dialogical shifts—was this a *good* reading of the Scripture? Put more technically, were the prosopological exegeses the earliest Christians deployed grounded in a valid hermeneutic?

As this question is posed, much of Christianity itself is suspended over a precipice, hanging by a slender thread, for the question touches upon matters of supreme concern to all it holds dear. For if the thesis argued throughout this book is correct, that a specific theodramatic reading technique, prosopological exegesis, was irreducibly essential to the development of the doctrine of the Trinity, then if this method cannot find adequate hermeneutical footing, Trinitarian dogma—as central as it is to every dimension of Christianity as currently conceived—might be undermined. Moreover, it also interfaces with a larger question that lies along a fault-line between Christianity and Judaism: Can the ancient Jewish Scripture really be considered *Christian* Scripture, so that it is appropriate for Christians to call it the "Old Testament," or is such a perspective inescapably supersessionist, so that nomenclature such as the Hebrew Bible, the Tanak, or the Jewish Scripture should be preferred?[1]

---

[1] These three terms—the Hebrew Bible, the Tanak, and the Jewish Scripture—are also problematic for the study of early Christianity. Hebrew Bible is inaccurate because the earliest Christians (who were, of course, Jews) preferred the Greek and other versions. Meanwhile Tanak is as perspectivally committed as Old Testament in the opposite direction because it affirms the validity and order of the Jewish canonical division (Torah, Prophets, and Writings) rather than the Christian. The term "Jewish Scripture" is perhaps as little more neutral inasmuch as it does not overtly commit to a specific canonical order and it correctly acknowledges the Jewish matrix in which Christianity emerged, but it does not accord well with contemporary English-language norms that position Judaism and Christianity as separate religions, making it appear as if this

If we moderns (or postmoderns) are acutely aware of disputes regarding how the ancient Jewish Scripture can legitimately be appropriated by subsequent believing communities, the situation was no different in the first and second centuries as Christianity, Judaism, and various sects drew upon the ancient Jewish Scripture in forging their self-identities vis-à-vis one another. Indeed, the legitimacy of prosopological exegesis was even discussed in an abstract, theoretical fashion as a subset of what constitutes a valid scriptural hermeneutic, especially by various so-called gnostic groups and Irenaeus. And as will become apparent, it is convenient that we have been collecting individual tiles of prosopological scriptural interpretation that combine to form a fresh portrait of the triune God throughout this volume, for Irenaeus's sophisticated answer regarding what constitutes a *good* reading pertains precisely to the manner in which individual tiles combine to form a mosaic. I submit that it is prudent to listen to what these early interpreters have to say as we seek to formulate our own answers regarding what constitutes an appropriate reading, even if we as contemporary readers of the ancient Jewish Scripture may ultimately want to press beyond them in formulating our own answers to this question. In fact, in due course I will give a list of guiding principles that I have found helpful.

GNOSTIC THEODRAMATIC EXEGESIS

Gnosticism refers to a broad, fluid intellectual and religious movement whose adherents generally shared the conviction that salvation, understood as escape from the evil material order, was contingent on obtaining esoteric knowledge. It thrived especially during the second and third centuries of the common era.[2] The gnostics frequently engaged in prosopological interpretation of the ancient Jewish Scripture, and, in order to grasp their maneuvers, it is imperative to have at least a rudimentary purchase on their belief-system.

body of literature belongs exclusively to the Jewish community but not the Christian. Much of the earlier debate regarding "Christianizing the Old Testament" and other Jewish/Christian issues are traced and synthesized by James Barr, *The Concept of Biblical Theology: An Old Testament Perspective* (Minneapolis: Fortress, 1999), 252–311; for an outstanding recent contribution, consider Christopher R. Seitz, "Old Testament or Hebrew Bible? Some Theological Considerations," *Word Without End: The Old Testament as Abiding Theological Witness* (Grand Rapids: Eerdmans, 1998), 61–74.

[2] The validity of Gnosticism as a blanket category description has been called into question by (among others) Michael A. Williams, *Rethinking "Gnosticism": An Argument for Dismantling a Dubious Category* (Princeton: Princeton University Press, 1996). Although Williams does helpfully point out the great diversity among such sectarian movements, the term "Gnosticism"—in my opinion—retains utility in referencing, albeit imprecisely, a variety of ancient worldviews that held much in common.

A Gnostic Story

For many devotees, the central tenets of Gnosticism could be explained via a story—and there were multitudinous variations on the story—about a most high God from whom emanated a contingent of lesser gods.[3] These gods coupled and produced still more lower gods until a fullness was attained. Yet one of these lesser goddesses, Sophia, reproduced apart from her male consort, bringing forth a malformed deity, causing both Sophia and her offspring to be removed from the fullness. Sophia, repentant, was allowed to return to the fullness, but her malformed offspring was not—indeed in his solitude and arrogance he came to regard himself as the most high God and proceeded, with the help of subordinate malignant spiritual powers, to create the physical universe.

This malformed yet arrogant god was called by a variety of names, such as the Demiurge ("the craftsman") and Ialdabaoth, and was frequently identified as equivalent to the God of the ancient Jewish Scripture. In other words, according to the basic Jewish-Christian version of the gnostic myth, Ialdabaoth, the God of the Old Testament, is the creator of the material order, but he is neither the most high God, nor the only God, nor a competent god, and the material universe is a malevolent, enslaving force that he uses to control human souls.

Within several versions of the gnostic myth, humans were first created as non-physical spiritual beings and were only subsequently imprisoned in a physical body by Ialdabaoth. Yet the gods who resided in the fullness were concerned about this state of affairs. They were proactive, granting some special humans (usually those in Seth's line as presented in Genesis) latent spiritual power that could be reawakened. Indeed, ultimately the gods residing in the fullness sent forth an ambassador, the Savior, Jesus the Christ in Christianized versions of the myth, to convey knowledge (*gnōsis*) to humanity, so that those having this latent spiritual power could be aroused. In becoming aware of the true state of divine–human affairs these specially endowed humans could ultimately escape from the material order and from the wicked heavenly powers that held them in bondage.

---

[3] The basic gnostic myth is perhaps best accessed in *The Apocryphon of John* and *The Hypostasis of the Archons* as discovered at Nag Hammadi. For an outstanding introduction to Gnosticism, including a reconstruction of the most common features in the gnostic myth, see Bentley Layton, *The Gnostic Scriptures: A New Translation with Annotations and Introductions* (ABRL; New York: Doubleday, 1987), 5–22. English translations of all the principal ancient texts can be found in this edition as well, and I follow Layton's translations for the Nag Hammadi texts in what follows.

Person-Centered Gnostic Interpretations

Many gnostic leaders found abundant evidence for their belief-system in the ancient Jewish Scripture, and one of their favorite interpretative techniques was prosopological exegesis. For example, in a text discovered at Nag Hammadi, *The Hypostasis of the Archons*, the arrogant craftsman god Ialdabaoth, thinking himself to be the only and the most high God, is made to borrow the words of Yahweh in Isaiah 46: 9 in order to say,

IALDABAOTH (speaking to HIMSELF): It is I who am god; there is none [apart
   from me].   (*Hyp. Arch.* 86)

Ialdabaoth is then rebuked by a voice issuing from the upper heavenly spheres, perhaps spoken by his mother Sophia or perhaps by another (cf. Irenaeus, *Haer.* 4. 35. 4), but, ignoring this voice, he only becomes increasingly blind to any higher reality as he pursues self-power. Ialdabaoth and the lesser spiritual rulers over whom he is chief, all of them together, then say,

IALDABAOTH AND HIS MINIONS (speaking to THEMSELVES): Come let *us*
   create a human being that will be soil from the earth.   (*Hyp. Arch.* 87)

This is a prosopological assignment that borrows from the "Come let *us* make humans in our image" language of Genesis 1: 26 and combines it with the description of the creation of Adam from the dust of the earth in Genesis 2: 7.[4] For the author of *Hypostasis*, Ialdabaoth and his subordinates have been posited as the "us" that truly spoke when humans were crafted from matter, the soil. Moreover, Irenaeus reports that essentially identical prosopological readings of these specific Old Testament passages—Isaiah 46: 9 and Genesis 1: 26—were held in common by several other gnostic leaders and subgroups: Ptolemy and the Valentinians (*Haer.* 1. 5. 4), Satorninos (*Haer.* 1. 24. 1), and other gnostics (*Haer.* 1. 30. 6; cf. 1. 29. 4).

Descriptions of Gnostic Reading Strategies

As reported by the earliest Fathers, who stridently opposed their interpretations, these various gnostic individuals and groups had a self-conscious reading strategy by which they sought to justify the validity of their prosopological assignments.[5] For example, Irenaeus attests that the Valentinians

---

[4] Cf. the reworking of Gen. 6: 7 so that it is not a speech by Yahweh alone, but is made to be a collective announcement by Ialdabaoth and his henchmen: "Come let us cause a flood with our hands and obliterate all flesh, from human being to beast" (*Hyp. Arch.* 92).

[5] Given the gnostic propensity for prosopological exegesis, it may that Irenaeus was more reluctant to use this method in comparison with his predecessors, as has been speculated by

apportioned the Old Testament prophecies to three different principal characters. That is, they interpreted as if some of the speeches in the Old Testament were delivered by the mother (i.e. Wisdom or Sophia), some by the seed (i.e. those humans endowed with a special spiritual substance), and some by the Demiurge.[6] Thus, for example, it is asserted by the Valentinians that when Jesus cried out, "My God, my God, why have you forsaken me?" (Mark 15: 34; Matt. 27: 46; citing Ps. 22: 1), he was really giving theodramatic voice to the words of Acamoth, who in the Valentinian version of the myth is the product of Sophia's thought and the mother of the Demiurge. In further describing gnostic hermeneutics, Irenaeus also reports the proclivity of a certain Satorninos for assigning alternative characters to explain the Old Testament. Satorninos affirms, "certain of the prophecies were spoken by the angels who created the world, others by Satan" (*Haer.* 1. 24. 2). The later (fourth-century) heresiologist Epiphanius describes the gnostic propensity for making theodramatic role assignments in more general terms, saying:

> whenever they find a passage capable of meaning something in opposition to themselves, they say that it has been spoken by the [malevolent] world spirit. But if any statement . . . can be adapted so as to be similar to their (sexual) desire, they transform it to conform to their (sexual) desire and say that it has been spoken by the spirit of truth.[7]

In this fashion Epiphanius asserts that the gnostics take any text that might oppose their preferred lifestyle and argue that the words were *actually spoken* by an evil spiritual being, and thus they claim that when the text is properly interpreted, it really supports their chosen lifestyle, and vice-versa. According to Epiphanius, then, gnostic exegesis is really *eisegesis* (reading into a text) since the gnostics use their preferred myth to assign speaking prosopa to the scriptural dialogues merely in order to promote debauchery.

And even if we are suspicious that Epiphanius, in his haste to bring down his gnostic opponents, may have exaggerated or misconstrued their sexual greed in making their prosopological assignments, at the same time it is self-evident that the gnostic prosopological assignments, drawn from their gnostic myths and applied to scriptural dialogues, result in an invalid reading of the Scripture. But why? Is it not the case that the proto-orthodox early Fathers are doing much the same thing, pulling from a triune Christian myth and applying it when assigning prosopa? We begin to see how the proto-orthodox Fathers might answer this charge in the fascinating exegetical debate between Origen and Heracleon.

Stephen O. Presley, "Irenaeus and the Exegetical Roots of Trinitarian Theology," in Paul Foster and Sara Parvis (eds.), *Irenaeus: Life, Scripture, Legacy* (Minneapolis: Fortress, 2012), 165–71, here 166.

[6] Irenaeus, *Haer.* 1. 7. 3.   [7] Epiphanius, *Pan.* 26. 6. 1–2; trans. Layton.

HERACLEON AND ORIGEN ON THEODRAMATIC INTERPRETATION

Origen's *Commentary on John* is punctuated throughout with his responses to the exegesis of a second-century gnostic named Heracleon. One example is particularly enlightening with regard to prosopological exegesis and the question of a valid hermeneutic. Heracleon, when exegeting John, had interpreted the words from Psalm 68: 10 LXX as cited in John 2: 17, "The zeal for your house will devour me" (Ps. 68: 10 LXX), in a theodramatic fashion. Origen is highly critical of the prosopological assignment made by Heracleon:

> It is especially careless of Heracleon, however, to think that the statement, "The zeal for your house will devour me" is placed in the mouth of the powers which were cast out and destroyed by the Savior [*ek prosōpou tōn ekblēthentōn kai analōthentōn hypo tou sōtēros dynameōn legesthai*], since he is not able to preserve the sequence of the prophecy in the Psalm [*mē dynamenos ton heirmon tēs en tō psalmō prophēteias tērēsai*] when he supposes that it was placed in the mouth of the powers which were cast out and destroyed.[8]

Origen opposes Heracleon's theodramatic role assignment here *not* because he disapproves of the prosopological method in general, on the contrary, Origen himself has determined that these words have been spoken by a different *prosopon*—here, David speaks "from the character of the Christ" (*ek prosōpou tou Christou*). Origen emphasizes that the only way Heracleon has been able to posit "the powers" as a collective theodramatic character is *by ignoring the narrative sequence of the psalm*. As far as Origen is concerned, for prosopological exegesis to be sound, not just any arbitrary character can be selected at whim, rather the exegete must pay attention both to *the sequential plotline* of the scriptural text being interpreted and also to *the exact words* utilized.[9] Yet, even when one pays attention to the basic plotline of this specific psalm, the Christ is nowhere directly mentioned, so is it not the case that Origen's prosopological assignment is equally suspect?

Origen seeks to safeguard himself against this charge by first of all testing whether or not specific lines within the larger Old Testament context, for him the entire psalm, can be reasonably explained by historical reference to David in relationship to the unfolding plotline of the psalm itself. If the lines *cannot* sensibly be construed as pertinent to what is known (or can reasonably be supposed) concerning the life of David, then Origen moves on to consider theodramatic solutions, such as positing that David might be adopting an

---

[8] Origen, *Comm. Jo.* 10. 223; Greek text in Blanc, SC 157; trans. Heine, FOTC.

[9] On the importance of fixing references on the basis of the exact words, cf. Origen's criticism in *Comm. Jo.* 6. 108–11 of Heracleon's prosopological assignments for Isa. 40: 3 in John 1: 23—"I am 'a voice of one crying out in the wilderness.'"

alternative *persona* such as that of the Christ, and then testing that theory against what is known about the life of Jesus from the Gospels.[10] So although the Christ may not be referenced in Psalm 68 LXX, numerous lines in the psalm, according to Origen, cannot possibly refer to the historical David— after all, when was David given "gall for food" (Ps 68: 22 LXX)?—but these details do fit specific idiosyncratic details in the life of Jesus (Matt. 27: 34, 48; Mark 15: 23, 36; Luke 23: 36; John 19: 28–9), so from Origen's vantage point the assignment is not arbitrary.

We might describe Origen's hermeneutic for fixing what he regards to be a valid prosopological assignment as having three dimensions.

1. *Literary Sequence*. A valid prosopological designation cannot violate the sequence of the prophecy in the immediate context. Although we should note that the boundaries of what constitutes the immediate context might not always be self-evident.

2. *The Primacy of the Ancient Prophet's Own Setting*. The identity of the speaker or addressee should first be sought on the prophetic horizon at the literary-historical level.[11] That is, if it is reasonable to suppose on the basis of the exact words spoken that the ancient prophet was speaking from his own person, then no alternative theodramatic person should be assigned.

3. *If Not the Ancient Prophet, Then a Theodramatic Character*. If a reader of the Jewish Scripture cannot reasonably suppose an ancient prophet (e.g. Isaiah or David) was speaking in his own person, then it is possible that the prophet had slipped into a theodramatic role and was speaking as that character in the divine drama. In such cases the identity of the theodramatic speaker and setting of the speech should be fixed by comparing the details of the speech with the literary-historical details of other known characters that appear in the great divine drama. It should be noted that Peter and Paul are depicted as using this exact same "if not the Hebrew prophet, then a theodramatic character" logic in Acts 2: 29–31 (cf. 2: 34) and Acts 13: 36 respectively. Moreover, the "if not the ancient prophet, then a theodramatic character" logic characteristic of prosopological exegesis is what is most damaging to the standard typological explanation for how it is that Jesus was found by early Christians to be the voice praying the psalms. Why? Because the sharing of a type demands that the respective Old Testament and New Testament passages participate in a

---

[10] For several helpful examples explaining Origen's prosopological method as applied to the Psalter, see Ronald E. Heine, *Reading the Old Testament with the Ancient Church: Exploring the Formation of Early Christian Thought* (Grand Rapids: Baker Academic, 2007), 159–63. On Origen as a scriptural interpreter, see Peter W. Martens, *Origen and Scripture: The Contours of the Exegetical Life* (Oxford Early Christian Studies; Oxford: Oxford University Press, 2012).

[11] On the various horizons and settings discussed here, see "Three Settings within the Theodrama" in Ch. 1.

common image (iconic mimesis), and the prosopological reasoning is precisely that the actors do *not* appropriately share that image.[12]

THE INTERPRETATIVE STRATEGY OF IRENAEUS

With Origen's response to Heracleon we have begun to see the contours of the debate that transpired in the early church regarding what constitutes a valid hermeneutic as it pertains to theodramatic interpretation of the ancient Jewish Scripture. The early Christians recognized, and the point was driven home by gnostic interpretation, that the prosopological method was dangerous inasmuch as the character assignments could be arbitrary and of very dubious validity. However, akin to Origen, Irenaeus was convinced that the prosopological technique could be reliably deployed if, and only if, it was rooted in a proper assessment of the macrofeatures of the Scripture.

Much like the varieties of Gnosticism explored above, most contemporary biblical interpretation today, both scholarly and popular-level, predominantly locates truth by means of external referentiality. That is, it is bent toward finding some "x" beyond the biblical text as the ultimate reality to which the text testifies, whether that "x" be history, psychology, science, or as in Gnosticism, a foundational story external to Scripture itself. The genuine importance of the words in the Scripture are to be found in their ability to point *through* the text and to testify to some external system that is regarded as the deeper reality—"this passage tells what actually happened" or "this text really speaks to us about the deep structures of the human psyche." Thus used, the Scripture is a vehicle that points at other realities, regardless of whether it does so truly as the devout proclaim, or falsely as skeptics conclude.

In contrast, for early Fathers such as Irenaeus, the Bible was true not only by virtue of its ability to point out truths external to the world of the text, but also by its ability, as O'Keefe and Reno put it, to "illuminate and disclose the order and pattern of all things."[13] As such, the Bible for the Fathers is not primarily a window *through* which one gazes on more primal truths, as if "what really happened" should be isolated, abstracted, and set up as the ultimate reality by which all else is measured and subjected. Rather external events and the

---

[12] For a richer discussion of the relationship between prosopological exegesis and so-called typology, see Matthew W. Bates, *The Hermeneutics of the Apostolic Proclamation: The Center of Paul's Method of Scriptural Interpretation* (Waco, Tex: Baylor University Press, 2012), 133–48, 248–53, and 340–1.

[13] John J. O'Keefe and R. R. Reno, *Sanctified Vision: An Introduction to Early Christian Interpretation of the Bible* (Baltimore: Johns Hopkins University Press, 2005), 7–13, here 13, have proven helpful in solidifying my thoughts on this topic.

happenings described in the Scripture are interpreted as part of a seamless, holistic, unfolding reality out of which the interpreter lives.

From within this framework Irenaeus explains his system for measuring how it is that certain prosopological assignments are valid and others, such as those proposed by the gnostics, are dubious. Thus, drawing on ancient literary theory, Irenaeus explains precisely what he believes has gone awry in the gnostic prosopological readings and establishes hermeneutical principles that he believes can support a valid prosopological interpretative strategy.

Rearranged Homeric Verses

The gnostics are akin, according to Irenaeus, to those who, "after having entirely fabricated their own system," transfer the sayings and names that are scattered hither and thither in a corpus of literature and rearrange them as suits their own purposes: "They act like those who would propose *hypotheses* which they chance upon and then try to put them to verse from Homeric poems, so that the inexperienced think that Homer composed the poems with that *hypothesis*, which poems in reality are of recent composition."[14] Irenaeus suggests that some of his contemporaries are in the habit of selecting snatches of Homer willy-nilly, after which they combine the lines to form a completely new overarching storyline or master plan for Homer's poems. They then attempt to hoodwink the unsuspecting into believing that their new amalgam is entirely Homer's own composition. Irenaeus acknowledges that this re-arrangement could trick a fool, but it would certainly not prove convincing to an experienced reader of Homer:

> Would not a simpleton be misled by these verses and believe that Homer composed them in that manner for that very *hypothesis*? Yet one who is well-acquainted with Homer's *hypothesis* will recognize the verses, but he will not recognize the *hypothesis*, since he knows that some of the verses were spoken by Ulysses, others of Hercules himself, others of Priam, others of Menelaus and Agamemnon.[15]

The experienced reader of Homer, by knowledge of the true hypothesis gained through sequential reading, can detect this faulty arrangement and show the whole to be an implausible interpretative rendering of Homer. So also, Irenaeus avows, the interpreter of the Scripture can do the same vis-à-vis the Bible and gnostic rearrangements.

> However, if the reader of Homer takes each verse and puts each one back into its own context, he will make the fabricated theme [*hypothesis*] disappear. In the

---

[14] Irenaeus, *Haer.* 1. 9. 4; trans. Unger (slightly modified).
[15] Irenaeus, *Haer.* 1. 9. 4; trans. Unger (slightly modified).

same way, anyone who keeps unchangeable in himself the Rule of Truth [Latin: *regulam veritatis*; Greek: *ton kanona tēs alētheias*] received through baptism will recognize the names and sayings and parables from the Scriptures, but this blasphemous theme of theirs he will not recognize.[16]

As Irenaeus further unfolds his hermeneutic, it becomes clear that for him any valid reading of a piece of literature, the Scripture included, necessitates that the reader be aware of the *hypothesis*, the *economy*, and the *recapitulation* of the work in question.[17]

Hypothesis. As the term was employed in Greco-Roman rhetorical schools, the *hypothesis* is the gist of a literary work, the master plan by which the sequence of events is arranged.[18] Quite succinctly, Sextus Empiricus says that when used in the literary sense, it refers to "the *peripeteia*, (or 'argument' or 'plot') of a drama."[19] For Irenaeus the hypothesis of the Scripture taken as whole is the Rule of Truth (*kanōn tēs alētheias*), which Irenaeus himself claims to have received in an unbroken line from the apostles. Although Irenaeus's variegated usage of the phrase does not easily lend itself to a precise definition, this Rule of Truth for Irenaeus is probably best described as a digest of the main plotline of the Scripture, such as can be found in *Against the Heresies* 1. 10. 1 (although conflated here with the term "economies"), and which also can be found outside Irenaeus's corpus in the condensations of the apostolic preaching in Acts chs. 2 and 13, Romans 1: 3–4, and 1 Corinthians 15: 3–5, all of which fed into or approximated early baptismal creeds such as the Apostles' Creed.[20] Indeed, the whole of Irenaeus's treatise *The Demonstration of the Apostolic Preaching*, or at least the outline it follows, is an excellent approximation of what Irenaeus means by hypothesis and the Rule of Truth.[21]

Some, such as O'Keefe and Reno, would further define the scriptural hypothesis for Irenaeus as "faith in Jesus Christ as the Son of God" or more simply just "Jesus Christ," but this seems to me to compress too much and to encroach on recapitulation (as it is described subsequently).[22] Frances Young, in her

---

[16] Irenaeus, *Haer.* 1. 9. 4; trans. Unger (slightly modified).

[17] In what follows I depend in part upon Robert Grant, *Irenaeus of Lyons* (London: Routledge, 1997), 46–53; Frances M. Young, *Biblical Exegesis and the Formation of Christian Culture* (Peabody, Mass.: Hendrickson, 2002), 19–21; and O'Keefe and Reno, *Sanctified Vision*, 33–41.

[18] Grant, *Irenaeus*, 46, defines hypothesis as, "the presentation (sometimes in a summary) of a plot or structure intended by an author such as Homer."

[19] Sextus Empiricus, *Adv. math.* 3. 3; trans. Bury, LCL.

[20] See the dated but still helpful contribution by Valdemar Ammundsen, "The Rule of Truth in Irenaeus," *JTS* 13 (1912): 574–80; for a recent synthesis, see John Behr, *The Way to Nicaea: The Formation of Christian Theology, Volume i* (Crestwood: NY: St Vladimir's Seminary Press, 2001), 33–43.

[21] See Irenaeus, *Epid.* 1, 3, and 52, as well as the remarks by John Behr (trans. and intro.) *St. Irenaeus of Lyons: On the Apostolic Preaching* (Crestwood, NY: St Vladimir's Seminary Press, 1997), 102 n. 1.

[22] O'Keefe and Reno, *Sanctified Vision*, 40–1.

book, *Biblical Exegesis and the Formation of Christian Culture*, captures admirably well the way the Rule of Truth (i.e. the hypothesis) functioned within Irenaeus's hermeneutic: "Neither the Rule of Faith nor the creed was in fact a summary of the whole biblical narrative. . . . They provided, rather, the proper reading of the beginning and the ending, the focus of the plot and the relations of the principle characters, so enabling the 'middle' to be heard in bits as meaningful."[23] Irenaeus believed that it was by adhering to the dominant plotline of the Scripture, the Rule of Truth or hypothesis, that one could be enabled to make sense of the subsidiary parts (see *Haer.* 2. 27. 1).

Economy. Economy (*oikonomia*) denotes the proper arrangement of affairs, and was applied in antiquity both to a well-run household and a well-crafted narrative or piece of rhetoric. If the hypothesis is the master plan for a whole literary work, then the economies are the bounds and the sequencing of the specific elements by which that master plan actually unfolds. Ancient rhetoricians and historians such as Quintilian, Diodorus Siculus, and Dionysius of Halicarnassus emphasized the necessity of a careful sequencing of events, the establishment of an economy or economies, when crafting a speech or literary narrative.[24] Since the ancient Jewish Scripture articulates a story, for Irenaeus the divine economy is the arrangement of the events described therein (*Haer.* 1. 10. 1; 3. 16. 6; cf. Eph. 1: 10; 3: 9; Philo, *Dec.* 53). According to Irenaeus, then, a good reading of the Scripture will fix the meaning and significance of any single event by locating it within the sequence of the whole economy as God has purposefully arranged it, and this is largely why gnostic interpretation fails (*Haer.* 5. 19. 2). For example, within the divine economy the event of the deliverance at the Red Sea can only be fully understood as part of a sequence of events that begins with the flood and is followed by Christian baptism. Seeking the meaning of what transpired at the Red Sea in isolation or out of sequence violates the divine economy.[25]

Recapitulation. In Greco-Roman rhetoric *recapitulation* (Latin: *recapitulatio*; Greek: *anakephalaiōsis*) refers to the end of a speech, when the speaker drives home the point with a summary of the strongest arguments. Irenaeus speaks of it when he describes the coming of Christ, "from heaven in the

---

[23] Young, *Biblical Exegesis*, 21.

[24] See Quintilian, *Inst.* 3. 3. 9; for further references, see Grant, *Irenaeus*, 49. Within rhetorical training, arrangement (usually termed *taxis*) was of paramount importance as one of the five principle steps in moving from invention to delivery.

[25] Yet as Kathy Eden notes (*Hermeneutics and the Rhetorical Tradition: Chapters in the Ancient Legacy and the Humanist Reception* [New Haven: Yale University Press, 1997], 27–32 esp. 28), ancient interpreters were well aware that any given literary arrangement might not be natural (chronological), but rather artificially arranged (e.g. starting *in medias res* rather than at the true beginning) to arouse an emotional response in the audience. However, even if the composition begins *in medias res*, the audience is still dependent on the chronological signals embedded by the author that are then sequenced by the reader in considering the meaning of the work as a whole.

glory of the Father *to recapitulate* all things" (*Haer.* 1. 10. 1). For Irenaeus the recapitulation of the Scripture entails the most central Christ events (the incarnation of the *Logos*, death on the cross, resurrection, ascension), in which Christ brought to a head all that had transpired within the divine drama thus far, reenacting the story *in nuce* in a virtuoso solo performance, summing it up expressly.[26] He serves as the unifying principle, bringing the whole divine economy forcefully and cohesively together as a resolved plot. Irenaeus uses two analogies to clarify how hypothesis, economy, and recapitulation interlock in supplying a valid method of scriptural interpretation, all of which helps show why he thinks proto-orthodox Christian prosopological exegesis is valid, whereas the gnostic version fails.

A King and a Building

The Mosaic of a King. For Irenaeus a literary *hypothesis* is like the image in the artist's mind that provides the plan and impetus to create a mosaic of a king. The *economy* is the well-ordered arrangement of the whole project, from the framework to the proper positioning of individual tiles, executed in accordance with the hypothesis. Thus, the economy is determined by the hypothesis. The *recapitulation* is the handsome face of the king, the most vivid, important portion within the economy of the portrait, fully unveiling the hypothesis of the artist to construct the portrait of a king. The problem is that someone can introduce a hypothesis contrary to the aim of the original artist, intending, Irenaeus suggests for sake of an example, to rearrange the stones and craft a dog. This alien hypothesis destroys the original economy through rearrangement, leading to an entirely different recapitulation at the center of the image—the snarling face of a mongrel rather than the noble visage of a king. This is precisely, according to Irenaeus, what the gnostics have done via their dubious scriptural interpretation—Christ the king has been transformed into a mangy mutt (*Haer.* 1. 8. 1; 1. 9. 4).

    A Building. Irenaeus invites us to consider scriptural interpretation as a building (*Haer.* 2. 27. 3). We might theorize, then, for Irenaeus that the *hypothesis* is like the architectural plan for a palace while the *economy* consists in the walls, floors, roof, and basic framework of the house. The *recapitulation*, then, Irenaeus affirms, is the cornerstone,[27] which stands at the center of the architectural plan (hypothesis) and determines the structural features (economies) of the house. In retrospect, a building inspector would know that the cornerstone (recapitulation) is the element that oriented and hence determined

---

[26] For a fuller treatment of recapitulation in Irenaeus, see Behr, *The Way to Nicaea*, 122–33.

[27] On Christ as cornerstone and recapitulation, see Irenaeus, *Haer.* 3. 5. 3; cf. 3. 12. 4; 4. 25. 1; O'Keefe and Reno, *Sanctified Vision*, 41.

the entire structure (economy) of the house and that it was designed to serve this central role by the architectural plan (hypothesis). As such the recapitulative cornerstone once found can serve as the "key" that explains the whole building in the most succinct manner possible.

Irenaeus on Proper Scriptural Interpretation

In summary, we might select this as the most compact self-expression that Irenaeus gives regarding his hermeneutical principles: "There is, therefore, as we have shown, one God the Father and one Christ Jesus our Lord, who comes through every economy and recapitulates in Himself all things."[28] That is, all of the Scripture concerns one God, the Father, and one Lord, Jesus Christ, as entailed in the hypothesis.[29] This Christ appears as a component within the arrangements and orderings (economies) that participate in the whole of the divine story, and he brings them forcefully to a head as the crucial element, gathering all the economies to a collective focus in the central events of his incarnational life, death, resurrection, and enthronement (as the recapitulation).

All this determines how Irenaeus makes his prosopological assignments when he reads a moment of dialogue in his Old Testament. First, when Irenaeus encounters conversation in the Old Testament, he undertakes a similar procedure to the three steps previously outlined for Origen, also culminating with the *"if not the ancient prophet, then a theodramatic character"* conclusion. For example, when treating the dialogue in Psalm 110 (109 LXX), Irenaeus exclaims, "these things were not said to David" (*Epid.* 49), before going on to posit an alternative prosopon. Second, however, it would seem that Irenaeus has added additional cross-checks to ensure the interpretation does not become arbitrary, asking: Does the assignment of this character align with the basic "master plan" (hypothesis) of God as we see that master plan embedded in specific sequential arrangements (economies) of the divine story, knowing that the story has been brought to a head (recapitulated) in Jesus' incarnation, death for sins, resurrection on the third day, and ascension? For Irenaeus, if a proposed prosopological assignment violates the overarching plot of the Scripture, its consecutive arrangement, or its culmination in Christ, then it is not valid.

---

[28] Irenaeus, *Haer.* 3. 16. 6; trans. Unger.

[29] Cf. Irenaeus's "one God" and "one Lord" language here with 1 Cor. 8: 6, which itself reworks the most central expression of Jewish monotheism, the "Hear O Israel, the Lord your God, the Lord is one" (Deut. 6: 4) of the Shema, moving it in proto-Trinitarian directions. For particularly outstanding analyses of how Paul interpretatively recrafts the Shema, see Gordon D. Fee, *Pauline Christology: An Exegetical-Theological Study* (Peabody, Mass.: Hendrickson, 2007), 88–94; N. T. Wright, *Paul and the Faithfulness of God* (2 vols. in 4 parts; Minneapolis: Fortress, 2013), ii. 3. 661–70.

PROSOPOLOGICAL OSCILLATION

As described above, the prosopological assignments made by Origen and Irenaeus are rooted in specific textual details and controlled by a sequential reading. Yet there is a further extension of the theodramatic method, employed by Tertullian, Origen, Jerome, Augustine, and others, that we might term *prosopological oscillation*. Sometimes these interpreters explained an Old Testament text by designating a theodramatic person as the sole referent, while allowing slippage within that one person in some fashion, so that another referent is brought in. This second referent is usually closely related to the first so that the identity of the two referents are felt to somehow nest (like a subset within a set in mathematics) or otherwise overlap. The actual person then selected as the immediate referent by the interpreter can move back and forth between the two referents (oscillate) as the interpreter deems necessary when attempting to make a cogent explanation of the passage in question.

For instance, an interpreter might appoint Christ as the speaker, while assigning part of the speech to *Christ himself as the head* and another part to *Christ as the body, that is, Christ as the church*. For example, since Christ is the bridegroom, Tertullian regards the bride, the church, to be contained within him, to such a degree that the church itself can become the addressee. For example, Tertullian states: "He [Christ] considers the church *to be in himself*, and concerning it the same Spirit says to him: 'You shall clothe yourself with all of them, just as an ornament upon a bride'" (*Marc.* 4. 11. 7 citing Isa. 49: 18). The "you" addressed here in Isaiah according to Tertullian is Christ the bride, that is, the church. Similarly Origen interprets Psalm 30: 2, "O Lord my God I cried to you and you healed me," as spoken by the Christ not in his capacity as head, but rather in the person of the body, the church.[30]

This person-centered oscillation was even discussed theoretically by Tyconius (*c.*380), a Donatist layman, in his *Liber Regularum*, which treats seven mystical principles of interpretation. While slightly faulting Tyconius for hubristically overstating the explanatory power of his rules and for his occasional misapplication, Augustine nonetheless gives Tyconius's seven principles a ringing endorsement, supplying a lengthy review and explanation of them in *De Doctrina Christiana* (3. 30–7 [42–56]). Tyconius calls his first rule "concerning the Lord and his body" and it illustrates theodramatic oscillation well. Tyconius notes that the "he bears our sins" of Isaiah 53: 4 is universally recognized by the church as pertaining to the Lord Christ, but that in his

---

[30] Origen, *Sel. Ps.* 29. 3 (PG 1292D–1293A). This example from Origen is per Heine, *Reading the Old Testament*, 163, who in turn depends on Marie-Josèphe Rondeau, *Les Commentaires patristiques du Psautier (3e–5e siècles):* i. *Les Travaux des Pères grecs et latins sur le Psautier. Recherches et bilan;* ii *Exégèse prosopologique et théologie* (2 vols.; Orientalia Christiana Analecta 220; Rome: Institutum Studiorum Orientalium, 1982–5), ii. 123.

judgment the words that follow, "And God wants to . . . let him see the light and to fashion him in wisdom," pertain not to the Lord Christ as the head, but to the Lord Christ's body, since it is the church not Jesus Christ that is in need of greater light and wisdom.[31] Similarly in Psalm 90: 11 LXX, Tyconius assigns Christ the head as the addressee to whom the psalmist speaks, "To his angels he has given command about you, that they guard you in all your ways," but what follows is construed as addressing Christ the body, that is, the church, "I will show him my salvation" (Ps. 90: 16 LXX), because this latter phrase is deemed more fitting for the church than for the Lord Jesus.[32] I will comment more specifically on the viability of prosopological oscillation as a legitimate exegetical strategy after synthesizing the overall discussion.

THEODRAMATIC INTERPRETATION AND NORMATIVITY

Drawing on the debate about hermeneutical normativity in antiquity but also moving beyond it, as a final reflection I would like to push past the confines of historical description of early Christian interpretative practices and offer the reader the fruits of my own methodological wrangling. I put forward the following as theses regarding the validity of early Christian theodramatic interpretation of the ancient Jewish Scripture, inviting the reader to engage my own position critically in forging or weighing her or his own hermeneutic.[33] I realize that many readers will not find my conclusions congenial, yet I hope that they will stimulate further discussion. I have organized the theses into three categories: enabling presuppositions, absolute blocks, and critical controls.

Enabling Presuppositions

Quite apart from that ultimate question, Did Jesus himself point in the direction of later Trinitarian developments?, the validity of early Christian

---

[31] Isa. 53: 11 as cited in Tyconius, *Reg.* 1. 1; trans. Froehlich. Some of Tyconius's other rules of scriptural interpretation are also conducive to slippage in the specific identity of the prosopological speaker—"concerning the Lord's bipartite body," "concerning species and genus," and "concerning the Devil and his body."

[32] Tyconius, *Reg.* 1. 3; trans. Froehlich.

[33] For a slightly different but largely complementary set of theses regarding how Scripture should be read in the church, consider the team-authored results of the fifteen scholars convened by the Center of Theological Inquiry in Princeton, New Jersey: The Scripture Project, "Nine Theses on the Interpretation of Scripture," in Ellen F. Davis and Richard B. Hays (eds.), *The Art of Reading Scripture* (Grand Rapids: Eerdmans, 2003), 1–5.

prosopological exegesis (and of any contemporary re-appropriations of the technique) of the ancient Jewish Scripture depends upon the following presuppositions. Whether or not any particular modern reader of this book will accept these presuppositions depends on the larger worldview or metanarrative that the reader currently inhabits. The employment of the prosopological method on the basis of these assumptions in the earliest church, however, is a datum that the intellectually virtuous reader will take into consideration as his or her worldview continues to undergo refinement, so such a datum, like any other important nugget of information, could prove worldview-shifting. True knowledge of the whole depends on particular details, and vice versa, as we refine our hypotheses about life in light of new data, spiraling, if we are epistemologically virtuous (i.e. honorable truth-seekers), toward the truth.[34] So although the following are probably best viewed as presuppositions of theodramatic interpretation, their truth value could also potentially come to be affirmed on the basis of a post hoc inspection of the elegant way theodramatic interpretation functions in the ancient sources when considered together with other evidence.

Regardless, if the following presuppositions are *not* true, then theodramatic interpretation as it was practiced in the early church *cannot* be affirmed as a suitable method of reading portions of the ancient Jewish Scripture, what is commonly (but anachronistically) termed the Old Testament. If they are true, then it may be a valid reading strategy for a given passage if other controls and conditions are met.

1. *The reality of a divine economy.* Theodramatic interpretation presumes that God providentially and in a foreordained fashion orchestrates all human affairs relating to salvation-history—past, present, and future. This includes past, present, and future events external to the ancient Jewish Scripture, events internal, and the literary process of inscripturation.

2. *Divine authorship of the ancient Jewish Scripture.* God is the ultimate author of the ancient Jewish Scripture, transcending but not negating human authorship. This has traditionally been called the inspiration of the Scripture.

3. *The unity and plot-arrangement of the ancient Jewish Scripture.* In theodramatic interpretation not only does the divine author stand behind the various books in the ancient Jewish Scripture, this divine author has invented a master plot (hypothesis) for the corpus so that the various books participate and contribute to one cohesively interconnected story. In other words the diverse scriptures are really a singular and divinely authored Scripture, crafted with divine authorial intentions that are in principle discoverable by a reader. I do not regard Catholic–Protestant–Orthodox–Jewish disputes about the boundary of the canon of the ancient Jewish Scripture,

---

[34] For an accessible primer on virtuous knowing, see W. Jay Wood, *Epistemology: Becoming Intellectually Virtuous* (Downers Grove, Ill.: InterVarsity, 1998).

that is, whether the so-called deuterocanonical or apocryphal books (e.g. Tobit, Judith) should be included in the canon or not, as seriously impeding the notion of a divinely invented master plot since the inclusion or exclusion of these books has only marginal impact on the basic overall plotline of the corpus when that plotline is reconstructed.

4. *Prophetic participation in the divine economy.* This thesis is really a subset of theses 1 and 2, but it is so fundamental that it merits separate mention. Theodramatic interpretation assumes: (1) that a prophet can receive genuine divine revelation; (2) the theodramatic world as a visionary or oracular manifestation into which the prophet can enter and take on a character;[35] and (3) the ultimate actualization of the theodrama as it is performed not by the prophet, but by the corresponding real-world human or divine persons.

Prophetic participation in the divine economy does not guarantee, however, that the prophet himself or the subsequent authors or redactors that inscripturated a given oracle understood fully the divine intention in granting a vision or oracle. On the contrary, even for the prophet participating in a theodramatic performance, some of the words spoken while "in character" might have remained enigmas and ambiguities at that time (cf. Irenaeus, *Haer.* 4. 26. 1). What was demanded of the prophet was not total comprehension of the received vision, but willing participation—to be carried along by the Spirit (cf. 2 Pet. 1: 20–1) as various speaking roles were given and adopted.

Accordingly, if these presuppositions are granted, in seeking the legitimate "meaning" any given prophetic utterance can bear, the meaning is not limited to the historical *Sitz im Leben* ("setting in life") of the prophet, nor to the literary

---

[35] For a statement on the ontological status of the theodramatic world, see my remarks in Ch. 1 n. 61 (cf. Ch. 1 n. 59 on the necessity of etic nomenclature). Additionally, one who is cautious about the validity of early Christian prosopological exegesis might ask: Even if we affirm that many early Christian Greek readers really *believed* the ancient Hebrew prophets to have uttered theodramatic oracles, could it be the case that this belief was simply mistaken? It might be argued, for instance, that the ancient Hebrew prophets were never genuinely stepping into something akin to a theodramatic role, rather the earliest Christians were merely anachronistically imposing a late, foreign Hellenistic reading strategy onto the much earlier Jewish Scripture. Indeed, such a claim has some heft, especially for those inclined to skepticism regarding God's superintendence of the divine economy, since prosopological exegesis seems to have grown principally out of developments in Greek drama and rhetoric that post-date much of the ancient Jewish Scripture. Yet, since prosopological reading is usually rooted in genuine dialogical shifts in the midst of ancient Israelite utterances, and given that the ancient Hebrew prophets were frequently known to perform symbolic actions physically as a complement to their verbal message (e.g. Isa. 20: 1–4; Jer. 19: 1–11; Ezek. 4: 1–5: 4; Hos. 1: 2–3), perhaps the distance between ancient Israelite oracular delivery and early Christian theodramatic appropriations is not as great as might first appear to be the case. In other words, despite the Hellenistic roots of the theoretical descriptions of prosopological exegesis, nevertheless prosopological exegesis draws upon transcultural and transtemporal patterns of communication (such as speech, dialogue, and performance). So in my judgment a hasty dismissal of the validity of early Christian prosopological exegesis of the ancient Jewish Scripture as an anachronism would be overly simplistic, even for those working solely within a historical-critical interpretative framework.

context of the book itself, nor to the ancient author who inscripturated the oracle, nor to the intention of the canonical editors. Rather since the divine author has inspired the oracle, the "meaning" can and should be assessed in light of God's intentions for the oracle vis-à-vis the whole divine economy on the prophetic, theodramatic, and actualized horizons (on these three levels, see Ch. 1). So, for example, if one grants the possibility of prophetic theodrama, one *cannot* say, "Isaiah could not literally be speaking in the person of Jesus of Nazareth because Jesus was not known by the historical Isaiah and is nowhere mentioned in Isaiah; therefore neither Isaiah the prophet, nor the Isaianic author(s), nor the canonical editors could possibly have envisioned Jesus as the speaker, all of which excludes this possible meaning."

When a prosopological assignment is made to explain a dialogical shift in the Scripture, the reader who posits this theodramatic utterance is not claiming that this is an additional "spiritual sense" built on the "historical sense," but rather that *the context that supplies the "literal sense" for the divine author is nothing less than the entire divine economy*. This is very close to an affirmation of what Catholic theologians have designated the *sensus plenior*, the fuller sense. That is, upon later inspection one can sometimes find a deeper meaning in the Old Testament intended by God but not necessarily intended by the human author. The difference is that in theodramatic interpretation, human intentionality is preserved inasmuch as the reader believes that the prophetic participant and human author(s) willingly participated in a theodramatic speech-performance, yet they simply may not have fully understood the significance of the role-playing or the full meaning of the prophetic utterance in light of the entire divine economy.[36]

In summary, if theodramatic scriptural interpretation, whether ancient or contemporary, is ultimately judged a valid reading technique vis-à-vis the ancient Jewish Scripture, then I submit that it is because the four presuppositions just discussed are true about God, the world, and Scripture.

Absolute Blocks

Yet even if one grants the truth value of the presuppositions above, as would this present author, I submit that theodramatic interpretation is nonetheless *not* a good reading in the following circumstances:

---

[36] *Sensus plenior* is defined by Raymond E. Brown and Sandra M. Schneiders, "Hermeneutics," in Raymond E. Brown, Joseph A. Fitzmyer, and Roland E. Murphy (eds.), *The New Jerome Biblical Commentary* (Englewood Cliffs, NJ: Prentice Hall, 1990), 1146–65, here 1157, as follows: "*Sensus plenior* is the deeper meaning intended by God but not clearly intended by the human author, that is seen to exist in the words of Scripture when they are studied in light of further revelation or of development in the understanding of revelation."

1. *The role assignment is based on a textual corruption.* Some theodramatic character assignments in earliest Christianity were fixed by readers on the basis of faulty manuscripts, such as when Isaiah 45: 1 was read prosopologically by Barnabas, Irenaeus, and others as concerning "my messiah, the Lord" rather than "my messiah, Cyrus" due to the corruption of *kyros* ("Cyrus") into *kyrios* ("Lord") in some early manuscripts. In such cases the theodramatic reading is neither valid nor fitting.[37]

2. *The role assignment or application is based on a serious mistranslation.* On occasion a person-centered reading achieved in the nascent church depends on unique features in the ancient Greek translation of the Jewish Scripture, the Septuagint, and these distinctive features cannot be supported by a reconstruction of the most likely Hebrew *Vorlage* ("precursor") to the Septuagint, or perhaps the Septuagint's translation is possible but remains a highly improbable construal. For example, the Hebrew of Isaiah 50: 7 is best translated, "I have set my face like flint" whereas Ps-Barnabas transforms it, "And he [God] established me as a firm rock" (*Barn.* 6. 3). Observe that the actor has changed. In the Hebrew and the Greek Septuagint the speaker talks in the first person, "*I* have set my face," but Ps-Barnabas has, "*God* established me," and this change in the verbal subject is crucial to the application by Ps-Barnabas, in which *God gifts* the speaker, the Son, with a body capable of enduring hardship. Although the role assignment itself is not based on a mistranslation or an excessively free rendering, the specific application does largely depend upon it, so I conclude that it is not a *good* reading.[38]

For those who accept the presupposition of the divine authorship of the ancient Jewish Scripture, the severity of a potential mistranslation or misapplication in the early church should, in my view, be assessed by comparing the

---

[37] There is decisive ancient manuscript evidence that much of the Bible underwent a lengthy and complex authorial, redactional, and canonical process, and that sometimes competing text-types and literary editions of certain books may even have been in existence from the beginning of the process (or at least very early). So, I am not suggesting that inspiration resides only at the fountainhead of the process. Rather most who affirm inspiration today see God's superintending hand at work throughout. In using the phrase "textual corruption," I am assuming that a given text can reach something nearing stability as authoritative Scripture for the community so that deviations are seen as problematic—that is, certain scribal alterations to the text are not accepted by the people of God as God-ordained. This is an exceedingly complex issue that cannot be fully discussed here. Even the notion of textual stability is quite difficult, especially for the OT. On the lack of complete textual stability and multiple literary editions, see Emanuel Tov, *Textual Criticism of the Hebrew Bible* (3rd rev. and exp. edn.; Minneapolis: Fortress, 2012), 174–90, 283–326; for a serious attempt to take account of this evidence in considering matters of canon and authority, see Lee M. McDonald, *The Biblical Canon: Its Origin, Transmission, and Authority* (Grand Rapids: Baker Academic, 2007).

[38] It is also remotely possible that at 6. 3 Ps-Barnabas was working with a corrupt text of the Septuagint since his text is clearly corrupt elsewhere, but he is closer to the standard text when citing Isa. 50: 7 in 5. 14, and per the Göttingen critical edition of the Septuagint, there is no further indication of such a corruption of Isa. 50: 7 in the extant witnesses.

underlying sense of the translation used (e.g. the Greek Septuagint) with that of the probable Hebrew *Vorlage*, as best as that can be reconstructed.[39] Generally speaking, in earliest Christianity prophetic inspiration was felt to happen on the level of visionary or oracular content, whereas the precise wording selected to house that divinely given content was freely determined by the human prophet,[40] so a translation can deviate substantially from the exact wording of the *Vorlage*, but still capture the underlying inspired meaning.

For instance, in Hebrews 10: 5 the Christ is designated as the speaker of the words, "a body you prepared for me" (a deviant form of Ps. 39: 7a LXX), but the Hebrew text instead reads, "ears you have dug out for me." Leaving aside, at least for now, the additional question of the authoritative nature of the interpretations found in the book of Hebrews as part of the New Testament for Christians,[41] in evaluating the quality of this prosopological reading of the ancient Jewish Scripture by the author of Hebrews, the contemporary theologian must assess whether or not the basic idea in the deviant text used by the author of Hebrews adequately represents that of the Hebrew *Vorlage*, realizing that the precise words used to clothe those ideas was secondary. Since "a body you prepared for me" and "ears you have dug out for me" in both cases refer to God's careful crafting of the physical body or some aspect thereof, the incarnational prosopological assignment made by the author of Hebrews of "a body you prepared for me" does not, at least to my mind, violate the idea in the Hebrew text, even if it is based on a questionable translation of the Hebrew. Thus, some but not all mistranslations or imprecisions in translation

---

[39] My current, provisional stance is that the ancient Hebrew consonantal text, once it reached a (relatively) stable form that would subsequently come to be regarded as canonical, should be regarded as more authoritative than subsequent Greek translations of the OT, even though the LXX was considered divinely inspired, and hence was heavily utilized, by the early church. (On the complexity of identifying such a stable canonical form, see n. 37 in this chapter.) This is to accept the basic position defended by Jerome in his debate with Augustine; it is also the view adopted by nearly all scholars today. Yet I am still pondering these matters; hence the "provisional" caveat. For an excellent discussion of the theological and historical complexities surrounding the relationship between the Hebrew Bible and the Septuagint, see Timothy M. Law, *When God Spoke Greek: The Septuagint and the Making of the Christian Bible* (Oxford: Oxford University Press, 2013).

[40] On the interplay between the visionary content and the linguistic framing in antiquity, see Plutarch, *Pyth. orac.* 5 [396c]; 7 [397c]; 21 [404b–c]; Dio Chrysostom, *Or.* 36. 1; Robert M. Grant, *The Letter and the Spirit* (New York: Macmillan, 1957), 5, 13–14; Bates, *The Hermeneutics of the Apostolic Proclamation*, 188–92.

[41] For most Christians, if any given NT author engages in a specific theodramatic reading of the OT, then that reading is prima facie valid and good since the NT is also divinely inspired. Be that as it may, in assessing what constitutes a good theodramatic reading of the ancient Jewish Scripture as approached first of all on its own terms, as I am attempting to do here, I prefer to disallow that preliminary authoritative closure in construing a particular reading as creditable. As my subsequent discussion shows, I believe hermeneutical closure for the ancient Jewish Scripture should first be established by measuring the fit between its hypothesis and the possible continuations of that story beyond the boundaries of the ancient Jewish Scripture itself. An evaluation of the inspired nature of the NT transpires subsequently.

are absolute blocks to an appropriate theodramatic interpretation, and fidelity to the underlying meaning must be assessed since inspiration resides on this level.

Critical Controls

If the presuppositions are granted and there are no absolute blocks, there is nonetheless no guarantee that a given theodramatic reading is a *good* reading of the ancient Jewish Scripture. After all, both the gnostic interpretations and the prosopological oscillations of the later church Fathers would grant essentially all these presuppositions and exclude these blocks, but along with Irenaeus, I believe that many such readings fail because prudent critical controls have been overrun. In my personal judgment, a good theodramatic reading of a specific passage in the ancient Jewish Scripture occurs when these conditions are met:

1. *The prosopological character assignments are rooted in genuine sites of dialogical shift, conversation, speech, or address in the ancient Jewish Scripture—* sites where positing a speaker or addressee on the sole basis of the prophetic horizon is problematic. This encapsulates the rule of Origen and Irenaeus— which indeed goes back to the book of Acts—that if the oracle contains spoken words that are difficult to construe on the prophetic horizon in the literary-historical context of the book itself (e.g. "you will not abandon me to the grave"—Ps. 15: 10 LXX in Acts 2: 27), then perhaps the prophet has slipped into the guise of an alternative character and is speaking theodramatically. If one believes in the reality of prophetic inspiration and the divine economy, it is not far-fetched to believe that certain vital actors in the economy, such as the anticipated royal messiah, might have made an advance appearance on the theodramatic stage in anticipation of their actualizing performance on the world stage. The vast majority of theodramatic interpretations that we have explored in this book fall into this category. For example, in Psalm 110: 1, when David says, "The Lord said to my Lord," as Jesus adroitly points out (Mark 12: 37), the Lord God *must be* talking to someone other than David, since David himself calls this person "my Lord." Any acceptable reading of this text whether Jewish, Gnostic, Christian, or otherwise, I submit, necessitates that the reader try to figure out the identity of the person to whom the Lord God is speaking—that is, a prosopological assignment is virtually demanded by the text itself.

2. *The hypothesis and the divine economy of the ancient Jewish Scripture are discerned on the basis of the chronological sequence of events in the ancient Jewish Scripture as a whole.* Consideration of this principle shows why gnostic readings of the ancient Jewish Scripture are self-evidently implausible: (1) the divine economy used by the gnostics is derived primarily outside Scripture rather than within Scripture; (2) the divine economy used by the gnostics generally ignores the sequence of events in the Scripture.

Looking now from a larger, constructive theological angle, it also must be acknowledged that the divine economy within the ancient Jewish Scripture includes unambiguous and multitudinous promises of a Davidic heir that will bring future restoration, a restoration that will occur beyond the bounds of the timeframe covered by the ancient Jewish Scripture itself (e.g. Isa. 55: 3; Jer. 23: 5–6; 30: 9; 33: 14–22; Ezek. 34: 23–4; 37: 24–5; Hos. 3: 5; Zech. 12: 8–13: 1 et al.). That is, the scriptural economy is unresolved, which compels the reader subsequently to test appropriate continuations to the story or endings in search of one that will cohere to the hypothesis and economy established. So, for example, when reading Psalm 2: 7, that the promised Davidic heir, the messiah, might be the addressee to whom God is reported to speak demands serious consideration *from within the bounds of the ancient Jewish Scripture itself*, not just when the Scripture is evaluated in a post-Christian light.

I find myself in disagreement here with Margaret Mitchell, although her work as a whole is helpfully stimulating, when she objects to Irenaeus's assertion that he has *discovered* the hypothesis in his Old Testament while his opponents have merely *invented* an alien hypothesis. Mitchell would prefer to frame all this in terms of a rhetorical/exegetical competition, with both sides putting forward contending hypotheses, arguing that both Irenaeus and the gnostics *invent* a hypothesis, for any asserted hypothesis is a human literary-critical construct. Thus for Mitchell when contemporary scholars side with Irenaeus against the gnostics, they are unhelpfully replicating his apologetic labels.[42] She is asserting, if I read her correctly, that it is somehow more charitable or fair to see Irenaeus and the gnostics simply as offering competing human constructs apart from any appeal to an actual divine hypothesis.

But Mitchell's position is no more nor less value laden than that of Irenaeus or his modern-day supporters. When Mitchell asserts that Irenaeus and the gnostics both invent a hypothesis for the ancient Jewish Scripture, this is of course correct, but it fails to take seriously the possibility that human hypothesis invention might truly be informed by a reconstructive discovery of the genuine divinely embedded hypothesis. And for those that accept the unity and inspiration of the ancient Jewish Scripture, the merit of any reconstructive discovery can be tested against a publicly available reality (i.e. the signals pointing to God's intentions available in the texts themselves).[43]

---

[42] Margaret M. Mitchell, *Paul, the Corinthians, and the Birth of Christian Hermeneutics* (Cambridge: Cambridge University Press, 2010), 25–6, 129–30.

[43] As evidence that the hypothesis/economy of the ancient Jewish Scripture should be treated as a human construct rather than divinely given, Mitchell, *Paul*, 26, asserts that if it were divinely given, then "all 'orthodox' interpreters would always agree, which of course they do not," but I find this reasoning specious. Consider an analogy from science. When a plethora of scientists, all working with epistemic virtue, acquire relevant data and formulate a descriptive theory, their findings that $e = mc^2$ should converge. However, if some scientists do not carry out their work in an epistemically honorable fashion, that is, they inadvertently fail to observe some of the data, or

As was discussed above, obviously theodramatic interpretation alone cannot prove the existence of a divinely implanted hypothesis in the ancient Jewish Scripture, rather this is a presupposition contingent on the unity and inspired nature of the ancient Jewish Scripture holistically conceived, and its validity must be weighed as a data point to be considered at the level of worldview formation and refinement.

3. *The apostolic proclamation, among other possibilities, is tested as a potentially fitting recapitulation, a capstone to the hypothesis and divine economy established in the ancient Jewish Scripture.* There are many contextual horizons against which one can read, but does the ancient Jewish Scripture itself give any clues regarding what context might be most suitable? The story of the ancient Jewish Scripture is a story that unsatisfyingly ends *in medias res,* with the anemically reduced people of God returned to the Promised Land, but the return is a far cry from the glorious future restoration announced by the prophets. The plotline established pleads for a fitting ending, so the most appropriate context for the whole will be one that looks to "read" subsequent history beyond the horizon of the ancient Jewish Scripture itself. There are several possible continuations to the story, all of which should be weighed, including the attempted Jewish revolution in the war against the Romans, the rabbinic movement, and the apostolic proclamation of the earliest church.

4. *In light of the validity of the apostolic proclamation as the recapitulation when tested, above all that Jesus was raised from the dead, the hypothesis and divine economy as derived from the ancient Jewish Scripture is extended to include the apostolic proclamation.* Not all readers will find this a legitimate critical control for determining *good* theodramatic interpretation of the ancient Jewish Scripture, preferring to locate it with the presuppositions or to disregard it all together as hubristic, supersessionist Christian nonsense. Along with Irenaeus, I disagree. For those that affirm that God has authored a divine economy that includes both the ancient Jewish Scripture and events external to Scripture, virtuous interpretation will take into account all the potentially relevant data, *even the data that goes beyond* that found in the ancient Jewish Scripture itself, since that story indicates that God's orchestration of all human affairs will continue into the future. The apostles make a truth claim about the

---

disregard data inconvenient to their preferred explanation, or refuse to consider that an established theory like $F = ma$ might need supplementation, or accidentally ignore the way their own measurements have affected the process, and then falsely conclude that $e^2 = mc$ or $e = m^2c^3$, then, that does not somehow disprove that the data, when studied with full-orbed epistemic virtue, would ultimately yield the conclusion $e = mc^2$ (or close approximations thereto). Likewise, given the complexity of the data, when various readers locate diverging literary hypotheses in the ancient Jewish Scripture, we cannot conclude that there is no single divinely intended, discoverable literary hypothesis. For all readers (this present author certainly included) have imperfect and varying levels of epistemic virtue in engaging the same publicly available data.

way the Christ-story completes the ancient Jewish Scripture, and that claim among many should be tested by the virtuous reader/knower.

The apostolic proclamation, which claims to extend and fulfill the master plotline established in the ancient Jewish Scripture, asserts that: (1) Jesus pre-existed with the Father, (2) took on human flesh in the line of David, (3) died for the sins of humanity "in accordance with the scriptures," (4) was buried, (5) was raised on the third day "in accordance with the scriptures," (6) appeared to many, (7) ascended, (8) was seated at the right hand of God as Lord, and (9) will come again as judge.

Given the presuppositions outlined above, I think *the best* reading of the ancient Jewish Scripture is that this Jesus Christ story is the fitting consummation of the divine economy established—he is the Davidic heir that fulfills the promises, the recapitulation, and hence a reading of the ancient Jewish Scripture which ignores his consummating force will not be the best construal of the encoded master plot. Of course, since I am a confessing Christian it is not surprising that I have come to this conclusion and I respect that others disagree, even those who have diligently and good-heartedly explored the same data set. Yet, I want to stress that this is not a merely private opinion disconnected from real-world data or a solipsism, since the conclusion is based on information available in the public arena—its viability is able to be assessed by anyone.

Further, I would affirm that if the ancient Jewish Scripture is read on its own, apart from testing whether or not the apostolic proclamation about Christ is the true capstone of the hypothesis and divine economy found therein, it does not demand *unique* Christian closure. However, the story internal to the Jewish Scripture itself strongly urges additional testing for plot continuation and closure beyond its own boundaries, and once the truth value of the apostolic proclamation is tested in light of other possible extensions or endings to the story, warranted plot resolution can be reached. Regardless of whether or not the reader agrees with the specific Christian denouement that I personally find compelling, for those that acknowledge divine inspiration, I want to assert resolutely that the postmodern tendency *not* to seek unique plot resolution in any direction—albeit even in the truly noble interests of tolerance, interreligious dialogue, or ecumenism—is not intellectually honorable in light of the text's own demands and ultimately smacks of wishy-washy anti-realism.[44]

The earliest Christians, but above all, the Apostle Paul and Luke the Evangelist, I submit, would both agree that the ancient Jewish Scripture could only be understood fully in the wake of the events surrounding Jesus

---

[44] On virtue and its relationship to the acquisition of knowledge, see Wood, *Epistemology*, 9–76.

Christ. For Paul, it is only when an interpreter is guided by the apostolic proclamation and sees the manner in which Jesus Christ brings the ancient Jewish Scripture to a climax that the veil is removed for that reader, not before (2 Cor. 3: 16; cf. 1 Cor. 15: 3–5; Rom. 1: 2–4).[45] Similarly, for Luke, even though, "beginning from Moses and all the prophets" the resurrected Jesus has already interpreted for the two travelers on the road to Emmaus "the things concerning himself in all the scriptures" (24: 27), it is only when the two travelers finally see the resurrected Jesus in the breaking of the bread that their eyes are opened, and they are able to exclaim, "Were not our hearts burning within us when he was speaking to us on the road, when he was expositing the scriptures for us?" (24: 32). The scriptures alone were not enough apart from the verifying reality of the resurrection, the keystone within the apostolic proclamation. Likewise, when Jesus appears to the eleven, he states, "it is necessary for all the things which have been written in the law of Moses and the prophets and the psalms to be fulfilled concerning me" (24: 44), but in order for the disciples to see the latent pattern in the scriptures, Jesus must do something further, he must either open the minds of the disciples (the traditional translation), or perhaps better, as I have argued elsewhere, he must explain for the disciples the divinely implanted *nous* of the scriptures, their "mind," that is, their "unitive sense" as intended by the divine author: "Then Jesus exposited the scriptures so that the disciples could understand the mind [*nous*] of them" (Luke 24: 45).[46] Either way, the disciples could not unlock the divinely given meaning of the ancient Jewish Scripture without first receiving from the resurrected Christ, indicating that the truths encapsulated in the apostolic proclamation were regarded in the earliest church as a necessary posthoc key to unlock what would come to be termed the Old Testament.

In considering the basis of my conclusion, does the apostolic proclamation undergird prosopological exegesis or is prosopological exegesis part of the "in accordance with the scriptures" portion of the apostolic proclamation that certifies the truthfulness of the early Christian testimony? For this present author, a choice between the two cannot be made, for they are mutually reinforcing when, beginning from either direction, a spiraling process of formulating theses and seeking verifications is undertaken.

5. *The entire extended apostolic divine economy (the ancient Jewish Scripture plus the apostolic proclamation) is, therefore, the literary-historical horizon from which a valid theodramatic character can be drawn by a reader while still respecting the ancient text; yet, for a good reading, a correspondence must exist between the description of the speaker or addressee in the ancient text and*

---

[45] I have written about this at length already in Bates, *The Hermeneutics of the Apostolic Proclamation*, esp. pp. 160–81.

[46] Matthew W. Bates, "Closed-Minded Hermeneutics? A Proposed Alternative Translation for Luke 24:45," *JBL* 129 (2010): 537–57.

what is known about the proposed theodramatic character as that character is revealed elsewhere in the divine economy. Once the apostolic proclamation has been tested and verified as the recapitulative key that sums up the hypothesis and economy of the ancient Jewish Scripture, then—and this is critical— characters that appear only within the extension to that story (e.g. Jesus of Nazareth or the apostles) are recognized as part of the literary-historical metatextual horizon within the bounds of which valid prosopological exegesis might transpire. Thus, when we discover that the speaker of Psalm 69: 10 says, "Zeal for your house consumed me," and we determine that the words are somewhat unsuitable if restricted to the prophetic horizon of David alone (in accordance with thesis 2), we should reflect upon the character description in the immediate context within Psalm 69 as well as upon the life-story of other major figures within the divine economy, especially Jesus of Nazareth, given the recapitulative force of his character within the master plot, to see if the prophet might have stepped into an alternative theodramatic character as he delivered his speech. The better the corroborating fit, the more plausible the proposed prosopological reading. Thus, the "literal sense" of these Old Testament prophetic texts must be sought within the bounds of the entire divine economy, including the apostolic proclamation about Jesus, even though the apostolic proclamation is not, strictly speaking, found in the Old Testament itself.

6. *In light of this extended apostolic divine economy, assigned prosopological characters should be restricted by the plausible limits of theodramatic prophetic vision.* One difficulty with what I have termed "prosopological oscillation" as described by Tyconius and practiced by Tertullian, Origen, Augustine, and others (as discussed previously in this chapter) is that it is hard to fathom how it could function as a genuine prophetic event. If a prophet is receiving visionary content, and is stepping into a theodramatic acting role (or is reporting an observed theodrama as an external spectator), it is difficult to imagine the *persona* the prophet is inhabiting or observing as oscillating between, for instance, Christ the head and Christ the body, as these Fathers would have it. In other words, granted the presupposition that a theodramatic utterance involves a genuine prophetic event, I suggest that any proposed explanatory role assignment should be tested by asking the question, How likely is it that a prophet could have seen or inhabited the proposed theodramatic sequence in a vision? At least to my mind, the oscillation of a single speaking person is difficult to imagine as a more probable occurrence within the bounds of a legitimate God-given prophetic vision than constancy, and thus the solution of prosopological oscillation as practiced by Origen, Tertullian, Tyconius, Jerome, Augustine, and many other Fathers, as whimsically entertaining and edifying as it might be, is nevertheless a faulty reading strategy vis-à-vis the ancient Jewish Scripture.

* * *

Early Christian interpretation of Old Testament dialogues covers the full spectrum of the divine life, from before creation to the final consummation. This final chapter broached the question of interpretative normativity via an exploration of gnostic prosopological exegesis and the response of Irenaeus and other early Fathers. Obviously, the validity of prosopological exegesis is bound up with questions regarding what constitutes a good reading of the Old Testament in general. Irenaeus's remarks about the hypothesis, economy, and recapitulation of Scripture were found to be a helpful initial guide. I have argued that while not all the specific examples of prosopological exegesis in the earliest church are equally convincing, the Old Testament texts so interpreted generally do feature legitimate "person-centered" difficulties that cannot be solved from within the bounds of the texts themselves, making the character assignments proposed by the earliest Christians plausible if certain presuppositions are granted. It has been suggested that when a reader seeks to make prosopological role assignments, the horizon against which the literal sense is best construed is the entire divine economy. It is hoped that the additional theses I have offered with respect to theodramatic scriptural interpretation—theses regarding enabling presuppositions, absolute blocks, and critical controls—will generate further reflection and discussion.

Epilogue: The Read God

As the earliest Christians pored over the ancient Jewish Scripture in light of their own experienced reality of the death, resurrection, and ascension of Jesus Christ, not to mention the outpouring of the Holy Spirit at Pentecost, they found that certain sites of dialogue in the Scripture demanded that the one God be identified as differentiated by multiple persons. Indeed, since the Gospel writers portray Jesus himself as undertaking prosopological exegesis on numerous occasions, it is at least plausible that this process in the early church was a continuation of Jesus of Nazareth's own theodramatic scriptural interpretation and performative actualization. For these early interpreters, as a prophet took on a theodramatic role, he was able to speak from the *prosōpa* (persons, dramatic characters) of God (the Father), the Son, and more rarely the Spirit, with all this facilitated through the Inspiring Agent, usually described as the Spirit. Extending the master plot and divine economy of the ancient Jewish Scripture in light of the apostolic preaching about Christ, the earliest Christians used that apostolic proclamation as a key to unlock the dialogical puzzles they found in what they would come to term the Old Testament.

TRINITARIAN BIRTH THROUGH OLD TESTAMENT DIALOGUE

As these dialogues were read by the earliest Christians, the metaphor of *prosōpon* or *persona* ("person"), and later *hypostasis* ("discrete individual being"), was taken to be the premier divinely authorized way to parse and differentiate identities and relationships with respect to the one God, and so the doctrine of the Trinity was born in an irreducibly essential fashion through interpretative reading, as this reading strategy combined with other factors (see Ch. 1). Hence, when theologians today depart from "person" language when speaking of the Trinity or Christological origins (e.g. Barth's *Seinsweise* or Bauckham's

Christology of Divine Identity), they risk cutting the doctrine off from its rootedness in the interpretation of the Old Testament in the New Testament and early church. This is why I currently prefer to speak of a *Christology of Divine Persons*. I am seeking to signal that prosopological exegesis, among other factors, was essential to how Jesus Christ was from our earliest Christian sources understood to be divine—namely, as the Son who converses with the person of the Father through the Spirit in a time-transcending fashion (with the Spirit also occasionally speaking directly as a person). I think more work remains to be done to ferret out precisely how a prosopologically oriented Christology of Divine Persons might interface with a Christology of Divine Identity and other possible models, but this must be left for future studies.

In the preceding pages we have sought to enter into the story of the divine persons as it is revealed in their scriptural dialogues. It is a story that stretches across the canvas of time, reaching back before creation, enfolding the incarnation, crucifixion, and enthronement of the Son, and culminating with conversations that anticipate the future new creation. As we have repeatedly observed, the theodramatic reading strategy employed by the earliest Christians did not immediately lend itself to conceptualizing the persons of the triune God in terms of subordination and procession, although neither are the persons so described inimical to such relational terms; rather, the divine persons thereby revealed show an unremitting personal concern for one another. Moreover, I believe the assumptions, details, and implications of prosopological exegesis substantially undercut scholarly theses that suggest a backward movement of Christology—that is, it undermines the idea that the first Christians did not regard Jesus as the preexistent Son of God but only came to regard him as such when he was adopted as Son at his resurrection, with Jesus' Sonship then retrojected in time. On the contrary, prosopological exegesis helps show that the Christology of our earliest Christian sources is as high as that of our later sources. Those who employed prosopological exegesis regarded Jesus as a preexistent *person*, the Son, and as such he was deemed capable of conversing with God the Father prior to his incarnation.

As a recapitulative theological summation, perhaps the boundlessly self-giving interior life of the persons of the Trinity in the earliest church is best captured in the following words which the author of Acts took as spoken by David via the Spirit, who had slipped into the character of the Christ:

THE CHRIST (speaking to GOD THE FATHER): I, the Son, kept seeing the Lord God, my Father, continually before me, for God is at my right hand lest I be shaken . . . . Because you, O my Father, will not abandon my soul to Hades, or permit your Holy One to see decay. You have made known to me the paths of life; you, O my Father, will fill me with joy in your presence.   (Acts 2: 25–8 citing Ps. 15: 8–11 LXX, paraphrased)

As such, the Son recalls the moment when the Father humbly appeared at his right hand, a reversal of the traditional positions, when the Son was in his hour of darkest need. The Son knew that the Father would not forsake him, instead he would bring the jubilant life-filled Son back into his own presence. And so the Father gives to the Son, as all three persons are bound together in an interpenetrating and endless spiral of divine self-giving love: Father, Son, Spirit—One God forever and ever.

References

Primary Sources: Selected Editions and Translations

Aland, Barbara, Kurt Aland, Eberhard Nestle, and Erwin Nestle (eds.), *Novum Testamentum Graece*. 27th rev. edn. Stuttgart: Deutsche Bibelgesellschaft, 2000.

The Ante-Nicene Fathers. 10 vols. Ed. Alexander Roberts and James Donaldson. 1885–7. Repr. Peabody, Mass.: Hendrickson, 1994.

Behr, John (trans. and intro.), *St. Irenaeus of Lyons, On the Apostolic Preaching*. Crestwood, NY: St Vladimir's Seminary Press, 1997.

Blanc, Cécile (ed. and trans.), *Origène. Commentaire sur sain Jean*. 3 vols. Sources chrétiennes. Paris: Cerf, 1966–75.

Charlesworth, James H. (ed.), *The Old Testament Pseudepigrapha*. 2 vols. New York: Doubleday, 1983.

Evans, Ernest (ed. and trans.), *Q. Septimii Florentis Tertulliani Adversus Praxean, Tertullian's Treatise against Praxeas*. London: SPCK, 1948.

Falls, Thomas B. (trans.), *St. Justin Martyr: Dialogue with Trypho*. Revised with a New Introduction by Thomas P. Halton. Fathers of the Church 3. Washington, DC: Catholic University Press of America, 2003.

Froehlich, Karlfried (ed. and trans.), *Biblical Interpretation in the Early Church*. Sources of Early Christian Thought. Philadelphia: Fortress, 1984.

Hall, Stuart G. (ed. and trans.), *Melito of Sardis On Pascha and Fragments*. Oxford Early Christian Texts. Oxford: Clarendon, 1979.

Heine, Ronald E. (trans.), *Origen, Commentary on the Gospel According to John*. Fathers of the Church 80, 89. Washington, DC: Catholic University of America Press, 1989, 1993.

Hill, Edmund (trans., intro., and notes), *The Trinity: The Works of Saint Augustine: A Translation for the 21st Century*. Hyde Park, NY: New City Press, 1991.

Holmes, Michael W. (ed. and rev.), *The Apostolic Fathers*. 2nd edn. Ed. and trans. J. B. Lightfoot and J. R. Harmer. Grand Rapids: Baker, 1992.

Irénée de Lyon: Contre les hérésies. Ed. and trans. Adelin Rousseau et al. 10 vols. Sources chrétiennes. Paris: Cerf: 1965–79.

Kennedy, George A. (trans.), *Progymnasmata: Greek Textbooks of Prose Composition and Rhetoric*. SBL Writings from the Greco-Roman World 10. Atlanta: Society of Biblical Literature, 2003.

Layton, Bentley, *The Gnostic Scriptures: A New Translation with Annotations and Introductions*. Anchor Bible Reference Library. New York: Doubleday, 1987.

Loeb Classical Library. Ed. Jeffrey Henderson et al. Cambridge, Mass.: Harvard University Press, 1911–.

Marcovich, Miroslav (ed.), *Iustini Martyris Apologiae pro Christianis*. Patristische Texte und Studien 38. Berlin: Walter de Gruyter, 1994.

Marcovich, Miroslav (ed.), *Iustini Martyris Dialogus cum Tryphone*. Patristische Texte und Studien 47. Berlin: Walter de Gruyter, 1997.

Nickelsburg, George W. E., and James C. VanderKam (trans.), *1 Enoch: A New Translation*. Minneapolis: Fortress, 2004.

Parry, Donald W., and Emanuel Tov (eds.), *The Dead Sea Scrolls Reader*. 6 vols. Leiden: Brill, 2004–5.

Patrologia graeca. Ed. J.-P. Migne. 162 vols. Paris, 1857–86.

Rusch, William G. (trans. and ed.), *The Trinitarian Controversy*. Philadelphia: Fortress, 1980.

Scheck, Thomas P. (trans.), *Origen, Commentary on the Epistle to the Romans*. Fathers of the Church 103–4. Washington, DC: Catholic University of America Press, 2001–2.

Schneemelcher, Wilhelm (ed.), *New Testament Apocrypha*. 2 vols. Trans. R. McL. Wilson. Rev. edn. Louisville, Ky.: Westminster John Knox, 1991.

Septuaginta, Vetus Testamentum Graecum. Ed. Alfred Rahlfs et al. 24 vols. Societatis Litterarum Gottingensis editum. Göttingen: Vandenhoeck & Ruprecht, 1931–.

Spengel, Leonardus (ed.), *Rhetores Graeci*. 3 vols. Leipzig: Teubner, 1854–6.

Unger, Dominic J. (trans. and annot.), *St. Irenaeus of Lyons: Against the Heresies*, with revisions by John J. Dillon and Irenaeus M. C. Steenberg. Ancient Christian Writers. Vols. i–iii of a projected 5 vols. Mahwah, NJ: Newman, 1992–.

Secondary Sources: Works Cited

Albl, Martin C. *"And Scripture Cannot Be Broken": The Form and Function of the Early Christian* Testimonia *Collections*. Supplements to Novum Testamentum 96. Leiden: Brill, 1999.

Alexander, Patrick H., et al. (eds.), *The SBL Handbook of Style*. Peabody, Mass.: Hendrickson, 1999.

Allison, Dale C., Jr. *Constructing Jesus: Memory, Imagination, and History*. Grand Rapids: Baker Academic, 2010.

Anatolios, Khaled. *Retrieving Nicaea: The Development and Meaning of Trinitarian Doctrine*. Grand Rapids: Baker Academic, 2011.

Anderson, R. Dean, Jr. *Glossary of Greek Rhetorical Terms Connected to Methods of Argumentation, Figures and Tropes from Anaximenes to Quintilian*. Contributions to Biblical Exegesis and Theology 24. Leuven: Peeters, 2000.

Andresen, Carl. "Zur Entstehung und Geschichte des trinitarischen Personbegriffes." *Zeitschrift für die neutestamentliche Wissenschaft und die Kunde der älteren Kirche* 52 (1961): 1–39.

Attridge, Harold W. *The Epistle to the Hebrews*. Hermeneia. Minneapolis: Fortress, 1989.

Attridge, Harold W. "Giving Voice to Jesus: Use of the Psalms in the New Testament," in Harold W. Attridge and Margot E. Fassler (eds.), *Psalms in Community: Jewish and Christian Textual, Liturgical, and Artistic Traditions*. SBL Symposium Series 25. Atlanta: Society of Biblical Literature, 2003, 101–12.

Aune, David E. *The New Testament in Its Literary Environment*. Library of Early Christianity 8. Philadelphia: Westminster, 1987.

Ayres, Lewis. *Nicaea and Its Legacy: An Approach to Fourth-Century Trinitarian Theology*. Oxford: Oxford University Press, 2004.

Balthasar, Hans Urs von. *Theo-Drama: Theological Dramatic Theory.* Trans. Graham Harrison. 5 vols. San Francisco: Ignatius, 1988–98.

Barnett, Paul. *The Second Epistle to the Corinthians.* New International Commentary on the New Testament. Grand Rapids: Eerdmans, 1997.

Barr, James. *The Concept of Biblical Theology: An Old Testament Perspective.* Minneapolis: Fortress, 1999.

Barrett, C. K. *A Critical and Exegetical Commentary on the Acts of the Apostles.* 2 vols. International Critical Commentary. Edinburgh: T&T Clark, 1994–8.

Barrett, C. K. *The Second Epistle to the Corinthians.* Peabody, Mass.: Hendrickson, 1997. Repr. from Black's New Testament Commentaries. London: A&C Black, 1973.

Barth, Karl. Church Dogmatics. 4 vols. Edinburgh: T&T Clark, 1956–75.

Bates, Matthew W. "Beyond Hays's *Echoes of Scripture in the Letters of Paul*: A Proposed Diachronic Intertextuality with Romans 10:16 as a Test-Case," in Christopher D. Stanley (ed.), *Paul and Scripture: Extending the Conversation.* Early Christianity and Its Literature 9. Atlanta: Society of Biblical Literature, 2012, 263–92.

Bates, Matthew W. "Beyond Stichwort: A Narrative Approach to Isa 52, 7 in Romans 10,15 and 11Q Melchizedek (11Q13)." *Revue biblique* 116 (2009): 387–414.

Bates, Matthew W. "A Christology of Incarnation and Enthronement: Romans 1:3–4 as Unified, Nonadoptionist, and Nonconciliatory." *Catholic Biblical Quarterly* 77 (2015): 107–27.

Bates, Matthew W. "Closed-Minded Hermeneutics? A Proposed Alternative Translation for Luke 24:45." *Journal of Biblical Literature* 129 (2010): 537–57.

Bates, Matthew W. "Cryptic Codes and a Violent King: A New Proposal for Matthew 11:12 and Luke 16:16–18." *Catholic Biblical Quarterly* 75 (2013): 74–93.

Bates, Matthew W. *The Hermeneutics of the Apostolic Proclamation: The Center of Paul's Method of Scriptural Interpretation.* Waco, Tex.: Baylor University Press, 2012.

Bates, Matthew W. "Prosopographic Exegesis and Narrative Logic: Paul, Origen, and Theodoret of Cyrus on Psalm 69:22–23," in Vasile Mihoc and Daniel Patte (eds.), *The Greek Fathers' and Eastern Orthodox Interpretations of Romans.* Romans through History and Culture 9. London: Bloomsbury (T&T Clark), 2013, 105–34.

Bauckham, Richard. *God Crucified: Monotheism and Christology in the New Testament.* Grand Rapids: Eerdmans, 1998.

Bauckham, Richard. *Jesus and the God of Israel: God Crucified and Other Studies on the New Testament's Christology of Divine Identity.* Milton Keynes: Paternoster, 2008.

Beale, Greg K. *The Book of Revelation: A Commentary on the Greek Text.* New International Greek Testament Commentary. Grand Rapids: Eerdmans, 2001.

Beale, Greg K. *Handbook on the New Testament Use of the Old Testament: Exegesis and Interpretation.* Grand Rapids: Baker Academic, 2012.

Beale, Greg K., and D. A. Carson (eds.), *Commentary on the New Testament Use of the Old Testament.* Baker Academic: Grand Rapids, 2007.

Behr, John. *The Way to Nicaea: The Formation of Christian Theology, Volume i.* Crestwood, NY: St Vladimir's Seminary Press, 2001.

Bird, Michael F. *Are You the One Who Is To Come? The Historical Jesus and the Messianic Question.* Grand Rapids: Baker Academic, 2009.

Blackwell, Ben C. *Christosis: Pauline Soteriology in Light of Deification in Irenaeus and Cyril of Alexandria.* Wissenschaftliche Untersuchungen zum Neuen Testament. Second Series 314. Tübingen: Mohr (Siebeck), 2011.

Bockmuehl, Markus. *Seeing the Word: Refocusing New Testament Study.* Grand Rapids: Baker Academic, 2006.

Bousset, Wilhelm. *Kyrios Christos: A History of the Belief in Christ from the Beginnings of Christianity to Irenaeus.* Trans. John E. Steely. Nashville: Abingdon, 1970.

Boyarin, Daniel. *Border Lines: The Partition of Judeo-Christianity.* Philadelphia: University of Pennsylvania Press, 2004.

Boyarin, Daniel. *The Jewish Gospels: The Story of the Jewish Christ.* New York: New Press, 2012.

Brown, Raymond E. *The Death of the Messiah: From Gethsemane to the Grave: A Commentary on the Passion Narratives in the Four Gospels.* 2 vols. Anchor Bible Reference Library. New York: Doubleday, 1994.

Brown, Raymond E., and Sandra M. Schneiders. "Hermeneutics," in Raymond E. Brown, Joseph A. Fitzmyer, and Roland E. Murphy (eds.), *The New Jerome Biblical Commentary.* Englewood Cliffs, NJ: Prentice-Hall, 1990, 1146–65.

Bruce, F. F. *The Acts of the Apostles: The Greek Text with Introduction and Commentary.* 3rd edn. Grand Rapids: Eerdmans, 1990.

Bultmann, Rudolf. *The Second Letter to the Corinthians.* Trans. Roy A. Harrisville. Minneapolis: Augsburg, 1985.

Bultmann, Rudolf. *Theology of the New Testament.* Trans. Kendrick Grobel. London: SCM, 1952–5.

Campbell, Douglas A. *The Deliverance of God: An Apocalyptic Re-Reading of Justification in Paul.* Grand Rapids: Eerdmans, 2009.

Capes, David B. *Old Testament Yahweh Texts in Paul's Christology.* Wissenschaftliche Untersuchungen zum Neuen Testament. Second Series 47. Tübingen: Mohr (Siebeck), 1992.

Chester, Andrew. "Jewish Messianic Expectations and Mediatorial Figures and Pauline Christology," in Martin Hengel and Ulrich Heckel (eds.), *Paulus und das antike Judentum.* Wissenschaftliche Untersuchungen zum Neuen Testament. Second Series 58. Tübingen: Mohr (Siebeck), 1991, 17–89.

Childs, Brevard S. *Isaiah.* Old Testament Library. Louisville, Ky.: Westminster John Knox, 2001.

Childs, Brevard S. "The *Sensus Literalis* of Scripture: An Ancient and Modern Problem," in Herbert Donner, Robert Hanhart, and Rudolf Smend (eds.), *Beiträge zur Alttestamentlichen Theologie: Festschrift für Walther Zimmerli zum 70. Geburtstag.* Göttingen: Vandenhoeck & Ruprecht, 1977, 80–93.

Cockerill, Gareth L. *The Epistle to the Hebrews.* New International Commentary on the New Testament. Grand Rapids: Eerdmans, 2012.

Collins, John J. "A Herald of Good Tidings: Isaiah 61:1–3 and Its Actualization in the Dead Sea Scrolls," in Craig A. Evans and Shemaryahu Talmon (eds.), *The Quest for Context and Meaning: Studies in Biblical Intertextuality in Honor of James A. Sanders.* Biblical Interpretation Series 28. Leiden: Brill, 1997, 225–40.

Collins, John J. *The Scepter and the Star: Messianism in Light of the Dead Sea Scrolls*. Anchor Bible Reference Library. 2nd edn. Grand Rapids: Eerdmans, 2010.

Crossan, John D. *The Historical Jesus: The Life of a Mediterranean Jewish Peasant*. San Francisco: HarperSanFrancisco, 1991.

Dachs, Hans. *Die λύσις ἐκ τοῦ προσώπου: Ein exegetischer und kritischer Grundsatz Aristarchs und seine Neuanwendung auf Ilias und Odyssee*. Erlangen: Junge & Sohn, 1913.

Davies, W. D., and Dale C. Allison, Jr. *A Critical and Exegetical Commentary on the Gospel According to Saint Matthew*. 3 vols. International Critical Commentary. Edinburgh: T&T Clark, 1988–97.

Dawson, David. *Allegorical Readers and Cultural Revision in Ancient Alexandria*. Berkeley: University of California Press, 1992.

Denton, Donald L., Jr. *Historiography and Hermeneutics in Jesus Studies: An Examination of the Work of John Dominic Crossan and Ben F. Meyer*. Journal for the Study of the New Testament: Supplement Series 262. New York: T&T Clark, 2004.

Dillard, Annie. *Pilgrim at Tinker Creek*. New York: Bantam Books, 1975.

Dodd, C. H. *According to the Scriptures: The Sub-Structure of New Testament Theology*. New York: Scribner's, 1953.

Downs, David J. "Prosopological Exegesis in Cyprian's *De opere et eleemosynis*." *Journal of Theological Interpretation* 6 (2012): 279–93.

Drobner, Hubertus R. *Person-Exegese und Christologie bei Augustinus: Zur Herkunft der Formel Una Persona*. Leiden: Brill, 1986.

Dunn, James D. G. *Christology in the Making: A New Testament Inquiry into the Origins of the Doctrine of the Incarnation*. 2nd edn. Grand Rapids: Eerdmans, 1989.

Dunn, James D. G. *Did the First Christians Worship Jesus?: The New Testament Evidence*. Louisville, Ky.: Westminster John Knox, 2010.

Dunn, James D. G. *Jesus Remembered*. Grand Rapids: Eerdmans, 2003.

Dünzl, Franz. *A Brief History of the Doctrine of the Trinity in the Early Church*. Trans. John Bowden. London: T&T Clark, 2007.

Eden, Kathy. *Hermeneutics and the Rhetorical Tradition: Chapters in the Ancient Legacy and the Humanist Reception*. New Haven: Yale University Press, 1997.

Ehrman, Bart D. *How Jesus Became God: The Exaltation of a Jewish Preacher from Galilee*. New York: HarperOne, 2014.

Ellingworth, Paul. *The Epistle to the Hebrews: A Commentary on the Greek Text*. New International Greek Testament Commentary. Grand Rapids: Eerdmans, 1993.

Emery, Gilles, and Matthew Levering (eds.), *The Oxford Handbook of The Trinity*. New York: Oxford University Press, 2011.

Evans, Craig A. "Jesus' Action in the Temple: Cleansing or Portent of Destruction?," in Bruce Chilton and Craig A. Evans (eds.), *Jesus in Context: Temple, Purity, and Restoration*. Arbeiten zur Geschichte des antiken Judentums und des Urchristentums 39. Leiden: Brill, 1997, 395–439.

Fee, Gordon D. *Pauline Christology: An Exegetical-Theological Study*. Peabody, Mass.: Hendrickson, 2007.

Fitzmyer, Joseph A. *The Acts of the Apostles: A New Translation with Introduction and Commentary*. Anchor Bible 31. New York: Doubleday, 1998.

Fitzmyer, Joseph A. "David 'Being Therefore a Prophet...' (Acts 2:30)." *Catholic Biblical Quarterly* 34 (1972): 332–9.

Fitzmyer, Joseph A. "Further Light on Melchizedek," in *The Semitic Background of the New Testament*. Grand Rapids: Eerdmans, 1997, 245–67. Repr. from *Journal of Biblical Literature* 86 (1967): 25–41.

Frei, Hans W. *The Eclipse of Biblical Narrative: A Study in Eighteenth and Nineteenth Century Hermeneutics*. New Haven: Yale University Press, 1974.

Gathercole, Simon J. *The Preexistent Son: Recovering the Christologies of Matthew, Mark, and Luke*. Grand Rapids: Eerdmans, 2006.

Gorman, Michael J. *Inhabiting the Cruciform God: Kenosis, Justification, and Theosis in Paul's Narrative Soteriology*. Grand Rapids: Eerdmans, 2009.

Grant, Robert M. *Irenaeus of Lyons*. London: Routledge, 1997.

Grant, Robert M. *The Letter and the Spirit*. New York: Macmillan, 1957.

Grenz, Stanley J. *Rediscovering the Triune God: The Trinity in Contemporary Theology*. Minneapolis: Fortress, 2004.

Grillmeier, Aloys. *Christ in Christian Tradition: From the Apostolic Age to Chalcedon (451)*. Trans. John Bowden. 2nd rev. edn. Atlanta: John Knox, 1975.

Hafemann, Scott J. "Eschatology and Ethics: The Future of Israel and the Nations in Romans 15:1–13." *Tyndale Bulletin* (2000): 161–92.

Hanson, Anthony T. *Jesus Christ in the Old Testament*. London: SPCK, 1965.

Harnack, Adolf von. *History of Dogma*. Trans. Neil Buchanan. Boston: Little, Brown, & Co., 1896–1905.

Hay, David M. *Glory at the Right Hand: Psalm 110 in Early Christianity*. Society of Biblical Literature Monograph Series 18. Nashville: Abingdon, 1973.

Hayes, John H. "The Resurrection as Enthronement and the Earliest Church Christology." *Interpretation* 22 (1968): 333–45.

Hays, Richard B. "Christ Prays the Psalms: Israel's Psalter as a Matrix of Early Christology," in Richard B. Hays, *The Conversion of the Imagination*. Grand Rapids: Eerdmans, 2005, 101–18. Repr. from "Christ Prays the Psalms: Paul's Use of Early Christian Exegetical Convention," in Abraham J. Malherbe and Wayne A. Meeks (eds.), *The Future of Christology*. Minneapolis: Fortress, 1993, 122–36.

Hays, Richard B. *Echoes of Scripture in the Letters of Paul*. New Haven: Yale University Press, 1989.

Heine, Ronald E. *Reading the Old Testament with the Ancient Church: Exploring the Formation of Early Christian Thought*. Grand Rapids: Baker Academic, 2007.

Helberath, Bernd J. *Der Personbegriff der Trinitätstheologie in Rückfrage von Karl Rahner zu Tertullians "Adversus Praxean"*. Innsbruck; Vienna: Tyrolia, 1986.

Hengel, Martin. *Judaism and Hellenism: Studies in Their Encounter in Palestine During the Early Hellenistic Period*. Trans. John Bowden. 2 vols. Philadelphia: Fortress, 1974.

Hillar, Marian. *From Logos to Trinity: The Evolution of Religious Beliefs from Pythagoras to Tertullian*. Cambridge: Cambridge University Press, 2012.

Holmes, Stephen R. *The Quest for the Trinity: The Doctrine of God in Scripture, History and Modernity*. Downers Grove, Ill.: IVP Academic, 2012.

Horsley, Richard A. (ed.), *Hidden Transcripts and the Arts of Resistance: Applying the Work of James C. Scott to Jesus and Paul.* Semeia Studies 48. Atlanta: Society of Biblical Literature, 2004.

Horsley, Richard A. *Jesus and the Powers: Conflict, Covenant, and Hope of the Poor.* Minneapolis: Fortress, 2011.

Horsley, Richard A., and John S. Hanson, *Bandits, Prophets, and Messiahs: Popular Movements at the Time of Jesus.* San Francisco: HarperSanFrancisco, 1985.

Hossfeld, Frank-Lothar, and Erich Zenger. *Psalms.* Trans. Linda M. Maloney. Vols. ii–iii of a projected 3 vols. Hermeneia. Minneapolis: Fortress, 2005–.

Hurtado, Larry W. *Lord Jesus Christ: Devotion to Jesus in Earliest Christianity.* Grand Rapids: Eerdmans, 2003.

Hurtado, Larry W. *One God, One Lord: Early Christian Devotion and Ancient Jewish Monotheism.* Philadelphia: Fortress, 1988.

Jewett, Robert. "The Redaction and Use of an Early Christian Confession in Romans 1:3–4," in D. E. Groh and R. Jewett (eds.), *The Living Text: Essays in Honor of Ernest W. Saunders.* Lanham, Md.: University Press of America, 1985, 99–122.

Jewett, Robert. *Romans: A Commentary.* Hermeneia. Minneapolis: Fortress, 2007.

Jipp, Joshua W. "Ancient, Modern, and Future Interpretations of Romans 1:3–4: Reception History and Biblical Interpretation." *Journal of Theological Interpretation* (2009): 241–59.

Juel, Donald. *Messianic Exegesis: Christological Interpretation of the Old Testament in Early Christianity.* Philadelphia: Fortress, 1988.

Kampling, Rainer. *Israel unter dem Anspruch des Messias: Studien zur Israelthematik im Markusevangelium.* Stuttgart: Katholisches Bibelwerk, 1992.

Keck, Leander E. "Christology, Soteriology, and the Praise of God (Romans 15:7–13)," in R. T. Fortuna and B. R. Gaventa (eds.), *The Conversation Continues: Studies in Paul and John: In Honor of J. Louis Martyn.* Nashville: Abingdon, 1990, 85–97.

Keener, Craig S. *The Historical Jesus of the Gospels.* Grand Rapids: Eerdmans, 2009.

Keith, Chris, and Anthony LeDonne (eds.), *Jesus, Criteria, and the Demise of Authenticity.* London: T&T Clark, 2012.

Kirk, J. R. Daniel. *Unlocking Romans: Resurrection and the Justification of God.* Grand Rapids: Eerdmans, 2008.

Koch, Dietrich-Alex. *Die Schrift als Zeuge des Evangeliums: Untersuchungen zur Verwendung und zum Verständnis der Schrift bei Paulus.* Beiträge zur historischen Theologie 69. Tübingen: Mohr (Siebeck), 1986.

Köstenberger, Andreas J. "John," in Greg K. Beale and D. A. Carson (eds.), *Commentary on the New Testament Use of the Old Testament.* Grand Rapids: Baker Academic, 2007, 415–512.

Kraus, Hans-Joachim. *Psalms.* Trans. Hilton C. Oswald. 2 vols. Minneapolis: Augsburg, 1988–9.

Kugel, James L. *Traditions of the Bible: A Guide to the Bible as It Was at the Start of the Common Era.* Cambridge, Mass.: Harvard University Press, 1998.

Law, Timothy M. *When God Spoke Greek: The Septuagint and the Making of the Christian Bible.* Oxford: Oxford University Press, 2013.

Lebreton, Jules. *History of the Dogma of the Trinity: From Its Origins to the Council of Nicæa,* i. *The Origins.* Trans. Algar Thorold. London: Burns Oates & Washbourne, 1939.

Lee, Aquila H. I. *From Messiah to Preexistent Son: Jesus' Self-Consciousness and Early Christian Exegesis of Messianic Psalms.* Wissenschaftliche Untersuchungen zum Neuen Testament. Second Series 192. Tübingen: Mohr (Siebeck), 2005.

Lewis, C. S. *Mere Christianity.* Rev. edn. New York: Touchstone, 1996.

Lieberman, Saul. *Hellenism in Jewish Palestine: Studies in the Literary Transmission, Beliefs and Manners of Palestine in the I Century B.C.E–IV Century C.E.* New York: Jewish Theological Seminary of America, 1962.

Lieu, Judith. *Image and Reality: The Jews in the World of the Christians in the Second Century.* London: T&T Clark, 1996.

Lieu, Judith. "Justin Martyr and the Transformation of Psalm 22," in Charlotte Hempel and Judith M. Lieu (eds.), *Biblical Traditions in Transmission: Essays in Honour of Michael A. Knibb.* Leiden: Brill, 2006, 195–211.

Lindars, Barnabas. *New Testament Apologetic: The Doctrinal Significance of the Old Testament Quotations.* Philadelphia: Westminster, 1961.

Luz, Ulrich. *Matthew.* Trans. James E. Crouch. 3 vols. Hermeneia. Minneapolis: Fortress, 2001–7.

McCready, Douglas. *He Came Down from Heaven: The Preexistence of Christ and the Christian Faith.* Downers Grove, Ill.: InterVarsity, 2005.

McDonald, Lee M. *The Biblical Canon: Its Origin, Transmission, and Authority.* Grand Rapids: Baker Academic, 2007.

McGrath, James F. *The Only True God: Early Christian Monotheism in Its Jewish Context.* Urbana, Ill.: University of Illinois Press, 2009.

Malina, Bruce J. and Jerome H. Neyrey. *Portraits of Paul: An Archaeology of an Ancient Personality.* Louisville, Ky.: Westminster John Knox, 1996.

Martens, Peter W. *Origen and Scripture: The Contours of the Exegetical Life.* Oxford Early Christian Studies. Oxford: Oxford University Press, 2012.

Meier, John P. "From Elijah-Like Prophet to Royal Davidic Messiah," in James D. G. Dunn et al. (eds.), *Jesus: A Colloquium in the Holy Land.* New York: Continuum, 2001, 45–83.

Meier, John P. *A Marginal Jew.* 4 vols. Anchor Bible Reference Library. New York: Doubleday, 1991–2009.

Metzger, Bruce M. *A Textual Commentary on the Greek New Testament.* 2nd edn. New York: United Bible Societies, 1994.

Meye Thompson, Marianne. *The Promise of the Father: Jesus and God in the New Testament.* Louisville, Ky.: Westminster John Knox, 2000.

Meyer, Ben F. *Critical Realism and the New Testament.* Allison Park, Pa.: Pickwick, 1989.

Meyer, Ben F. *Reality and Illusion in New Testament Scholarship.* Collegeville, Minn.: Michael Glazier, 1994.

Mitchell, Margaret M. "Patristic Rhetoric on Allegory: Origen and Eustathius Put 1 Samuel 28 on Trial." *Journal of Religion* 85 (2005): 414–45.

Mitchell, Margaret M. *Paul, the Corinthians, and the Birth of Christian Hermeneutics.* Cambridge: Cambridge University Press, 2010.

Moltmann, Jürgen. *The Crucified God: The Cross of Christ as the Foundation and Criticism of Christian Theology*. Trans. R. A. Wilson and John Bowden. New York: Harper & Row, 1974.

Noble, Paul R. "The 'Sensus Literalis': Jowett, Childs, and Barr." *Journal of Theological Studies* NS 44 (1993): 1–23.

Novenson, Matthew V. *Christ among the Messiahs: Christ Language in Paul and Messiah Language in Ancient Judaism*. Oxford: Oxford University Press, 2012.

Offermanns, Helga. *Der christologische und trinitarische Personbegriff der frühen Kirche: ein Beitrag zum Verständnis von Dogmenentwicklung und Dogmengeschichte*. Berne: Herbert Lang; Frankfurt am Main: Peter Lang, 1976.

O'Keefe, John J., and R. R. Reno. *Sanctified Vision: An Introduction to Early Christian Interpretation of the Bible*. Baltimore: Johns Hopkins University Press, 2005.

Parsons, Mikeal C., and Martin M. Culy. *Acts: A Handbook on the Greek Text*. Waco, Tex.: Baylor University Press, 2003.

Peppard, Michael. *The Son of God in the Roman World: Divine Sonship in Its Social and Political Context*. New York: Oxford University Press, 2011.

Pervo, Richard I. *Acts: A Commentary*. Hermeneia. Minneapolis: Fortress, 2009.

Plummer, Alfred. *A Critical and Exegetical Commentary on the Second Epistle of St. Paul to the Corinthians*. International Critical Commentary. Edinburgh: T&T Clark, 1915.

Presley, Stephen O. "Irenaeus and the Exegetical Roots of Trinitarian Theology," in Paul Foster and Sara Parvis (eds.), *Irenaeus: Life, Scripture, Legacy*. Minneapolis: Fortress, 2012, 165–71.

Puech, Émile. "Notes sur la manuscript de XIQMelchîsédeq." *Revue de Qumran* 12/48 (1987): 483–513.

Rahner, Karl. *The Trinity*. Trans. Joseph Donceel. New York: Seabury, 1974.

Ratzinger, Cardinal Joseph. "Concerning the Notion of Person in Theology." *Communio* 17 (1990): 439–54.

Rondeau, Marie-Josèphe. *Les Commentaires patristiques du Psautier (3e–5e siècles) i. Les Travaux des Pères grecs et latins sur le Psautier. Recherches et bilan; ii. Exégèse prosopologique et théologie*. 2 vols. Orientalia Christiana Analecta 220. Rome: Institutum Studiorum Orientalium, 1982–5.

Rowe, C. Kavin. *Early Narrative Christology: The LORD in the Gospel of Luke*. Grand Rapids: Baker Academic, 2009. Repr. from Berlin: de Gruyter, 2006.

Sanders, E. P. *Jesus and Judaism*. London: SCM, 1985.

Schenck, Kenneth. "2 Corinthians and the Πίστις Χριστοῦ Debate." *Catholic Biblical Quarterly* 70 (2008): 524–37.

Schreiber, Johannes. *Die Markuspassion: Eine redaktionsgeschichtliche Untersuchung*. Beihefte zur Zeitschrift für die neutestamentliche Wissenschaft 68. Berlin: de Gruyter, 1993.

The Scripture Project, "Nine Theses on the Interpretation of Scripture," in Ellen F. Davis and Richard B. Hays (eds.), *The Art of Reading Scripture*. Grand Rapids: Eerdmans, 2003, 1–5.

Seitz, Christopher R. "The Trinity in the Old Testament," in Gilles Emery and Matthew Levering (eds.), *The Oxford Handbook of The Trinity*. New York: Oxford University Press, 2011, 28–39.

Seitz, Christopher R. *Word Without End: The Old Testament as Abiding Theological Witness*. Grand Rapids: Eerdmans, 1998.

Shotwell, Willis A. *The Biblical Exegesis of Justin Martyr*. London: SPCK, 1965.

Skarsaune, Oskar. *The Proof from Prophecy: A Study in Justin Martyr's Proof-Text Tradition: Text-Type, Provenance, Theological Profile*. Supplements to Novum Testamentum 56. Leiden: Brill, 1987.

Slusser, Michael. "The Exegetical Roots of Trinitarian Theology." *Theological Studies* 49 (1988): 461–76.

Small, Brian C. "The Characterization of Jesus in the Book of Hebrews." Ph.D. diss., Baylor University, 2012.

Stanley, Christopher D. *Arguing with Scripture: The Rhetoric of Quotations in the Letters of Paul*. London: T&T Clark, 2004.

Stegman, Thomas D. *The Character of Jesus: The Linchpin to Paul's Argument in 2 Corinthians*. Analecta biblica 158. Rome: Pontifico Istituto Biblico, 2005.

Stowers, Stanley K. *The Diatribe and Paul's Letter to the Romans*. Society of Biblical Literature Dissertation Series 57. Chico, Calif.: Scholars Press, 1981.

Stowers, Stanley K. "Romans 7:7–25 as Speech-in-Character (προσωποποία)," in T. Engberg-Pederson (ed.), *Paul in His Hellenistic Context*. Edinburgh: T&T Clark, 1994, 180–202.

Studer, Basil. "Zur Entwicklung der patrististichen Trinitätslehre." *Theologie und Glaube* 74 (1984): 81–93.

Theissen, Gerd, and Dagmar Winter. *The Quest for the Plausible Jesus: The Question of Criteria*. Trans. M. Eugene Boring. Louisville, Ky.: Westminster John Knox, 2002.

Tilling, Chris. *Paul's Divine Christology*. Wissenschaftliche Untersuchungen zum Neuen Testament. Second Series 323. Tübingen: Mohr (Siebeck), 2012.

Tov, Emanuel. *Textual Criticism of the Hebrew Bible*. 3rd rev. and exp. edn. Minneapolis: Fortress, 2012.

Trier, Daniel J. *Introducing Theological Interpretation of Scripture: Recovering a Christian Practice*. Grand Rapids: Baker Academic, 2008.

Turner, Max, and Joel B. Green (eds.), *Between Two Horizons: Spanning New Testament Studies and Systematic Theology*. Grand Rapids: Eerdmans, 2000.

Vanhoozer, Kevin J. *The Drama of Doctrine: A Canonical Linguistic Approach to Christian Theology*. Louisville, Ky.: Westminster John Knox, 2005.

Wagner, J. Ross. "The Christ, Servant of Jew and Gentile: A Fresh Approach to Romans 15:8–9." *Journal of Biblical Literature* 116 (1997): 473–85.

Wagner, J. Ross. "Faithfulness and Fear, Stumbling and Salvation: Receptions of LXX Isaiah 8:11–18 in the New Testament," in J. Ross Wagner, C. Kavin Rowe, and A. Katherine Grieb (eds.), *The Word Leaps the Gap: Essays on Scripture and Theology in Honor of Richard B. Hays*. Grand Rapids: Eerdmans, 2008, 76–106.

Wagner, J. Ross. *Heralds of the Good News: Paul and Isaiah in Concert in the Letter to the Romans*. Supplements to Novum Testamentum 101. Leiden: Brill, 2002.

Wainwright, Arthur W. *The Trinity in the New Testament*. London: SPCK, 1962.

Wallace, Daniel B. *Greek Grammar Beyond the Basics: An Exegetical Syntax of the New Testament*. Grand Rapids: Zondervan, 1996.

Watson, Francis. "The Triune Divine Identity: Reflection on Pauline God Language, in Disagreement with J. D. G. Dunn." *Journal for the Study of the New Testament* 80 (2000): 99–124.

Watts, Rikk E. "Consolation or Confrontation? Isaiah 40–55 and the Delay of the New Exodus." *Tyndale Bulletin* 44 (1990): 31–59.

Watts, Rikk E. "Mark," in Greg K. Beale and D. A. Carson (eds.), *Commentary on the New Testament Use of the Old Testament*. Grand Rapids: Baker Academic, 2007, 111–249.

Wenham, Gordon J. *Genesis*. 2 vols. Word Biblical Commentary 1–2. Dallas: Word, 1987–94.

Westermann, Claus. *Genesis*. Trans. John J. Scullion. 3 vols. Minneapolis: Augsburg, 1984–6.

Wilckens, Ulrich. *Der Brief an die Römer*. 3 vols. Evangelisch-katholischer Kommentar zum Neuen Testament. Neukirchen-Vluyn: Neukirchener, 1978–82.

Williams, Michael A. *Rethinking "Gnosticism": An Argument for Dismantling a Dubious Category*. Princeton: Princeton University Press, 1996.

Wimsatt, W. K. and Monroe D. Beardsley. "The Intentional Fallacy," in William K. Wimsatt (ed.), *The Verbal Icon: Studies in the Meaning of Poetry*. Lexington: University of Kentucky Press, 1954, 3–18.

Wood, W. Jay. *Epistemology: Becoming Intellectually Virtuous*. Downers Grove, Ill.: InterVarsity, 1998.

Wright, N. T. *Jesus and the Victory of God*. Minneapolis: Fortress, 1996.

Wright, N. T. *The New Testament and the People of God*. Minneapolis: Fortress, 1992.

Wright, N. T. *Paul and the Faithfulness of God*. 2 vols. in 4 parts. Minneapolis: Fortress, 2013.

Yarbro Collins, Adela, and John J. Collins. *King and Messiah as Son of God: Divine, Human, and Angelic Messianic Figures in Biblical and Related Literature*. Grand Rapids: Eerdmans, 2008.

Young, Frances M. *Biblical Exegesis and the Formation of Christian Culture*. Peabody, Mass.: Hendrickson, 2002. Repr. from Cambridge: Cambridge University Press, 1997.

Young, Frances M. "The 'Mind' of the Scripture: Theological Readings of the Bible in the Fathers." *International Journal of Systematic Theology* 7 (2005): 126–41.

Zizioulas, John D. *Being as Communion: Studies in Personhood and the Church*. Crestwood, NY: St Vladimir's Seminary Press, 1985.

Index of Biblical References

Distinct references to the Septuagint (LXX) have only been maintained when the versification of the LXX differs from the standard versification found in the *New Revised Standard Version* of the Bible.

Old Testament
Genesis
  1: 1 172
  1: 26–7 45, 82
  1: 26 80, 82, 179
  2: 7 179
  2: 8 55 n. 27
  2: 18 80
  3: 22 80, 82
  3: 24 55 n. 27
  6: 7 179 n. 4
  11: 4 80
  11: 7 80
  14: 18–20 59
  19: 24 163
  22: 2 64 n. 47

Exodus
  3: 6 46
  4: 22–3 102
  19: 16–20 173
  20: 18–19 173
  23: 20 89 n. 7

Deuteronomy
  6: 4 21, 188 n. 29
  9: 19 173
  32: 21 100 n. 36
  32: 35–6 142 n. 6
  32: 43 69, 151 n. 19

1 Samuel
  16: 6 162 n. 13
  16: 12 162 n. 13
  16: 13 48 n. 13

2 Samuel
  2: 4 48 n. 13
  5: 3–5 48 n. 13
  7: 14 69
  19: 22 162 n. 13
  22: 3 141 n. 6, 142 n. 6

1 Kings
  8: 27 121

Psalms
  2 62, 66, 76, 80, 160, 166–9
  2: 2 63 n. 45, 168

  2: 3 62 n. 45
  2: 4–5 62 n. 45
  2: 5–9 62–3, 68, 80
  2: 6–9 70, 161 n. 9
  2: 6 62 n. 45, 63 n. 45, 68 n. 55, 77
  2: 7–9 68, 79
  2: 7–8 70–1, 78, 167
  2: 7 50 n. 18, 51 n. 21, 54 n. 25, 63, 64–73,
    76–7, 78 n. 72, 79–80, 84, 92 n. 17, 109 n.
    48, 162, 168, 170, 197
  2: 8–9 168
  2: 9 168
  2: 10 168
  15: 8–11 LXX 153, 155, 204
  15: 10 LXX 72–6, 154, 196
  15: 11 LXX 155
  16: 10 74
  17 LXX 149–50
  17: 5–6 LXX 150
  17: 5 LXX 150
  17: 7 LXX 150
  17: 18–19 150
  17: 50 LXX 150–3
  21 LXX 112, 118 n. 7, 126–7, 130–1, 133,
    136–40, 144 n. 9
  21: 2 LXX 27–30, 118 n. 7, 144 n. 9
  21: 7–9 LXX 131
  21: 7 LXX 118 n. 7
  21: 8–9 LXX 130
  21: 15 LXX 134 n. 37
  21: 16 LXX 133 n. 35
  21: 17 LXX 133 n. 35, 134 n. 38
  21: 18–19 LXX 134 n. 37
  21: 19 LXX 133
  21: 21 LXX 134 n. 38
  21: 22 LXX 137, 145
  21: 23–5 LXX 137
  21: 23 LXX 137–41, 144 n. 9, 145–6
  21: 25 LXX 137 n. 1
  22 126–7, 129 n. 28, 130 n. 29, 131 n. 31,
    133 n. 35, 137 n. 2
  22: 1 127–30, 180
  22: 16 133 n. 35
  22: 18 133 n. 35
  22: 25–32 137 n. 2

Old Testament: Psalms (*cont.*)
23 LXX 165
24 165
30: 2 189
34: 18 LXX 139 n. 4
34: 19 LXX 116
39: 7–9 LXX 86
39: 7 LXX 1 n. 1, 86
39: 7a LXX 195
39: 7–9 LXX 87
39: 8 LXX 30 n. 50
40: 6–8 86
40: 6 1 n. 1
41: 2 LXX 139 n. 3
41: 3 LXX 88, 139, 139 n. 3
44: 7–8 LXX 163, 165, 170, 171 n. 27
68 LXX 6, 116–17, 118 n. 7, 119, 124, 182
68: 2–7a 117
68: 5 LXX 116–17
68: 7–10 LXX 123
68: 8 LXX 124
68: 10 LXX 6, 119, 121 n. 15, 122,
　　124–5, 149, 181
68: 10a LXX 123
68: 10b LXX 123
68: 22 116
69: 201
69: 9 6 n. 9
69: 10 201
71: 17 LXX 55
72: 17 55
77: 2 LXX 100 n. 35
90: 11 LXX 190
90: 16 LXX 190
96: 7 LXX 69
101: 26–28 LXX 165 n. 21, 170–4
101: 26 LXX 30 n. 50, 82, 172
109 LXX 44, 51, 53, 61–2, 80, 161,
　　166–7, 188
109: 1 LXX 44, 49, 52 n. 22, 53, 61, 160, 161
　　n. 10, 163, 166–7, 170
109: 2 LXX 53, 166
109: 2–3 LXX 53
109: 3 LXX 53, 54 n. 25, 54 n. 26, 61 n. 40,
　　78 n. 72, 80, 84, 105, 161 n. 9
109: 4 LXX 55, 69 n. 56, 70
109: 5–6 LXX 167 n. 23
110 44, 51 n. 20, 47, 52, 55, 59, 60, 61 n. 44,
　　62–3, 66, 84, 160, 162, 166, 188
110: 1 27, 51 n. 21, 52, 59 n. 37, 60 n. 39, 61,
　　90 n. 10, 169, 196
110: 3 54 n. 25
110: 4 52
114–15 LXX 147–50
114: 1–9 LXX 148
114: 3 LXX 150

114: 4 LXX 148
115: 1 LXX 147–8, 153
116 147
116: 1 LXX 152 n. 19
117: 22 LXX 143
118: 22–3 88 n. 6
135: 15–18 46

Isaiah
2: 10 100 n. 36
2: 19 100 n. 36
2: 21 100 n. 36
7: 1–8: 10 143
7: 14 143
8: 5–11 143 n. 8
8: 13–14 143
8: 14 142
8: 16–18 141, 144
8: 16 143–4
8: 17–18 141, 143 n. 7, 144, 146
8: 17 141–2, 145–6
8: 18 141, 142 n. 6, 145–6
8: 19 143 n. 8
9: 6 143
11: 10 152, 159
12: 2 142
20: 1–4 192 n. 35
28: 16 88 n. 6
40: 3–5 90 n. 10
40: 3 89 n. 7, 90 n. 10, 91, 181 n. 9
40: 13 100 n. 36
41: 8 97 n. 28, 97 n. 30
42: 1–9 79, 96, 97 n. 30, 98, 100
42: 1–4 80, 96, 96 n. 27, 97–100
42: 1 64 n. 47, 79–80, 97, 99 n. 33, 100
42: 2–3 97, 99 n. 34
42: 3 99 n. 34
42: 4 97
42: 5–7 80, 99–100
42: 5 96–7
42: 6–7 96–8, 99 n. 32
42: 6 103 n. 39
42: 8–9 97–8, 100
42: 19 105 n. 41
44: 9–20 46
45: 1 27, 61 n. 43, 194
45: 23 100 n. 36
46: 9 179
48: 4 105 n. 41
48: 8 105 n. 41
49: 1–12 97 n. 30, 101–2, 110
49: 1–9 101
49: 1–4 101
49: 1 105
49: 1a 104
49: 1b–4 104

49: 1b 104 n. 40
49: 3 97 n. 28, 97 n. 30, 102, 105
49: 4 102
49: 5–6 54 n. 26, 105–6
49: 5 101, 104 n. 40, 111 n. 52
49: 6–7 96
49: 6 103, 106 n. 44, 108–9
49: 7 101, 107–8
49: 8–12 108
49: 8–9 109
49: 8 103 n. 39, 106 n. 44,
   108–9
49: 18 189
50: 4 111 n. 52
50: 6 34–5, 88
50: 7 88, 194, 194 n. 38
50: 8 88
51: 6 171
52: 7 60, 92
52: 13–15 107–8
52: 14 107 n. 46, 108 n. 46
52: 15 107 n. 46
53 111–13, 131 n. 30,
   165 n. 20
53: 1 50 n. 16, 112
53: 4–6 113
53: 4 189
53: 6 101
53: 7–8 111, 113
53: 8 113
53: 11–12 113
53: 11 190
53: 12 113
55: 3–5 74–5
55: 3–4 75
55: 3 72–5, 76 n. 68, 197
55: 4–5 74
55: 4 74–6
55: 5 74–6
56: 7 118 n. 8, 119
58: 6 94 n. 24
61: 1 93
61: 1–2 93–6, 109–10
61: 2 60, 93
65: 1–2 125–6
65: 1 126
65: 2 125–6
65: 7 125
66: 5 100 n. 36
66: 15 100 n. 36
66: 22 173

Jeremiah
7: 11 118 n. 8
9: 24 100 n. 36
19: 1–11 192 n. 35

23: 5–6 197
30: 9 197
33: 14–22 197

Ezekiel
4: 1–5 192 n. 35
34: 23–4 197
37: 24–5 197

Daniel
2: 44–5 88 n. 6
7: 9–14 59 n. 37
7: 13–14 46, 49, 161 n. 10
9: 25 92, 93 n. 19
9: 26 93

Hosea
1: 2–3 192 n. 35
3: 5 197
11: 1–2 102
11: 1 102

Joel
2: 32 100 n. 36

Haggai
2: 6 172–3
2: 7 173

Zechariah
12: 8–13: 1 197
14: 5 100 n. 36

Malachi
3: 1–2 89
3: 1 89 n. 7, 90, 91
3: 2–3 89
4: 5 90

Old Testament Apocrypha
4 Ezra (or 2 Esdras)
3: 6 55 n. 27

New Testament
Matthew
1: 22–3 143
3: 3 91 n. 13
4: 1–11 102
4: 13–16 143
2: 15 102
3: 17 63, 99 n. 33
8: 17 113
11: 5–6 94
11: 10 89–90
11: 11–21 120
11: 14 90 n. 11
12: 13 99
12: 14 116
12: 15–16 99
12: 18–21 99

New Testament: Matthew (*cont.*)
12: 18 97
12: 22 99
13: 31 116
13: 35 100 n. 35
16: 21 129 n. 27
17: 5 63 n. 46, 99 n. 33
17: 10–12 90 n. 11
17: 23 129 n. 27
19: 28 15, 48 n. 13, 162
20: 19 129 n. 27
21: 13 118 n. 8
21: 18–19 120
21: 19 158 n. 4
21: 42–5 88 n. 6, 143
22: 41–6 44
24 120
25: 31–2 100
25: 31 48 n. 13, 162
26: 28 99 n. 32
26: 61 121
26: 63–4 49, 116 n. 10
27: 34 116
27: 35 133
27: 40 121
27: 43 130
27: 46 127
27: 48 116 n. 2
28: 18–20 100
28: 19 5

Mark
1: 1–3 92 n. 16
1: 2–3 30 n. 50, 89 n. 9, 90 n. 12,
    91 n. 15
1: 1 91 n. 15
1: 2 89–90, 120
1: 3 89 n. 7, 91
1: 11 63
3: 6 115, 144
3: 27 88
6: 15 90 n. 11
8: 31 115, 129 n. 27
9: 7 63 n. 46, 71 n. 60
9: 11 90 n. 11
9: 30–1 115
10: 33–4 115
11: 11–21 120
11: 11 120
11: 15–29 116
11: 16 120
11: 17 118 n. 8
11: 56 94
12: 10–11 88 n. 6, 143
12: 18–27 46
12: 27 47
12: 28 53 n. 23

12: 35–7 30 n. 50, 44, 49, 51 n. 20,
    53 n. 23, 62, 66
12: 35 47
12: 36 49, 66
12: 37 196
13 120
14: 24 99 n. 32
14: 58 121
14: 61–2 15, 49, 161 n. 10
14: 62 15 n. 7
15: 23 116 n. 1, 182
15: 24 133
15: 34 127, 180
15: 36 116 n. 1, 182
15: 37 122
15: 39 15

Luke
1: 17 90 n. 11
1: 32–3 48 n. 13
1: 32 162
1: 33 162
1: 78 55 n. 29
2: 48–9 65 n. 51
3: 4 91 n. 13
3: 6 91 n. 13
3: 22 63, 162
4: 16–21 94
4: 18–19 94, 110, 118
4: 18 95
4: 21 94
7: 22–3 94
7: 27 89–90
9: 22 129 n. 27
9: 35 63 n. 46, 162
9: 51 115
13: 32 129 n. 27
17: 24–5 129 n. 27
18: 31–3 116
18: 33 129 n. 27
19: 46 118 n. 8
20: 17–18 88 n. 6, 143
20: 37 73 n. 64
20: 41–4 44
21 120
22: 20 99 n. 32
22: 37 113
22: 67–70 49
22: 69–70 161 n. 10
23: 34 133
23: 35 130
23: 36 116 n. 2, 182
24: 7 73 n. 63
24: 27 200
24: 32 200
24: 36–49 140 n. 5
24: 41–3 140 n. 5

24: 44–5 140 n. 5
24: 44 200
24: 45 113 n. 56, 200
24: 46 73 n. 63

John
  1: 1 16
  1: 14 121
  1: 21–5 90 n. 11
  1: 23 91 n. 13, 181 n. 9
  2: 13–22 118
  2: 16 121
  2: 17 116 n. 1, 119, 122, 123, 181
  2: 19 129 n. 27
  2: 21 121
  2: 22 121 n. 14, 122
  5: 15 144
  5: 18 115
  5: 21 121 n. 14
  6: 39–40 121 n. 14
  7: 19–25 116
  7: 46 15
  8: 37–40 116
  8: 58 15, 158 n. 4
  10: 30 5
  11: 53 116
  12: 38 112
  12: 41 112
  14: 10 15
  15: 13 125
  15: 20–5 116
  15: 25 117–19
  16: 32 129
  19: 23–4 133 n. 33
  19: 24 133
  19: 28–9 116 n. 2, 182
  19: 28 133 n. 35
  19: 30 122
  19: 37 133 n. 35
  20: 19–29 140 n. 5
  21: 12–13 140 n. 5
  21: 14 121 n. 14

Acts
  1: 9 161
  2 162, 185
  2: 22–36 72 n. 61
  2: 24–8 153
  2: 24 73 n. 63, 121 n. 14, 150, 153
  2: 25–8 155, 204
  2: 25 154 n. 24
  2: 27 196
  2: 28 155
  2: 29–31 182
  2: 29 154
  2: 30 154
  2: 31 154

2: 32–7 166
2: 32 73 n. 63
2: 33–5 61
2: 33 161, 163
2: 34–5 160
2: 34 154–5, 182
2: 35 160
2: 36 161–2
3: 22 73 n. 63
3: 26 73 n. 63
4: 11 88 n. 6, 143 n. 7
5: 37 66 n. 53
7: 37 73 n. 63
8: 26–40 110
8: 30–5 113
8: 30–1 113
8: 32–4 111
8: 32–3 111
8: 34 111, 165 n. 20
10: 41 73 n. 63
13 185
13: 22–4 73
13: 32–7 162
13: 32–5 71–2, 76
13: 32–3 72–3, 74 n. 65
13: 33 72, 76
13: 34–5 74
13: 34 73 n. 63, 73 n. 64, 75
13: 35 154
13: 36–7 72
13: 36 182
13: 47 106 n. 44, 109
16: 25 152 n. 20
17: 3 73 n. 63
17: 31 73 n. 63
21: 38 66 n. 53
25: 16 37 n. 64

Romans
  1: 2–4 200
  1: 3–4 78 n. 73, 157–60, 185
  1: 3 22 n. 25, 57 n. 32, 158–9
  1: 4 159, 162
  1: 7 124 n. 19
  1: 9 22 n. 25
  2: 1–5 31 n. 55
  2: 17–29 31 n. 55
  3: 1–9 31 n. 55
  3: 25 125
  3: 27–4: 2 31 n. 55
  3: 30 15
  5: 8 124 n. 19
  5: 10 22 n. 25
  7: 7–8: 2 31 n. 55
  8: 3 22 n. 25, 57 n. 32, 158
  8: 9–11 152
  8: 14–17 151

New Testament: Romans (*cont.*)
  8: 15 78 n. 73
  8: 23 78 n. 73
  8: 29 22 n. 25, 78 n. 73
  8: 35 124 n. 19
  8: 39 124 n. 19
  9–11 146 n. 10
  9: 4 78 n. 73
  9: 32–3 88 n. 6, 143 n. 7
  10: 6–8 57 n. 32
  10: 6 31 n. 55
  10: 13 100 n. 36
  10: 16 50 n. 16
  10: 20–1 126
  11: 9–10 116–17
  11: 19 31 n. 55
  11: 25–7 99
  13: 7–8 46 n. 8
  14: 11 100 n. 36
  15: 1–12 149
  15: 2–3 6
  15: 3–4 123 n. 16
  15: 3 57 n. 32, 123, 125, 149
  15: 5–6 150
  15: 7–9 150
  15: 7–9a 150
  15: 8 150 n. 17
  15: 9–12 150
  15: 9 149, 150 n. 16, 150 n. 17, 151–3
  15: 10–12 151 n. 19, 152 n. 19
  15: 10–11 151
  15: 12 159
  15: 21 107 n. 46

1 Corinthians
  1: 9 22 n. 25
  1: 31 100 n. 36
  2: 16 100 n. 36
  3: 11–13 173
  6: 14 121 n. 14
  7: 31 171
  8: 6 57 n. 32, 188 n. 29
  10: 4 57 n. 32
  10: 22 100 n. 36
  11: 25 99
  12–14 152
  12: 1–3 151
  12: 11–13 151
  13: 12 37 n. 64
  14: 15 152 n. 20
  15: 3–5 101, 185, 200
  15: 25 169
  15: 26 169
  15: 27 169
  15: 28 22 n. 25, 169
  15: 45–7 57 n. 32
  15: 47 158

2 Corinthians
  1: 11 37 n. 64
  1: 19 22 n. 25
  3: 6 99
  3: 16–17 152
  3: 16 200
  4: 7–15 146
  4: 13–14 147
  4: 13–14a 149
  4: 13 57 n. 32, 148, 150
  5: 18–6: 2 109
  5: 20 109 n. 49
  5: 21 57 n. 32
  6: 1–2 108
  6: 2 106 n. 44, 108 n. 47, 109
  8: 9 57 n. 32, 158
  10: 1 37 n. 64
  10: 17 100 n. 36
  13: 11 124 n. 19
  13: 14 15, 124 n. 19

Galatians
  1: 16 22 n. 25
  2: 20 22 n. 25, 124 n. 19
  3: 1–9 151
  3: 11 73 n. 64
  4: 4 57 n. 32, 91, 158,
    158 n. 4, 159
  4: 5 78 n. 73
  4: 6 5, 151
  4: 14 22 n. 25
  4: 24–7 99

Ephesians
  1: 5 78 n. 73
  1: 10 186
  3: 1–6 99
  3: 9 186
  5: 19 152 n. 20

Philippians
  1: 19 152
  2: 6–11 78 n. 73, 160
  2: 6–8 57 n. 32, 159
  2: 7 158 n. 4, 159
  2: 10–11 100 n. 36

Colossians
  1: 15–20 26, 57 n. 32
  3: 16 152 n. 20

1 Thessalonians
  1: 4 124 n. 19
  1: 10 22 n. 25
  2: 16 124 n. 19
  3: 13 100 n. 36

2 Thessalonians
  1: 7 100 n. 36
  1: 9 100 n. 36

1: 12 100 n. 36
2: 1–2 46 n. 8

2 Timothy
2: 8 159 n. 7
2: 13 169

Hebrews
1: 2 171
1: 3 174
1: 5–14 170
1: 5 69, 72 n. 61, 164, 170, 174
1: 6 69
1: 8–9 163–5, 170, 171 n. 27
1: 8 164 n. 17
1: 9 164
1: 10–12 165 n. 21, 170, 173
1: 10 30 n. 50, 31 n. 50, 172
1: 13 164, 166 n. 22, 170
2: 5 69 n. 57
2: 11–13 140, 146
2: 11–12 138
2: 12–13 143 n. 7
2: 12 138–9, 141, 151
2: 13 141, 144–5
2: 13a 141
2: 13b 141
2: 14 146
3: 7 86 n. 4, 165
5: 5–6 69 n. 56
5: 5 69, 72 n. 61, 80
5: 6 70
5: 7 148
6: 20 70
7: 16 174
7: 21 55
7: 26–7 174
9: 9 132 n. 32
9: 20 99 n. 32

10: 5–10 70 n. 57
10: 5–9 86 n. 1
10: 5–6 55
10: 5 1, 50 n. 17, 86, 195
10: 6–7 87
10: 7 30 n. 50, 31 n. 50
10: 8–10 86 n. 2
10: 10 87
10: 15 165
10: 29 99 n. 32
10: 30 142
11: 19 132 n. 32
12: 18–21 173
12: 24 99 n. 32
12: 26–9 172
12: 26 173
12: 29 173
13: 5–6 30 n. 50, 31 n. 50
13: 20 99 n. 32
13: 23–4 146 n. 10

James
5: 13 152

1 Peter
1: 2 15
2: 4–8 88 n. 6, 143 n. 7
2: 21–5 113

2 Peter
1: 20–1 192
3: 13 173

Revelation
2: 26–7 169
5: 10 169
12: 5 168
19: 15 168–9
20: 6 169
21: 1–2 173

Index of Other Ancient Sources

Arius
Letter to Eusebius of Nicomedia
5 79 n. 75

Athanasius
C.Ar.
1. 54 112 n. 54

Augustine
Doctr. chr.
3. 30–7 189
Trin.
1. 1 3 n. 3, 4 n. 5, 38 n. 66, 38 n. 67
2. 4 3 n. 3
9–11 135 n. 39
15. epilogue 38 n. 68

Cicero
Cat.
1. 11. 27 31 n. 51

Clement of Alexandria
Str.
6. 15 61 n. 43

Clement of Rome
1 Clem.
1. 1 37 n. 64
16. 2 112, 132 n. 30
16. 15–16 131
16. 17 131 n. 30
36. 4–5 80
36. 4 70
36. 5 61 n. 44, 166 n. 22
36. 6 166
47. 6 37 n. 64

The Dead Sea Scrolls
CD
7. 18–20 48 n. 12
12. 23 48 n. 12
1Q Hoyadoth 60 n. 39
1QHymns 60 n. 39
1QIsa^a
42: 1 97 n. 30
49: 1 104
49: 1a 104 n. 40
49: 1b 104 n. 40
49: 6 103 n. 39
1QS
8. 14 91 n. 14
9. 10–11 48 n. 12
9. 19–20 91 n. 14

1QSa
2. 11–20 48 n. 12
11Q13 53, 59–60, 92–3
4Q521 93
Frg. 2 93 n. 21
4Q176
Frgs. 1–2. i .4–9 91 n. 14

Dio Chrysostom
Or.
36. 1 195 n. 40

Epiphanius of Salamis
Pan.
26. 6. 1–2 180 n. 7
30. 13. 7–8 63 n. 47

Eusebius of Caesarea
Dem. ev.
376 97 n. 30

The Gospel of the Ebionites
Frg. 63 n. 47

The Gospel of the Hebrews
Frg. 63 n. 47

Hippolytus
Haer.
9. 12 36 n. 62
Noet.
7 37 n. 63
11 37 n. 63
12 126 n. 22
14 37 n. 63

The Hypostasis of the Archons
General 178
86 179
87 179
92 179 n. 4

Ignatius of Antioch
Eph.
18. 2 159 n. 5
20. 2 159 n. 5

Irenaeus
Epid.
1 185 n. 21
3 185 n. 21
36 159 n. 5
43 55 n. 29
47 163, 164 n. 16, 165 n. 19
48–9 61 n. 44

48 54 n. 26
49–50 32 n. 57
49 61 n. 43, 71 n. 59, 80, 133 n. 36,
    166–7, 188
51 54 n. 26, 106 n. 42
52 185 n. 21
53 54 n. 26, 95 n. 25
55 82 n. 80
67 33 n. 60, 123 n. 17
68 88
69–70 112 n. 55
79 126, 134 n. 37
80 133 n. 33, 134 n. 37
82 116 n. 2
85 61 n. 44, 133 n. 36
88 88
92 126
Haer.
1. 5. 4 179
1. 7. 3 180 n. 6
1. 8. 1 187
1. 9. 4 184 n. 14, 184 n. 15, 185 n. 16, 187
1. 10. 1 186–7
1. 24. 1 179
1. 24. 2 180
1. 29. 4 179
1. 30. 6 179
2. 6. 1 126
2. 27. 1 186
2. 27. 3 187
2. 28. 7 61 n. 44
3. 5. 3 187 n. 27
3. 6. 1 164 n. 16
3. 9. 1–2 90 n. 10
3. 10. 5 61 n. 44, 90 n. 10
3. 11. 6 96 n. 27, 97 n. 30
3. 12. 4 187 n. 27
3. 12. 8 112 n. 55
3. 16. 3 159 n. 5
3. 16. 6 186, 188 n. 28
3. 19. 2 116 n. 2
4. 3. 1 170, 171 n. 26
4. 20. 10 99 n. 34
4. 23. 2 112 n. 55
4. 25. 1 187 n. 27
4. 26. 1 192
4. 33. 12 116 n. 2
4. 35. 3 116 n. 2
4. 35. 4 179
5. 12. 2 97 n. 29
5. 19. 2 186

Jerome
Comm. Isa.
4 63 n. 47

Josephus
Ant.
17. 271–2 66 n. 53

17. 273–6 66 n. 53
17. 278–85 66 n. 53
18. 63–4 67 n. 53
20. 169–71 66 n. 53
20. 200 67 n. 53
B. J.
2. 56 66 n. 53
2. 261–3 66 n. 53
2. 433–4 66 n. 53
2. 652–3 66 n. 53
5. 30–3 66 n. 53
5. 309 66 n. 53
7. 29–36 66 n. 53

Justin Martyr
Dial.
13. 2–9 112 n. 55
24. 4 126 n. 21
26. 2 100 n. 37
32. 3 163
34. 1 129
34. 6 55 n. 29
36. 2 132 n. 32
36. 5 163
36. 6 37 n. 63
42. 2 133 n. 36
52. 1 132 n. 32
56. 14–15 163, 164 n. 18
56. 14 164 n. 16
62. 1–3 82 n. 81
62. 3 82 n. 81
63. 3 54 n. 26, 61 n. 42
63. 4 164 n. 16
64. 5 55 n. 29
64. 6 55 n. 29
65 100
76. 7 61 n. 42
77. 4 132 n. 32
78. 10 132 n. 32
83 61 n. 42
83. 1–4 163
83. 3 166
83. 4–84. 1 54 n. 26
83.4 166
86.3 164 n. 16
88.8 37 n. 63, 63 n. 47, 70 n. 58
90.2 132 n. 32
97–106 137 n. 2
97. 2 126 n. 21
97. 3 132, 133 n. 34
97. 4 131
98. 1 131
99. 1–2 118 n. 7
99. 1 131–2
99. 2 132
101. 2–3 118 n. 7
102. 5 133 n. 35
103. 6 63 n. 47

Justin Martyr: *Dial.* (*cont.*)
104. 1–2 133 n. 34
104. 1 133 n. 35
105. 1 132
106. 1 137 n. 2, 140
113. 6 132 n. 32
114. 1 33 n. 60
114. 2 123 n. 17, 126 n. 21,
   132 n. 32
121. 1 55 n. 29
121. 4 106 n. 43
122. 3–6 99 n. 32
122. 3 100 n. 37
122. 5 109 n. 48
123. 8–9 100 n. 37
123. 8 97 n. 30
135. 1–3 97 n. 30, 100 n. 35
135. 2–3 100 n. 37
1 Apol.
17. 1–2 46 n. 8
35. 3 126 n. 21
35. 5 133 n. 34, 133 n. 35
35. 7 133 n. 35
35. 8 133 n. 34
36. 1–3 123 n. 17
36. 1–2 32, 33
37. 1–39. 1 37 n. 63
38. 1 126 n. 21, 131
38. 2 34, 35
38. 4 133 n. 34, 133 n. 35
38. 6 131
42. 1–2 33 n. 60
45. 1 163
45. 2–4 61 n. 42
45. 3 166
45. 5 166
49. 1–4 37 n. 63
49. 3 126 n. 21
50. 2–11 112 n. 55
50. 5 133 n. 36

Marcellus of Ancrya
On the Holy Church
9 38 n. 69

Melito of Sardis
Frag.
15 61 n. 44
Pascha
35 132 n. 32
40–2 132 n. 32
64 112 n. 55
79–80 116 n. 2
82 61 n. 44
93 116 n. 2
101 88

Odes of Solomon
28. 14 133 n. 35
28. 18 133 n. 35

31. 4 141
31. 9 133 n. 35

1 Enoch
48. 1–3 55
48. 3 55
48. 4–6 55
62. 7 55 n. 28

Origen
Cels.
2. 37 116 n. 2
8. 12 38 n. 69
Comm. Jo.
2. 75 38 n. 69
6. 108–11 181 n. 9
6. 196 68 n. 55, 95 n. 26,
   126 n. 22
10 .222 119
10. 223 181
10. 246 38 n. 69
13. 5 71 n. 60
Comm. Rom.
2. 11. 2 32 n. 57
8. 6. 11 126 n. 22
Philoc.
7. 1–2 32 n. 57
Princ.
4. 3. 1 3 n. 3
Sel. Ps.
29. 3 189

Philo of Alexandria
Cher.
127 17 n. 10
Conf.
146 17 n. 10
Dec.
53 186
Fug.
101 17 n. 10
Opif.
19–25 17 n. 10
Sacr.
8 17 n. 10
Spec. Leg.
1.81 17 n. 10
Somn.
1.215 17 n. 10

Plutarch
Pyth. Orac.
5 (396c) 195 n. 40
7 (397c) 195 n. 40
21 (404b–c) 195 n. 40

Psalms of Solomon
17. 21–5 168 n. 24

Ps-Barnabas
Barn.
4. 8 99 n. 32

5. 1 87
5. 5 82
5. 9–10 88
5. 13 134 n. 38
5. 14 88
6. 2–4 143 n. 7
6. 2 88 n. 6
6. 3 88, 194
6. 6 134 n. 38
6. 10 132 n. 32
6. 12 82
6. 13–16 152
6. 15 88
6. 16–19 140
6. 16 139 n. 4
6. 16a 139
6. 16b 139
7. 3 116
12. 4 126
12. 10 61 n. 43, 166 n. 22
12. 11 61 n. 43
14. 5–7 99 n. 32
14. 6 96, 106
14. 7–9 95
14. 7 96
14. 8 106
14. 9 109
17. 2 132 n. 32

Ps-Clementine
  Hom.
  18. 13 61 n. 43

Quintilian
  Inst.
  3. 3. 9 186 n. 24
  9. 2. 32 31 n. 51

Sextus Empiricus
  Adv. math.
  3. 3 185 n. 19

The Sibylline Oracles
  1. 367 116 n. 2
  6. 25 116 n. 2
  8. 248 168 n. 24
  8. 303 116 n. 2

The Talmud
  b. Pesaḥim
  54a 59 n. 37
  b. Sanhedrin
  38b 59 n. 37
  j. Taʿanit
  4. 8 (68d) 66 n. 53

Targum Isaiah
  42: 1 97 n. 30
  49: 1 104
  49: 1a 104 n. 40
  49: 1b–4 104 n. 40

49: 5 104 n. 40
49: 6 103 n. 39

Targum Neophyti
  Gen 3: 24 55 n. 27

Targum Ps-Jonathan
  Gen 2: 8 55 n. 27

Tatian
  Oratio ad graecos
  4. 1 46 n. 8

Tertullian
  Adv. Jud.
  10. 4 116 n. 3
  13. 10–11 116 n. 3
  Marc.
  3. 5. 2–3 33 n. 60
  3. 5. 2 123 n. 17
  3. 6. 6 105 n. 41
  3. 7. 2 134
  3. 17. 1 107 n. 46
  3. 17. 4 99 n. 34
  3. 19. 5 134
  3. 20. 3 71 n. 60
  3. 20. 4–5 106 n. 43
  3. 20. 5–7 75 n. 66
  3. 22. 6 137 n. 2, 140 n. 5, 152 n. 21
  4. 11. 7 189
  4. 22. 1 71 n. 60
  4. 22. 9 71 n. 60
  4. 23. 8 99 n. 34
  4. 38. 3 46 n. 8
  5. 9. 7–8 54 n. 26
  Prax.
  11 27–8, 32–3, 95 n. 26
  11. 7 164 n. 18

The Testament of the Twelve Patriarchs
  T. Job
  33. 3 59 n. 37

Theophilus of Antioch
  Autol.
  2. 10–11 82 n. 82
  2. 10 61 n. 44
  2. 18 82 n. 82
  2. 20 82 n. 82
  2. 22 82 n. 82
  2. 35 97 n. 29
  3. 14 46 n. 8

2 Enoch
  25. 3–4 55 n. 27

Tyconius
  Liber Regularum
  1. 1 190
  1. 3 190

Valentinus
  On the Three Natures
  Frg. 38 n. 69

Index of Modern Authors Cited

Albl, Martin C. 125 n. 20, 143 n. 7
Alexander, Patrick H. 3 n. 3
Allison, Dale C., Jr. 15 n. 7, 43 n. 5, 48 n. 13, 64 n. 47, 66 n. 53, 94 n. 23
Anatolios, Khaled 13 n. 3, 36 n. 62, 135 n. 39
Anderson, R. Dean, Jr. 31 n. 52
Andresen, Carl 28, 41 n. 1
Attridge, Harold W. 29, 30 n. 47, 69 n. 57, 86 n. 5, 121 n. 15, 137 n. 2, 151 n. 18, 153 n. 22
Aune, David E. 42 n. 2
Ayres, Lewis 13 n. 3

Balthasar, Hans Urs von 5 n. 8
Barnett, Paul 147 n. 12
Barr, James 177 n. 1
Barrett, C. K. 73 n. 63, 111, 147 n. 13
Barth, Karl 12 n. 1, 25, 203
Bates, Matthew W. 30 n. 48, 30 n. 49, 31 n. 50, 32 n. 57, 34 n. 61, 41 n. 1, 46 n. 9, 50 n. 16, 59 n. 35, 59 n. 36, 60 n. 39, 72 n. 61, 93 n. 19, 113 n. 56, 117 n. 4, 123 n. 16, 123 n. 17, 126 n. 23, 127 n. 24, 148 n. 14, 150 n. 16, 157 n. 1, 160 n. 8, 183 n. 12, 195 n. 40, 200 n. 45, 200 n. 46
Bauckham, Richard 2, 22–6, 91 n. 15, 92, 100 n. 36, 128, 129 n. 28, 137 n. 2, 203–4
Baur, F. C. 16
Beale, Greg K. 53 n. 23, 59 n. 34, 169
Beardsley, Monroe D. 58 n. 33
Behr, John 10 n. 14, 13 n. 3, 38 n. 69, 185 n. 20, 185 n. 21, 187 n. 26
Bird, Michael F. 94 n. 23
Blackwell, Ben C. 124 n. 18
Bockmuehl, Markus 59 n. 34
Bousset, Wilhelm 18
Boyarin, Daniel 19 n. 18, 22
Brown, Raymond E. 81 n. 78, 130 n. 29
Bruce, F. F. 73 n. 63
Bultmann, Rudolf 18, 18 n. 14, 48 n. 11, 147 n. 12, 158 n. 2

Campbell, Douglas A. 32 n. 55, 148 n. 14
Capes, David B. 25 n. 38
Carson, D. A. 59 n. 34
Chester, Andrew 48 n. 12
Childs, Brevard S. 81–2, 105 n. 41
Cockerill, Gareth L. 69 n. 57, 142 n. 6
Collins, John J. 21–2, 48 n. 12, 51, 54 n. 25, 77 n. 69, 78 n. 71, 93

Crossan, John D. 42, 48 n. 11, 89 n. 8
Culy, Martin M. 72 n. 62

Dachs, Hans 30 n. 48, 31 n. 54, 32 n. 57
Davies, W. D. 64 n. 47
Davis, Ellen F. 190 n. 33
Dawson, David 81 n. 78
Denton, Donald L., Jr. 42 n. 3
Dillard, Annie 4, 4 n. 7
Dodd, C. H. 53 n. 23
Downs, David J. 29 n. 42
Drobner, Hubertus R. 29 n. 42
Dunn, James D. G. 2–3, 11, 20–2, 24, 48 n. 11, 48 n. 13, 56 n. 30, 57, 78 n. 71, 78 n. 72, 161–2
Dünzl, Franz 13 n. 3

Eden, Kathy 186 n. 25
Ehrman, Bart D. 2, 11, 22, 51–2, 57 n. 32, 74 n. 65, 78 n. 71, 158 n. 3, 159 n. 6, 159 n. 7, 161–2
Ellingworth, Paul 69 n. 57, 86 n. 5
Emery, Gilles 12 n. 2
Evans, Craig A. 120 n. 12

Fee, Gordon D. 188 n. 29
Fitzmyer, Joseph A. 74 n. 65, 93 n. 19, 154 n. 23
Frei, Hans W. 81 n. 78

Gathercole, Simon J. 30 n. 50, 31 n. 50, 51 n. 20, 55 n. 29, 70 n. 57, 90 n. 12, 100 n. 35
Gorman, Michael J. 124 n. 18
Grant, Robert M. 113 n. 56, 132 n. 32, 185 n. 17, 185 n. 18, 186 n. 24, 195 n. 40
Green, Joel B. 10 n. 13
Grenz, Stanley J. 12 n. 1, 39 n. 71
Grillmeier, Aloys 28 n. 42

Hafemann, Scott J. 123 n. 16
Hanson, Anthony T. 29, 30 n. 50, 86 n. 1, 101 n. 38, 108 n. 47, 123 n. 16, 126 n. 23, 148 n. 14, 150 n. 16, 152 n. 19, 173 n. 28
Hanson, John S. 67 n. 53
Harnack, Adolf von 3, 16–17, 19
Hay, David M. 59 n. 37, 61 n. 44
Hayes, John H. 78 n. 71
Hays, Richard B. 9, 29, 53 n. 23, 72, 75 n. 67, 127, 148 n. 14, 154, 190 n. 33

Heine, Ronald E. 182 n. 10, 189 n. 30
Helberath, Bernd J. 29 n. 42
Hengel, Martin 19 n. 17
Hillar, Marian 18 n. 16
Holmes, Stephen R. 12 n. 1
Horsley, Richard A. 46 n. 9, 67 n. 53
Hossfeld, Frank-Lothar 54 n. 25, 147 n. 11
Hurtado, Larry W. 20–3, 26–7, 78 n. 73

Jewett, Robert 18, 158, 159 n. 7
Jipp, Joshua W. 158 n. 2
Juel, Donald 60 n. 37

Kampling, Rainer 90 n. 12
Keck, Leander E. 152 n. 19
Keener, Craig S. 48 n. 13
Keith, Chris 43 n. 5
Kirk, J. R. Daniel 159 n. 7
Koch, Dietrich-Alex 123 n. 16
Köstenberger, Andreas J. 117 n. 5
Kraus, Hans-Joachim 147 n. 11
Kugel, James L. 4 n. 6, 55 n. 27

Law, Timothy M. 195 n. 39
Lebreton, Jules 14
LeDonne, Anthony 43 n. 5
Lee, Aquila H. I. 51 n. 21, 54 n. 25, 64 n. 48
Levering, Matthew 12 n. 2
Lewis, C. S. 14
Lieberman, Saul 19 n. 17
Lieu, Judith 19 n. 18, 131 n. 31, 137 n. 2
Lindars, Barnabas 78 n. 71
Luz, Ulrich 64 n. 49

McCready, Douglas 50 n. 15
McDonald, Lee M. 194 n. 37
McGrath, James F. 13 n. 4, 20, 20 n. 19
Malina, Bruce J. 37 n. 65
Martens, Peter W. 182 n. 10
Meier, John P. 15 n. 7, 42, 48 n. 13, 67 n. 53
Metzger, Bruce M. 72 n. 62, 164 n. 15
Meye Thompson, Marianne 65 n. 51
Meyer, Ben F. 43, 58 n. 33
Mitchell, Margaret M. 81 n. 78, 197, 198 n. 43
Moltmann, Jürgen 12 n. 1, 128–9

Neyrey, Jerome H. 37 n. 65
Noble, Paul R. 81 n. 78
Novenson, Matthew V. 48 n. 12

Offermanns, Helga. 28 n. 42
O'Keefe, John J. 183, 185, 187 n. 27

Parsons, Mikeal C. 72 n. 62
Peppard, Michael. 77 n. 70, 78 n. 71, 78 n. 72, 78 n. 73
Pervo, Richard I. 74 n. 65, 111 n. 51

Plummer, Alfred 147 n. 12
Presley, Stephen O. 29, 180 n. 5
Puech, Émile 92, 93 n. 19

Rahner, Karl 8, 12 n. 1, 38 n. 66
Ratzinger, Cardinal Joseph 29 n. 42
Reno, R. R. 183, 185, 187 n. 27
Rondeau, Marie-Josèphe 28 n. 42, 29, 111 n. 53, 189 n. 30
Rowe, C. Kavin 162 n. 12
Rowe, Eric 38 n. 69

Sanders, E. P. 120 n. 12
Schenck, Kenneth 148 n. 14, 148 n. 15
Schneiders, Sandra M. 81 n. 78, 193 n. 36
Schreiber, Johannes 51 n. 20
Seitz, Christopher R. 83, 177 n. 1
Shotwell, Willis A. 132
Skarsaune, Oskar 126 n. 21
Slusser, Michael 29, 41 n. 1, 112 n. 54
Small, Brian C. 32 n. 56
Stanley, Christopher D. 147 n. 13
Stegman, Thomas D. 148 n. 14
Stowers, Stanley K. 31 n. 55, 32 n. 55
Studer, Basil 29 n. 42

Theissen, Gerd 43 n. 5
Tilling, Chris 25 n. 38
Tov, Emanuel 194 n. 37
Trier, Daniel J. 10 n. 13
Turner, Max 10 n. 13

Vanhoozer, Kevin J. 5 n. 8

Wagner, J. Ross 143 n. 7, 150 n. 16, 150 n. 17
Wainwright, Arthur W. 15
Wallace, Daniel B. 86 n. 3, 164 n. 17
Watson, Francis 124 n. 18
Watts, Rikk E. 78 n. 72, 89 n. 9, 91 n. 15, 105 n. 41
Wenham, Gordon J. 81
Westermann, Claus 80 n. 76
Wilckens, Ulrich 150 n. 16
Williams, Michael A. 177 n. 2
Wimsatt, W. K. 58 n. 33
Winter, Dagmar 43 n. 5
Wood, W. Jay. 191 n. 34, 199 n. 44
Wright, N.T. 2, 15 n. 7, 19 n. 18, 23–6, 43, 48 n. 11, 48 n. 13, 120, 188 n. 29

Yarbro Collins, Adela 21–2, 51, 54 n. 25, 77 n. 69, 78 n. 71
Young, Frances M. 72 n. 61, 113 n. 56, 185–6

Zenger, Erich 54 n. 25, 147 n. 11
Zizioulas, John D. 39 n. 71

Index of Concepts and Other Names

Aelius Theon 31 n. 53
angel 20, 22 n. 25, 26 n. 39, 60, 69, 170, 174, 180, 190
Apollonius of Alexandria 31 n. 54
apologetics 14–15, 197
apologist 5, 16, 17 n. 11, 46 n. 8, 82
apostolic proclamation 82, 101, 109, 122–5, 198–201, 203
Aristarchus of Samothrace 31 n. 54
Arius 79 n. 75, 174
Athanasius 112
atonement 60, 87, 101, 113, 125,
Augustine 2–4, 37–8, 134 n. 39, 135 n. 39, 189, 195 n. 39, 201

baptism 5, 90–3, 185–6; see also Jesus Christ

Callistus 36 n. 62
Christ, see Jesus Christ
Christology:
    adoptionism 11, 18, 20, 68, 74, 76–9, 84, 158, 159 n. 6, 160–2, 204
    backward movement of 2, 56–8, 77–9, 204
    of Divine Identity 2, 22–5, 92, 176, 203–4
    of Divine Persons 2, 7, 24, 91, 176, 204
    early high 2, 24, 90–2
    mediators 3, 16–17, 19–26, 175
    see also Jesus Christ
Cicero 31
Clement of Alexandria 61 n. 43, 123 n. 17
Clement of Rome 37 n. 64, 61, 67, 69–70, 80, 112, 131, 166
Council of Constantinople 11, 13, 24, 26, 39, 175
Council of Chalcedon 21
Council of Nicaea 11, 13–14, 21, 24, 26, 36 n. 62, 39, 175
covenant 89, 96, 98–9, 103 n. 39, 108, 109 n. 48, 110, 114,
creation 4, 7, 8 n. 10, 16–17, 38, 53–5, 79 n. 75, 80, 82, 128, 140, 169–74, 178–80, 202, 204
cross 5–8, 15, 33, 35, 88, 115–16, 122–35, 148–51, 153–56, 166, 169
crucifixion, see cross
cry of dereliction 127–37, 140, 144 n. 9, 155, 180

demiurge 178, 180
Dio Chrysostom 195 n. 40
Diodorus Siculus 186

Dionysius of Halicarnassus 186
divine agency 3, 21–3, 26
divine economy 35, 70, 82–3, 94, 169, 186–7, 191–203

Epiphanius of Salamis 63 n. 47, 180
Eusebius of Caesarea 97 n. 30
exégèse prosopologique 29

filioque 39
forsakenness 127–30, 134–6, 144 n. 9, 155–6

Gnosticism 8, 38 n. 69, 71 n. 60, 119, 170, 177–81, 183–4, 186–7, 196–7, 202
God:
    as addressee 1, 6, 27, 33, 86–8, 102, 107, 117–19, 122, 124, 131–2, 136, 138–9, 148–9, 151, 155, 204
    oneness 13, 15, 36 n. 62, 37–8
    as single principle 38 n. 70
    as single prosōpon 36 n. 62
    as speaking person 44–5, 49–50, 52–6, 61, 63–71, 74–5, 77, 79–84, 90, 96–110, 125, 161–3, 168

Hades 148–50, 153–6, 204
Hell, see Hades
Hellenism 3, 14 n. 5, 16–20, 31, 42, 92 n. 17, 158, 192 n. 35
Heracleon 119, 180–1, 183
Heraclitus 30
Hermeneutics, see Scripture: methods of interpretation
historical Jesus 11, 13–17, 18 n. 13, 21, 41–56, 60–2, 64–7, 89–90, 93–5, 118–22, 130, 176, 203
historical method 10–11, 41–4, 56–9, 67
Holy Spirit, see Spirit
Homer 3, 30, 31 n. 54, 32 n. 57, 184–5
homoousios 16, 39, 92
hypostasis 16–17, 38 n. 69, 39, 50, 203

Ialdaboath 178–9
identity 2, 15, 22–5, 64–7, 89, 92, 103, 105, 119, 176, 203–4
Ignatius of Antioch 159 n. 5
image 17, 45–6, 72 n. 61, 80, 82, 154, 179, 183, 187
incarnation, see Jesus Christ
intertextuality 56–9, 74–6, 109 n. 35

Irenaeus of Lyon 27, 29, 32 n. 57, 33 n. 60, 54
    n. 26, 55 n. 29, 61, 67, 70–1, 80, 82, 88, 90,
    95, 96 n. 27, 97 n. 29, 99 n. 34, 106, 112 n.
    55, 116 n. 2, 123 n. 17, 126, 133, 134 n. 37,
    159 n. 5, 163, 164 n. 16, 165–7, 170–1,
    177, 179–80, 183–9, 192, 194, 196–8, 202

Jerome 63, 189, 195, 201
Jesus Christ:
    as addressee 27, 44–5, 49–50, 64–5, 68–70,
        71 n. 60, 77, 82, 91, 97 n. 29, 98–100,
        102–3, 106 n. 44, 107 n. 46, 108–9, 113,
        160–71
    anointing 48, 63, 92–6, 162–4, 167
    baptism 63–71, 76–80, 99 n. 33, 100
    begottenness 7, 11, 39, 44–5, 50, 52–4, 61 n.
        40, 62–80, 84, 92 n. 17, 106, 135, 161–3,
        167–8
    enthronement 8, 48, 50 n. 18, 52–3, 67,
        69–71, 74, 76–80, 84, 117, 123, 148, 151,
        157–63, 165, 166 n. 22, 167–8, 170, 188, 204
    history, *see* historical Jesus
    incarnation 1, 22, 25, 37 n. 66, 50 n. 17, 54
        n. 26, 57 n. 31, 69–70, 85–9, 95, 128, 139,
        157–60, 170, 187–8, 195, 204
    messiah 1, 6, 9, 11, 18, 20–2, 25 n. 38, 28, 30
        n. 47, 33, 35–6, 44, 47–57, 59–62, 63 n.
        45, 66 n. 53, 67 n. 53, 69–71, 74–80, 86,
        88, 90, 92–5, 102, 109 n. 48, 113, 116–19,
        122–7, 129–34, 138, 143, 148–64, 166–7,
        181–2, 189–90, 194–7, 204
    mission 22, 85, 64–6, 88–9, 95–6, 98,
        102–10, 113, 115, 118 n. 7, 121 n. 15
    passion 6, 29 n. 47, 34, 116, 122,
        126–35, 148
    preexistence 5–7, 11, 17–18, 20, 22, 30 n.
        50, 44, 50–80, 88–90, 94, 100 n. 35, 119,
        144, 150 n. 16, 158, 160–2, 166, 199, 204
    priest 20, 48 n. 12, 54–6, 60, 62, 69, 70,
        85, 167
    resurrection, *see* separate entry
    return 165–9, 199
    Servant 79, 96–110, 111 n. 52, 113, 115–16,
        131 n. 30, 150–1
    Son of God, *see* separate entry
    Son of Man, *see* separate entry
    as speaking person 6, 8, 29–30, 64–71,
        76–9, 86–8, 90 n. 12, 94–5, 102, 104–5,
        116, 122, 131, 136–56, 169, 181–2,
        189–90, 195, 204
    vocation, *see* Jesus Christ: mission
Justin Martyr 27, 29, 32–6, 37 n. 63, 46 n. 8,
    54 n. 26, 55, 61, 63 n. 47, 67, 70, 82, 97,
    99–100, 106, 109, 112 n. 55, 118 n. 7, 123
    n. 17, 126–7, 129, 131–3, 137 n. 2, 140,
    146, 163–6

Kerygma 100–1, 113

law (of Moses) 116, 140–1, 143–4, 200
logos 16–17, 18 n. 16, 20, 29, 32–3, 82, 88,
    175, 187

Marcellus of Ancrya 36 n. 62, 38 n. 69
Marcion 71 n. 60
Melchizedek 55, 59–60, 92, 93 n. 19, 167
messenger 89–90, 92,
messiah, *see* Jesus Christ
metaphor 3–4, 8 n. 10, 25, 34, 36 n. 62, 37–40,
    54, 78, 118, 134, 155, 175, 203
Middle Platonism 17, 18 n. 16, 20
mimesis 72 n. 61, 183
modalism 36 n. 62, 38
Monarchianism 36 n. 62, 40
Monotheism 3, 13 n. 3, 16, 17, 19–27, 100,
    188 n. 29

new creation 8, 171–4, 204

Octavian 77 n. 70
Origen 3 n. 3, 17, 32 n. 57, 38, 67, 68 n. 55, 71
    n. 60, 95, 116 n. 3, 119, 126 n. 22, 180–3,
    188–9, 196, 201

passion, *see* Jesus Christ
Pentecost 150, 153–5, 160–3, 203
perichōrēsis 121 n. 14, 152
person, *see* prosōpon
Philo of Alexandria 17, 30, 80, 186
preexistence, *see* Jesus Christ
priest, *see* Jesus Christ
prosopographic exegesis 28
prosopographische Schriftexegese 28
prosopological exegesis:
    ancient descriptions 57–8
    background 31–2
    criteria 59 n. 35
    definition 3, 31, 33, 36
    ontological status 61
    previous scholarship 28–30
    settings 34–6
    time 33–4, 50–1
prosopological oscillation 189–90, 201
prosōpon:
    background 31–40
    definition 36–7
    relationship to other terms 16, 36–40,
        175, 203
prosopopoeia 29 n. 47, 31–2
Ps-Barnabas 61, 82, 87–8, 95–7, 99 n. 32, 101,
    106, 109, 116 n. 2, 125–6, 132 n. 32,
    133–4, 139–40, 143 n. 7, 146, 166 n.
    22, 194

Ps-Plutarch 30
Ptolemy 179

Q 57 n. 32, 89
Quintilian 31 n. 51, 186

recapitulation, *see* Scripture
reception history 9, 41, 43, 56–9, 61 n. 44, 63,
    64 n. 49, 67–8, 112–13, 139, 158–9
rescue, *see* salvation
resurrection 11, 14, 17–18, 20–1, 46–7, 50 n.
    18, 69, 72–4, 76–7, 78 n. 71, 84, 100, 103,
    106, 108, 122, 137–8, 140, 145–6, 149, 151,
    153–4, 157–60, 163, 187–8, 200, 203–4
revelation 4–5, 8 n. 10, 37–8, 113, 191–3,
    196–201
right hand 27, 35–6, 44, 47, 49, 52, 59, 61, 77,
    100, 123, 153–6, 160–3, 165, 167, 199,
    204–5
Rule of Faith 185–6

Sabellianism 36 n. 62
salvation 7, 25, 87, 91 n. 13, 92, 103–9, 117,
    118 n. 7, 124 n. 18, 129–32, 134–40,
    144–9, 151, 153, 15–6, 177, 190–1
Satorninos 179, 180
Scripture:
    authorial intention 83
    context 1, 45, 47 n. 10, 53, 54 n. 26, 70, 74
        n. 65, 75, 81–2, 89, 96, 99, 102, 105 n. 41,
        109, 121, 125, 131 n. 30, 138, 139 n. 3,
        142–3, 147, 162, 173, 181–2, 193, 196,
        198, 201
    economy 35, 70, 82–3, 94, 169, 185–8,
        191–3, 196–203
    historical sense 81–2, 183, 192–3
    hypothesis 184–8, 191, 195 n. 41, 196–9,
        201–2
    inspiration 3, 6, 32–3, 40, 49, 66, 83, 94,
        12–3, 136, 149, 151–2, 155, 164 n. 18,
        165, 171, 175, 191, 193, 194 n. 37,
        195–9, 203
    literal sense 81–3, 183, 192–3
    methods of interpretation of 3, 5, 81–4,
        113, 175–202
    mind 113, 199–200
    narratival sense 81–2, 183, 192–3
    recapitulation 83, 185–8, 198–9,
        201–2, 204
    sensus plenior 83, 193
    typology, *see* separate entry
servant, *see* Jesus Christ
Shema 21, 188 n. 29
solution-by-person 31 n. 54, 41, 44, 62, 66,
    74–5, 80, 83–4, 96, 101, 106, 110, 130
Son of God 11, 22, 74 n. 65, 77–8, 157–160,
    162, 204

Son of Man 18, 20, 46–7, 49, 55, 161 n. 10
Spirit:
    as inspiring agent, *see* Scripture: inspiration
    procession 7, 11, 39, 135, 163 n. 14,
        175, 204
    as speaking person 27–8, 163–5, 170–1
Stoicism 17
subordination 7

Tatian 46 n. 8, 140 n. 5
temple 44, 55, 65 n. 65, 89, 116, 118–23, 139,
    173, 181, 201
Tertullian 13, 27–9, 32–3, 37 n. 63, 46 n. 8, 54
    n. 26, 67, 71 n. 60, 75 n. 66, 95, 99 n. 34,
    105 n. 41, 106 n. 43, 107, 116 n. 3, 123 n.
    17, 133–4, 137 n. 2, 140 n. 5, 152 n. 21,
    164 n. 18, 189, 201
Theodrama:
    actualized setting 35–6, 50, 77, 94–5,
        116–17, 122, 142, 145–6, 152, 161, 167,
        169, 172, 193
    definition 5 n. 8, 32–6
    ontological status 33 n. 59, 34 n. 61, 192
    performative utterance 95, 117–18, 122,
        129–34, 196, 203
    prophetic setting 34–6, 50, 52, 70, 86, 104,
        111, 161, 167, 171, 193
    prosōpon, *see* separate entry
    theodramatic setting 34–6, 50 n. 18, 53–4,
        67–8, 69 n. 57, 70–1, 76, 80, 84, 87,
        102–3, 106, 109, 151, 154, 161, 163, 165,
        166 n. 22, 167–8, 170–1, 193
    time 33–4, 50–1
    script 30 n. 50, 34, 49, 62, 94, 116, 129–34,
        136, 140, 148, 155
Theophilus of Antioch 46 n. 8, 61, 82, 97 n. 29
Tiberius 46, 77 n. 70
transfiguration 63 n. 46, 64–6, 69, 71 n. 60, 79,
    99 n. 33, 100
Trinity:
    economic/immanent 8, 12 n. 1, 24, 134
    mediatorial figures 16–17, 19–26
    prosopological exegesis 26–40
    psychological analogy 135 n. 39
trito-prosopon exegesis 126 n. 23
Tyconius 189
type 9, 100 n. 35, 154
typology 9, 29 n. 46, 72, 100 n. 35, 108 n. 47,
    117, 123 n. 16, 126–7, 141, 142 n. 6, 148,
    154, 161, 182–3

Valentinus 38, 179–80

Wirkungsgeschichte 56–9, 64 n. 49, 67
wisdom 20, 23, 26, 55, 82–3, 175, 178–80, 190
worship 21, 39, 55, 69, 102, 120, 151,
    155, 172

Printed and bound by CPI Group (UK) Ltd, Croydon, CR0 4YY